Plymouth Blitz

About the Author

Michael C. McLaughlin is an Associate Fellow of the Royal Historical Society and a member of the Historical Association, the Old Plymouth Society, the British Association for Local History, the North American Conference on British Studies, the International Churchill Society and the Devon Family History Society. He also holds memberships in Phi Beta Kappa and Phi Alpha Theta.

He wrote *Voices from the Blitz: The Portland Square Air Raid Tragedy* to commemorate the 85th anniversary of the tragedy in partnership with the Old Plymouth Society. His research on the Plymouth Blitz has appeared in the *Plymouth Herald* and in scholarly and professional journals including *The Historian*, *The Journal of Mortality*, *Omega*, *Their Finest Hour*, *Devon Family Historian*, and the *Journal of the Institute for Cemetery and Crematorium Management*.

A graduate of the College of the Holy Cross in Worcester, Massachusetts and the University of Notre Dame in South Bend, Indiana, Michael is pursuing his doctoral studies at the University of Plymouth. He has spent the past twenty years working in Catholic education and currently serves as Head of Middle School at Austin Preparatory School in Reading, Massachusetts. In addition to his historical research, he writes curriculum resources and travel features. He enjoys travelling, writing, and cooking. Michael lives in Reading, Massachusetts, with his wife Jessica.

His website is: www.michaelwriteshistory.com

Plymouth Blitz

The Bombing of Portland Square and the Devastation of a City

Michael C. McLaughlin

PHAROS

First published in 2026 by Pharos
an imprint of Pelagic Publishing
20–22 Wenlock Road
London N1 7GU, UK

www.pharospublishing.com

Plymouth Blitz: The Bombing of Portland Square and the Devastation of a City

A CIP record for this book is available from the British Library

EU Authorised Representative: Easy Access System Europe –
Mustamae tee 50, 10621 Tallinn, Estonia, gpsr.requests@easproject.com

ISBN 978-1-78427-673-7 Hbk
ISBN 978-1-78427-674-4 Pbk
ISBN 978-1-78427-675-1 ePub
ISBN 978-1-78427-676-8 PDF

Cover image: Britain's Home Front 1939–1945: Air Raid Damage. Firemen, weary but undaunted, hang a Union Jack on a lamp-post after the two-night attack on Plymouth.
© IWM (HU 36253)

Typeset in Minion Pro by S4Carlisle Publishing Services Ltd, Chennai, India

For my family: my anchor to the past, my compass in the present, and my sail for all that is yet to come.

Lord, keep us safe this night,
Secure from all our fears,
May angels guard us while we sleep
'Til morning light appears.

John Leland

This verse from the hymn 'Lord Keep us Safe this Night' was adopted as a prayer in the Portland Square Air-Raid Shelter by members of the Deaf Community.

Contents

Preface

Pat Twyford, journalist with the *Western Morning News* observed that war 'came to our door'.[1] The attacks on Plymouth reached a climax in 1941 as part of a coordinated German assault on port cities. No one was spared the carnage that Hitler's Luftwaffe, the Nazi air force, inflicted. Over the course of seven nights, 20 and 21 March and 21, 22, 23, 28, and 29 April, the blitz obliterated Plymouth's commercial district, administrative centre, and several neighbourhoods.

In the early hours of 23 April, St George's Day, a direct hit on the Portland Square Air-Raid Shelter resulted in the death of at least seventy-one men, women, and children.[2] It was the greatest single loss of civilian life in an air raid in Plymouth. Major and Mrs Lang and Maggie Cornelius were among the casualties that evening. Their sons Anthony and Basil became orphans and were taken in by other members of the family.

The Cornelius family's tragedy in the Second World War mirrored the trials fellow citizens experienced on the home front. The chaos of war shattered not only the landscape of their city but also the make-up of their family.

By the end of the Second World War, approximately 1,174 civilians in Plymouth had been killed as a result of air raids by the Luftwaffe. Thousands more were left homeless from the impact of the torrent of high-explosive bombs and incendiary devices that decimated the city and the Royal Dockyard at HMNB *Devonport*. After London, Plymouth was, proportionally, one of the most heavily bombed cities in England.

The blitz was a watershed moment in the history of Plymouth. Tragedy united all citizens as victims. Emerging from the ashes of destruction, Plymouth adopted the defiant call of *Resurgam*, 'I will rise again', as its watchword.[3]

In coping with this disaster, surviving members of the Cornelius family grappled with questions of what happened on that fateful April night. It would compel Anthony Cornelius to research the events surrounding the incident for the next eighty years and ultimately result in the installation of a memorial to all who perished at Portland Square.

Today, the Portland Square Memorial is situated next to the Portland Square Building on the University of Plymouth campus. The statue casts its shadow near the very place that the Cornelius family once called home.

The bombing at Portland Square is often referenced in accounts of the Plymouth Blitz, but the incident is usually reduced to just a few sentences. This book aspires to chronicle that moment in detail. First, we will explore Plymouth's growth and trace the development of Portland Square. Adopting a micro-historical approach, we will meet the Cornelius family and experience the early months of the war through their lens. To frame the Portland Square incident, the narrative will detail the start of the Plymouth Blitz in March. We will then reconstruct the scenes of the raid, rescue, and recovery at Portland Square in April before addressing the management of events that took place in the aftermath of this catastrophic tragedy. Finally, an examination of the quest to memorialise the dead will bring the Cornelius family narrative and the Portland Square incident full circle.

I hope that the history that I will share with you in these pages may help you to explore this tragedy and its place within Plymouth's darkest days. I share the Cornelius family story as the anchor to this narrative to provide a personal lens through which to wrestle with the human impact that is often lost behind the facts and statistics of war.

Indeed, as we continue to watch the real cost of conflict and its impact on civilian life across the world today, we remember the toll that modern warfare levies on ordinary individuals and communities. While researching and writing this book, the nearly daily news coverage of the indiscriminate bombing of residential areas in the assault on Ukraine and the hostilities in the Middle East suggest that the world has not yet learned from the annals of history.

In his research about what happened to his parents at Portland Square, John 'Anthony' Cornelius, whom you will meet in these pages, wrote about his motivation for investigating this event. 'I'm doing this mainly for my two grandchildren so they will get to understand, in some small way, what happened to their great grandparents.'[4]

Though I am not a Cornelius by blood, I had the great fortune to marry into the Cornelius family. I embrace the mantle as our family's newest storyteller.

In taking on the responsibility to shed light on the Cornelius family's story and realise John's desire for his grandchildren, and now great-grandchildren, I also endeavour to honour the other lives lost. Though names may differ, the threads of common experiences unite our narratives into a shared history of heart-wrenching tragedy and inspirational fortitude.

Michael C. McLaughlin
2026

Acknowledgements

His Majesty the King for allowing me to make use of certain files within the Royal Archives at Windsor.

Thank you to the following: the National Archives at Kew Palace; the Imperial War Museum Archives; the Ministry of Defence; the British Library; the Nancy Astor Archive housed at the University of Reading; the Winston Spencer Churchill Archives housed at Churchill College, Cambridge; the Trustees of the Mass Observation Archive housed at the University of Sussex; Curtis Brown of London; Reach Licensing and the *Western Morning News*; Newspapers.com; the Plymouth Library; and The Box Plymouth.

I am grateful to Deborah Lister of DW Research and Archive Services. Deborah was a valued partner throughout this journey. She served as my eyes 'on the ground' in visiting The Box to obtain documents and was a tremendous cheerleader of this project.

I appreciate several individuals who shared reflections and entrusted me with them. I especially thank Peter Chapman; Simon Edwin for the account of his father Stanley Hollett; Deborah Horton, daughter of Barbara (Cundy) Mills; and the family of William P. Johns.

The images in the text are printed with the permission of the Dunham, Cornelius, and Hill families; Rita Boswell; Peter Chapman; Deborah Horton, Pete Joll; Frances Payne; Maggie Pugh; Chris Roberts; Anna Ost; Chris Robinson and the Plymouth Barbican Trust; Steve Johnson and Plymouth Cyberheritage; Plymouth: The People's Blitz; *Plymouth Herald*; and The Box Plymouth.

I am thankful to those in Plymouth's historical circles who have expressed interest in my project and have encouraged me throughout the process with words of wisdom or a document to inspire my writing: Andy Phillips of the *Plymouth Herald*; Gloria Dixon of the Old Plymouth Society; Chris Robinson; Vivien Warne and Friends of Ford Park Cemetery; Helen Charlesworth; Anne Corry; Jennifer Hobbs; Jackie Rees, widow of Tony Rees; Harry Bennett of the University of Plymouth; and Steve Johnson.

I was able to share my research with scholars in related fields and am thankful for their validation and support. The Old Plymouth Society; the British Association For Local History; David Freeman of the International Churchill Society and *Their*

Finest Hour; the UK Historical Association; Devon Family History Society; Julie Rugg of the University of York; the editors of *Omega*, *Mortality*, and the Institute of Cemetery & Crematorium Management; and the *Plymouth Herald*.

My ever-enthusiastic friend Luke Liddle and the team at Buckingham Education and the Independent Schools Cultural Alliance for your pride in and celebration of my work.

I am appreciative of my colleagues at Austin Preparatory School in Reading, Massachusetts, for indulging me in my storytelling and reading excerpts along the way.

Nigel Massen has been a valued mentor and thoughtful editor. I am honoured to be associated with the launch of Pharos Publishing. I am so appreciative of the entire team, especially David Hawkins and Sarah Stott.

My mom Karen and dad Frank for their incredible support of my education and to my sisters and their families.

I am grateful to the family that I have married into for allowing me to tell this important story. Thank you to the Cornelius, Hill, and Dunham families—most especially to Rosanne: may you rest in peace.

Ever present in my work was the late John Anthony 'Did' Cornelius. I did not have the opportunity to meet him but feel as if I have come to know him through his memoir and advocacy for the Portland Square Memorial. I can't help but think that he would have found this process fascinating.

Last, and certainly far from least, I am most blessed by the constant patience, support, perspective, wisdom, and inspiration of my wife Jessica. It would not be an afternoon at our home without this book making its way into the conversation. Jess, thank you for championing this endeavour, for reading countless drafts, and for encouraging me to keep focused. I am lucky to be on this journey with you. I love you.

Map of Portland Square and its environs, 1894. From *Map of Plymouth-Devonshire CXXIII.8.18*. [Courtesy the British Library Collection]

Chronology

1919	Treaty of Paris formally ends the Great War
1921	British Territorial Forces reconstituted as the Territorial Army, a reserve force
1924	British Committee of Imperial Defence establishes Air Raid Precautions Subcommittee
30 January 1933	Adolf Hitler becomes Chancellor of Germany
26 February 1935	Formal establishment of the Luftwaffe as a third wing of the German military
1937	Air Raid Precautions Act passed in Britain
March 1938	Hitler annexes Austria through the Anschluss
1938	Munich Crisis
March 1939	Hitler violates the Munich Agreement by occupying all of Czechoslovakia
Spring 1939	Britain begins to expand the Territorial Army
June 1939	Portland Square Air-Raid Shelter listed as part of Plymouth's Air Raid Precautions Plan; construction intensifies
1 September 1939	Germany invades Poland
3 September 1939	Britain declares war on Germany
Autumn 1939	Construction of the Portland Square Air-Raid Shelter expands
1939/1940	Phoney War
9 April 1940	Nazi invasion of Denmark and Norway
10 May 1940	Nazi invasion of Belgium, Luxembourg, the Netherlands, and France; Churchill declared Prime Minister in England
26 May–4 June 1940	Evacuation of British troops at Dunkirk
22 June 1940	France surrenders
Summer 1940	Battle of Britain for air supremacy; Luftwaffe focuses on RAF assets
6 July 1940	First air raid on Plymouth at Swilly Road
7 September 1940	Beginning of the London Blitz
27–28 November	Plymouth's most severe air raid to date

28 December	Plymouth's deadliest air raid to date
14 January 1941 and 13 February 1941	Heavy raids on Plymouth
20 March 1941	Royal Visit of King George VI and Queen Elizabeth to Plymouth
20–22 March 1941	Plymouth Blitz begins, with attacks targeting the administrative and commercial districts
21 April 1941	Blitz on Plymouth resumes
22/23 April 1941	Portland Square is hit just after midnight
23 April 1941	Rescue and recovery efforts at Portland Square; the Luftwaffe strikes again
28 April 1941	Communal funeral for Portland Square; the Luftwaffe returns for two more nights
2 May 1941	Churchill visits Plymouth
3 May–9 June 1941	A further ten minor air raids on Plymouth
30 April 1944	Final Luftwaffe air raid on Plymouth, the city's fifty-ninth attack
8 May 1945	Victory in Europe Day

Introduction
22 April to 23 April 1941

The frightening memories of the devastating aerial raids that struck Plymouth a month earlier were still fresh. Over the span of those two horrific March nights, Nazi Germany's Luftwaffe, its air force, dropped thousands of bombs that decimated the port city's commercial and administrative core. This was the German blitzkrieg, or lightning war, in action: a calculated strategy of rapid, overwhelming force intended to paralyse Germany's adversaries and secure swift domination. Yet Plymouth—and Britain—were not about to surrender.

Plymouth was a battleground. The German offensive on the night of 20 March scarred the city. The bombardment levelled stores, schools, churches, and municipal buildings. Hundreds of homes were damaged or in ruins. The attack wrought havoc on utilities. The destruction crippled supply chains. Before the city could begin to assess the extent of the damage, the Luftwaffe returned on 21 March for a second night of heavy bombardment. Pandemonium reigned as the shock and scale of the devastation overwhelmed the city's emergency response system. The death toll of these two nights—336—more than doubled the combined total fatalities—146—from all previous raids on Plymouth.[5]

In the days that followed, the skies were mercifully clear of enemy planes. It seemed that the threat of another aerial assault had passed.

Plymouth licked its wounds while addressing a new set of challenges. After quenching the fires and razing unstable buildings, the city needed to re-establish mechanisms for administrative functions. Utilities needed to be restored. Alternative premises were required to provide a marketplace where residents could purchase food and other necessities. A potential humanitarian crisis loomed as the Emergency Response Committee faced the task of feeding and billeting the many who lost their homes as well as managing the increasing number of citizens who evacuated Plymouth nightly for the sanctuary of the countryside.

Just as Plymouth was settling into the rhythm of a new way of life, Hitler's Luftwaffe returned and delivered another crushing blow. Just after dark on 21 April, German pilots breached the English Channel and descended on Plymouth in full fury. They brought a strike force of 120 aircraft. The objective of this mission was to lay waste to the Royal Navy's dockyards and expand the impact zone of the March attack by targeting residential districts. This was not just military strategy; it was psychological warfare.

The following night, 22 April, the German strike force returned. Plymouth would relive the hell inflicted in March and which other cities had also endured: successive nights of targeted bombing to simultaneously destroy buildings, disrupt life, and demoralise the civilian population. Air-raid sirens blared out as the first wave of planes was detected. The raid followed the Luftwaffe's successful blueprint. The first phase involved dropping thousands of incendiary devices with the intention of creating mayhem and taxing resources as crews raced to contain the fires. This action would also mark out the target field for the squadrons arriving to execute the second stage of the attack: the bombardment.

As the inferno raged, residents hurriedly gathered precious belongings such as jewellery and documents and sought refuge. Some took to private bunkers in their gardens or underneath stairwells or in cupboards in their homes. Others made their way to one of the many municipal communal air-raid shelters strategically positioned throughout Plymouth.

Maggie Cornelius. [Dunham family]

Major William John Lang Cornelius, 1930s [Dunham family]

The neighbourhood of Portland Square in Drake's Ward was home to one of the largest of these shelters. At 42 Portland Square, Lang and Maggie Cornelius were just sitting down to a late dinner when the air-raid sirens went off. It had promised to be a quiet night as both of their sons—Anthony, 13, and Basil, 6—were away with Maggie's mother Emma Hill at her countryside cottage.

Emma had grown increasingly nervous about staying in Plymouth proper. The business that her late husband had left to her was a heap of rubble, another casualty of the March raids. The death of one of Anthony's neighbourhood friends Ronald Walters, who was killed when bombs struck near Portland Square in that same raid, contributed to her unease. She packed up the boys, but could not persuade Maggie and Lang to make the trek. As a war veteran and now member of the Home Guard, Lang felt a duty to remain in Plymouth—and Maggie wasn't prepared to leave him. Furthermore, Maggie was heavily pregnant and was expecting to enter into a nursing home to give birth to their third child any day. And so, that night, Lang and Maggie found themselves alone for a dinner of pasties with only their cat to keep them company.

As the warbling sirens blared their warning cry, the couple pondered their next move. They decided that rather than remain in their home, they would instead make their way across the street to the large communal air-raid shelter under the park at the centre of Portland Square.

Lang gathered a few belongings, papers, and valuables into a valise while Maggie put on her grey tweed coat to face the chilly evening and the cold, damp conditions that awaited them in the shelter. She affixed a silver brooch of St Christopher, the patron saint meant to guard against sudden death, to her lapel. The cat would need to look after itself; animals were not permitted in the shelter anyway. They braced themselves for the sights and sounds of Plymouth under siege. Bright flares descended over the rooftops. The Luftwaffe was releasing incendiary devices to torch the city.

Lang assisted Maggie the short way across the road to the shelter and down the stairs to safety. Once inside the shelter, they turned to the left and found a place to sit on the wooden benches next to some of their neighbours from Portland Square and families from nearby Victoria Street. There, they waited.

Outside, the hellish glow from the inferno created by the thousands of incendiary devices illuminated Plymouth. The conflagration acted as a signalling beacon for the Luftwaffe bomber pilots now on their final approach across the once impenetrable English Channel. The eerie wail of the air-raid sirens and the incessant drone of enemy planes circling above reverberated through the brisk night air.

In the shelter, Lang looked down at his watch: midnight. It was the start of a new day: St George's Day, 23 April, celebrates England's patron saint. In legend, St George defeated a dragon. Tonight, it seemed that a dragon's fiery breath threatened to consume Plymouth.

Above the embattled city, a Luftwaffe pilot pulled the lever to release his payload as his plane descended low over a large reservoir in Drake's Ward. A heavy-calibre bomb dropped from his hold and tore through the sky. The trajectory sent it pummelling towards the centre of the park at Portland Square—and the packed air-raid shelter beneath it.

Impact.

The bomb pierced through the thick, reinforced concrete and plunged into the earth beneath the Portland Square Air-Raid Shelter. There was a moment of silence. Then, a massive explosion when the bomb detonated. Soil and concrete erupted violently skyward and crashed down. The blast conjured up a swirling plume of debris and the acrid smell of destruction.

When the dust settled, it revealed a gaping crater. Something darker settled too. In the raw silence that followed, death had spoken: bodies buried, lives erased, a neighbourhood forever altered.

1

Before the Blitz: How the Royal Navy Built the City

Long before German bombs fell on Plymouth, it was naval ambition, not wartime devastation, that shaped the city's foundations. Plymouth is a large port city located in the county of Devon in south-west England. Its modern metropolitan area comprises what were once three independent towns: Devonport, East Stonehouse, and Plymouth itself. These communities, stretching west to east along the waterfront, did not simply grow beside each other; they grew with and because of the Royal Navy. The Navy's expanding footprint not only bound these towns into a shared strategic purpose but also spurred waves of urban growth, forging not just a city but a strategic cornerstone of the British Empire.

Plymouth's geographic advantage

Plymouth has long benefited from a combination of natural geographic strengths and strategic positioning. It sits between the rivers Tamar and Plym at the point where they flow into Plymouth Sound, a deep, sheltered, natural harbour. Beyond this protected cove are the English Channel and the Western Approach. The region thus provides both easy access to the open sea and a well-defended anchorage. Given this geography, it is of little wonder that the Royal Navy has long considered the area to be an asset in its portfolio.

Early maritime significance

Sutton Pool, the original port of Plymouth, was home to a squadron of the English fleet in the Elizabethan Age. It was from this harbour that Plymouth's native son Sir Francis Drake set sail against the Spanish Armada in 1588. Vice-Admiral Drake famously insisted on first finishing his game of boules, a form of lawn bowling, on the grassy knoll of the Plymouth Hoe before boarding his ship. Drake's resounding victory over Spain was consequential and marked England's rising prowess as a naval power.

The settlers who established Sir Walter Raleigh's ill-fated colony of Roanoke, Virginia, departed from Plymouth in 1585. Though not a crown-sponsored expedition, a generation later, in 1620, the Pilgrim founders of Plymouth Colony in Massachusetts set sail for the New World from Plymouth aboard the *Mayflower*. Legend has it that just like tourists visiting the Barbican district today, the pilgrims patronised Jacka Bakery in the heart of the historic port. It is said that the pilgrims enjoyed the goods at Jacka's so much that the ship's purser added a few orders to their provisions for the Atlantic crossing.

A turning point: the rise of Devonport

England's growing colonial ambitions in the seventeenth century required a large-scale rethinking and expansion of naval infrastructure throughout the realm, including at Plymouth.

In 1690, William III (r. 1689–1702) and Mary II (r. 1689–1694) ordered the establishment of a new royal dockyard. The layout of Plymouth could not accommodate the new maritime needs of the Crown. The medieval port of Sutton Pool was at capacity, and the city itself was a warren of cobbled streets and narrow lanes compacted around the harbour. The River Plym and Cattewater estuary could only offer shallow anchorage owing to silt deposits, thereby limiting the possibility for developing facilities for larger vessels there.

To meet immediate needs and anticipate future demands, surveyors explored alternate sites for new construction. They determined that the undeveloped banks of the Hamoaze, the muddy estuary of the River Tamar to Plymouth's west, could accommodate the space needed to execute the royal vision.

The new complex was a comprehensive effort to establish a self-sustaining naval hub. The campus was primarily designed to support the construction and outfitting of wooden warships with facilities such as a stone-stepped drydock, a smithy, and workshops to manufacture rope, rigging, and sail. A network of channels, locks, basins, and slipways would enable a crew of skilled tradesmen to repair and maintain the fleet. A complex of barracks and officers' quarters would house sailors in training, awaiting assignment, or on leave. A hospital, chapel, and administrative offices rounded out the first wave of development. The complex and the adjoining residential area for civilian labourers and their families would be known as Plymouth Dock, or more colloquially the Dock.

During the following century, the Dock expanded northward along the Tamar. Salt marshes were filled in, and a town was born. Further development meant not only an expansion of naval facilities but also commensurate growth of infrastructure to support the growing civilian population. The building frenzy included schools, churches, housing, places of commerce, and, of course, plenty of pubs. Employment opportunities and public amenities attracted more people to the area which, in turn, spurred further growth.

Military investment and urban growth

Throughout the Georgian eighteenth century, Britain 'ruled the waves'. The naval works at the Dock were vital to the business of building Britain into an empire. For example, Captain James Cook began his three famous voyages from its wharves. The first expedition resulted in his mapping of New Zealand and Cook's sighting of Botany Bay and Sydney Harbour in Australia. On later voyages, Cook returned to the Pacific, where he surveyed Hawai'i and charted much of the American north-west.

The renewal of threats from Britain's ancient adversary France with the rise of Napoleon necessitated defensive measures to the Dock. Though the decisive Battle of Trafalgar in 1805 eliminated Napoleon's ambitions to challenge Britain's supremacy at sea and crushed his designs to launch an invasion, the Royal Navy nevertheless invested in erecting a series of defences at Plymouth to address any vulnerability in the early nineteenth century.

A stone breakwater nearly a mile long was built in 1812. This was intended to protect against the most valuable, and most threatening, aspect of the region's geography: access to the open waters of the Atlantic Ocean. The breakwater was designed to combat the forces of nature by shielding ships from strong ocean currents and tides pushing north into Plymouth Sound. To accomplish this engineering feat, ships ferried nearly 4 million tons of quarried stone to build a protective wall in the 10-metre deep waters.

The breakwater also factored into the Navy's defensive strategy to protect the Dock from enemy ships. The position of the breakwater across the middle of the Sound meant that any hostile ship would be funnelled to the narrows on either shore. These routes placed potential aggressor ships squarely in the deadly range of coastal redoubts. Further defences such as chains and metal nets stretching between the beach and the breakwater made the environs beneath the surface just as treacherous. If a vessel made it through this gauntlet unharmed, the bastion on Drake's Island was positioned to engage the assailant before it could sail up the Tamar and harass the naval works.

British ships, on the other hand, found a much more welcoming reception. In addition to servicing ships of the line, one of the Dock's other responsibilities was provisioning the fleet. Plymouth Sound was the westernmost principal port for vessels sailing from England and the first anchorage on the return voyage home. Warehouses that spread along the banks of the Tamar stored and supplied rations of food, fresh water, liquor, clothing, and other equipment. A distillery, which remains in business in Plymouth's Barbican today, furnished the fleet with a specialised high-proof gin for officers to enjoy aboard.

The Royal William Victualling Yard centralised this massive supply operation, thereby increasing organisational efficiency. It was built during the reign of the sailor-king William IV (r. 1830–1837) in the town of East Stonehouse on the peninsula of Devil's Point. The development physically linked Plymouth and the Dock.

If the Dock was to serve as a centre for shipbuilding, East Stonehouse was to function as a depot for provisions. The Yard complex included a multitude of warehouses, workshops, mills, breweries, distilleries, bakeries, cooperages, and slaughterhouses. In time, a rail system provided a conduit for goods to be shipped into the Yard and keep the storerooms stocked. The operation of these facilities required a large, dedicated workforce and, with that, the need for additional housing and municipal services for those labourers. The Admiralty sponsored new, purpose-built neighbourhoods. Once again, the expansion of naval facilities stimulated urban growth.

The growth of the dockyard, however, caused a reversal of fortune for Plymouth proper. The Dock had initially relied on Plymouth for its labour supply and civic administration. In time, the Dock itself became home not only to officers, sailors, and cadets but also to a skilled civilian labour force and their families, the families of sailors at sea, and a population of pensioners. Indeed, at the start of the nineteenth century, the Dock's population exceeded that of its neighbour.

The residents of the Dock demanded recognition of their community as a separate municipal entity. Sailors and labourers alike felt pride in their role in the national story, especially during the Napoleonic era. In 1823, George IV (r. 1820–1830) incorporated the Dock into an independent, separate town: Devonport. Queen Victoria (r. 1837–1901) contributed to the identity shift as well. On one of her visits, she renamed the naval works Devonport Dockyard.

To celebrate its independent status and further distinguish itself from old Plymouth, Devonport erected a series of monuments and municipal buildings, including its own town hall, library, and post office.

Industrial expansion

The technology of the Industrial Revolution boomed during the Victorian Age and initiated the next phase of the dockyard's expansion, this time driven by steam and steel. The Royal Navy innovated, adapted, and expanded. Steam engines enhanced the manoeuvrability of ships that had previously relied exclusively on wind and sail power. The vessels themselves also evolved, transitioning from wooden to iron-clad to metal. Rather than modifying existing facilities to design, construct, and support these new ships, a purpose-built complex, Keyham, was commissioned instead. The campus expanded the footprint of the naval base. Keyham became an innovation hub, supporting advancements in naval engineering that would keep the British fleet at the vanguard.

While innovation propelled growth at the dockyard, shifting global threats prompted a renewed focus on the region's defences.

The Palmerston line

Later in Victoria's reign, France re-emerged as a naval rival. New global powers asserted themselves too. The evolving landscape prompted Britain to assess its defences anew. In 1860, the Royal Commission on the Defence of the United Kingdom recommended the construction of a series of coastal batteries to provide a more comprehensive network of protection.

Devonport's defences included a ring of purpose-built fortifications throughout the harbour and around the dockyard to protect the area from both naval and overland assaults. Known as Palmerston Forts for their association with the prime minister who championed their construction, the expenditure for these precautionary defences underscored Devonport's strategic importance. Fort Bovisand and Fort Picklecombe secured the narrows of the breakwater. Additional redoubts situated high above the water, such as the Knowles Battery atop Knowles Hill and Fort Stamford on Mount Batten Peninsula, were in time equipped with heavy, long-range artillery to act as a further deterrent to foreign ships.

The Empire's engine room

The naval arms race of the late nineteenth century further catalysed growth. Following German unification in 1871, Britain faced a rising continental power that poured resources into military expansion, including a modern navy. To maintain supremacy at sea, the Royal Navy had to keep innovating. During the reign of Edward VII (1901–1910), shipyards produced larger, faster vessels capable of projecting British power across the globe. These cutting-edge warships demanded equally modern facilities.

In response, the Navy nearly doubled the size of the Keyham campus between 1896 and 1907. New dry docks, workshops, and support buildings pushed the complex to its industrial limits. Engineers dredged the Plymouth Sound and extended jetties deeper into the Tamar to accommodate the new fleet. With these improvements, the entire Channel Squadron could be anchored within reach of Devonport, with ample capacity for fuelling, outfitting, and repairing vessels as well as housing their crews.

A changing cityscape

As Devonport continued to grow, Plymouth invested in municipal services such as schools, libraries, and hospitals to keep pace. Plymouth developed a commercial centre with department stores such as Yeo's and Spooners and the flagship store of E. Dingle & Co. Ltd to carry goods that were produced for the consumer mass market.

On Plymouth's waterfront, the long peace of the nineteenth century resulted in the transformation of the area west of the Royal Citadel from a garrison to a grassy expanse for recreation. Hoe Park featured a dancehall and bandstand, while the Tinside Lido below allowed for wading and sunbathing. Promenade Pier provided various amusements with shops, concessions, and venues for concerts and sport over the water.

Though these amenities were a benefit for city-dwellers, Plymouth itself was grappling with a housing shortage. A longer-term solution was needed.

The suburban shift

Residential development in Plymouth was largely restricted to Sutton Pool until the start of the nineteenth century. New residential areas were needed to relieve the pressures of population growth and to accommodate a growing and aspirational middle class seeking better living conditions that befitted their status.

This demand created lucrative opportunities to redevelop open land north of Plymouth into residential districts, reshaping Plymouth's layout and expanding its boundaries beyond the historic core. The deedholders of these vast estates cashed in on the growing demand for housing. Developers seized the opportunity to parcel off tracts of land and market the area to the emerging middle class. These new residential areas offered a refuge from the crowded Barbican district. Here, there was greater space for the households and lifestyle that white-collar professions and new fortunes commanded.

A growing public transportation network that included buses, trams, and local trains made it possible for people to reside in these suburban areas and commute into the central commercial and administrative areas of Plymouth or offices in Devonport and East Stonehouse for work.

By the twentieth century, what was previously a collection of naval infrastructure and pockets of civilian neighbourhoods had coalesced into a single urban unit. There was an unbroken line of development from the River Tamar to the River Plym. The grand boulevard of Union Street connected the three towns of Devonport, East Stonehouse, and Plymouth. Over time, the Navy's building projects and additional housing gradually filled in the remaining spaces between these communities, erasing the boundaries that had separated them. A transportation web further unified the region. That unity would soon be formalised.

Three towns, one city

While socio-economic changes were driving this urban transformation, conflict was heating up across the Channel on the continent. A blend of militarism, entangling alliances, imperial ambitions, and nationalism contributed to mounting tensions between the European powers. This volatility jeopardised the peace of the long nineteenth century and pushed nations to the precipice of war.

With the need for greater coordination and administrative efficiency between Devonport, East Stonehouse, and Plymouth if war should, in fact, break out, the three separate townships were incorporated into a single entity in 1914. While the naval base would retain the name Devonport, the unified city would be named after the most historic of the three boroughs: Plymouth.

2
Portland Square

Ordnance Survey map, 1933: detail of Drake's War and Portland Square. [Reproduced with the permission of the National Library of Scotland]

Portland Square and the growth of Plymouth

As Plymouth grew, new neighbourhoods emerged that reflected the city's changing identity. Portland Square began as a quiet experiment in urban refinement. It offered a striking contrast to the crowded lanes and salt-weathered warehouses of the Barbican district on the waterfront. With its private green at the centre and uniform façades encircling it, the Square embodied the aspirations of a rising middle class. Here were order, symmetry, and social aspiration—evidence that Plymouth's growth was not only outward but also upward.

The area that would become Portland Square was laid out in 1811.[1] At the time, the area was referred to as 'New Town', and maps of the period refer to the development by this name.[2] The Square occupied land to the west of Tavistock Road.

The Regency-era urban planners of Portland Square appeared to take their cue from contemporary land developers such as Thomas Cubitt in London. Homes with uniform, stately exteriors bordering tree-lined squares, like those laid out in the capital's fashionable Belgravia district, signalled affluence and elegance. Indeed, London-based architect John Foulston was commissioned to design several buildings in Plymouth. He remained in the region and became the foremost architect and urban planner of the period, leaving his mark on the character of Plymouth's public buildings and private homes.

Portland Square would primarily consist of rows of three-storey residences encircling a central private park. The first structures rose along the western, southern, and eastern edges. By 1850, the perimeter was complete.[3] In the intervening decades, the area south of Portland Square experienced substantial development with the infilling of streets and buildings. As a result, Portland Square was no longer physically separated from the rest of Plymouth.

In time, New Town was no longer a fitting descriptor for this area of Plymouth. The city was continuing to expand through further waves of new construction that enveloped outlying settlements. New Town was surrounded by newer developments. Portland Square and its environs were rebranded. As the area largely encompassed the former site of Sir Francis Drake's Elizabethan-era mills, the name Drake's Ward was adopted. The old mill ponds north-east of Portland Square were converted into a reservoir to provide clean water for the population moving into the area. Delineating the ward's northern border was the aptly named thoroughfare of North Road.

Plymouth's growing confidence in its future was evidenced in its bold investments in transportation. Rather than simply reacting to expansion, the city proactively shaped it. The construction of North Road Station, Plymouth's principal railway station today, was a statement of intent. Designed to handle both passenger and freight traffic, it linked Plymouth not only to Devonport and Cornwall but also to the wider national rail network. Additional stops such as Mutley Station followed. These were laid out with the expectation that neighbourhoods such as Drake's Ward would continue to grow. The city's infrastructure was not just practical, it was aspirational; and it positioned Portland Square at the very heart of Plymouth's evolving urban landscape.

Changes to Portland Square

By the 1880s, the Square's inaugural homes were already over fifty years old and overdue for a refresh. The pace of new construction around Portland Square prompted residents to invest in the modernisation and upkeep of their homes.

Some of Plymouth's foremost architects were contracted for renovations at multiple residences. For example, property owners invested in conveniences such as plumbing for interior lavatories. Others replaced windows or gave a facelift to the exteriors. Several owners expanded their home's footprint or reconfigured floorplans. Additional structures such as workshops, wash houses, warehouses, cottages, and stables replaced rear gardens.[4] This wave of home enhancements ensured properties remained competitive with the influx of newer construction.

The addition of public amenities further enhanced the property value of homes and the appeal of an address in this corner of Drake's Ward. Adjacent to Portland Square, Sherwell Congregational Church was opened in 1864, and an adjoining school was opened in 1867. Further up the road on North Hill, the Anglican church of St Matthias the Apostle, distinguished by its 120-foot crenelated limestone tower, was consecrated in 1887. The reservoir was reimagined as Drake's Place Reservoir and Pleasure Gardens in 1891. The public retreat, accessible from the north-eastern corner of Portland Square, included a 200-foot colonnade that provided shade. Above, a wide terrace invited visitors to promenade while they surveyed the ornamental fountains. With amenities such as these close at hand, Portland Square remained a highly desirable address for members of the growing middle class.

Who lived in Portland Square?

Portland Square's residents encompassed a spectrum of white-collar professions, from businessmen, doctors, and scientists to music teachers and artists. *Eyre's Post Office Plymouth & Devonport Directory* of 1895 provides a list of residents whose middle-class professions and prosperity contributed to the neighbourhood's social fabric of progress and promise.[5]

At the turn of the century, business leaders established homes alongside neighbours whose enterprises allowed them to ascend the ranks of financial success. William Hamley, who operated a thriving timber business, lived at No. 1. Next door, Robert Relf and his son George Robert were the contractors responsible for major railway developments in Devonshire during this period and the maintenance of Sutton Harbour. John Ham, a builder, lived at No. 13, and his son occupied No. 8. Alfred Latimer, the son and later partner of the *Western Daily Mercury* proprietor Isaac Latimer, resided at No. 9. John Thomas Fouracre lived at No. 14. He was a prominent stained-glass artist whose works adorned many churches and public buildings, including the Plymouth Guildhall. Henry Hearder Yeo at No. 17 made his fortune in the canvas sail trade. Herbert Fripp, the solicitor partner of Were and Fripp, lived at No. 31.

Members of the scientific and medical community found their place at Portland Square too. Dr Robert Oxland, Fellow of the Chemical Society, resided at No. 32. Oxland had devised a process for extracting tungsten, among other advancements. William and James Square, both Fellows of the Royal College of Surgeons, occupied three houses, 14, 22, and 29, as homes and private surgeries following in the footsteps of their father William Square, who also operated a practice from Portland Square. Louis Sexton, a dental surgeon, resided at No. 19 with his father William, also a dentist. Henry Mayne operated his dental practice from No. 15.

Educators contributed to the intellectual atmosphere of the neighbourhood. Indeed, several residents were members of the Plymouth Athenaeum, which dedicated itself to the promotion of scholarship in a variety of fields. Henry Richard Babb, Headmaster of the Plymouth School of Art, lived with his family at No. 21. Emily Minhinnick, at No. 36, was an early education expert and ran a kindergarten.

Portland Square was also a respectable address for spinsters and widows from affluent families. Elizabeth Lampen lived at No. 3. For many years, the Portland Hotel operated from No. 20. The Prideaux sisters, Augusta and Lucy, came from a banking family and lived on the premises with several domestic servants. Emily Sophia Spooner, whose family established Spooner's Department Store, resided at No. 23.

The area housed social institutions too. Miss Dorcas Body's Ladies' School, a finishing school for young women, was located at No. 30. In 1909, No. 26, the former home of India rubber merchant George Richard Barrett and his family, became the home of the Friendless Girls Help Association. Its mission was to care for orphaned girls and equip them with skills to earn a living as domestic servants.

As Portland Square residents' own stories reflected, upward social and economic mobility was possible through self-improvement and the opportunities created by the Industrial Revolution. In the late nineteenth century, the middle class was expanding to include additional occupations and professions that required education and specialised skills. A middle-class lifestyle was not just a distant dream; it was now an attainable goal within reach for a broader segment of society.

Plymouth continues to grow

As the twentieth century dawned, the tide of Plymouth's urban sprawl continued to push beyond Portland Square. Houndiscombe Farm was sold off and redeveloped as a residential area known as Mutley Ward. The railway station at Mutley Road, built in anticipation of this growth, connected residents to the rest of the metropolitan area. Schools such as Hyde Park School, Gunnerside, and Plymouth College were built during this period to educate children living in this growing part of Plymouth.

Houndiscombe House, the palatial estate built by former mayor William Derry, and the open space of its lawns and gardens were among the hold-outs to urbanisation. But after Derry's death in 1903, even this grand estate succumbed to the pressures and potential of development. The home was razed, and developers laid out streets filled with 'long rows of terraced houses that continued up and over the steep roads to infinity'.[6] The homes included bow windows, a distinctive architectural feature found in properties built during this time.

By the 1930s, Mutley Ward was largely complete. One indicator of this growth was encroachment towards the Plymouth, Devonport, and Stonehouse Cemetery. The precursor to today's Ford Park Cemetery, this was located north of the historic city limits. Indeed, cemeteries often existed outside cities for hygienic reasons. There was a financial reason too: property inside city walls was too valuable to allocate as a final resting place for the deceased. By the early twentieth century, development had reached and surrounded the cemetery, symbolising how the city had engulfed what was once considered its rural fringe.

By the 1930s, Portland Square was firmly integrated into the heart of Plymouth. The city's expansion had redrawn its map, but it also redrew social contours of neighbourhoods such as Portland Square. Once a quiet enclave for the well-to-do, it now housed people from a broader economic spectrum and pulsed with the rhythms of modern urban life: children rushing to new schools, workers boarding trams, and families navigating a faster-paced world.

The streets and houses remained the same, but the world in and around Portland Square was changing. A new urban middle class moved in, bringing fresh energy that reshaped what it meant to live there.

Pre-war Portland Square

In the 1930s, Portland Square continued to be an attractive neighbourhood. William Johns was a teenage Air Raid Precautions volunteer during the Second World War. He recounted the layout of the area in his memoir: 'Portland Square had the geometry of tall buildings and elegant facades. Each house fronting a private park of

Aerial view of Portland Square and its environs. [Chris Robinson, *Plymouth Before the War from the Air, Then & Now*]

Homes fronting Portland Square, with their characteristic bow windows. [Steve Johnson, Plymouth Cyberheritage]

well mown grass, cultivated flowers and rustling beach trees. Its aura and style was of middle class opulence.'[7]

Stanley Hollett lived at 4 Portland Square on the south side of the park. He described the spacious dimensions of the grounds: 'the "square" itself which was oblong and about 400 × 200 ft in size and was beautiful with large trees around the perimeter and internally lots of which were oak, and the ground under the trees was always covered in long grass, with the whole area surrounded by 5'0 high cast iron railings.'[8]

The oasis-like park exuded an air of exclusivity. Throughout much of the 1930s, its use was a benefit reserved for those who resided in one of the homes on Portland Square and was, in essence, an extension of their living space. Anthony Cornelius, who lived at No. 42, recalled: 'Until the iron fence was taken away at the beginning of WWII access to the Square was only permitted for home owners.'[9]

Former residents of Portland Square recalled the park's rural character. Stanley remembered how peaceful it was in the summer, especially with its grounds carefully maintained, 'It was always very peaceful and tranquil in the summer months, and being private ground it always looked at its best.'[10] Noreen Wise, née Harris, who lived across Portland Square at No. 19, described it as almost pastoral: 'The whole square was really fine with a large central garden surrounded by railing and

I remember sheep grazing there, unbelievable in the centre of a city!'[11] Stanley agreed, noting that 'it was common to see sheep + cattle grazing there prior to coming to market. I remember as a child seeing lambs born there in the spring.'[12]

Fronting the park, several of the properties retained their earlier grandeur and were home to individuals with fortunes to match. Mr William Weeks Hamley took up residence in Portland Square in the mid-1890s and immediately renovated the rear of the property to accommodate his burgeoning business. Hamley lived there until his death in 1940. Anthony recalled this affluent neighbour and his luxury car: 'They lived at No. 1 Portland Square right opposite my house. Mr. Hamley owned a big timber business and he had a Bentley or Rolls with a chauffeur. I was very impressed.'[13]

Barbara Mills, née Cundy, who lived at No. 27, vividly remembered some of the more eccentric neighbours: 'Can you remember the Conicks, the antique dealers that lived the far end of the Square in quite a big house and lived there for many years. I can remember being invited with my sister and a friend to her dog's birthday party (Duchess the dog was called). It was always a very dark and gloomy looking house.'[14] The Conicks lived at No. 20, which had formerly housed the Portland Hotel.

In addition to private residences, several buildings were used as offices. Stanley recalled several companies including Western Counties Brick, Hamley's Timber Importers, Janes Outfitters, and Plymouth City Waterworks. Stanley's own residence doubled as the location of his father's business. The family's back garden contained a series of workshops and storerooms that opened onto Victoria Street, the rear street that ran parallel to the south of Portland Square. Mr. Hollett was a builder and employed tradespeople in private projects throughout Plymouth and surrounding towns.

William remembered businesses and private medical practices operating from several properties: 'The doctor's consulting room, unsullied by panel patient in muffler and cloth cap, a discreet dental surgery, the occasional brass plate of a solicitor.'[15]

Anthony recalled one such physician, Dr James Elliot Square. 'I remember that he used to wear a trilby hat and had a goatee (unless I'm dreaming).'[16] In addition to his work as a surgeon at the nearby Royal Eye Infirmary, Dr Square ran a practice in his father's old Portland Square surgery and was, like Anthony's father Lang, involved with the administration of St Matthias's Church.

Portland Square appeared to be an elegant neighbourhood, especially when contrasted with the apartment-style housing of the working class a block away on Victoria Street. The level of wealth that some imagined was based solely on appearances—and appearances can be deceiving.

To a casual observer such as William, the stately homes and private park certainly conveyed a sense of wealth and privilege. As an outsider, William assumed that all the households on the Square functioned like the genteel homes of a bygone day: 'That all should know their station the tradesman's entrance was in the rear. "Below Stairs" the menials cooked and sallied forth to their chores and at night would when dismissed silently climb the carpeted stairs to cheerless attic rooms.'[17] Some households, like the Hamleys at No. 1 and Miss Hicks at No. 31, employed servants to carry out some of these tasks. In general, however, this reality was more reminiscent of the Portland Square of a generation earlier.

Though framed by elegant Regency homes, Portland Square was more than anything in the 1930s a neighbourhood that was home to a modest, hard-working community. As wealthier families relocated to more spacious suburban houses, Portland Square came to reflect the rise of a more diverse middle class. This expanding group included artisans, civil servants, and technicians, many with skilled roles that provided financial stability, if not the occasional luxury. Residents held a wide range of jobs, from engineers and skilled tradesmen at Devonport Dockyard to clerks, teachers, trade agents, and furniture dealers. One neighbour was an advocate for the deaf; another worked in the fur trade. These people enjoyed a degree of comfort but lived within practical limits.

By the 1930s, substantial wealth and the trappings associated with the upper crust lifestyle were more the exception than the norm. While middle class, most families living on Portland Square were not a part of that elite, uppermost echelon of society who could afford—or might even require—domestic assistance, such as the staff that the Hamleys employed. Instead, wives, widows, and older female family members contributed to their household's economy by attending to domestic tasks such as cooking and cleaning. The 1939 Register records many women in Portland Square as performing 'unpaid domestic duties'.

The Square's façade still whispered of wealth, but its social make-up continued to shift. In addition to middle-class households, other residents held more modestly compensated positions such as chauffeur and delivery driver, baker's assistant, and apprentice gardener. Even Minnie Weeks, the cook and housekeeper to Viscount Waldorf Astor, the Lord Mayor of Plymouth, and his wife Lady Nancy, MP for Plymouth Sutton, kept a room here.[18]

These residents could afford to live in Portland Square because many of the once-grand homes were gradually subdivided. The opportunity to rent out spare rooms or individual flats within larger houses lowered the financial threshold required for residency. 'I was later to find it was not as "posh" as I had first believed, many of the houses had been divided into self contained flats,' reflected William.[19] Noreen Wise and her family lived in one such flat:

> The first home I remember is 19 Portland Square in what had once been an elegant Regency house. We had the ground floor flat, a living room, scullery, two bedrooms and a conservatory. There was a walled garden with two pear trees but we did not have a bathroom and there was just a cold water tap in the kitchen. We bathed in a zinc bath in front of the living room fire. The front door had stained glass panels and there was a boot scraper.[20]

The Cornelius residence had a similar feel, having been renovated over time to accommodate modern conveniences and take in lodgers to help foot the bills. Lodgers occupied a suite of two to three 'sunny' rooms with a kitchenette and bath.[21]

'No. 42 Portland Square was a rambling, not an attractive-looking building,' Anthony remarked. 'It did, however, offer all kinds of exploring expeditions for a small kid.' He vividly recalled the layout of his home:

> We occupied the ground floor and one room on the second floor (my brother's and my bedroom). The ground floor consisted of a kitchen (scullery), breakfast room, a small triangular-shaped room, a large sitting room and a large room opening onto the back garden. The sitting room and this room were divided by a wide arch with a curtain. The room opening onto the garden was my parents' bedroom. The triangular room became a nursery for, first me, and later my brother. Eventually we both moved upstairs to the second floor. At the time of her death my mother was expecting another child and I suspect that this room was assigned again the role of a nursery. The rest of the house my parents rented out.[22]

While indoor plumbing was a convenience, piped hot water remained a luxury. 'We did have access to the bathroom on the third floor for our weekly baths! Otherwise all hot water had to be heated in kettles on the gas stove,' Anthony recalled. 'We had one inside toilet on the third floor and one outside toilet for the ground floor in the back garden. It was cold having to "spend a penny" in the winter!'[23]

During Anthony's childhood, his home's utilities transitioned from gas to electricity:

> Until the late 1930s the house was lit by gas. I remember having to change the gas 'mantles'—a small filament cone that fitted over the gas jet and, by glowing, illuminated the room. There was a marble fireplace and I used to sit in front of the fire in the winter picking out shapes in the striations of the marble. Until we had electricity one of my chores, as I got older, was to take the wet cell battery, which powered the wireless, up to the local branch of the electric company on Tavistock Road to have it charged and to bring back a fully charged battery. I think the charge lasted about a week.[24]

An army of purveyors supplied the neighbourhood with food and other necessities. Noreen's recollections of these services paint a portrait of Portland Square as being a hub of activity around delivery time:

> Bread was delivered by a horse drawn van by a man in a brown coat with a leather bag of money over his shoulder, milk was brought to the door in churns and measured into the housewife's jug. Fresh fish was brought in a hand cart

> and there was a barrel organ pushed by a little bald man in a bright blue suit and red scarf complete with a monkey on a chair.[25]

Anthony similarly remembered these deliveries, especially the horses that drew the carts:

> We also had periodic visits from the 'rag and bone' man with his horse-drawn cart. Until the late 1930s the milk man also had a horse-drawn cart. This was later replaced by an electric-driven cart. The milk bottles still rattled in the metal crates so we always knew when the milk man was near. The horses seemed to choose the street outside our house as the point where they did their business. I remember this quite clearly as my mother used to dash outside and collect the manure for our garden. As I got older this chore fell to me. Looking back on it I suppose we had one of the best fertilized gardens in Plymouth.[26]

The Holletts' garden might have also been a worthy contender for the title. Stanley's recollections of the fruits and flowers in bloom reinforce the image of Portland Square as an idyllic sanctuary in the heart of an industrious military port city:

> I spent my very young years in our lovely garden (as well as being a nuisance in the workshops) where we had a summer house, and when in season we could pick plums, apples, loganberries, raspberries, while we enjoyed the sun as it was south facing. We had a large tabby cat who was called Peter who I used to play with and he was a very friendly animal and loved to be made a fool of. My mother used to grow tomatos [*sic*] in the greenhouse, and lovely chrysanthemums and dahlias and roses with various other flowers. It seemed we used to have lovely summers in those days as we spent a lot of time there.[27]

Portland Place East ran alongside the Corneliuses' home, linking the Square with the bustle of Tavistock Road. From there, residents had easy access to the city centre's markets, vast department stores, and other amenities. Though Portland Square was largely peaceful, signs of city life were never far away. 'Portland Square was a quiet neighbourhood except it was one of the Plymouth Corporation bus routes,' Anthony recalled. 'I remember the big double-deckers turning the very tight corner outside our home.'[28]

Victoria Street

Victoria Street and Victoria Lane ran behind the southern edge of the Square. 'We just called it "the lane,"' Anthony recounted. 'It was a narrow winding street that connected Portland Square with Coburg Street, almost in the city centre.'[29]

Peter Chapman, born on 28 September 1934, lived in the Victoria Buildings flats at No. 6. The family included mother and father William and Lilian as well as their four sons, Stanley, Richard, Lesley, and Peter. Peter, the youngest of the lot, remembered the warm personality his mother contributed to their home, 'My mother was always laughing & happy, kept an immaculate home & made everyone welcome.' Peter's father had an important role to play too. William, literally, brought home the bacon. 'My father, being a slaughter man, there was never a shortage of food, maybe not of the best cuts from a beast, but plenty!' [30]

Peter recalled the labyrinthine layout of the eight interconnected units that made up the structure:

> Victoria Buildings was built on a slope with 8 flats. It had a 'U' shaped plan. Numbers 1, 3, 5, & 7 were on the lower south side. Numbers 2, 4, 6, & 8 on the north side. It was built of red brick with a slate roof. On the east side, which joined the north & south sides, were three landings joining 3 & 4, 5 & 6, 7 & 8 with steel pillars & railings on each landing. They each had individual flush toilets for each flat & a shared wash house with a copper boiler in the inner lower corner, a cold water tap, a drain & a mangle. A large window faced east. Numbers 1 & 2 each had a washhouse on the ground floor. Sandstone stairs led from one level to the next on the north side of the landings. [31]

The flats themselves were without trappings and amenities.

> Each flat had a passageway & four rooms supplied by gas & electricity but no running water. The water for daily use was kept in the room used for cooking in a water can which was filled from the tap in the washhouse. There was a fireplace in one of the living rooms with a Devon grate on which to cook.[32]

While Victoria Buildings may have lacked some of the material comforts of Portland Square, its warmth derived from a close-knit sense of community. 'Families, friends & neighbours were very close & helpful to each other,' recounted Peter.

Although he called No. 6 home, many of Peter's most formative childhood experiences unfolded just next door. He spent much of his childhood in the care of his neighbours the Sherlocks at No. 7. So familial was the relationship between Peter and these neighbours that he affectionately called them Granfer and Gran. Mrs Sherlock's sister, Beatrice Cook, lived there too. When Peter contracted diphtheria and needed to convalesce away from Plymouth, it was Beatrice Cook who took him out to the Cornish countryside to recover. [33]

The rudimentary nature of some conveniences provided enough of a contrast with the comfortable life on Portland Square to perpetuate some prejudicial perceptions. 'We looked on "the lane" as a rough place, almost a slum in our minds. I was not allowed to play or even socialise with boys from there. Most of the buildings were tenements,' Anthony wrote.[34] This area was a precarious place for him. 'I was frequently chased by some of the bigger boys—"ruffians" my parents called them.'[35]

Stanley, on the other hand, had more pleasant memories of Victoria Street. As the Holletts' construction workshop and warehouses were accessible from Victoria Street, the area was familiar territory to Stanley. So too were the people who lived there: 'Now I was going to school I was allowed to play with other children who I had got to know there and who lived in the adjacent streets, and there was always plenty to amuse us.'[36] Stanley was friendly with the boys and girls who lived on Victoria Street. They included schoolmates such as Kenneth Allen, Ron and Phyllis Pepper, and Peter Chapman's brother Leslie.

***

This close-knit world of Portland Square and Victoria Street, one built on family ties, neighbourly warmth, and the steady rhythms of ordinary life, was about to be profoundly upended.

When the Second World War broke out, Plymouth's strategic value placed it in the crosshairs. The city was transformed into a battle zone. Ordinary neighbourhoods such as Portland Square could not escape the extraordinary trials of war. The private park in Portland Square would be dug up to house a concrete shelter, and the Halwell Street lumber yard behind Victoria Buildings would be converted into a makeshift mortuary. The army of purveyors pared down their wares and collected ration coupons. The friendly sounds of neighbours greeting one another would be replaced with the warbling shrill of the air-raid siren.

In time, the distinction between the home front and the field of combat would all but vanish. Citizens would endure the dangers of war first hand—and many, including those who called Portland Square and Victoria Street home, would become its casualties.

3

The Cornelius Family of 42 Portland Square

The Cornelius family's story mirrors that of many Plymouth households, rooted in maritime tradition. For generations, their lives were shaped by the rhythms of naval service and the demands of a port city that stood on the front lines of Britain's military history. The family's connections to the Royal Dockyard at Devonport and the Royal Navy were integral to the Corneliuses' history, heritage, and identity.

One forebear in the Cornelius family tree is William Cornelius (*c.*1774–1852). William served in the Royal Navy during Britain's prolonged wars with Napoleonic France, a time when the nation's very survival seemed at stake. He was present on the HMS *Royal George* on the 'Glorious 1st June' in 1794, when four French ships were captured. He was also aboard on 23 June 1795, when *Royal George* captured three French frigates.[1]

The family took particular pride in William's role as an Able Seaman aboard HMS *Prince* during the legendary 1805 Battle of Trafalgar. Though *Prince* arrived late, simply being associated with that pivotal moment in British history became a point of enduring familial pride, cherished lore that was proudly passed down from one generation to the next. Trafalgar was, of course, the legendary naval battle off the coast of Spain that quashed Napoleon's challenge to British supremacy on the seas and ended the threat of a French invasion. Famously, Vice-Admiral Horatio Nelson inspired his fleet with the signal 'England expects that every man will do his duty.' At the height of the battle, Nelson was gunned down aboard his flagship HMS *Victory*. He was mortally wounded, but his triumph secured his place as Britain's most celebrated naval hero.

Just as the Cornelius family's naval heritage reflected a broader Plymouth experience, so too did their passage through the blitz. Tracing their experience reveals how the air raids did not merely strike Plymouth from above but reached deep into the homes and histories of its people, upending lives and reshaping them forever.

William Cornelius & Son

Four generations after Trafalgar, William's descendant and namesake William Cornelius (1869–1947) was living at 21 Cecil Street in Plymouth. He was a skilled tradesman who operated a watchmaking and jewellery business. On 9 October 1893, he married Elizabeth Sarah Maria Lang from Bow. Sarah moved into William's lodgings, and the couple began to make a home and build their family. On 28 November 1896, still at Cecil Street, they welcomed their first child, a son they named William John Lang. He was affectionately nicknamed 'Lang' after his mother's maiden name. A second son, George James Benjamin Ivor, followed a year later.

In 1901, the family moved to the less congested, more suburban area of Mutley. This new ward of Plymouth would be the setting for Cornelius family life in the early twentieth century. The family relocated to 17 Kingsley Road, just north of the railway line and the Royal Eye Infirmary.

The Corneliuses' home was convenient to Mutley Station. The transportation network provided William with the flexibility to reside in Plymouth while working in Devonport. In William's case, his specialised mechanical skills in making and repairing watches were transferable to lucrative employment at the naval base. He was employed as an electronics fitter and later draughtsman, part of the corps of skilled civilian workers contributing to the new class of Edwardian warships.

Cornelius family portrait. Left to right: William Sr, Lang, Olga, Sarah, Ivor, Elizabeth. [Dunham family]

Thanks to his steady income, William was able to access the trappings of the aspirational middle-class lifestyle. William's elevated pay meant that he could dedicate time and resources to endeavours such as social organisations and scholarly pursuits. He held leadership roles in the Masonic Lodge, St Matthias's parish, and the Plymouth Philatelic Society. These activities reflect a middle-class ethos: success was not merely a personal achievement, but a responsibility to contribute to the betterment of the wider community.

Within a couple of years, the Cornelius family had outgrown their home. The couple's third child, Elizabeth Sarah Mary Ruth, was born in 1903. When the vacant land adjoining Houndiscombe Farm was redeveloped into a residential district, the Cornelius family moved. The *Plymouth Directory* for 1905–06 records the Cornelius family as having relocated from Kingsley Road to 5 Maple Grove. The move was perfectly timed as the family welcomed a fourth child, Olga Annie Lang, in 1907.

Still convenient for William's commute to Devonport, 5 Maple Grove was also a central location for the family's other activities and the extended Cornelius family. Their parish church, St Matthias's, stood atop North Hill, a short walk east. In the other direction, following North Road west past North Station, William's parents, William and Thomasina, lived at 12 Staddon Terrace.

For Lang, the new neighbourhood offered access to educational opportunities. The boy was enrolled at the new Hyde Park School, which opened in 1904. The 1908 Admission Register for Regent Street School records him as pupil number 1,910. Lang later attended Plymouth and Mannamead College, where he won prizes in the third and fourth forms and earned two honours from the Royal Drawing Society.

After completing school, Lang entered professional life as part of Plymouth's civil service corps. In 1913, aged 17, Lang began working at the Post Office in Devonport as a 'learner'. He was apprenticed to the telegraph department and received technical training on how to operate the new technology.

Like so many young men of his generation, Lang enlisted in the British Army when the First World War erupted on the Continent. In August 1916, he joined the 28th Battalion Royal Fusiliers, 'The Public School Battalion', in Edinburgh. In October, he transferred to the Royal Engineer Signals and was stationed at Fenny Stratford in Buckinghamshire for training. Later, Lang transferred to Newport Pagnell, Biggleswade, and Hitchin for further technical courses.

Lang deployed in September 1917. He served with the 21st Corps Signal Company, Royal Engineers. His training and practice as a telegraphist with the Post Office provided him with the practical expertise to perform vital communications tasks for the Army.

Lang progressed through the ranks. He served as a private until his promotion to lance corporal in June 1918, which came with elevated responsibilities as a Supervisor of the Army Signals. Though the Armistice ended the First World War on 11 November 1918, the mobilised British forces continued to operate in select

Lang Cornelius on active service at Mt. Carmel, October, 1919. [Dunham family]

locations to advance British interests. During this campaign, Lang was promoted to Second Corporal in January 1919. He was also named Superintendent of the Army Signals. Lang would be promoted to the rank of corporal in July 1919 and sergeant a month later in August.

Lang's service was as a member of the Egyptian Expeditionary Force, a strategic reserve supporting British campaigns in North Africa and against the Ottoman Empire in the Middle East. Lang was an avid amateur photographer and documented his activities during these years. His photographs depict him throughout Egypt and the Middle East installing and operating military communications infrastructure. Indeed, his Army Form B199A makes note of his military familiarity with the coastal area from Gaza to Beirut and his 'knowledge of Damascus, Jerusalem, Jaffa, and Haifa'.[2]

Lang was discharged in January 1920 and was awarded the British War Medal and Victory Medal. He came back to Plymouth and his family home at Maple Grove. With his refined communications skills, Lang regained employment with the General Post Office (GPO) in the telegraph division.

Though Lang resumed many aspects of his old life, much had changed, including the people around him. Not long after his return, someone caught his attention and captured his heart: his neighbour, Marjorie 'Maggie' Hill.

The Hill family

Percy Hill (1879–1940) rose to wealth by following in the footsteps of his family's trade as a proprietor of a pawnbroking business. Venturing out on his own early on, Percy operated a shop at 7 Holburn Street in Prince Rock while maintaining bachelor's quarters at 71 Lisson Grove in Mutley Plain.

He married Emma Prentice (1876–1964), the daughter of a London accountant, in 1899. They established their home close to their business on Prince Rock.

Percy and Emma's first child Marjorie Clarissa, known in the family as Maggie, was born on 14 March 1901, at the family home on 4 Holburn Street. Six more children followed over the next decade: Geoffrey Paul Strathmore, Madeline Elizabeth, William Charles Manning, Gloria Adelaide, Percy Arthur Patrick, and Doreen Mabel Mortimer.

Children of the Hill family, *c.*1914. Left to right: Gloria, Geoffrey, Maggie, Doreen (seated), Madeline, Pat (seated), Charles. [Hill family]

Around 1903, the family moved their shop and home a few blocks from Holburn Street to larger premises at the corner of St John's Road and Alma Street. Staff such as Albert George Lang were employed to help operate the shop. To keep the household running smoothly, the Hills employed several domestic servants: a nurse, a cook, and someone to provide general assistance in the nursery. Tasks included taking care of the children, cooking, and washing. Classified listings from the time indicate that the family sought applicants who were experienced, had good references, were trustworthy, and abstained from alcohol.[3]

In time, a larger home eventually became necessary to accommodate the Hills' growing brood of children and the small army that Mrs Hill hired to help rear them. Their prosperity on the rise, the family purchased Elm Croft in Laira on the road out of Plymouth in about 1909.

Advertisements in the *Western Morning News* classified section are indicative of the Hills' growing affluence and provide insight into what Percy and Emma valued. A governess was sought to take charge of the four eldest children. Applicants were required to be proficient in music, French, and needlework, and to be a congregant of the Church of England.[4] The ideal candidate would also be 'bright and active'.[5] A teenaged assistant was also sought to support the governess and help with general

The Hill family and household at Elm Croft, *c.*1911. [Hill family]

The Hill family and household in the garden of Elm Croft, *c.*1911. Left to right: Gloria, Geoffrey, Charles, Maggie, Nell (dog), Miss Gould (governess), Pat, Ellen (maid), Madeline, Emma. [Hill family]

domestic duties.[6] This position was later described as a 'Mother's Helper', with the expectation that the applicant be 'willing' and 'fond of children'.[7] Other servants attended to the general tidiness of the home. Among the family's live-in domestic help were May Pethick and Lilian Landells, a governess called Miss Gould, and a lady's maid named Ellen.

The Hill family purchased 2 Maple Grove in Mutley in about 1914. Situated on a corner plot, the property had originally belonged to one of the development's founding investors, making it one of the more substantial and desirable residences in the new neighbourhood.

Another sign of the family's affluence was their investment in Maggie's education. Channelling discretionary income into private schooling, particularly for daughters, was a clear indicator of upward mobility and social ambition. With a curriculum that emphasised etiquette, refinement, and accomplishments in the arts and languages, education prepared a young woman for a range of social opportunities and enhanced prospects for a favourable marriage.

Maggie attended school at Beaconsfield Convent in Plymouth, which was housed at a palatial rural estate some distance north of Mutley. The Catholic Ursuline Sisters of France ran the property as a boarding school for well-to-do French girls. When the First World War broke out, the student body changed from French boarders to primarily English day students. Maggie was among those who took classes in the old mansion and benefited from modernised classrooms in a newly extended academic wing.

Maggie's mother Emma provided a model of putting that social training to use. She hosted social gatherings and fundraisers at the Hills' Maple Grove home.[8] Card tournaments of whist and bridge brought respectable society to their home in support of causes such as nursing and healthcare. Through these philanthropic events, Emma revealed not only her passion for social causes, but also a sense of responsibility to use her position for the good of her community, an impulse very much in keeping with the values of the middle class.

Beyond the social realm, Emma also demonstrated the economic value of an education. She assisted Percy in running the family business; unsurprising, given her upbringing as the daughter of a London accountant. Indeed, after Percy's death in 1940, Emma would successfully manage the pawnbroker's on her own. Emma also independently owned property in the village of Crapstone outside Plymouth. She generated additional income by operating the cottage, named Restormel after the Cornish castle,[9] as a bed and breakfast for families on holiday. For a time, her sister Mabel managed the property and hosted such guests as Geoffrey Shakespeare, MP, and his family.[10]

Percy took advantage of the opportunities that the family's wealth provided for personal amusements. A member of the Plymouth Philatelic Society, he used his business network to trade in rare and antique stamps.[11] He was also a pioneering motorist and was among the first in Plymouth to own and operate a private vehicle. Such was his fascination with cars that Percy served as president of the Plymouth and District Motor Cycle Club from 1909 to 1910. Indeed, when the family moved to Mutley, he immediately sought additional space in which to garage his motorbike and sidecar.[12]

Percy and Emma built a comfortable life for their family. Their home at 2 Maple Grove stood as a symbol of that upward climb. Just across the street lived the Cornelius family. They moved in similar social circles and shared common values, but it was the quiet bond forming between Lang and Maggie that would eventually unite the two households.

Lang Cornelius of 42 Portland Square

When Lang Cornelius returned to Maple Grove after the First World War, he courted Maggie Hill. There were many opportunities for the Cornelius and Hill families to interact, from their shared parish community of St Matthias's to the simple reality of daily life when they lived just across the street from each other.

Plymouth in the 1920s offered no shortage of diversions for young sweethearts: dancehalls, cinemas, and cafes as well as various seaside amusements such as the Promenade Pier and the spacious Hoe with its bandstand overlooking the Plymouth Sound.

Lang and Maggie married on 21 November 1923 at St Matthias's Church. A family friend, the Rev. Ernest Barrington Woodman, rector of King's Nympton, Devon, officiated at the service. It was a grand affair. Maggie wore an ivory charmeuse

The wedding of Lang and Maggie Cornelius at St Matthias's Church, North Hill, 21 November 1923. [Dunham family]

and lace gown trimmed with orange blossoms and pearls, an ornate train, and a hand-embroidered veil. Her mother wore a blue velvet dress and coat of oriental design while her mother-in-law wore a black and lace dress with a matching hat surmounted by ostrich feathers. After a reception at the Hills' home, family and friends gathered for dancing at the Cooperative Café.[13]

Upon returning to Plymouth from their honeymoon to London and the coast, the happy couple initially lived with relatives before eventually settling into their own home on Portland Square just a couple of blocks south of their parents' homes on Maple Grove. Though Portland Square retained some single-family homes, many had been subdivided into flats. With plenty of space to themselves, Lang and Maggie rented out spare rooms on the upper floors to lodgers to help with their finances.

The wireless watchman

Each day, Lang's half-mile commute to work took him to Guildhall Square, the heart of Plymouth's administrative quarter. Lang worked at the GPO on Westwell Street in the wireless communications division. Drawing on his pre-war apprenticeship at Devonport Post Office and the experience he gained with the Army's Signals, Lang oversaw telegraph communications and radio licensing.

As a wireless inquiry officer, Lang ensured that Plymouth residents complied with regulations around operating telegraphs and radios, his military service providing him with a unique perspective on the importance of effective and regulated communication. His work included investigating violations of illegal devices and improper licensing, while his technical expertise on the installation, operation, maintenance, and mechanics of this technology positioned him as an expert witness. He was called upon to share his findings in several incidents that escalated to formal legal enquiries.[14]

Philatelic pursuits: stories in stamps

Philately, the collection and study of postage stamps, is a hobby that requires an investment of both time and money. The acquisition of rare stamps can be costly, requiring not just discretionary income but also disposable means. The time and financial resources involved were themselves indicators of middle-class privilege.

Perhaps owing to his work at the GPO, it is not surprising that in his spare time Lang was an avid stamp collector. He specialised in postage stamps of Egypt. Given his campaigns in the Middle East, his collection reflected his worldly life experiences. Lang followed his father William's—and eventually his father-in-law Percy Hill's—lead as an active member of the Plymouth Philatelic Society and, like William, served as an elected committee member to guide the society's activities.

Lang's knowledge of stamps and the stories told through their art was extensive. In 1936, he delivered a lecture at the Athenaeum on the Falkland Islands. The lecture featured a stamp display about a Devon-bred sailor being the first Englishman to site the Argentinian islands. Lang had spent years acquiring the materials, including copies of the various stamps and other artifacts connected to the story.[15]

A year later, he delivered a talk entitled 'Great Britain Philatelic Bric-a-Brac'. In his lecture, Lang described the pleasure derived from collecting stamps and learning the stories behind them. To the casual observer, the hobby was little more than sticking stamps in a book; but for someone like Lang, it was more like a puzzle that brought together elements of history and culture. He encouraged collectors to look beyond the stamps themselves to the stories they told: 'Unless we aim at collecting not only stamps, but also such information as we are able to, in relation with those stamps, then I am afraid the man in the street will continue to view us and our stamps with tolerance, instead of the keen interest which we have a right to expect.'[16]

Steward of St Matthias's

Just as Lang exercised leadership in his professional and social endeavours, he also played an active role in the leadership of his parish community of St Matthias's on North Hill. He was a lay reader and participated in the rites of the liturgy. He and his father both served on the Parochial Church Council (PCC). Lang was elected as the treasurer and served in that capacity throughout the 1930s. Lang's responsibilities included the accounting of the weekly collection from the congregation. Lang's son Anthony recalled accompanying his father on many occasions: 'I used to go into the vestry each Sunday night and help (!) him count the collection.'[17] Holding this position of responsibility in the parish, Lang wasn't just counting coins; he was also safeguarding the financial future of the parish.

In 1936, in addition to his role as treasurer, Lang also served as the people's warden. A liaison between church leadership and the congregation, he was responsible for listening to the concerns of fellow parishioners. That year, one issue so divided the parish that it ultimately resulted in the resignation of the vicar. A contingent of parishioners, including, it seems, Lang, advocated for lifting restrictions on how the church hall could be used, hoping to generate much-needed income to reduce the parish's growing debt. The PCC was also concerned that there were not enough social activities to attract and retain younger parishioners. Their proposal to open the hall for community events reflected broader generational shifts: younger and more progressive parishioners were eager for social engagement, while more traditional voices feared a decline in moral standards. The vicar, the Rev. A. Murray Thom, disagreed with the use of the hall for what he considered activities of a 'moral risk' such as dances, plays, and card tournaments. Finding himself completely at odds with the PCC and his congregation, Thom ultimately chose to resign from his post.[18]

Lang worked closely with the new vicar, the Rev. Sydney Alfred Bill, on efforts to inspire a new vitality in the church community. Over the next two years, owing to additional social activities, many of which were held at the church hall, the parish community grew, and the parish's debt was settled. When Bill was appointed Bishop of Lucknow, India, in 1939, Lang coordinated the parish's gift of an engraved ecclesiastical ring to commemorate the appointment. Lang attributed the vibrancy of the church community, in particular the increase in a younger demographic within the congregation, to Bill's leadership: 'When Mr. Bill came here just over two years ago, he saddled himself with a heavy responsibility. It is a very different situation at the present time. The spiritual and social life of the parish has increased to a marvellous degree during the last two years.'[19]

A month later, Lang was responsible for the arrangements for installing Bill's successor, the Rev. Roger Welchman, on 24 February, the feast day of the parish's patron St Matthias. The ceremony occurred in conjunction with Bill's consecration as bishop on the other side of the world. This feat required tremendous coordination on an international scale.[20]

Now the vicar's warden, Lang held an important leadership position from the outset of Welchman's tenure and would be a trusted confidant to the vicar. In time, the two became close friends.

Lang's activities reflect his personal convictions and the broader patterns of civic engagement among the professional middle class of his generation. He was able to direct time, money, and mental energy towards his parish not for personal gain, but out of a sense of duty.

Lang's volunteering reflects his desire, and a middle-class ethos, to use his time and talents for the advancement of the greater good. These values would continue to shape the next chapter of his life, including his sons' upbringing.

John 'Anthony' Cornelius

Lang and Maggie's family grew with the addition of two sons. John Anthony was born on 13 March 1928 and David Basil was born on 16 November 1934. John, affectionately called Anthony by his family, was an inquisitive, observant, and well-loved boy.

Anthony attended primary school close to Portland Square and was responsible for navigating his way there each morning:

> My earliest school days were at Gunnerside School in North Road. This was a prep school run by the Misses Stranger – Hilda and Phoebe. Can't say I remember much about those days. I used to walk there from Portland Square and had to cross a very busy road (for those days). I do remember that there were a lot of girls there and I think there were some boarders.[21]

From left to right: Sarah Cornelius, Anthony Cornelius, Maggie Cornelius, Bow, *c.*1933. [Dunham family]

He later followed in his father's footsteps at Plymouth College. 'After Gunnerside I went to the Plymouth College prep school, headmaster E.C.A. Firman.'[22] Anthony was an accomplished athlete and fared well in the school's annual athletic contests. In 1938, he placed first in the under 12 division in the 100-yard dash and first in the 440-yard sprint. He would defend those titles in 1939 and add the high jump to his list of accomplishments.[23]

His new school meant a slightly longer walk, but it was one that took him past the homes of his grandparents. 'This again was within walking distance from Portland Square (no school buses in those days) and I used to pass No. 2 Maple Grove. It was a relatively long walk, about 20 minutes. Used to walk home at lunch time and then back to school in the afternoon.'[24]

Reflecting on his education, Anthony had little to say about the curriculum. 'I don't remember much about Prep school other than having to learn the multiplication tables up to 12X.'[25]

What stood out more were the friendships he formed:

> At prep school, I became friends with several boys: David Griffin, son of Stanley Griffin, a Plymouth builder and undertaker, the Butland Brothers (Derek and Desmond) from Yelverton, Derek Wilcox, whose father was in the

Lang and Anthony Cornelius. [Dunham family]

> Merchant Navy, Ivor Osborn, whose father was a builder in Coburg Street, and Lawrence Vanstone, whose father was an architect. Others I can visualize but can't remember their names.[26]

When school was not in session, Plymouth offered young Anthony and his friends plenty of activities. Portland Square's central location provided him with easy access to many places to explore in his free time:

> Portland Square was close to the city centre with its large department stores (Spooners, Dingles, Costas, Yeos, etc.), the Guildhall, General Post Office (where my father worked), Council offices, markets, etc. As I got older I was allowed to walk down to the large market to buy fish for [my cat]. I remember it was a Mrs. O'Leary who had a fish cart there. We were also relatively close to Plymouth Hoe. Sometimes a few friends and I used to walk up there to see the Royal Navy warships come through the Sound to the Devonport Dockyard.[27]

Restormel Cottage, *c.*1938. Left to right: Mabel Solmon, Doreen Hill, Anthony Cornelius, Percy Hill, Emma Hill. Restormel was Emma Hill's private retreat outside Plymouth, where she took her grandsons just before the April raids that had such an impact on Portland Square. [Dunham family]

Anthony had a keen interest in science, and the pharmacy near his home helped to nurture that curiosity: 'The chemist on the corner of Portland Place East and Tavistock Road was Roper Lewis. I was always fascinated with the big, coloured bottles. I dearly wanted a microscope and chemistry set that was in the window. I can't remember if I ever got it.' The pharmacist made an impression as well. 'Mr. Lewis was a tall, distinguished-looking gentleman. I remember he had a lady assistant. The dispensary was behind the shop.'[28]

During school holidays, Anthony often visited the weekend home of his maternal grandmother Emma Hill, which provided an escape from the hustle and bustle of life in the port city. Anthony looked back with fondness on his visits to Restormel and the people he spent time with:

> We had great times there. There was a large veggie garden at the back of it that my Uncle Pat [Percy & Emma's youngest son] used to cultivate. I remember he had a trenching tool, a relic from WWI, and I used to help digging veggie beds. There was also a large wood at the rear of the garden (looked like a jungle

> to us!). I remember when Barry, one of Uncle Al's [Alastair Davey, husband of Emma's daughter Madeline] nephews from Brazil stayed with us, we built a tree house in the woods.[29]

The visits were also an opportunity to socialise with schoolmates such as Derek and Desmond Butland: 'When I stayed with my grandmother in her bungalow at Crapstone I used to walk over to Yelverton and meet up with the Butlands and go riding on one of their ponies.'[30]

That same rural retreat would later save Anthony's life. It was at Restormel, removed from the heart of Plymouth, that he and his younger brother took refuge during the height of the German blitz in April 1941.

***

For Lang Cornelius and his family, the rhythm of life resounded with the warmth of close-knit relationships and the cadence of community. But the pleasant melody of this existence would be interrupted when the storm clouds of another war began to gather. The familiar tune of daily life would soon be accompanied by the discordant tones of uncertainty—and by Plymouth's own preparations for the impending conflict.

4

Bunkering Down for War: Air-Raid Shelters in Plymouth

The English Channel had long served as England's most reliable defence against the military ambitions of mainland Europe. Since the Norman invasion of 1066, the water provided a formidable barrier, dissuading or defeating attempts by foreign powers to invade England's shores. From the medieval era to more modern times, the Channel had protected the island from the machinations of its continental rivals. England, guarded by its seas, had grown accustomed to a sense of insularity; a confidence that the homeland was secure as long as the Channel remained unbreeched.

As the twentieth century dawned and new technology emerged, this ancient defence began to lose its relevance.

The First World War accelerated the arms race that ignited the conflict in the first place. Both sides sought to develop weaponry to break the stalemate on the Western Front and secure victory: tanks, chemical weapons, and air power. The face of warfare was changing. No longer would armies and navies alone decide the fate of nations; the skies had become a new battlefield. Towards the end of the First World War, Britain itself experienced raids from German Zeppelin airships and Gotha bombers. Continued aerial advancements would render the Channel's protection increasingly obsolete, and the United Kingdom would have to adapt to this new world.

The advent of aircraft expanded the zone of battle, drawing civilians into the theatre of war. Speaking on the need for civilians to brace themselves for the impending war in 1939, Sir John Anderson, Air Raid Precautions Chief, warned that no corner of the nation should consider itself immune to attack: 'I am quite sure that people have even now no real appreciation of what this country would have to face if engaged in another European war. We still think in terms of war off the premises, so to speak. We cannot bring ourselves, therefore, to realise that the front line might be just outside our own door.'[1] His warning signalled a turning point. Civilians would become, in a sense, combatants too, participants in a war that would be brought to their homes from above.

A new German threat: the Luftwaffe

The Treaty of Versailles put an end to the First World War in 1919. The aim of the peace process was to put 'the war to end all wars' in the rear-view mirror and create a 'lasting peace' for Europe. Germany was made to assume full responsibility for the carnage of the conflict. Signed in the same palace where Kaiser Wilhelm I had been proclaimed as the Emperor of Germany, the Treaty aimed to dismantle the German state. As a punishment for its role in the war, Germany would surrender territory, pay hefty reparations, and undergo a programme of disarmament. Many of the Treaty's 440 terms sought to curtail Germany's military ambitions by imposing strict limitations on the size of and further investment in its armed forces. These terms, however, would ultimately serve as the lightning rod for renewed nationalism in Germany a decade later.

Adolf Hitler and the Nazi Party rose to power amid the political and economic turmoil that Germany experienced after the war. With them came a deliberate and systematic campaign to reclaim Germany's position in Europe through rebuilding the nation's military might. Painting the Versailles Treaty as grossly unfair and the government that agreed to it as weak and ineffectual, Hitler used the terms of the Treaty as a catalyst to fuel resentment and rally people to the Nazi cause. Once in power, he repudiated the agreement. In violation of the sanctions, Germany embarked on a massive rearmament programme that would soon restore the nation's place as a dominant military power. This act of open defiance went unchecked. Fearing another all-consuming conflict, the nations of Europe adopted a policy of appeasement rather than taking Hitler to task.

One prong of the revitalised Nazi war machine was the institution of a new air force, the Luftwaffe. The creation of the Luftwaffe as a separate and distinct branch of the armed forces signalled a significant development in military strategy, one that acknowledged the growing importance of air power in modern warfare.

Hermann Göring's appointment as commander-in-chief of the Luftwaffe laid the foundation for its rapid growth. Göring was a member of Hitler's inner circle. His appointment sent a clear message about the value that the Nazi leadership pinned to developing air supremacy. Göring's political clout—indeed, Hitler would later anoint Göring as his successor—was such that he could marshal whatever financial, material, and personnel resources were necessary to achieve his objective. This contributed to the accelerated development of Luftwaffe as Göring was able to utilise his political position in the service of his military role.

Göring's ascent mirrored the Nazi Party's own rise. Göring leveraged his early loyalty to Hitler into increasingly influential political positions within the regime. An early and ardent follower of Hitler, he was given command of the paramilitary Brown Shirts and was beside Hitler at the attempted Beer Hall Putsch in 1923. In securing a seat in the Reichstag in 1928, Göring became the de facto spokesperson of Nazism in political circles. As the Nazi Party gained more representation in the Reichstag, Göring's influence increased. He was made President of the Reichstag in 1932, placing him in position to facilitate the Nazi takeover of the government and, ultimately, delegate total authority to Hitler in 1933.

The Nazi regime laid the groundwork for a powerful air force through a series of strategic organisational moves. Göring was appointed Commissioner of Aviation in January 1933. In March, the Nazi Party set up the German Air Sports Association to act as an umbrella for all private and national aviation organisations, effectively serving as a front to conceal the establishment of the military Luftwaffe. The next month, the Reich Aviation Ministry was formed. Göring was its chair. This Ministry would have oversight of all aspects of aviation from the design and manufacture of aircraft to the training of pilots and development of strategy. In May, the Army's Military Aviation division was placed under the Ministry's jurisdiction. In September, the parallel civilian and military divisions of the Ministry were combined, ostensibly to improve operational efficiency by eliminating redundancy and streamlining resources. Four new departments were created which facilitated growth and directed additional resources towards military purposes: research, construction, training and staffing, and central command.

The pilots who would make up the core of the Luftwaffe trained clandestinely during the interwar period. Even before Hitler's power grab in 1933, pilots honed their aviation skills under the ruse of intending to fly commercial, not military, aircraft. Secret training bases operated with the support of the Soviet Union. The arrangement provided pilots with the opportunity to train in combat-ready planes and for military leaders to develop strategy for how to deploy this new fighting force. During this period, pilots and personnel alike deepened their understanding of the capabilities of aircraft and how this technology could alter the face of modern warfare. The foundation set, the growth accelerated once Hitler and the Nazi Party were at Germany's helm.

The Luftwaffe was officially established in name in 1935. This was the result of another reorganisation of the Reich Air Ministry. All military functions were now placed under a new Air Force High Command. A new, imposing building in Berlin would serve as the Luftwaffe's headquarters.

The next task was to define the role that this new military asset would play. The deployment of the Luftwaffe's Condor Legion during the Spanish Civil War provided a real-world combat environment to test aircraft designs and tactical manoeuvres. As a result of the experience, leadership saw the capabilities of the Luftwaffe operating as tactical support for army or naval missions as well as an independent force. Ultimately, the Luftwaffe's role would be a blend of the two.

The public witnessed the devastation wrought on the civilian home front population. Coverage in the press of tragedies such as the bombing of Guernica received widespread attention. The rules of warfare had changed. Civilian populations were now squarely in the crosshairs: they would not just be collateral damage but rather often the military's intended target.[2]

By the late 1930s, the theoretical scenarios of sustained, large-scale aerial attacks that were imagined, discussed, and debated in Britain were now a reality. German aircraft possessed the capability to cross the Channel to conduct targeted raids on British cities and towns. The British would have to confront the sobering truth that the English Channel was no longer enough to keep the horrors of war at bay. The era that had seen England secured behind its watery bastion was coming to an end. The entire realm was now susceptible to the skies above. This new aerial threat required a comprehensive response in terms of both military strategy and civilian preparedness. Investment in the RAF and anti-aircraft technology would be essential for contesting Nazi air supremacy. Concurrently, on the ground, the government would also need to take urgent steps to protect the civilian population.

Air Raid Precautions in the United Kingdom

In the wake of the First World War, Britain's military strategists and politicians recognised that future conflicts would include an increased emphasis on aerial warfare. The spectre of more advanced aircraft, capable of carrying heavier payloads over greater distances, loomed large. The devastating potential of this new theatre of combat, coupled with the rapid evolution of aviation technology in the interwar period, compelled authorities to reassess and bolster civilian defence strategies.

To investigate these mounting concerns, the Committee of Imperial Defence established a subcommittee in 1924. This new body, aptly named Air Raid Precautions (ARP), was tasked with evaluating the potential impact of aerial attacks. Under the leadership of Sir John Anderson, the committee investigated emerging aerial weapons technologies and strategies. Its members also considered what measures could be instituted to enhance civilian safety. They evaluated measures such as the implementation of blackout regulations, the practicality of mass evacuations, and the construction of infrastructure such as air-raid shelters.

Britain's approach to air-raid precautions evolved from talk to action in 1935. This shift was prompted by Nazi Germany's 1935 declaration of the establishment of the Luftwaffe and the nation's continued defiance of the Treaty of Versailles. In response, Whitehall created the Air Raid Precautions Department in March to implement Anderson's committee's recommendations and launch a sweeping campaign to fortify the home front.

The Air Raid Wardens' Service was created in 1937. A volunteer force, this was intended to implement ARP directives at a local level. Wardens were to be responsible for monitoring compliance with blackout regulations and would be on the front lines of their communities, providing information, enforcing safety measures, and assisting with emergency response. Thousands joined Plymouth's ranks.

The landmark passage of the 1937 Air Raid Precautions Act and its adoption in 1938 marked a transition from theoretical planning to practical implementation. It standardised procedures, ensuring greater consistency in training, equipment, and protocols. Local authorities had a statutory responsibility to develop and implement ARP schemes tailored to their specific areas. Recognising the significant costs associated with these measures, the Act also established a mechanism to underwrite these initiatives. The Act effectively set Britain's nationwide effort to prepare for any potential German aerial action into motion.

The 1938 Munich Crisis brought Europe closer to precipice of war. This centred around Nazi Germany's demand for the annexation of the German-speaking Sudetenland region of Czechoslovakia. Whether the nations of Europe would accede to Hitler's demands to appease him or would check those ambitions by defending Czechoslovakian sovereignty contributed to an atmosphere of imminent conflict.

Diplomatic tensions escalated in September. Fearing the outbreak of hostilities, Whitehall enacted emergency measures. Adhering to a prevailing concern of airborne gas attack, the government accelerated the distribution of gas masks to the civilian population. Local authorities, including those in Plymouth, intensified efforts to dig open-air trenches in public spaces such as parks and squares. These efforts were intended to provide some measure of protection, if only psychological, for civilians during an air raid.

The Munich Agreement on 30 September succeeded in preventing the outbreak of war. Prime Minister Neville Chamberlain famously celebrated that he had secured the foundation for a lasting peace in Europe.[3]

While Chamberlain had claimed victory, other camps contended that it was no longer a matter of if war could be avoided but rather when war would come—and whether Britain would be ready when it did.

Following the Munich Crisis, Whitehall conducted a threat assessment of different regions of Britain. At the outset of 1939, Plymouth was categorised as a 'neutral' area.[4] This classification meant that Plymouth occupied a middle ground in terms of vulnerability. HMNB *Devonport* was a target of strategic importance. Plymouth, by extension, was also at risk. Yet Plymouth lay outside the likely range of the Luftwaffe bases in Germany. Strategists determined other sites were more likely first-tier targets. Plymouth's designation—seeming to be out of immediate danger yet not completely immune—meant that the city needed to be ready yet could also entertain discussion about how best to implement measures.

The experience of being on the brink of war, coupled with the certainty that it would eventually come, underscored the urgency of continuing to make preparations.

Anderson shelters

A central pillar of the national preparedness plans was providing shelters for civilians. Whitehall concluded that every household in a vulnerable area should have some form of protection from aerial attack.[5] To achieve its objective, the government mass-produced shelter kits and facilitated their distribution. These shelters came to be known as 'Anderson shelters' after Sir John Anderson, the Home Secretary who was ultimately responsible for Britain's civil defence preparations.

The Anderson shelters were of a compact yet practical design. The corrugated metal structures measured 4.5 feet by 6 feet (1.4 by 1.8 metres) and were at least 6 feet (1.8 metres) from floor to ceiling. As such, the shelter could house four to six persons. While it could not shield against the impact of a direct hit, it was graded to withstand secondary impact: 'Such a shelter should provide reasonable protection against blast and splinters from the nearby explosion of a medium-sized high explosive bomb, and against the collapse of the superstructure.'[6] Cynics seized on this, and characterised the shelter programme as little more than a symbolic scheme designed to temper fears and anxiety about the coming conflict rather than to offer any real protection.[7]

Families would be responsible for constructing their shelter. Citizens would excavate a hole in their garden, insert the corrugated iron panels, and affix the roof. The shelter would then be insulated with earth. Families could enhance the shelter by outfitting the interior with seating or makeshift beds.

The initial distribution scheme for Anderson shelters was based on financial means. Families with an annual income of £250 or less were eligible to receive a shelter free of charge. Initial estimates suggested that about 30,000 Plymouth residents would qualify for this. The city was first to conduct a house-to-house inquiry to determine if a family qualified for a shelter and had the space to erect it. This process was anticipated to take seven months.[8] Those earning more than £250 could purchase a government-issued shelter for £8, but only after distribution to qualifying families was complete.[9] For households in this income bracket, sourcing an individual shelter through the private market was perhaps the most practical and expedient option.

Despite the relatively simple design and plans for the Anderson shelters, their installation proved more complex. Some Plymouth residents were unclear about the construction process. They expressed frustration: 'We are anxious to get on with the job and get our shelters together, but we have received no instruction as to how to erect them. It is no good fooling around with the stuff unless you know how to do the job properly.' To provide direction, Plymouth Corporation set up a sample shelter on Catherine Street to demonstrate proper construction techniques.[10]

Believing that the aerial threat to Plymouth was distant or unlikely, other citizens were more complacent and delayed constructing their shelters. An editorial in the *Western Morning News* opined that Plymouth residents and leaders had adopted a 'distance fallacy' and failed to recognise that modern aircraft were indeed capable of striking Plymouth. While it was the responsibility of city officials to pursue a policy of preparation rather than 'procrastination', the author wrote, it was likewise incumbent on the average 'man on the street' to contribute to the city's preparedness and 'do his share'.[11] This call to action would be repeated throughout the summer through information services and civic programming.[12]

In the end, only the outbreak of war itself, it seemed, would compel the procrastinators to act.

Communal shelters

While Anderson shelters provided a measure of protection, they were not a universal solution. Many lived in circumstances that made a garden shelter impractical or impossible. For example, there were homes that lacked the adequate space needed for an Anderson shelter. 'There were a large number of people living in the centre of the city and elsewhere who didn't have gardens,' recalled Larry Stevens who grew up in Plymouth.[13] Residents in flats faced a particular challenge. These families usually had no private outdoor space at all.[14]

Moreover, Anderson shelters could only offer a refuge for people when they were at home. Residents were vulnerable when at work, school, or simply out and about. These limitations highlighted a crucial gap in the air-raid defence strategy. A more comprehensive approach was needed to ensure the safety of all residents, regardless of their housing situation or daily activities.[15] Plymouth accelerated its investigation into the construction of communal shelters for the public in both the city's commercial core and congested residential areas.

The Air Raid Precautions Act vested local authorities such as Plymouth Corporation with sweeping powers to execute civil defence directives, including providing adequate public shelters for civilians. One of the most significant provisions was the power to requisition or purchase property. This stipulation empowered local authorities to secure suitable locations for public shelters, whether by commandeering existing structures, renovating buildings, or acquiring land on which to construct purpose-built ones.

In the winter of 1939, the Plymouth ARP Committee and City Council met to set policy regarding the city's permanent communal shelter system. This was intended to take a systematic approach to construction to avoid the haphazard excavation of trenches that had occurred during the Munich Criss the previous summer. Plymouth City Councillor H.G. Philips opposed the construction of any more open-air trenches as a 'waste of money'. Instead, he advocated investing in enclosed subterranean structures: 'Deep shelters can be built in proportion for about a third of the cost of trenches. The population would also feel secure and be secure. They would not look on air raids as a nuisance, and not as a thing of terror.'[16]

While waiting on directives from the Home Office in London about regulations concerning the construction specifications for these shelters and how the initiative would be funded, Plymouth set about assessing its needs and capacity. As an initial step, a survey of basements was proposed with the thought that some of these spaces could satisfy the anticipated requirements of the city.[17]

Instructions soon came from Anderson and his ARP group regarding what to do about the existing open-air trenches. It was suggested that these could be repurposed as the initial excavation work for more permanent shelter structures. First, the condition of the trenches would need to be evaluated.[18] In Plymouth, city leaders directed the city engineer to survey those locations and make an assessment. This report would then be used to determine which trenches would be refilled and which other ones would be deepened to house large, communal structures with concrete sidings and ceilings.[19]

The proposal was met with both criticism and concern. Some objected to the projected financial implications of the plan. This camp asserted that the shelters were an unnecessary endeavour because of the prevailing sentiment that other locales were more likely targets for a German attack than Plymouth.[20] Others deemed the timeline for the project too slow and contended that Plymouth was a significant military target that would certainly be in the scopes of Germany's attack plans. Former mayor Solomon Stephens, then serving as chairman of Plymouth's Air Raid Precautions Committee, attempted to strike a balance between both extremes: 'We have to remember that preparation for A.R.P. is new in this country,' he said. 'It is better to do something slowly which will not disfigure the city and which will afford full protection to the city.'[21]

Portland Square prepares

'Ever since the threat of war,' remembered Stanley Hollett, 'lots of air raid shelters had been built, on the streets, and lots of places were underground—like our beloved Portland Square.'[22] What had been a space for strolling and summer play would soon become something else entirely: a subterranean sanctuary built of reinforced concrete that was capable of protecting hundreds of people.

While many of the homes surrounding the Square could accommodate private Anderson shelters in their gardens, many residences housed more people than could take refuge in those structures. The need for a public shelter was even more critical for residents of the apartment buildings on the adjoining Victoria Street. It was imperative that these people should also have a place to take refuge during an aerial attack.

Plymouth Corporation thus commandeered the Square's private park as a site for one of the public shelters needed to satisfy civil defence requirements.

In June 1939, Portland Square was listed among the sites submitted to the Home Office as part of Plymouth's comprehensive plans to comply with ARP mandates.[23]

The shelter would serve as the principal public shelter for Drake's Ward. Initial estimates determined that the Portland Square Air-Raid Shelter could comfortably house 750 persons and be constructed at a cost of £3,450.[24]

The construction of shelters such as the one at Portland Square was carried out in earnest throughout the summer of 1939. Stanley remembered that the grounds were 'excavated and concrete tunnels constructed and then covered over, and this would give shelter to over 600 people'.[25]

The site was already partially excavated from the trenches dug during the 1938 Munich Crisis. While these existing trenches were incorporated into the designs, industrial excavators were brought in to accelerate the work. Fresh concrete was poured into moulds, and a series of prefabricated concrete block structures, often reinforced with steel girders, were fitted into place.[26]

Once a shelter was completed, crews backfilled trenches and covered the top with dirt. Like the Anderson shelters in private gardens, the top layer of hard-packed soil further insulated the shelter from the effects of a bomb while also restoring a sense of normality to the environs by concealing the bunker.

Shelters followed strict government specifications. Underground shelters were expected to be topped by at least 1.5 feet (.5 metre) of earth. The seating galleries were to be approximately 65 to 80 feet (20 to 25 metres) long with a height of 5.5 to 6.2 feet (1.7 to 1.9 metres). Galleries were to be 4.5 feet (1.4 metres) wide.[27] In practice, the galleries felt narrower because the addition of wooden benches alongside both walls effectively meant that citizens would sit knee to knee during an alert.

The air-raid shelter at Portland Square conformed to the national standard. The structure was made of reinforced concrete and had a curved ceiling.[28] It was 6.2 feet (1.9 metres) high and 4.5 feet (1.4 metres) wide.[29] Jim Brown, ARP warden for Portland Square, remembered that the shelter complex was divided into four compartments or pocket shelters that were connected by smaller communications tunnels.[30]

Indeeed, the schematic for larger shelters was configured to limit damage from a bomb. Portland Square utilised a perpendicular design scheme: 'This trench was laid out to a plan of tunnels or "galleries," each running at right angles to one another, to prevent blast shooting from one end of the shelter right through to the other. Basically, shelters worked on a damage limitation plan.'[31] If one section of the shelter sustained a direct hit, the other sections would not be as severely impacted.[32]

Additional shelter safety features included debris curtains and escape hatches. The curtains were heavy fittings that were able to be drawn across the entrance to the shelter once a raid began. This feature was supposed to stop debris and shrapnel from coming into the shelter if a bomb exploded close to the entrance. Escape hatches were located throughout the structure. These outlets offered alternative exits from the shelter if any egress route was obstructed.[33] Further, the Corporation promised that the shelters would be soundly constructed, 'The new ones envisaged in the scheme proper will be of steel and concrete.'[34]

Public shelters were also outfitted with seating, lighting, and provisions for sanitary needs.[35] 'In the big shelters, which are costly structures, everything possible is done to make them comfortable so that in the event of their use in an emergency they shall not be merely a "hole in the ground." Seats are provided, and the shelters are electrically lit.'[36]

The concrete burrow

The pace of shelter construction accelerated at the end of August. With shelters more widely viewed as 'a vital necessity', the intensity of work reflected a heightened sense of urgency. On 1 September, the same day that Germany invaded Poland, it was reported that work on Plymouth's public shelters was happening around the clock with crews rotating onto job sites in twenty-four-hour shifts.[37]

Drawing on a verse from the Gospel of Matthew, a *Western Morning News* editorial mused about the sanctuary that these shelters might now provide for Plymouth's citizens as war with Germany dawned: '"The foxes have holes and the birds of the air have nests," and man himself now has his concrete burrow to go to earth.'[38]

5

'This country is at war'

On 3 September, the United Kingdom declared war on Germany after the British ultimatum for Germany to commit to withdraw its troops from Poland was ignored.[1] Prime Minister Neville Chamberlain communicated the news to the nation from the Cabinet Room of 10 Downing Street. That evening, King George VI addressed the Empire, acknowledging the gravity of the moment and expressing his steadfast hope about the future:

> There may be dark days ahead, and war can no longer be confined to the battlefield, but we can only do the right as we see the right, and reverently commit our cause to God. If one and all we keep resolutely faithful to it, ready for whatever service or sacrifice it may demand, then with God's help, we shall prevail.[2]

'Those who were not anxiously standing by their wireless sets were at church,' reported the *Western Morning News* in Plymouth. 'There was no excitement – just a subdued acceptance of the situation.'[3] At St Augustine's Church, word of Chamberlain's announcement was met with voices raised in prayer as the community joined together to sing a hymn and the National Anthem.[4]

Anthony Cornelius was spending the last of the summer holidays at his grandmother's country retreat in Crapstone when war was declared: 'I had little concept of what that news meant. However, I soon realised that something was up when my gas mask arrived and had to go through numerous drills to learn how to use it.'[5] His neighbour Stanley Hollett recalled listening to the news on the wireless in his home at Portland Square. 'Very few people had any ideas of the horrors that were to come to our city of Plymouth.'[6]

The Portland Square project expands

The state of war accelerated progress on public air-raid shelter construction projects throughout Plymouth. By the middle of September, more headway had been made. The Portland Square shelter was initially intended to accommodate 650 people, but the scope of the project was expanded so that the site would be able to provide protection for at least 1,000. Construction would continue throughout the autumn to complete this extension. When finished, the complex at Portland Square would be one of the largest public shelters in Plymouth.[7] As one curious citizen who surveyed several shelters to inspect the work and compare them observed, 'The one over in Portland-square, over which I was courteously shown, was really excellent.'[8]

Though it was generally accepted that shelters were essential for public safety, there was also a recognition that the construction process and the structures themselves were changing the face of the city—and Portland Square was no exception. For example, Barbara Cundy remembered that the ornate fencing that bordered the park was removed: 'when the war came all the railings were taken down and the air raid shelter was made.'[9]

When the project expanded, an editorial entitled 'Trees and Trenches' in the *Western Morning News* expressed concern about the fate of Portland Square's characteristic trees, painting the construction work as a struggle between nature and human necessity:

> An interesting struggle of Nature against man is going on in Portland-square, Plymouth. As progress is made with the work on the trenches being constructed there, so the larger chestnut, sycamore, and other trees, hitherto undisputed tenants of the small area of earth, find their very existence threatened. Tons of soil are being dug away from their roots and piled high round their trunks. As yet, however, they have shown no signs of giving in.
>
> One or two, which were in the direct line of operations, had to be cut down at the start, the rest are in a flourishing state. A few leaves here and there are turning brown, and some are falling to the ground, but that is merely the advent of autumn.
>
> The real testing time will come when the trees will be trying to obtain nourishment from the soil for their next year's growth. In the spring we shall see the result of their endeavours. It is to be hoped they are successful, for Portland-square would be a barren sight without its trees.[10]

This waiting, watching, and wondering for the 'real testing time' of spring reflected a broader sense of suspended judgement and questions about the state of war with Germany. Indeed, the Wehrmacht, the unified armed forces of Germany, slowed down as autumn gave way to winter. After its 'lightning' conquest of Poland, Hitler's forces appeared to go into hibernation. Indeed, the winter of 1939–40 would come to be characterised as the 'phoney war' owing to the lack of any substantive military activity.

From phoney war to real war: shifts in air-raid shelter policy

Troublingly, reports emerged of vandalism and theft in Plymouth's newly completed public shelters almost immediately. 'Under cover of darkness, electric light bulbs have been removed, fittings tampered with, and seats damaged,' officials noted.[11] Lord Mayor G.S. Scoble, soon to be replaced by Viscount Waldorf Astor, expressed deep concern over this 'senseless damage' and 'petty pilfering', reminding citizens of their responsibility to maintain the shelters and take the threat of a Nazi aerial assault seriously.[12] He warned that the vandals' actions could have 'very serious consequences if these shelters have to be used suddenly', emphasising that the shelters were public property intended for everyone's safety.[13] 'There seem to be some people who do not yet realize that there is a war on,' he admonished.[14]

The months of inaction eroded the initial wartime urgency. Though there were gas mask and air-raid drills at schools, black-out restrictions, the onset of rationing, and the scheduled testing of air-raid sirens, no bombs had fallen. The air raids seemed to be more figments of Whitehall's fear-mongering imagination than a reality that the people of Plymouth—or Britain—would ever endure.

At the end of winter, while an apocalypse was about to be unleashed upon Europe, Plymouth was seemingly absorbed in the minutiae of local matters. An editorial in the *Western Morning News*, a continuation of a letter published in the autumn about the trees in Portland Square, focused not on Britain's state of war and Plymouth's preparedness for it, but rather on providing an update about landscape aesthetics and the maintenance of the park:

> When the construction of A.R.P. shelters in Portland-square, Plymouth, was undertaken last autumn, doubt was expressed in this column as to whether the trees would survive the spoliation of many of their roots and the removal of large quantities of soil. Care was taken that the trenches should run the length of the narrow avenues between the row of trees, but even so it was plain that nature would have something of a battle against the works of man.
>
> It can now be fairly said that the trees are coming out on the winning side. About a fortnight ago, the large chestnut tree at one corner shot out a few tentative buds. Now tiny leaves are appearing. Several of the other trees are following suit. Soon we may hope for a wealth of greenery to replace the dinginess of winter.
>
> It will be recalled that when authorities decided to use the square as a shelter site they promised the trustees that they would repair the railing which surround it, and also return the ground. Work on the railings has already started, and no doubt the turf will not be far behind. Already there is a new appearance of tidiness about the place, and when everything is completed residents in the neighbourhood will have reason to be grateful for the considerate treatment they have received from the governing authorities.[15]

This focus on beautification suggests a naïveté about the dire situation facing Britain. The writer's cheerful attention to 'tiny leaves' and anticipated 'wealth of greenery' and the satisfaction expressed about the 'new appearance of tidiness' read like a profound failure to grasp the magnitude of what being at war with Nazi Germany actually meant. That municipal authorities in Plymouth were dutifully honouring and prioritising promises about landscape restoration, and that citizens were noting this with approval, signal a community still operating largely within the framework of peacetime bureaucracy. Within months, Plymouth would face devastation that would render such concerns trivial.

The events of spring 1940 abruptly dispelled any remaining questions about Nazi Germany's ambitions. On 9 April, German forces struck to its north, overwhelming Denmark in mere hours before launching an assault on Norway. A month later on 10 May, the same day that Winston Churchill took office as Britain's prime minister and Minister of Defence, the Wehrmacht unleashed its full fury westward with breakneck speed. Luxembourg fell in less than a day. The Netherlands capitulated after just four days of resistance. Belgium held out for only eighteen.

The French Army similarly collapsed with stunning speed as German armoured columns sliced through the Ardennes and raced to the Channel coast. British forces, deployed to stand with their allies against the Nazi tide, found themselves outflanked. They were ultimately trapped and cornered on the beaches. Only through what would be coined the 'Miracle at Dunkirk' did British troops manage to evacuate across the Channel to safety. On 14 June, Paris fell, and the French signed an armistice on 22 June. The tables had turned in a mere six weeks. At the end of it, Britain was left standing alone against Nazi Germany's dominion over continental Europe.

The German Wehrmacht aggressively leveraged this momentum. It launched the first campaign fought entirely by aircraft: what became known as the Battle of Britain. Fought between July and October 1940, Germany sought to gain control of British airspace in preparation for a possible invasion. Early German attacks focused primarily on Royal Air Force (RAF) targets, including airfields, radar stations, aircraft factories, and infrastructure, to weaken Britain's capacity to defend itself. Although these attacks inflicted significant damage, they failed to eliminate the RAF or secure German control of the skies. As a result, the Luftwaffe increasingly shifted its focus away from military objectives and toward the terror bombing of British cities, setting the stage for the Blitz.

By the summer of 1940, the illusion of Plymouth's distance from the war had finally collapsed. *Western Evening Herald* correspondent Pat Twyford captured the situation: 'There was no longer any question in anyone's mind as to the vulnerability or remoteness of Plymouth as far as air attack was concerned. Plymouth was bang in the front line.'[16]

With Nazi forces in control of northern France, airfields in Vannes, Rennes, and Tours placed much of southern England within easy range of enemy bombers.

The logistics that would have made an aerial assault on Plymouth complicated—distance, fuel constraints, reduced payloads—no longer applied. Overnight, Plymouth was no longer on the periphery but rather situated directly in the Luftwaffe's strike zone. The city's significance to the war effort only increased the eventuality of a German attack. As the largest naval base in Western Europe, HMNB *Devonport* supported vital Atlantic convoy operations, hosting vessels in need of refuelling, resupply, and repair. Indeed, in the summer of 1939, Luftwaffe reconnaissance missions had mapped Plymouth's military and industrial infrastructure in forensic detail, surveillance that Nazi strategists would use to plan their eventual campaign on the city.[17]

Recognition and readiness

The stops and starts of preparing for war at last gave way to a mounting sense of urgency in Plymouth. With the Nazi threat positioned just across the Channel, citizens finally heeded the call to prepare themselves for aerial attack. Nearly half of the Anderson shelters that had been erected in Plymouth were found to be installed incorrectly. The winter had been unkind to these subterranean sanctuaries. Improper drainage had resulted in waterlogged floors and rendered some structures unfit for use. Residents endeavoured to take corrective action.

Other residents who had entirely delayed the installation of their Anderson shelters now rushed to set them up.[18] Indeed, as the last troops were evacuated from the beaches of Dunkirk, residents overwhelmed Plymouth Corporation offices with a flood of requests for assistance with erecting their shelters. What months of official planning and public notices could not accomplish, the fall of Europe had brought into sharp clarity: the realisation that Plymouth stood in the line of fire and that citizens needed to be ready.

This changing military landscape likewise transformed public sentiment towards communal air-raid shelters. Just a year earlier, Plymouth's citizens had debated the construction of public shelters. Even towards the end of the winter, these shelters were dismissed as 'white elephants', perceived as more costly to maintain than the value they promised to provide.[19] By the spring, this scepticism had faded. Now, citizens sanctioned expenditures for shelter upkeep and demanded that additional public shelters be built. That call would soon be answered with the construction of surface shelters strategically located down the middle of roads in some of Plymouth's most densely populated areas.[20]

Yet, even as anxiety rose, active public engagement varied. Indeed, the general public demonstrated little willingness to take personal ownership. For example, a pattern of passive criticism was evident in discussions over directional signage. Citizens complained that pointers to shelters and first-aid posts were 'vague' and 'indefinite', merely pointing 'somewhere' without specific street names or locations.[21]

Even when suggesting remedies, such as the seemingly simple task of adding street names 'when the signs are repainted', the public's approach remained one of identifying what others should do.[22]

The challenge of public indifference was compounded by continued acts of vandalism. In some cases, vandals caused significant damage. In one place, they reportedly moved 3 tonnes of rocks into one shelter's tunnels, ultimately making them impassable.[23] To mitigate vandalism, officials proposed locking the shelters; however, this measure created its own set of challenges connected with access. A subsequent appeal for volunteer 'key keepers' was intended to address that. Colin Campbell, town clerk and ARP controller, indicated that this position required no skill: 'They need not be trained A.R.P. workers, but simply people living near the shelters who would be responsible for the key.' Only eight people responded to a call for 800 positions, a mere 1 per cent of the required number.[24] That so few volunteered spoke volumes.

Similar calls went out to recruit citizens who lived or worked in the vicinity of a public air-raid shelter, presumably one that they and their families would be using, to help manage their local shelter and assist in 'preserving order and preventing panic'.[25] This request was also met with silence. The prevalence of signs stating 'there is no guard for this air-raid shelter' served as an admission of an 'apathetic public'.[26]

This collective shirking of responsibility underscored a deeper issue. While civil defence was a shared necessity, some seemed to treat it as someone else's responsibility.

Or might this collective paralysis have been a symptom of a deeper tension and undercurrent of fear, an awareness that the war across the horizon would test the city in ways still unimaginable?

Had Plymouth done enough? And would it be enough? In Portland Square, the trees stood in their uneasy defiance, sheltering a community perhaps still not ready for the storm that was to come. But that storm was coming. Indeed, for Major Lang Cornelius of No. 42, it had already begun.

6

A Wartime Portrait of a Father and Son

The summer of 1938 was filled with anticipation for young Anthony Cornelius. Just as he accompanied his father to the vestry of St Matthias's Church on Sunday evenings, Anthony occasionally tagged along with his father to the headquarters of the Territorial Army (TA) at the Drill Hall. The pair would board a tram near their Portland Square home at Tavistock Road, change at the busy Derry's Clock intersection, and then catch a shuttle to the bustling military centre of Devonport.[1]

Summer exercises for the 43rd Wessex Divisional Signals of the TA offered Anthony a glimpse into Lang's military world and a temporary escape from the ordinary happenings on Portland Square. The exercises became an adventure, with young Anthony watching Major Cornelius at work. As Anthony remarked, the experience provided 'great fun for an 11-year old!'.[2]

In June, the Terriers, as the Signals were called and referred to themselves, set up camp in Cornwood, a village just outside Plymouth, to practise their skills with tactical drills. Under the command of Major Cornelius, the troops prepared and tested equipment, laid cable lines to connect two centres of communication, and practised setting up and operating wireless devices across Dartmoor.[3]

Later in the summer, Major Cornelius was responsible for organising another war games exercise. The day was an opportunity to test out new equipment that mechanised the laying of communications cable. Held in early August, the exercise challenged the detachment to establish communications between a fixed headquarters and a mobile column.[4]

Neither father nor son could have guessed how soon those drills would become more than just practice.

Lang rises through the ranks of the TA

The TA emerged in the aftermath of the First World War. Originally conceived as the Territorial Force at the start of the war and reconstituted by the Territorial Army and Militia Act of 1921, the TA was meant to augment Britain's national defence. Comprising of civilians, the TA was envisaged as a reserve force. While the British Expeditionary Force (BEF) would serve as the nation's combat troops, the TA would provide reinforcement and act as a support mechanism. In a war, TA divisions would join regular army units and be deployed in waves on an as-needed basis.

During the 1920s, the TA offered a pragmatic solution for maintaining a degree of military readiness even as agreements were made about disarmament and demilitarisation. It functioned as a strategic safety net in that it allowed for rapid expansion and mobilisation in the event of future conflict without maintaining a large standing army in peacetime.

Lang Cornelius's background in communications made him suited to the work of the TA Signals. This was a specialist technical unit responsible for providing essential battlefield telecommunications systems. Having previously served with the 21st Corps Signal Company of the Royal Engineers during the First World War, Lang had both military communications and leadership experience. He continued to serve as part of the British strategic forces in the Middle East through 1920.

Likewise, his career with the GPO's telegraph division in Plymouth provided him with additional practical experience in communications systems. Lang's understanding of communications infrastructure aligned with the Signals' focus of installing, maintaining, and operating telecommunications equipment in support of the infantry. With their need for trained engineers, the Signals unit found in Lang a professional who not only understood technical intricacies but also had first-hand experience in navigating the environments and situations where these communications technologies and skills would be utilised.

Lang was granted a TA Commission as second lieutenant with the 43rd Wessex Divisional Signals on 10 September 1925. In 1927, he was promoted to lieutenant and then elevated to the rank of captain in 1929. He was named a major on 10 April 1934.[5]

Lang's involvement with the TA extended beyond its military functions. The TA served as a social institution of sorts, particularly for veterans of the First World War such as Lang seeking to maintain their service connections. Local newspapers regularly reported on these social gatherings. Lang immersed himself in this aspect of TA life, attending the annual TA officers' dances in Plymouth during the early 1930s with other members of the Cornelius and Hill families.[6] These events, designed to promote relationships within the ranks and generate broader interest in the TA, reflected the organisation's understanding that social cohesion and networking might enhance critical recruiting efforts.

A detachment of Lang's No. 1 Company was selected to serve as part of the military guard of honour for the coronation of King George VI at Westminster Abbey in May 1937. As they stood to attention along the streets of London, these men were placed at the very heart of one of the most significant ceremonial events of the interwar period. Though the day was marked by driving rain, the atmosphere teemed with pride and enthusiasm. Lang observed that 'although we got soaked to the skin, the celebrations were worth going to see—it was a sight we shall never forget'.[7]

Despite such opportunities, the TA faced persistent challenges of funding and recruitment. Lang was committed to addressing these issues throughout the 1930s. Presiding over the December 1932 company dinner, Lang reported that while the unit maintained its military readiness, it was not at full strength. In particular, it faced a shortage of skilled operator recruits. Previously, the Post Office had provided a steady pipeline of professionals, like Lang, with technical aptitude. That personnel reserve was now tapped. The shortage necessitated a shift towards more internal training programmes.[8]

At the January 1934 dinner, Lang praised the company's successful recruiting efforts. In his address, Lang emphasised how TA service developed both 'elements of discipline and good citizenship' that benefited civilian employers, advocating for greater workplace accommodations that might further increase TA participation.[9] Lang's strategic thinking and efforts to expand capacity were formally recognised with his promotion to major that April.

As the decade progressed, Lang's role and responsibilities focused more and more on recruitment initiatives. At the January 1935 company dinner, he applauded the unit's unprecedented success in recruitment initiatives. He noted that the company had achieved 'the happy position of having a waiting list of recruits'. Specialist positions, such as electricians and instrument mechanics, however, remained difficult to fill. He reported that a number of members had transitioned into the regular Army, a testament to the TA's effectiveness as a pipeline and training ground for active service. Lang particularly praised the growing cooperation of Plymouth's business community in providing release time for TA service.[10] Lang's remarks underscored the ongoing evolution of the company's recruitment strategies and the increasing importance of community collaboration to sustain them.

A special TA recruitment task force was convened in 1937 to coordinate efforts and resources.[11] Lang's contribution was to strengthen the TA's relations with Plymouth's business community. He promoted the mutual benefits of TA service for businesses, their employees, and the TA.[12] These efforts coincided with the increasing urgency across Britain to expand TA numbers as international tensions mounted and signs pointed towards war.

At the 1938 company dinner, Lang highlighted the impact of the task force's efforts. While acknowledging the perennial challenges of resources and facilities, Lang could attest to significant progress in numbers and military readiness.[13] He thanked and praised those employers who had extended additional leave and pay privileges to TA members, which had the effect of even more men joining the TA—numbers that would continue to swell over the succeeding year.

Major Cornelius: a father on the front

By March 1939, the escalating expansionism of Nazi Germany had reached an inflection point. Brazenly moving beyond the earlier annexation of the Sudetenland, Germany completely occupied Czechoslovakia. Hitler's flagrant violation of the Munich Agreement shattered any remaining illusions of diplomatic restraint. Would Hitler stop there? Europe's policy of appeasement had failed. Hitler's decisive act made it abundantly clear that war was not a distant possibility but an imminent danger.

Within two weeks of the Nazi occupation, British Secretary of State for War and MP for Plymouth Devonport Leslie Hore-Belisha announced plans to dramatically increase the numbers of the TA. The signal was clear: Britain knew it could no longer rely on diplomacy alone. A shift was under way among the politicians in Whitehall, one that acknowledged military force might soon be the only viable response.

The TA's expansion strategy was urgent yet methodical. The core of the expansion plan centred on a duplication strategy: existing units were tasked with over-recruiting, with the goal of creating parallel, second-line divisions. Once sufficient numbers were achieved, the original unit would split into two. This strategy ensured that new units included a complement of veteran reservists. In essence, the goal was to share the resources of institutional knowledge, leadership, and experience so that all units would be evenly trained and ready.

Major Cornelius played a central role in driving a surge of recruits for his unit. He organised a citywide drive in which a convoy of the Signals' motorised assets toured the streets and staged interactive demonstrations. The displays drew public attention and highlighted the unit's modern capabilities and communications technology. The campaign proved effective. Enlistments rose sharply and contributed to reducing the unit's manpower deficit by nearly a quarter in just a week. To speed the intake process further, Cornelius even opened his own home in Portland Square as an auxiliary office for processing recruits into the company.[14]

Throughout the spring, the unit engaged in a steady programme of training designed to prepare recruits for the demands of modern warfare. This culminated in July with a large-scale war games exercise intended to test the men's technical skills in a realistic combat setting. For the Signals, this meant not only demonstrating proficiency in wireless, line, and visual communication, but doing so under the pressures and uncertainties of a battle scenario.

Major Cornelius designed and coordinated the two-part exercise, which unfolded under torrential rain in Tavistock, conditions that added further challenge to the day. The scenario imagined a conflict between the invading forces of 'Yellowland' and the defending state of 'Wessexia'. In the first phase, the Signals were tasked with relaying a complex series of messages between fixed points using wireless sets, mechanical cable layers, and dispatch riders. The second phase required them to maintain this traffic while on the move, adjusting to the demands of a mobile battlefield.

The exercise was a success. New recruits gained valuable, tangible experience in their skills, while more seasoned men faced additional tests designed to stretch their abilities. The day not only reinforced technical skills and practical lessons but also strengthened cohesion within the unit. Just as importantly, it highlighted those individuals capable of assuming greater responsibility at a moment when the formation of a parallel division would soon require men who were prepared to step into leadership roles.[15]

In August, the unit travelled to Corfe Castle in Dorset for a fortnight of intensive training.[16] The camp combined advanced technical instruction with continued recruit development. This provided the men an experience beyond what could be achieved in Plymouth while also creating a degree of consistency across the TA. This programme proved particularly timely as the division neared the point at which it would cleave in two.

By the end of the month, the 43rd had reached the recruitment levels necessary to split, leading to the creation of a second-line duplicate: the 45th (West Country) Divisional Signals. The split coincided with the Nazi invasion of Poland on 1 September. Personnel from the 43rd were reassigned to the 45th as part of the TA restructuring programme.

Major Cornelius was embodied with the 45th Divisional Signals on 2 September. The immediate priority was thorough yet accelerated training. All efforts were focused on preparing the division for its anticipated mobilisation to France in the spring of 1940. Given the major's role in designing and coordinating the Signals' training exercises, he was a natural choice to assist the newly formed 45th in structuring its routines and achieving operational readiness.

With the 45th now established, the unit dispersed from Plymouth to training sites throughout the region. Anthony soon faced the moment of farewell, watching his father depart for Crediton, north of Exeter.

Lang penned a letter home to Anthony on 13 November 1939. Written on official 45th Divisional Signals stationery—its motto *Certa Cito*, 'Swift and Sure', emblazoned at the top—the letter spoke directly to Lang's young son:

> Dear old Boy,
> I hope you are behaving yourself + being a real help to Mummy now that I am away + since Basil has not been well.
>
> Yes, thank you. My cold is very much better.
>
> I haven't seen any cards 'Soldiers of the king.' I have some 'Uniforms of the Territorial Army' like the one in this letter + I shall be bringing them home with me. I will send you some duplicates later, but I have not yet got the set. Keep any you may have very clean so that we can perhaps fill up the gaps.

There is a small P.O enclosed for you. Don't spend it now, but save it for Xmas when I hope to be home with you all for a whole week. We must try + have a jolly time since I cannot get home for Nov 28th. Do you know that date?

Must hurry now + post this for the mail so that you may get it tomorrow Tuesday morning.

Look after Mummy + Basil.

With love + kisses to you three from your Daddy.

xxxxxxx[17]

Lang's letter reveals a profound paternal intimacy. He affectionately refers to Anthony as 'old Boy' and alludes to his own forthcoming birthday on 28 November. The letter is laced with fatherly encouragement, urging Anthony to be on his best behaviour, to be 'a real help to Mummy', and to take on the responsibility to 'look after Mummy + Basil'. The letter also demonstrates Lang's efforts to maintain the close relationship he enjoyed with his son. The two had a shared interest in building collections, and the details about Lang's efforts to curate sets of cigarette cards speak to this: the collectable cards included detailed coloured illustrations of regimental uniforms. Lang's efforts to search for these, send duplicates to Plymouth, and his instructions for Anthony to keep his own collection 'clean' so they could 'fill up

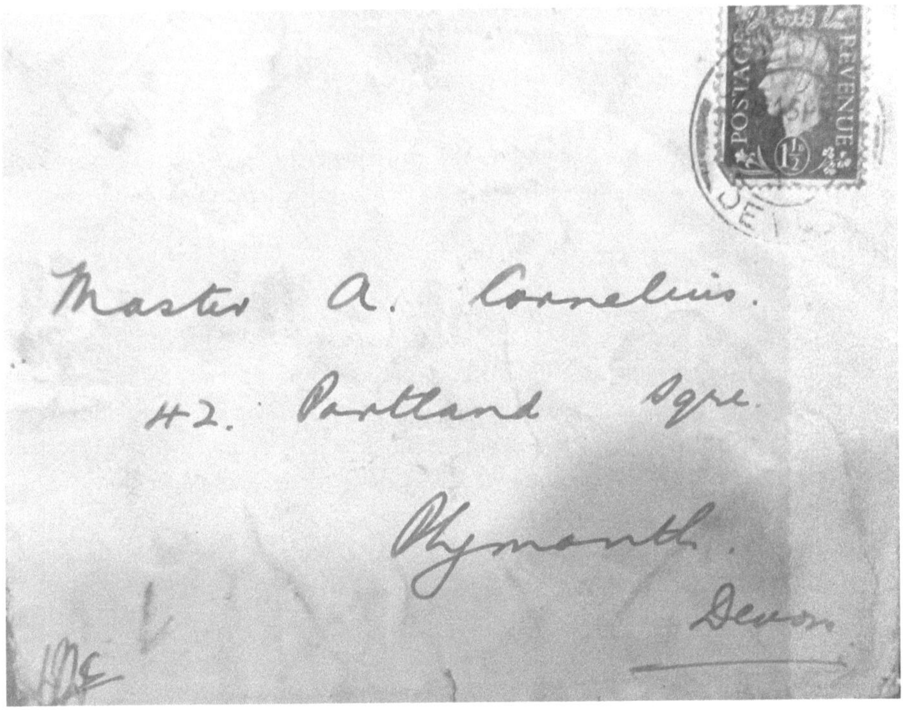

Envelope addressed to Anthony Cornelius containing letters from Lang, 1939. [Dunham family]

the gaps' together upon his return, point to an attempt to preserve a semblance of normality amid the growing uncertainties of war.

In February 1940, Lang was briefly deployed to France—from 13 February to 21 February—in support of the BEF. The presence of the BEF was meant to bolster French forces and deter further German manoeuvres. It seemed to work, at least briefly. The winter of 1939–40 was a period marked by military inaction on both sides after the initial declaration and mobilisation towards war in the autumn.

Lang's letters home from France pulsed with paternal love and gentle encouragement. Noting 'with the BEF' on the top of his note, Lang wrote to Anthony on 18 February 1940 of snowball fights and souvenir trinkets, promising rewards for academic achievement and encouraging his son to keep his stamp collection, another mutual hobby, in good order:

> Well! My son, I hope you are quite fit again, and back at school. Don't forget what I promised you, a really good present if you come out 1st, 2nd, or 3rd this term. So do try. You would love it here with plenty of snowballing. I cannot write very much as paper is short, but I thought you would like a short note from me to keep. I am bringing along a wee souvenir – it is very small, but comes from here which is the main thing.
>
> Look after Mummy + Basil, until I come. And keep your stamp album clean + tidy.
>
> Cheerioh! Your loving Daddy xxxxxxx[18]

Another letter on the same day and on the same paper to Lang's younger son Basil echoed these themes—encouragement to do well in school, promises of a prize, and some fatherly humour:

> Darling Basil,
> Well! My little man. How are you now. Back at school with Miss Slater again I hope, sitting at your nice little desk. Please tell Mummy to give my best regards to Mr. Welchman when she sees him next time. I am bringing along a little memento and a coin for you next time I am on short leave which I hope won't be very long. This can only be a short letter because of paper, but, like Anthony, I know you will wish to keep it, coming from here. Would you like a nice cold snowball? If so, come here + I'll give you one.
> Cheerioh! Little chappie
> Your loving Daddy xxxxxxx[19]

Lang was soon recalled to England and returned to Plymouth. The souvenir referenced in his letters was packed carefully in his bags: a gyroscope with its base fashioned from a miniature Eiffel Tower. Years later, Anthony would recall the toy with nostalgia, remembering how he would wind the gyroscope, release it, and watch it balance on the tower's base.[20]

On 3 April, Lang's father-in-law Percy Hill died. The funeral was held on 6 April at St Matthias's Church and was conducted by the Rev. Roger Welchman. Lang joined Maggie at the service. Maggie's mother, Percy's widow Emma, was indisposed and could attend neither the funeral nor the burial that followed at Ford Park Cemetery.[21] Percy's death had a lasting impact on Lang, who now had added concerns about his grieving family and the future of the Hill's pawnbrokerage business, which Emma now managed alone. Emma was so distraught after Percy's death that she sold much of their household furniture and other belongings at auction.[22]

Shortly after the burial, Lang rejoined his unit—which was preparing for redeployment to France. But the evolving landscape of the war necessitated a change to this assignment. As previously mentioned, Germany invaded Denmark and Norway on 9 April, then Belgium, France, Luxembourg, and the Netherlands simultaneously on 10 May. The speed with which the Low Countries fell and with which the German Army pushed into France, put a stranglehold on Paris, and pinned the combined British and French forces to the Channel coast erased any hope for the Allied command. Retreat became the order of the day.

Thus, while the War Ministry focused on evacuating the trapped Army from peril in France in late May, Lang and the 45th were assigned to Kent to provide critical defensive coverage in the event of a Nazi invasion.

The strain of military life

Lang's letters from this later spring period lay bare the weight of military life. They reveal an older man wrestling with the psychological toll of yet another war. There was a deeper struggle too—the emotional toll of uncertainty and separation from his young family. Amid the unfolding drama of the Dunkirk evacuation, Lang's letters home to his wife Maggie reveal the personal impact of war.

Writing late into the night on 30 May from Sevenoaks, Kent, Lang exposed his struggles:

> My beloved darling,
> Just a brief note before I turn in. Am afraid I have some unfortunate news to relate. For some months past I have not felt equal to the strain of this kind of life as we are finding it now, and I've been feeling that the task I was called upon to do was beyond my strength. Ever since your Dad passed on I have not felt the same.

The CO fetched me in his room yesterday + was very nice about things, but said he felt compelled to tell the G.O.C. he did not consider I could stand up to the job. I have got to admit he is right. We all of us have a limit, and I honestly feel I have reached mine. I shall be 44 next Nov, and I feel I cannot stick it. I get very nervy + jumpy at times and once or twice I've had broken nights. I expect I shall have to see the General soon and L.B. thinks they may find a more suitable job for me elsewhere. However, darling, don't lose heart. It will I am sure be all for the best + pray that I may get a billet nearer home.

L.B. himself is very morose at times + Pat Tottendell even says he feels the strain. It is possible that one or two more may be shifted as well shortly. I've got a feeling Gerald may be included – but I don't know.

I try so hard to keep pace with this hectic life but its useless hoodwinking oneself to hard facts.

So soon as I know anything definite I will write or wire. Please don't tell anyone yet, because it is not definite.

Had a letter today from Mother. Please tell her I've received it + will be writing again later. We still have no news, but there are many rumours, so we just rub along from day to day.

Have just had a nice bath and its nearly 11.30 pm so will close + get down to it.

God bless you, my three darlings. Please pray hard for me sweetheart, that I may be given a good job suitable to me nearer home. Ask Roger to offer up a prayer for me during this difficult time (but don't tell him why, please).
Nightie night
With all my love and kisses
Ever your living Hubby + Daddy
Billie xxxxxxx
A xxxxxxx
B xxxxxxx[23]

In this intimate letter, Lang reveals his fears and frailties. The recent loss of his father-in-law seems to have punctured whatever emotional resilience he had maintained. He reflects on his own limitations. Lang's increasing age and the escalating demands of military service have conspired to overwhelm him. Though post-traumatic stress disorder would not be clinically defined for years, Lang's visceral reactions to the psychological landscape of war were symptomatic responses to the trauma he endured in his youth and now seemed to be reliving: broken nights, a nervous disposition, and emotional exhaustion. Prayers, letters from home, and the prospect of a new assignment that was closer to Plymouth seemed to bring him a sense of relief.

In the days following, Lang continued to navigate the uncertainty of his position with a mixture of hope and worry. Writing to Maggie again on 1 June, he expresses his persistent concerns about what his possible reassignment might entail and how it might impact his family:

My beloved darling,

In case I do not get much time tomorrow I will write this short note now. Have not yet received the parcel of clothes. Hope it arrives on Monday in case I have to make a hurried move elsewhere. There is no news further in this matter. The recommendation at present is for an administrative job with a training unit or an area job. This is only the first step. It will be for the higher authority to decide. My one fear is whether I may have to revert to rank of Captain. I sincerely hope not and pray not.

Am enclosing a 1/- P.O. cash for the boys. Had a shock today when pay list arrived, as most of us have only received 18 days pay + allowances instead of 31, owing to change of area. However, I hope the balance will come soon, but then I suspect they will take a slice out for income tax. So be very careful darling with the cash – the situation is critical until I know what the monthly deduction is going to be.

Am attending church parade tomorrow as last Sunday. L.B. will not be there so shall be reading lesson again I suspect. The vicar paid an official call here at teatime + I had a chat with him afterwards.

Hope to go to evening service at St. Nicholas as last Sunday.

The doctor has now received some vaccine so shall probably be done on Monday noon + get it over.

Still no news from the P.O. re promotion. They are a long time deciding.

Had a nice letter from Ruth yesterday, offering to send me a parcel if I required it or knitting, so shall reply saying "very many thanks" but nothing required at the moment.

Jove! If they happened to send me to the West it would be ok. Lets hope so.

Well my darling, my heart aches every day + night with longing to be with you + the boys again, even if only for a short spell. It would certainly break the strain a bit.

Must close now beloved, and get to bed as its getting late + I feel the need for rest. It's been awfully bad here today, with tendency to thunder, but so far it has kept off. We had a storm with very little rain earlier in the week which lasted 4–5 hours + then cleared up.

I hear Plymouth is pretty crowded these days, according to Mrs. Nash who has come up for the weekend. I disapprove of the ladies being here – there are several now, but I think it rather foolish at present. Still, it is their affair.

Nightie night, my darlings, God bless + keep us all safe – reunite us all soon in Peace to the world.

With all my love and kisses. Ever your loving hubby + Daddy,
Billie xxxxxxx
A xxxxxxx
B xxxxxxx[24]

Lang's letter reads like a careful report about his daily happenings and interactions. Between these observations, though, he continues to express his anxieties about his position within the TA and the potential personal impact of any change. Lang seemed acutely aware of his diminishing capacity and recognised the need to restructure his responsibilities. The recommendation from the divisional brass for Lang to take on an administrative job would allow him to continue serving—and for the division to continue benefiting from his leadership—while accommodating his limitations. Lang approached the news with a mix of cautious optimism and apprehension. He hoped that the new assignment might include relocating closer to home and family. However, he worried that the change might necessitate a demotion to the rank of captain with a commensurate reduction in pay. Further, having achieved the rank of major and played a leadership role with the Signals for the past decade, this potential reduction in rank may have stung his professional pride.

No records or letters chronicle how his conditions deteriorated over the summer. On 10 September 1940, however, Lang relinquished his commission on account of ill health and was thus invalided from the TA. He returned to his family in Plymouth and resumed his work at the GPO.

Committed to honouring his civic duty to serve his country, Lang volunteered to join the newly-instituted Home Guard. This was formed of volunteers who were either too young, too old, or otherwise unable to serve in the regular armed forces or reserves. They played a crucial role in providing additional support on the home front. Lang was a part of the 21st (33rd GPO) Battalion, Devon Home Guard, which was made up of GPO employees and was tasked with protecting that organisation's communications equipment.[25] For Lang, joining the Home Guard provided a meaningful way to continue to contribute to the war effort despite his medical discharge.

Lang's homecoming to Portland Square brought little reprieve. Though he had returned home, he was no further from the reach of war. If anything, he was now even closer to it. The Luftwaffe's aerial assault over Plymouth was transforming the port city into a battlefield of its own.

7

Attacks from the Air

On Saturday 6 July 1940, Plymouth experienced its first Luftwaffe attack.

That morning, Sylvia (née Nicholas) Whitton had returned home to Swilly Road to visit her younger siblings—Dot, Ivy, Fern, and Joe —after having celebrated her honeymoon on the Isle of Wight. Her sisters played with their dolls in the yard.[1] Next door, Mr Harry Swinburne sat on his front step polishing his shoes. Children from the adjoining homes enjoyed the summer sun.

Just before noon came the sound of aircraft engines, high above. The drone of the enemy engine was unmistakable. Those watching the skies searched for signs of the enemy raider. There, against the blue summer sky, the intruder appeared as little more than a glinting speck, artfully weaving between wisps of cloud cover in a triangular pattern over the city.[2]

Air-raid sirens wailed, and everyone ran for cover.

Then came a sound no one had heard before, but everyone had dreaded: the menacing whistle of the first bomb ever dropped on Plymouth. Several landed on the homes on Swilly Road and claimed Plymouth's first air-raid victims.

Blanche Ellnor, 33, had brought her children to their garden shelter at the start of the alert. After some time, she left and returned inside her home, a decision that proved tragic. A neighbour, Henrietta Mould, recounted the scene in a letter to her daughter Audrey: 'She thought it was such a long time before the all-clear … so she ran back to put her dinner in the oven, and a bomb dropped right on the house.'[3] The blast flung Mrs Ellnor's body into the next garden.

When crews arrived on the scene, they encountered Fern searching through the debris for the dolls that Dot and Ivy had been playing with. The blast had knocked Dot into the Nicholases' half-finished Anderson shelter, and Ivy was propelled in right behind her, the extreme force of the explosion tearing her clothing. Emergency personnel dug both of the young girls from the rubble. Sylvia suffered a gash on her neck and a dislocated shoulder. Their brother Joe, 13, was also wounded. The blast severely damaged his ear and caused additional injury. He was taken to the Prince of Wales Hospital, Greenbank, where he died two days later.[4]

Emergency services responded to the incident in full force. Mould recalled the large crowd that descended upon the blast site: 'ARP workers, police and soldiers, ambulances, doctors and nurses you can imagine what the scene was like.'[5] It was one of utter devastation. A reporter for the *Western Morning News* captured the wreckage: 'Above, a wall leaned drunkenly against the staircase top. Beds were white with plaster from bared ceiling laths; broken glass lay everywhere, curtains and their poles were twisted as though a hurricane had blown through the house.' In a neighbouring home, 'Pictures hung at strange angles, and not a corner of any room had escaped the falling masonry.'[6]

The third victim, Harry Swinburne, 58, was discovered buried under the rubble of the ruined homes. The randomness of survival would become a cruel hallmark of the blitz—his wife had been shopping in the city, while their young son David had taken shelter with neighbours and escaped unharmed.

As the dust settled, one warden, brushing debris from his uniform and adjusting his tin hat, grimly observed, 'That's the first taste. [...] but I'm afraid it's only a taste.'[7] His words would prove prophetic.[8]

A city under siege

Over the next fortnight, Plymouth would endure its initiation into this new form of warfare as the Luftwaffe launched a further seven strikes between 7 and 21 July.

The tempo quickened mercilessly in the days following that first raid. On Sunday afternoon, 7 July, as families gathered for afternoon tea, another German bomber descended over Plymouth. The raid demonstrated the enemy's brazen confidence as the attack again took place in broad daylight. The bombs struck at the junction of South Milton Street and Home Sweet Home Terrace. The rehearsed air-raid drills seemed to prove their worth as most residents had already reached the safety of nearby shelters. Five, including a policeman and soldier dutifully protecting others, were killed.[9]

The following morning brought no reprieve when Devonport suffered its turn under fire. A bomb plunged through the Royal Sailors' Club in Morice Square: it exploded in the kitchen and reduced the dining room to rubble. Mass casualties were narrowly avoided; the dining room had been filled with sailors enjoying a hearty breakfast only minutes before the attack. Sidney Slee, aged 54, a butcher, was not as fortunate, however. He was killed in his shop when it sustained a direct hit.[10]

The next days painted a grim picture of Plymouth's new normal. After a day of reprieve, 10 July saw bombs falling across Exeter Street and the recreational Hoe district, with the enemy adding a cruel flourish by machine-gunning civilians as they ran for cover.[11] Though none were struck by bullets, five lives were lost to the bombs. Two days later, on 12 July, the Germans expanded their reach, raining down explosives on residential areas across the city. The RAF station at Mount Batten was the primary target for a raid on 15 July.

This merciless pattern continued throughout the month. After a relatively minor raid on 20 July, Plymouth found itself trapped in an exhausting sequence of alerts the following day. Five separate waves in the span of twenty-four hours kept citizens in a perpetual state of anxious vigilance.[12] Kent Tugwood, 4, was one of two casualties that day. The boy had been battling the flu, and tragically, he had been taken back home after one alert because his parents believed that the comforts of home would be better for their son's health than the conditions of the shelter.[13]

The July raids definitively answered any lingering questions about the city's vulnerability and offered a preview of what was to come. There would be no rest for Plymouth's citizens: they would now order their lives by the sounds of air-raid sirens. Evenings that were once peaceful became punctuated more frequently by the drone of enemy aircraft and the terrifying explosion of bombs. The Luftwaffe was waging an assault on civilian morale through fear: nobody and no locale was out of range. The intentional bombing of civilian targets further blurred any distinction between the home front and the front lines of war.

Witnessing war at home

Though the bombs fell elsewhere, war had crept into daily life at 42 Portland Square.

Upstairs, lodger Isadore Gasson found himself accused of failing to observe the nightly blackout restrictions. He appeared in court to contest the charge. There, he produced a green curtain as evidence that no light had escaped his window. The charge was dismissed.[14]

Meanwhile, downstairs, Anthony Cornelius recalled standing at the kitchen door wearing his toy tin helmet and scanning the sky for signs of the enemy aircraft: 'My father was rather nervous and wanted me to come indoors. I remember looking up and seeing searchlights and seeing a kind of silvery confetti coming down. I found out later they were bombs.'

Anthony recalled how, for him, the early alerts and summer Luftwaffe raids seemed to be more of an inconvenient disruption to daily life than any real danger:

> The raids started off as so called nuisance raids. The barrage balloons would go up, a few German planes would come over, nothing happened. I think we all got lulled into a sense of false security. We saw "con trails" (condensation trails left by the exhaust of the plane's engines) high in the sky and said "Jerry is at it again." Not much more than that. We continued on our way, probably to school.[15]

Anthony approached the situation with a child's sense of invincibility and amusement. 'For a kid it was quite an exciting time,' he reflected.[16] 'Life for a 12 year old boy in those days was full of adventure. Girls had not been invented.'[17] When the all-clear sirens sounded, Anthony and his friends scoured the city for bomb fragments. 'We would walk the streets looking for shrapnel and bits of incendiary bombs.'[18] What was terrifying for adults became, in his young eyes, an opportunity for exploration:

> On the way to school, I would look for incendiary bomb fins and eventually amassed quite a collection. The bombs were quite small, about two feet long and about four inches in diameter. They were made of thermite and would ignite when they landed and would burn intensely for several minutes. The fins were made of steel and therefore survived the fire.[19]

The dangers of war were momentarily forgotten as Anthony and his friends revelled in building their collection, finding wonder in the very thing that also caused so much worry. But the illusion of safety could not last. The war was no longer a story broadcast on the wireless; it was falling from the sky, echoing in the streets, and pressing in from every direction.

The increasing frequency of air raids transformed daily life. Anthony's boyish enthusiasm couldn't mask the physical and psychological toll. As the raids intensified, the thrill faded. He began to flinch at loud noises and found himself increasingly unsettled. 'The air raids were, in some respects, a frightening time for me,' he recalled. His anxiety, which had been heightened by loud noises, was only magnified by the terrifying din of war: 'I was always very nervous of thunderstorms and the sound of heavy antiaircraft guns and bombs exploding did nothing to calm me.'[20]

Plymouth goes underground

The Luftwaffe raids became a grim routine as summer gave way to autumn. Plymouth's network of public shelters filled with those seeking refuge from the Nazi terror in the skies above. Nights that should have been spent comfortably at home were instead frequently spent in the damp, crowded quarters of the city's subterranean air-raid shelters as the Luftwaffe changed tactics. Residents of Portland Square and the surrounding streets trudged to the air-raid shelter beneath the park, bunkering down with neighbours and praying that they could endure another sleepless night without losing everything.

The Chapman family on Victoria Street was one of those that were obliged to use the Portland Square shelter. Peter, the youngest of the four Chapman brothers, remembered the first time that he took shelter there:

> The first time I entered on the south side, a veteran of the First World War was sat picking at his clothes. This is what they did in the trenches picking out lice. He was called Craig & the urchins unkindly referred to him as "picking 'em

> out Craig." Being freshly built, it smelt of cement. I can only recall the south & east sides which each had an entrance in the middle of the site. The shelter had dome shaped tunnels. On each side of the tunnels were wooden slatted seats on which to sit & sleep. There was an escape hatch on the east tunnel. The tunnels had electric lighting.[21]

Peter's recollection captures the raw, industrial nature of underground spaces such as the Portland Square Air-Raid Shelter—the fresh cement smell and basic furnishings emphasising their utilitarian design.

Anthony recounted his childhood impressions of the shelter: 'You went down some steep steps to get inside and turned left or right, it was lit by electric light I think. For a kid it was quite an exciting time.'[22] He would have visited the shelter regularly with his family:

> We spent many nights in the shelter and I remember those hard wooden seats, the dim lighting, and the dank smell. We used to sit just inside the entrance that faced East toward Tavistock Road. I remember I had a tin hat – a toy – and I used to wear it religiously when the sirens went. Fat lot of protection it would have given me but of course we never thought of those things then.[23]

Noreen Wise who lived on the opposite side of the Square, remembered the environment as uncomfortable and how it wore on her family: 'We spent so many nights in that cold shelter on the hard slatted benches, we were so cold, tired, and frightened.'[24]

The Portland Square shelter became like a second home for those who utilised it. The shelter developed its own unique rhythms and routines as people sought ways to cope with the nightly uncertainty of air raids. The communal atmosphere offered temporary respite from the terror.

As Arthur Davis, a boy from Victoria Street whose family also sheltered at Portland Square, reflected, the shelter functionally transformed into something akin to a social club. Children found distraction in games while adults passed the anxious hours playing cards.[25]

'When the raids were particularly bad,' recalled Noreen, 'we would have sing songs to keep our spirits up.'[26] Larry Stevens, whose family also made regular use of the shelter, noted that these songs included popular tunes such as *Run Rabbit Run*, *The White Cliffs of Dover*, and *The Quartermaster's Store*. 'There were also times,' Larry reflected, 'when people were too weary to sing and just sat in silence hoping that the next bomb was not for them.'[27]

This shared experience proved so compelling that some residents chose the public shelter over their private Anderson shelters, preferring the comfort of companionship with neighbours to the prospect of facing the frightening raids alone.[28]

Through these activities and support, shelter occupants created moments of normality, temporarily pushing aside the dark reality of the conflict raging above ground.

From summer to school

London bore the brunt of the Luftwaffe's concentrated fury in the autumn of 1940, and Plymouth's residents found themselves drawn into an uneasiness of more intermittent air raids. The sporadic nature of these attacks necessitated planning and emergency drills to teach residents about how to keep themselves safe in different situations.

Anthony recalled how vigilance and raid preparedness impacted his school day at Plymouth College:

> Back at school, I remember the Headmaster telling us we had to remain 'cool, calm, and collected' whatever we thought that meant. Our air raid shelter was in the locker room in the basement. The rule was if the air raid siren went on our way to school or to home we were to proceed immediately to whatever was nearest. I remember being caught several times around the halfway point. Decision time for a 12-year old! If the alert went while we were in school we all trooped down to the basement and had to remain there until the all clear went. We missed a lot of tiresome lessons that way! I remember many times that the alert went while we were on the playing field. Being kids we were in no rush to get to the shelter; we wanted to see the action in the form of flak bursts overhead.
>
> On the playing field was an RAF barrage balloon station staffed by WAAF (Women's Auxiliary Air Force) personnel. We always knew when something was about to happen when we saw the balloon released from its moorings and was floated upwards. The balloon was made of some kind of rubberized fabric and it was filled with helium (I think). The idea was that it would ascend to several thousand feet while still tethered to the ground by its steel cable. The presence of the cable would, it was hoped, discourage enemy bombers from flying low over the city, thus making their bomb aiming less precise. It's questionable if it worked. It was, however, a great morale booster to see Plymouth's defence rising into the air but it was equally frustrating to see enemy fighters shoot them down![29]

Autumn in the air-raid shelters: from public outcry to public action

Over time, the constant use of air-raid shelters revealed both deficiencies in their physical conditions and the social strains of communal life underground. As residents descended into designated shelters, they confronted a host of challenges: overcrowding, poor ventilation, inadequate sanitation, and the seepage of groundwater. Similarly, social tensions boiled over in the confined spaces. The challenges of maintaining order and civility in these cramped conditions would become as pressing a concern for city authorities as the physical conditions of the shelters themselves. These challenges, while initially tolerated as a necessary inconvenience, would soon spark both public outcry and eventual public action to address the reality of living—and coexisting—in the underground communal air-raid shelters.

Plymouth journalist Pat Twyford recalled surveying the city's shelters and finding many of them in an unsatisfactory condition:

> I remember doing a tour of the underground shelters because there was so much complaint about their condition in wet weather. I found many of them leaking badly, with walls dropping wet, and the floors in some places where there was a lack of proper drainage with anything from six inches to a foot of water. There were at least two where it was utterly impossible to get through the entrance without waders.[30]

The lack of adequate sanitary facilities sparked a wave of further frustrations. The shelters' chemical toilets produced odours described as 'nauseating', something that the poor ventilation only exacerbated, and often did not have adequate privacy provisions. The recently built smaller surface shelters, on the other hand, did not have any such sanitary facilities, a deficiency that drew additional complaints from residents who took refuge there.[31]

As nights of bombing continued, communal shelters began to blur the line between emergency refuge and nightly residence. Families with private shelters had been encouraged to make them comfortable with chairs and provisions. Why could those utilising the public communal shelters not do the same, especially if they were returning to the same shelter night after night? Individuals left bedding, furniture, and personal belongings in the shelters to stake claims on preferred spots, treating these public spaces as private territory. Some even took to utilising the public shelters as their nightly sleeping quarters, whether there was an active alert or not.[32]

With overcrowding in the shelters came new concerns. Lord Mayor Waldorf Astor issued pointed instructions to address some of them, 'Dogs ought not to be taken into public shelters, and people should not smoke while seeking protection in them.'[33] Dogs brought into the shelters could become dangerously agitated by the terrifying sounds of aircraft overhead and thus pose a risk to shelter occupants. The close confines and poor ventilation made smoking a nuisance. Smokers also congregated near doorways, restricting airflow and blocking shelter access. This behaviour revealed how some individuals treated the shelters as a personal domain and without consideration for the larger public good.

It was clear that additional rules and regulations would be necessary to govern this new public space in Plymouth and throughout Britain. The Ministry of Health established national guidelines to maintain order and safety. Publicised through posters and signage, they were likewise shared in the press. These guidelines covered a range of topics and reflected the need for cooperation and consideration in close quarters. Regulations banned smoking anywhere in or around the shelter entrances and people were instructed not to congregate there. Another rule prohibited citizens from bringing their pets into shelters, while taking in beds and furniture was also forbidden. Shelter infrastructure was to be preserved, with clear rules against any damage to the amenities. Sanitary facilities were designated for emergency use only during air raids, not as a public convenience for passers-by. Overall, the Ministry emphasised the need for calm, orderly conduct, requiring shelter occupants to maintain quiet and disciplined behaviour when occupying the space.[34]

Later in the war, the Ministry of Health's 'Keep Fighting Fit' campaign recast these regulations as helpful 'health hints' rather than as prescriptive ordinances. Colourful posters included cartoon illustrations alongside reminders about personal hygiene, the daily cleaning and airing of clothing and bedding, ventilation, and taking personal responsibility for the cleanliness of public shelters.[35]

Yet creating rules and a code of conduct proved far easier than enforcing them. Though tasked with maintaining order, shelter wardens possessed no real authority to enforce these regulations. Indeed, their attempts at implementation were occasionally met with outright defiance as citizens ignored their efforts and took 'no notice of them'.[36] The situation could escalate quickly and even turn violent. For example, when Plymouth shelter warden Margaret Hamilton asked a husband and wife to put out their cigarettes, the wife verbally accosted and physically assaulted Hamilton and another warden.[37]

In an effort to maintain and improve the conditions of the shelters, some well-meaning citizens sought to raise money from those who were making use of them. In some cases, boxes for a voluntary donation were installed at shelter entrances or individuals took up collections. Proponents argued these donations would provide shelter users with a meaningful way to express gratitude, particularly in cases where private property owners had opened their shelters to the public.[38] However, critics opposed this approach, especially in public communal shelters, viewing it as insensitive to the dire circumstances that brought people to seek protection in the first place: soliciting donations from individuals during moments of extreme vulnerability was seen as inappropriate and potentially coercive. Critics proposed that alternative fundraising methods might instead be pursued via more conventional channels such as subscriptions or direct appeals.[39]

What was truly needed, however, was not just improved infrastructure but a shift in the public's mindset: a willingness of shelter occupants to prioritise the good of the community over individual preferences and convenience:

> There was a need for the public, particularly those who had been disregarding the comfort and welfare, and even the safety of the lives of other people, to

> take heed of the simple rules made for the use of shelters, and to understand that unless they conformed to the reasonable requests put forward other steps would have to be taken to ensure the comfort and safety of those who used the shelters.[40]

Of course, if citizens were unwilling to change on their own and comply with the rules set out for the public good, more drastic measures, such as police intervention or fines, would need to be pursued.

October 1940 marked a turning point in shelter conditions throughout the United Kingdom with the appointment of Herbert Morrison as Home Secretary and Minister of Home Security. Like Anderson before him, Morrison exercised sweeping oversight of civil defence, including the communal air-raid shelters.

Public shelters had initially been designed with the assumption that they would be used intermittently and for short periods of time. Wartime reality, however, was different. Citizens frequently found themselves spending long stretches of time in these spaces day after day. As a result, the communal shelters were woefully inadequate. Making improvements to them a priority, Morrison empowered local authorities to address substandard conditions by installing bunks for sleeping, ensuring requisite supplies, and increasing staffing. He deputised Ellen Wilkinson, MP, to manage the shelter improvement initiative. Wilkinson took a personal interest in this assignment, visiting locations throughout Britain, including Plymouth, to assess conditions for herself and make tailored recommendations.[41]

The Ministry of Home Security issued engineering guidance in December to redress structural deficiencies. Circular 290 included a covering letter outlining recommendations about shelter design, construction, renovations, and maintenance: 'These notes contain modifications which in the light of actual experience it has been found to be desirable to introduce in the standard designs of surface, trench and basement shelters, together with observations as to the certain measures which it is considered should be undertaken as regards to existing shelters of these types.'[42] The circular included new design schematics aimed at strengthening structures and mitigating dampness. For existing structures, such as those in Plymouth, the circular outlined measures to remedy defective mortar, reinforce weak roofs, and correct water infiltration.

Thus, renewed efforts emerged to enhance shelter conditions and habitability. Infrastructure improvements were made and construction defects repaired. The installation of water pumps addressed flooding.[43] Shelter amenities such as better lighting systems, enhanced sleeping arrangements, and improved sanitary facilities were also promised and delivered.[44] Coal-fuelled stoves were installed to address the dank and chilly conditions.[45] A practice of regular disinfection mitigated public health concerns about flu, sore throats, and other communicable illnesses.[46] Larger shelters were also provisioned with first aid posts complete with sick bays and medical personnel as part of a national scheme sponsored through the Ministry of Health.[47]

Winter warfare

Throughout the late autumn, alerts and attacks continued in Plymouth but were relatively minor, especially when contrasted with raids in cities such as Birmingham, Coventry, Manchester, and Liverpool, and the continued barrage of London. The raids generally involved a single plane or small detachment of aircraft and resulted in comparatively limited damages or casualties. An exception was the raid on 27–28 November involving over 100 German aircraft. A witness described the attack as 'the most fantastic and fearsome that Plymouth had yet experienced'.[48]

Yet for all the Luftwaffe's might that evening, it would take only a few planes striking key targets in the opening minutes to cause the most damage. The raid began at 7.30 p.m., and clear weather conditions gave German crews the advantage of visual bombing. The Royal Air Force base at Mount Batten, including its facilities for Sunderland seaplanes, was the primary objective for the mission.

Flying low over Plymouth Sound through heavy defensive fire, one of the first bombers released four flares as it approached Mount Batten. Two fell into the water, one struck a bridge, and the fourth hit an airplane hangar that immediately erupted in flames. The blaze served as a beacon for the following waves of bombers.

Minutes later, another crew succeeded in striking one of the RAF oil tanks at Turnchapel. The impact triggered a massive explosion. For the next hour, the concentration of Luftwaffe planes over Plymouth reached its peak. Successive waves of bombers sustained the attack until about 3 a.m.

Firefighters battled extraordinary conditions. The heat was so intense that water from hoses evaporated before it could reach the flames, and toxic fumes forced crews to retreat. When one tank exploded, boiling oil rained down, claiming the lives of several firefighters. In time, reinforcements arrived from outside Plymouth to help.

The fire raged for five days. The column of billowing smoke loomed over Plymouth and was visible for miles across the surrounding countryside. The public feared that the flames would serve as a beacon for another German attack. Surprisingly, the Luftwaffe did not exploit the advantage, deploying its forces on Liverpool, Southampton, and London instead.[49]

A deadlier raid occurred a month later on the night of 28–29 December. The attack left eleven dead and twelve critically wounded. The toll on property was severe too: the raid reduced seventeen homes to rubble, with another 300 severely damaged. Plymouth experienced some of the heaviest calibre munitions in the German arsenal. For the first time, the attack included several 500-pound bombs. A single 1-tonne bomb failed to detonate, landing beneath a house on Woldson Street, where it was later safely removed by the Bomb Disposal Squad.[50]

Attacks intensified in the new year. With the Luftwaffe reallocating assets ahead of Germany's campaign against the Soviet Union, its tactics in Britain shifted. Coastal cities such as Plymouth were targeted more frequently. British radar defences that could disrupt attacks on cities farther north proved less effective on the coast. Furthermore, by the time an incoming raid was detected in these more southerly locales, never mind by the time the RAF could scramble assets, the German sorties would have already hit their marks and the planes started their return course to France.

Plymouth experienced two significant attacks in early 1941, both of which surpassed the magnitude of any earlier raid.

On 14 January, a three-hour raid seriously damaged the city's electrical and gas infrastructure. A squadron of two dozen Luftwaffe planes caused tremendous carnage. There were twenty-six fatalities. Property was devastated: sixty homes were levelled and 400 sustained serious damage. Another 2,000 properties endured minor scrapes. Public property was hit too. The City Hospital and Prince of Wales's Hospital sustained direct hits. The roof of Sherwell Congregational Church on the edge of Portland Square was set ablaze, rendering the entire building unfit.[51]

Stanley Hollett recounted the terrifying scene he encountered as he made his way home through Plymouth from a narrow escape at the Plaza Cinema:

> Outside was like Fairyland with hundreds of incendiarys [*sic*] all over the Barbican, it was like daylight with all hell let loose, and looking up you could see the undersides of some of the aircraft reflecting from the fires and even see the black cross markings under the wings. I was a couple of weeks off my 13th birthday and my only thought then was to get home quick, so I ran up the narrow lane at the side of the cinema, and continued up Green Street, then up Gibbon Street and left to Sherwell Arcade where there were several fires that had taken a hold, including Sherwell Church which was beyond saving as the main roof had started to fall in by then.[52]

By the time he reached his own street, the destruction from the night hit even closer to home:

> I carried on to my home in Portland Square only to find the house next door (No 5) was going up in flames. There were anti aircraft guns banging away and tracer bullets and shells going all over the place and was the heaviest raid we had up to then. I ran indoors and went downstairs to the basement which we used as our refuge and my mother said where the hell have you been I've been worried stiff, and our neighbours from next door were also there who didn't have a clue their house was burning down, but by this time it was too late to save anything.[53]

A month later, the night of 13 February was another unlucky moment for Plymouth. Early in the evening, spotters detected a large formation of about seventy Luftwaffe bombers en route to Cardiff and Liverpool. After attacking those cities, the bombers headed back towards their French bases, their course taking them back over Plymouth. Presuming that these planes had dropped all their bombs on their northern targets, Plymouth officials did not activate the air-raid siren. Tragically, several planes still had bombs in their holds and jettisoned them as they flew over. The Royal Eye Infirmary in Mutley was among the properties damaged.[54] Among the dead were several families from Alfred Road near HMNB *Devonport*: Violet Trotman and her children, Pamela and Leonard; Joseph Henry and Edith Watts and their children, Terence and Ruth; and elderly siblings Richard and Emmeline Shears.[55] Pat Twyford wrote that they were all 'caught in their beds and buried under tons of debris.'[56]

Politicians visited Plymouth in the wake of these attacks. In early March, Lady Astor hosted fellow MP Ellen Wilkinson, the woman whom Home Secretary Morrison had deputised to oversee matters pertaining to air-raid shelters, to inspect Plymouth's shelter network. Wilkinson toured numerous shelters of varying type and size, finding many to be dry and in good condition, especially in light of months of frequent use. Giving her stamp of approval, she praised their construction and maintenance: 'On the whole I think Plymouth has done a pretty good workmanlike job with its shelters. [...] You have not tried any experiments, and have kept pretty well to Home Office standards, but within that standard you have done a sound job.' Compared with other sites, Plymouth's shelters were, Wilkinson noted, 'paradise', but there was, of course, still room for improvement. Some shelters were damp, and she provided recommendations to rectify this and to enhance shelter conditions, particularly for children, with the retrofitting of additional stoves and bunks.

Wilkinson's visit was also intended to fortify citizens' resolve and to offer support for the work of public officials as the air-raid crisis continued. She spoke at a luncheon for the Plymouth Mercantile Association, during which she appealed to the patriotic characterisation of the war as an existential battle for good. Wilkinson challenged her audience to embrace 'the very highest cause to which human life can be dedicated – the case of freedom and liberty'. She remarked that it served no constructive purpose to grieve and criticise, but also acknowledged that individuals and the city had endured loss and warned that additional difficulties lay ahead. Commending the efforts of the city's leadership, Wilkinson encouraged others to recognise and support that work and be prepared to contribute more. Citizens could not rely on ARP services alone; they too would need to take individual action, and do so without the expectation of reward.

Lord Astor shared his assessment of the city's experience to date. 'We have been extremely lucky in Plymouth. We have had air-raids, but when you compare them with the magnitude of raids in other places, you are bound to see we have been lucky.' He seemed convinced that Plymouth's worst was in the rear-view mirror.

Wilkinson, on the other hand, did not seem as confident. Instead, she declared the city was still a likely target for the Luftwaffe: 'Plymouth is definitely on the danger list as a result of the fall of France.' She had good reason to be 'anxious there should be good shelters in Plymouth'. Given her role, Wilkinson appreciated the bigger picture and recognised that danger persisted. She ominously forecasted that Plymouth was 'one of those towns which may need its civil defences'.[57]

Indeed, they would. The city's luck, as Lord Astor characterised it, was about to run catastrophically dry.

8

Pageantry amid the Peril: The Making of a Royal Visit

Lady Astor strolled through the streets of Plymouth with a special mission in mind. The next day, 20 March, the first day of spring, the city would host two special visitors. It would be a day of public appearances and fanfare meant to celebrate service, sacrifice, and solidarity. Just as the spring promised rebirth after winter's hardships, this event offered a similar renewal for the beleaguered city itself, a fresh beginning after challenging times. Lady Astor would play a central role in all the pageantry planned for the day—a tremendous opportunity to amplify her profile both with her constituents and on the national stage—but it would be her visitors who would be the talk of the town.

While passing by a florist's shop, a delicate posy of daphne caught Lady Astor's discerning eye. The vibrant blossoms captivated her, and she imagined the bouquet would be a perfect gift to present to one of the visitors upon their arrival in Plymouth. She entered the shop and inquired about acquiring a spray for the following morning. To her dismay, the florist was not able to obtain any more blossoms to create a new arrangement; however, the florist was able to put her in touch with Mrs Duke Young, a local gardener who was extremely proud of her garden's three daphne shrubs.

Lady Astor telephoned Mrs Young, and requested that she 'pick her daphne for the "greatest lady in the land"'.[1] Lady Astor did not share the name of the intended recipient, but given Lady Astor's words and given that the request came from that quarter, Mrs Young could very well have deduced her flowers' likely recipient. Indeed, details of the forthcoming visit had already been announced on the wireless.[2] Upon hanging up the phone, Mrs Young hurried out into her well-cultivated garden, carefully picked the remaining daphne, and sent the blossoms to Plymouth.

That evening, the visitors' train enjoyed a quiet night on a remote railway siding in the Devon countryside. The following morning, the train resumed its journey and arrived in Plymouth exactly as scheduled at 10.30 a.m.[3]

Lady Nancy Astor, MP of Plymouth and Lady Mayoress, exhibited selfless dedication to the city during the blitz and used her position to advocate for residents, improve conditions, and boost morale. [*Plymouth Herald*]

Lady Astor waited on the platform at Millbay Station with the beautiful arrangement of fresh daphne in her hand. She looked striking in her black gown, a full-length mink coat, and a petite black hat trimmed with mink to pull her ensemble together.[4] Lord Astor was convalescing with a bout of the flu at their country estate at Cliveden, so it was up to her to head the reception delegation. Deputy Lord Mayor Modley joined her, his polished livery collar of office sparkling in the morning sun. High-ranking officers from the different services, their uniforms pressed to perfection, stood to attention.[5] Railway office staff waited on adjoining platforms to participate in the morning's festivities.[6]

As the train steamed into the station, the excitement among the welcome party and the assembled crowd was palpable. The carriage doors opened. When the principal occupants alighted from the train, the crowd cheered.

The couple was instantly recognisable: King George VI and Queen Elizabeth.

A long-awaited visit

The tableau that played out on 20 March was one that Lord and Lady Astor had, like Mrs Young and her daphne blossoms, been cultivating for some time.

Waldorf Astor, 2nd Viscount Astor, and his wife, Lady Nancy Astor, were prominent figures in early twentieth-century British society and politics. Born into the immensely wealthy American Astor family, Waldorf moved to England, where he became a politician, newspaper proprietor, and, later, a philanthropist. His wife, Nancy, also American-born, encouraged his political ambitions and then entered politics herself as MP for Plymouth, becoming the first woman to take a seat in the House of Commons after Waldorf inherited a peerage and entered the House of Lords. Lady Astor was known for championing social reforms, particularly temperance, though her political career was also marked by controversial views. The Astors were fixtures of London high society, their wealth and influence centred on their residence at 4 St James's Square and their country estate, Cliveden in Berkshire.

Lord Astor was named Lord Mayor of Plymouth shortly after the war began. In August 1940, leveraging their connections, the Astors began petitioning Buckingham Palace to host Queen Elizabeth for a visit to Plymouth. Such an occasion would be a cause for celebration.

Lady Astor was confident that the visit would transpire and proactively made requisite safety arrangements. As part of her preparations, she investigated adding a private air-raid shelter to their home to provide a refuge for the Queen in the event that an alert should sound during the visit. She sent a note to the town clerk, Colin Campbell, requesting an 'adequate' air-raid shelter at Elliot Terrace. She proposed that one could be engineered by reinforcing an area of the basement and requested that a Plymouth Corporation surveyor visit the property to make an assessment.[7] These preparations ultimately proved premature.

When the German aerial assault on London began in September 1940, the royal focus naturally shifted to the capital. The Blitz on London began on Black Saturday, 7 September. After the opening salvo, the Luftwaffe pummelled London for fifty-six of fifty-seven consecutive nights. London reeled from the assault. Given the prolonged intensity of these attacks, the Crown attended to the besieged capital.

As autumn progressed, the Luftwaffe expanded its zone of interest and targeted other major cities, and with greater ferocity than Plymouth had experienced to date. Given these circumstances, the promised visit to Plymouth was no longer a royal priority.

Queen Elizabeth's acting private secretary Captain Arthur Penn sent Lord Astor a letter to explain the situation. Penn wrote that the Queen regretted cancelling, describing the visit as 'a project which Her Majesty had every hope of fulfilling'. Penn apologised, highlighting how circumstances shifted what was possible or prudent in the royal diary—and where the Crown needed to devote its attention: 'so much has happened since then to change the activities both of the King + of the Queen that all their programmings have been, as you may imagine, wholly disarrayed'. Penn tempered the Astors' expectations: 'there does not seem for the moment any likelihood of this pleasure being put into effect'.[8]

With London and other locales under attack, Plymouth, and the Astors, would have to wait.

Making a case for Plymouth

Autumn 1940 had witnessed London's transformation into an urban battlefield of unprecedented devastation. The relentless attack culminated with the December inferno that was branded as the capital's Second Great Fire. St Paul's Cathedral, that icon of the London skyline that Churchill commanded be preserved at any cost, stood wreathed in smoke and flame.[9] The image gripped the nation's attention and came to symbolise the Blitz; yet London was far from alone in bearing the brunt of German aggression.

At the start of 1941, Plymouth weathered its own crucible of fire and steel, and had the scars to prove it. Lady Astor witnessed the plight of Plymouth's citizens first hand. When she returned to the city after the January raid, she immediately went to the site of the bombings. The *Western Morning News* reported that she visited a number of locations before daybreak to support emergency personnel and offer assistance to those impacted. 'So many of the victims live in my constituency', she said, 'that I have had quite a busy day doing things to help.' She praised the people of Plymouth for how they were facing the situation. 'No moaning, no groaning, but just patient, courageous endurance,' Astor observed. 'Grit and determination to stick it have been evinced everywhere.'[10] Indeed, the Mass Observation report for April 1941 assessed the morale in January as 'exceptionally good', though nervousness about future attacks was also noted. [11] Even though attitudes were optimistic, something more, it seemed, was needed.

It was important that others witness Plymouth's devastation and how its citizens were navigating the aftermath. While it had been appropriate for the King and Queen to remain in London as a symbol of steadfast leadership during the autumn, it was vital that other battered cities also feel the royal presence. And they did. The royal couple's winter visits included: Merseyside on 6–7 November, Coventry on 16 November, Southampton and Portsmouth on 5 December, Birmingham on 12 December, Bristol on 16 December, Liverpool on 18 December, Sheffield on 6 January, Portsmouth on 6 February, and Manchester on 14 February. Though smaller in scale than the raids elsewhere, the bombardment and resulting hardship in Plymouth provided a compelling case for the Astors to renew their request to place a royal visit back on the table. As at other locales, the royal presence would serve as an acknowledgement of the city's experience.

With the most intense raids seemingly over, Plymouth was focused on its future. A royal visit could do more than console; it could inspire resolve and catalyse the city's rebuilding process. The royal visit was valuable political currency, and the Astors were intent that Plymouth would benefit from it.

Thus, Lord Astor reopened his dialogue with the Palace. Using Arthur Penn as an intermediary, he sent the Queen a new invitation in early February. On 20 February, Penn replied on her behalf, but remained non-committal: 'I know that Her Majesty would much like to visit Plymouth if it can be fitted into a rather difficult programme.'[12] The note was, in essence, a cordial way to bow out of Lord Astor's request.

Captain Penn's note did not, however, suffice for Lady Astor. Her patience for the courtiers who managed the royal diary seemed to unravel. On 23 February, she sent Captain Penn her own letter. She retorted to his words by quipping 'don't tell me about a difficult programme' and indicated she would not accept excuses. Then, drawing on her experience in Parliament, she laid out her case. She referenced the royals' visits to other locales, and she positioned Plymouth as a unique case owing to HMNB *Devonport.* In this regard, Lady Astor asserted that Plymouth was perhaps more worthy of the Crown's attention than some other cities because of its military contributions to the war effort: 'Plymouth has suffered more from Naval losses than any town in the Kingdom.' She continued her argument by reminding Penn of Plymouth's blitz experience and, ironically as her letter was doing just that, about not having bemoaned the situation: 'just because we don't squal [*sic*] it doesn't mean that we have not had our blitzes. They began long before London and have gone steadily on.' In Lady Astor's calculus, Plymouth exceeded the threshold that warranted a royal visit.

Determined to employ every possible argument in making her case, Lady Astor's closing remarks gave a more personal justification for the visit. She asserted she did not request that the Queen visit because of her own role in Parliament, a move that might have been perceived as political. Rather, she insisted that the visit would signal the Crown's appreciation for her aristocratic husband and for his work as Plymouth's lord mayor.[13]

The visit takes shape

Five days later, on 28 February, the Astors received the desired news. Captain Penn indicated a royal tour of the south-west was likely to occur during the week of 17 March. Plymouth would be included on the itinerary. Most significantly, the visit would also include the King. Penn indicated that an official programme had not been worked out—after all, the trip itself was still not confirmed—but wanted to keep the Astors apprised, or perhaps mollify Lady Astor and keep her at bay.[14]

The Astors were optimistic and prepared accordingly. Lord Astor replied to Penn's letter the next day. He shared that he had conveyed the news to Admiral Sir Martin

Dunbar-Nasmith, Commander-in-Chief of Plymouth and the Western Approaches, and noted Lady Astor's willingness to meet with royal household staff in London to assist with planning.[15] Internal household notes among the Astors' staff on 3 March reference the likelihood of Plymouth welcoming 'two Very Royal Personages'.[16]

Managing the royal engagement would be no small feat. Though the visit was essentially engineered by and at the behest of the Astors, Lady Astor undoubtedly felt pressure. Even at short notice, a standard of excellence would be expected. If the royal couple were indeed coming, Plymouth needed to be ready.

On 8 March, with the visit still unconfirmed, much less what the itinerary might entail, Lady Astor asked Penn for a status report: 'I wonder whether you can give us any more information about the possible, or I hope I may describe it as prospective visit?' She shared her availability to meet Penn to discuss details and added a postscript about which dates might work better for the event owing to other engagements already planned for the city.[17]

Whether it was Lady Astor's letter that helped to finally move the needle of the palace machine or not, the logistics for the anticipated tour of the south-west coalesced in the following days. A forty-page manual entitled 'Great Western Railway Notice No. 10' was drawn up and distributed to divisional superintendents and engineering staff throughout the rail network. This included the movements of the Royal Train and provided timetables for 18 to 21 March as well as detailed instructions for locomotive traffic.[18] It was clear that the engine was, quite literally, gathering steam.

Plymouth prepares to host the Crown

On 10 March, Lord Astor received confirmation from Sir Alexander Hardinge, Private Secretary to the Sovereign, that the royal visit would definitely take place: 'This is just to let you know that the King and Queen propose to visit Plymouth on Thursday, March 20.' Plymouth would be the final leg of an itinerary that would include visits to the bombed Welsh cities of Swansea and Cardiff on 19 March. Hardinge outlined the contours of the day's programme: 'Their Majesties will arrive by train from the West, and will be ready to start between ten and half past. It is the King's intention to visit Naval Establishments, Docks, etc., while The Queen can go elsewhere in the City.' In a nod to the Astors' role as hosts, Hardinge referenced aspects of the agenda in which their input would be welcomed: 'I gather that in the afternoon The King and Queen will go together to some of the Clubs, etc., about which Lady Astor has spoken to them.'

A postscript urged discretion: 'I expect you know that nothing must be said in advance about Their Majesties' visits.'[19] Of course, keeping the visit a secret, especially with all the planning and preparation that would need to be hastily done, was easier said than done.

With only ten days to prepare, military officials, municipal administrators, and palace courtiers quickly devised a programme that reflected the formulaic template used successfully in other locales. As they did so, they operated under the principle that royal visits are moments of carefully crafted political theatre. From the sites visited to the people introduced, every element is curated to convey specific messages and reinforce particular narratives. Reporting about the day's visit would contribute to shaping and memorialising that messaging.[20]

The itinerary for the day in Plymouth would reinforce the Crown's solidarity with its war-weary subjects and reflect the monarchy's genuine interest in their well-being. The success of the visit hinged on a balance of ceremony and intimacy. Public pageantry would alternate with personal exchanges, allowing the royal couple to fulfil dual roles: as inspirational symbols of national power and as empathetic individuals who validated personal suffering, sacrifice, and loss.

Like set pieces, visits aboard vessels or to affected neighbourhoods, a ceremonial inspection of civic organisations, a luncheon and tea, and tours of social service agencies were slotted into the day's programme.[21] The agenda aimed to maximise the royal couple's exposure across all segments of society, ensuring that their presence would reach the widest possible audience. The visit would provide an opportunity for the King and Queen to witness and validate civilian sacrifice first hand—and for civilians to witness them bearing witness.

Throughout their day, the royal pair would interact with a representative sample of the population. The programme would thus allow citizens from all walks of life to either personally encounter the monarchs or see themselves represented in the groups with which the Crown engaged. As a result, citizens could see their own lived experiences reflected in these publicised interactions, as if they too had conversed with the Crown and had their experiences acknowledged.

Spreading the word

Once the structure for the day had been decided, a classified memorandum about the visit was released to select parties on 18 March from the office of Admiral Dunbar-Nasmith, Commander-in-Chief of Plymouth. The memo and accompanying schedule, precise to the minute, expressed the royal couple's wish that their visit provide them with an opportunity to interact with a large number of individuals: 'The visit is to be without ceremony, it being Their Majesties' desire to see as many of the personnel as possible with the minimum interference with work or routine.' The memo further stipulated how to dress, whether or not coats would be worn, and which vessels and institutions would fly the Royal Standard. The reminder for personnel to carry their gas masks with them throughout the visit indicated the Navy's persistent concern about a German gas attack, despite the Luftwaffe not utilising such tactics in previous raids in Plymouth or elsewhere in Britain. The memorandum concluded by urging recipients to use discretion about what to share, and with whom, and cautioned that 'the visit is not to be made known generally until Thursday morning, 20th March'.[22]

While there was an information embargo at HMNB *Devonport*, details flowed more freely in civilian quarters. Part of this stemmed from the flurry of correspondence sent from the offices of the lord mayor and town clerk inviting individuals to participate in different parts of the programme. The Lord Mayor's Office deputised organisations to select representatives to participate in a ceremony on Guildhall Square. The groups included the Guildhall Working League, War Aid Supply Depot, Women's Voluntary Services, and a handful of other organisations.[23] The town clerk invited dignitaries to watch this inspection from a special enclosure.[24] These invitations sparked conversations and contributed to specifics being circulated among the public.

News spread further as sites on the itinerary prepared for their role. On 18 March, a representative of the Young Men's Christian Association (YMCA) phoned Lady Astor to learn if the 'rumour' were true and promised the facility would be 'spotless'. That same day, the YMCA inquired about the length of the visit and the nature of the programme.[25] Similarly, Virginia Settlement House staff proposed a tour route through its 'rambling' complex. They inquired about the propriety to 'offer a cup' of tea to the King and of 'the Mothers to sing something quite informal? "For they are jolly good fellows"??'[26] These preparations and eager inquiries about protocol indicate that information was being shared and discussed broadly.

As the final plans came together, efforts to make the broader population aware of the visit were put into motion. Tension between restricting the flow of information and ensuring public participation, however, presented a challenge.[27] The decision to share details was, unquestionably, a security risk. Hitler had dubbed the Queen as 'the most dangerous woman in Europe'; indeed, Queen Elizabeth and King George VI topped the list of individuals that German assets were directed to apprehend should they ever have the opportunity.[28]

Recuperating at Cliveden, Lord Astor appealed to Hardinge for permission to release information about the visit. 'Have we your permission to broadcast through the Plymouth re-diffusion the general programme of Their Majesties in Plymouth on Thursday morning?' Astor inquired.[29] After all, the monarchs' ability to make an impact depended entirely on meeting people, making public knowledge of their movements essential.

Rediffusion was a wired radio network that distributed content to individual subscribers. It was intended to be used for emergency purposes to broadcast important news from the Ministry of Information during the war. For Lord Astor, the royal visit warranted making use of a Rediffusion relay: 'I do not see how otherwise we can guarantee to have the necessary number of people out in the streets, whether along the route which they [the King and Queen] are to follow, or in the bombed districts which they are to visit.'[30] The wired configuration of the network theoretically made Rediffusion more secure than over-the-air broadcasts which could have been picked up by German intelligence. Permission was duly granted.

Mass Observation reporters described the broadcast and its intention of maximising public participation and attendance:

> On the morning of the King's visit messages were put out over the system with the authorisation of the Town Clerk (and some say he actually delivered them) at about five minutes to 7 a.m. and five minutes to 8 a.m. – i.e. just before the peak listening periods for B.B.C. news. These messages are said to have detailed the routes. In consequence, a large proportion of the town were informed in advance of the visit and its details, facts generally undisclosed and not in any way publicized until well after the visit was over.[31]

As Astor hoped, word of the visit spread quickly throughout Plymouth. Indeed, a core element of the network was that subscribers were encouraged to share news with neighbours. With approximately one in ten households subscribing to Rediffusion, it was estimated that news could be relayed to the entire population of Plymouth at a moment's notice, and certainly more effectively than if mobile loudspeakers were used: 'If people were asked to pass on the news, in five minutes the whole town could be informed of something which had occurred only a little time before.'[32] An occasion such as a royal visit would have been news excitedly exchanged. But might too much information have been shared too early and too broadly?

If German intelligence services had been able to listen in, they would have had full access to the day's agenda. In the estimation of the Regional Commissioner assessing matters after the visit, municipal authorities had made 'little attempt to keep the impending visit secret', thus elevating the risk for the King and Queen—and, indeed, for all of Plymouth.[33] Mass Observation researchers concluded that greater oversight of the Rediffusion network would be needed in the future to avoid similar missteps: 'Our impression is that there is a complete local muddle over the role and responsibility for emergency use of Rediffusion. This was one of many cases where too much was left to the decision of the Town Clerk.'[34]

After the visit, an intelligence report documented concerns about the general flow of information. For example, while commending HMNB *Devonport* brass for their efforts to contain intelligence, municipal civil defence personnel were criticised for failing to adopt the same standard: 'There is no doubt that through the indiscretion of civil defence personnel the visit of the King and Queen was made known throughout the city much sooner than was considered advisable by the service authorities.'[35] Indeed, the report pointed out that news about the visit was the talk of the town on Wednesday 19 March, a full day before the King and Queen were due in Plymouth. The report highlighted a concerning example of how even ordinary housewives spoke with accuracy about intimate details of the day: 'Telephone interceptions reveal that one lady spent the morning telephoning the news to her friends, actually mentioning the fact that their Majesties were to arrive at Millbay Station at 10.30 hours next day.'[36] Any effort by the Palace to keep particulars confidential was rendered ineffective by the casual conversations of Plymouth's own citizens.

Despite his machinations in helping to bring about the visit and his efforts to promote it, Lord Astor would ultimately not participate in the momentous day. He anticipated being well enough to make the journey from Cliveden to the coast to take part in the festivities; indeed, on 18 March, he requested that his valet arrange for his preferred barber to be at Elliot Terrace early on Thursday morning for a last-minute trim.[37] However, his health again took a sudden turn. On Wednesday 19 March, it was decided that the viscount would remain in Berkshire. Lady Astor would step in as the official host of the day.

With the clock ticking on 19 March, it was time for Lady Astor to put the finishing touches on the day—sourcing an appropriately fitting bouquet to present to the Queen.

Across the English Channel, the Luftwaffe were also making final preparations for 20 March.

The airfields of France

As destructive as the January and February raids had been, those attacks paled in comparison to what the Luftwaffe command coordinated for Plymouth on 20 March. As the Luftwaffe had done elsewhere, the strike was planned as a one-two punch: two successive nights of concentrated bombing on the same target. Reichsmarschall Hermann Göring himself would direct and track the progress of the operation from the comfort of his personal train carriage.[38]

It is entirely plausible that Göring knew about the royal visit to Plymouth and adjusted plans accordingly. The royal movements in the south-west were not a state secret. Their visit to Swansea and Cardiff on 19 March was publicised as part of the daily Court Circular and noted in other papers. The specifics of the Plymouth itinerary were common knowledge among residents in the days, rather than hours, leading up to the visit. An attack that might endanger, harm, or even result in the death of the British sovereign would undoubtedly have tipped the scales. Such action had the potential to create propaganda gold for the Nazis in simultaneously undermining British morale and projecting an image of Germany's military supremacy.

Whether Göring actually knew of the royals' exact whereabouts or not, Plymouth was an ideal target for the ongoing psychological and physical war that the Luftwaffe was waging. It was home to a strategically important military base, densely populated, and comparatively intact. An attack on the scope and scale that Göring designed would demonstrate the continued strength of the German war machine.

The Luftwaffe's specialised pathfinder force was scheduled to be a part of the evening's raid. Though the clear weather forecast made these planes redundant, Göring's decision to use them maximised operational success. Once they located their targets, the pathfinder squadrons would release thousands of incendiaries. The ensuing fires would tax Plymouth's emergency response teams and also act as a signal beacon for the successive waves of Heinkel bombers that would follow as phase two of the raid.

The bomber units of Luftflotte 3 received the night's mission objectives. Göring ordered the main force to attack Plymouth. Sorties destined for other locales were directed to input the coordinates for Plymouth as a contingency if they failed to reach their intended targets. Crews spent the morning of 20 March preparing for the evening ahead. They conducted test flights around the airfields and reported to the depots to receive their payload of munitions.[39]

***

Meanwhile, in Plymouth, with the Royal Train now at Millbay Station and the monarchs preparing to begin their tour, residents were focused on the revelry of the day's festivities, blissfully unaware of the Nazis' designs to wreak devastation on their city later that same day.

9

The Crown Comes to Town: 20 March 1941

The Court Circular, the public diary of royal activities, makes note of the royal visit to Plymouth in its chronicle.[1] A couple more sentences about the day are recorded in the private diary of King George VI.[2] While the visit was covered in the local press and documented by British *Pathé*, the narrative about the day has generally been attached to and overshadowed by the events that happened only hours after the King and Queen departed from Plymouth.

The royal visit was, in essence, the finale to an era. Sadly, the Victorian city that welcomed the Windsors and served as the backdrop to the fanfare of the occasion would be unrecognisable a day later. Within hours of the royal tour, Guildhall Square would be illuminated not by patriotic fervour but by the flames of Nazi incendiary bombs. That night, the Luftwaffe launched the opening salvo of the series of seven devastating night-time raids that would become known as the Plymouth Blitz. In the span of a single day, Plymouth experienced both the height of ceremonial splendour and the depths of wartime destruction.

The royal visit to Plymouth is, however, worthy of independent exploration as a case study of the Crown's personal diplomacy. The following discussion primarily turns to a moment-by-moment chronicle that illuminates how the Crown celebrated the importance of solidarity, service, and resilience through both pageantry and personal conversations.

The monarch's military morning

Amid the fanfare of the royal arrival at Millbay Station, Lady Astor stepped forward to present her spray of daphne to the Queen.

The Queen's 'radiant' ensemble won the attention of Plymouth's residents. She was described as wearing a Regis blue ensemble complete with a coordinating coat, pearl and diamond stud earrings, and four strands of pearls.[3] A sapphire and diamond clasp held a corsage to her jacket lapel and matched a smaller clasp in her hat. A pair of fox fur-trimmed gloves, silk court shoes, and an envelope-shaped handbag accessorised the outfit. The Queen worked with the royal couturier Norman Hartnell to develop the look.[4] The head-to-toe blue was a vibrant choice that ensured visibility even at a distance. After all, being seen was fundamental to the day's objective.

The King wore his uniform as Admiral of the Fleet, demonstrating solidarity with the sailors of the Royal Navy and Plymouth's maritime heritage. Indeed, the military would be the focus of the morning's itinerary.

After the reception formalities, the royal motorcade proceeded to HMNB *Devonport*. Throngs of spectators enthusiastically welcomed the royal entourage. A reporter from the *Western Morning News* described the joyful scene, 'cheering crowds lined the footpaths, and Union Flags of all sizes twinkled from the hands of adults and children alike'.[5] The atmosphere of public celebration demonstrated how the Crown's presence had the capacity to transform war-weary citizens into a jubilant crowd united in patriotic pride.

As the senior peer in the region, Piers Edgcumbe, 5th Earl of Mount Edgcumbe, greeted the King and Queen at Millbay Pier. The Queen shook the earl's hand and exchanged pleasantries.[6] Other dignitaries on hand included the director of the Great Western Railway and his administrative team.

The royal pair inspected the officers and men of the Minesweeping Flotilla, a defensive squadron that was responsible for locating and neutralising German sea mines. This important work ensured the safe passage of merchant and naval vessels passing through the waters around Plymouth. The King and Queen spoke with these servicemen and commended them for their bravery in the face of their hazardous work.[7]

As scripted and precise as the morning was, it was not without the occasional technical difficulty. For example, when the two naval dispatch riders revved the engines of their motorcycles to lead the motorcade to HMNB *Devonport*, one of the motorcycles stalled. Needing to keep to schedule, the procession departed with a sole rider at the front of the column. In due course, the second rider was able to restart his motorcycle and regain his position as the motorcade passed through the gates into the yard.[8]

The Devonport leg of the day underscored the King's role as Head of the Armed Forces. He reviewed troops at the Royal Marine and Royal Naval Barracks, while platoons from ships and training establishments such as the Royal Naval Engineering College and HMS *Defiance* also participated.[9]

The motorcade then drove along the quayside and passed several ships including HMS *Exeter*. This Plymouth-built ship was celebrated for its victorious role in the Battle of the River Plate, the first major naval engagement of the war.

The Admiral Superintendent arranged for the couple to walk through workshops vital to the maintenance and repair of the fleet. Of particular interest to the pair was how women were contributing to the war effort. They spoke to a group operating aluminium-cutting machines.[10]

The King and Queen then separated to follow individual itineraries, maximising their impact by covering more ground.

King George VI, Admiral of the Fleet

First, those with the longest service in various departments at the dockyard were presented to the King. What an honour for those men to have their longevity acknowledged by their monarch, the moment reinforcing the bond between the Crown and those who served it.

The King then presided over an investiture ceremony at the Flagstaff Steps. The parade ground was filled with crews representing the British, Canadian, Polish, Free French, and Norwegian Navies. Aleksander Hulewicz, former Commanding Officer of the Polish Navy Destroyer ORP *Grom* (Thunder), was granted the Distinguished Service Order. His heroic efforts had involved conducting a search and rescue mission for downed British pilots while contending with an aerial attack that put his own safety in peril.[11]

Applause erupted as Hulewicz saluted King George and received his regalia. The significance of the award extended beyond the individual, though: by honouring a Polish naval officer, the ceremony highlighted the collaborative military efforts of the exiled Allied nations and the shared commitment to resisting Nazi tyranny. Despite being displaced, European nations refused to accept defeat and continued to contribute to the fight against a common enemy.

The King's visit continued with an inspection of several vessels docked at the quayside. A reporter for the *Western Evening Herald* praised one crew's efforts to have their vessel 'looking spick and span as though just out of the dock' for the review. The crew had just returned from patrolling duties in the Channel: 'There was nothing to show that only a short while before the men had been at action stations.'[12]

Further down the docks, the King boarded an American destroyer in service under the Lend-Lease Act, a nod to the American contributions to Britain's efforts. The ship was manned entirely by Canadian sailors, underscoring the integral role of the Empire in the war effort.[13] The King conversed with officers and crew. His familiar nature and personal engagement demonstrated a sincere interest in the well-being of the crew and appreciation for the dedication of their service.

Queen Elizabeth surveys damage

While the King inspected the Navy, the Queen travelled with Lady Astor to survey some of the damaged residential areas close to HMNB *Devonport* and speak with citizens who had been affected.

When the crowd caught sight of the Queen's car departing the North Gate, it erupted in joyous applause: 'As the car with the Royal insignia moved slowly through the streets, cheers rolled upon cheers in deafening waves. But it was from the women that the cheers came the loudest, women in their everyday dress, with babies clutching their shoulders, with children clinging to their skirts.'[14] Again, the presence of royalty fostered enthusiasm and provided the opportunity for a morale-boosting moment.

Devastation tempered the atmosphere of the morning. Neighbourhoods bore the wounds of war with damaged buildings and rubble-strewn streets. Many of the remaining homes no longer had conveniences of power, heat, or running water.

The plight of Plymouth was one that others, even, to a degree, the Royal Family, also endured. Indeed, Buckingham Palace had been bombed several times during the autumn air raids on London, which had resulted in them seeming to share the harsh realities of war with their subjects.

An enthusiastic welcome greeted the Queen when she arrived at her destination. 'Cheering crowds, almost entirely women and children, many waving paper Union Flags, greeted the Royal car as it drew up at the end of Nepean-street. Her Majesty alighted to smile and wave in acknowledgement before entering the street which had suffered so severely.'[15]

Queen Elizabeth was scheduled to meet with residents of Nepean Street, where several homes had been razed and more were deemed uninhabitable. Individual conversations with residents were not simply sympathetic exchanges; they were powerful, authentic moments that showed the Crown validating the people's experiences. These intimate interactions, reported in detail by the *Western Morning News*, suggested that no hardship nor sacrifice went unnoticed by the Crown.

One encounter took place with Mr and Mrs Heap, an elderly couple who had called 15 Nepean Street home for thirty-six years. Learning that they had neither gas nor water, the Queen inquired, 'Really, has everything been broken then?' Lady Astor interjected, with admiration for their resolve, 'Not quite, Ma'am, their spirit is unbroken.' Before moving along, the Queen extended a compassionate gesture. Taking Mrs Heap's hand in her own, she expressed her prayers for the couple: 'I do hope you will be able to live peacefully now.'[16]

Another visit was to the Andrews family at No. 19. An air-raid warden, Mr Andrews wore his uniform of blue dungarees and tin helmet. He waited with his family where their home once stood, and relayed a harrowing account of the raid that had destroyed their residence. When the air-raid sirens had started to wail, Andrews had escorted his wife and children to a neighbour's shelter to take refuge. He then went about his duties to ensure that other neighbours also took safety precautions. A bomb landed in the vicinity as he was conducting this vital work, and falling debris prevented him from returning to the shelter to check on his family. Andrews' dedication to duty and the fortitude he displayed during those critical moments exemplified the commitment of ordinary citizens to safeguard their community, and won praise from the Queen.

The Queen took particular interest in the Andrews' two-year-old daughter Ruth who was perched on her father's shoulder during the exchange. The Queen remarked, 'She's a lovely little girl – she doesn't look as if she has been bombed. It was a marvellous escape, and I am so glad that you are all right.'[17]

The Andrews' neighbour, Mrs Heardman of 21 Nepean Street, also shared her experience. When one raid began, the entire family had sheltered in a corridor at the rear of their home, except for one invalid daughter who took refuge in a cupboard under the stairs. After the raid, the girl was moved to one of the city hospitals. Mrs Heardman was still visibly shaken by the ordeal and shared her emotions with the Queen, who offered words of comfort: 'It is a terrible experience. We all look for better times. I hope you will soon feel better.'[18]

In exchanges like these, the Queen followed a similar conversational pattern. She acknowledged a specific hardship faced by the family, commended their resilience, and offered a personal word of encouragement and comfort. Through these representative encounters, other civilians could arguably see their own suffering acknowledged and access the Queen's message of hope: just as these families would rebuild their homes and lives, so too would others.[19]

Before returning to the naval base, the Queen participated in several other brief engagements. She met the staff of Ford House and visited the Royal Naval Hospital to speak with officers, servicemen, and medical staff.[20]

Over the course of the morning, the number of citizens turning out on the streets grew as word about the royal visit spread: 'Though the visit was intended to be secret and informal the news spread swiftly and the streets were lined with cheering people.'[21] This enthusiasm would only continue to build as citizens made their way to Guildhall Square to participate in the second phase of the day's programme.

Midday meal

After their hour of separate activities, the King and Queen reunited. The pair had a quieter moment with a small luncheon at Admiralty House on Mount Wise with HMNB *Devonport* brass just after 1 p.m. At the conclusion of the luncheon, Admiral Dunbar-Nasmith's senior staff and senior Dominion naval officers were presented on the Admiralty House Terrace.

A final, and particularly impressive, military salute involved a detachment from the Royal Indian Army Service Corps, which lined the path to the motorcade. Coverage from the *Western Morning News* made exceptional note of the soldiers' 'turbaned' heads and praised the men for journeying 'thousands of miles at the call of their King-Emperor.'[22]

Having completed the morning's military-focused programme, the King and Queen began the civic part of their visit to Plymouth. The centrepiece was to be a grand parade at Guildhall Square to celebrate those personnel who had helped Plymouth endure the Luftwaffe's winter aerial attacks.

Parade on Guildhall Square

Guildhall Square teemed with participants and onlookers in advance of the 2.30 p.m. ceremony. The Mr Gossip column in the *Western Independent* captured the scene: 'George Street, Plymouth, as full of life as it was never to be again. School children line the pavements, waving Union Jacks.'[23] The *Western Morning News* detailed how citizens packed the area and stood shoulder to shoulder, some even finding perches high above the crowd: 'The approaches to the Guildhall and the forecourts of the municipal buildings were thronged, and people were kept from overflowing on to the roadway by a good-natured police cordon. Clusters of onlookers were even on vantage points of the Guildhall roof.'[24]

At last, the car bearing the royal couple arrived. The arrival ignited an eruption of patriotic fervour: 'A ripple of cheering heralded the King and Queen's

King George VI and Queen Elizabeth at Guildhall Square, 20 March 1941. The parade and walkabout was the highpoint of the civilian part of the day's visit. The blitz on Plymouth would strike the same spot later that evening. [*Plymouth Herald* and Chris Robinson, used with permission from Pat Twyford, *It Came To Our Door*, revised edition, 2005]

approach. Flags waved and dipped in the wind, and as the Royal car ran into the Guildhall-square the crowd seemed for a moment as if it would surge round it in a demonstration of loyalty.'[25] The public display and general celebratory atmosphere evidenced the positive impact that the monarchs' presence was having.

Lady Astor and Deputy Lord Mayor William Modley headed the receiving party as the royal couple ascended the dais in front of the Guildhall's doors. The bells of Plymouth's mother church, St Andrew's, pealed the hymn 'Abide with Me' across Guildhall Square.[26]

Police Superintendent Alexander Hawkins was responsible for organising the parade, which involved over 1,000 public safety personnel. On his signal, the pageantry unfolded: 'Plymouth's civil defence army – the wardens, firemen, and rescue workers – in their workaday blue tunics, nurses with white caps and cloaks nodding in the wind, Air Force Defence Cadets in uniforms, and then representatives of women's work organisations from every part of the city.'[27] Rather than a performative ceremony for the Crown, the parade was instead an opportunity for the royals to recognise and celebrate the efforts of ordinary people who mobilised in support of Plymouth.

After the parade, the royal pair walked among the formations and conversed with participants. These interactions allowed the King and Queen to learn first hand how different organisations were contributing to public welfare and to validate this important work.[28]

For example, the King spoke with William Mead, superintendent of the Auxiliary Fire Service, about the important work of the fire parties. The King also spoke with a group of Air Force cadets, chatting with the commanding officer and several of the recruits.

Another anecdote centred around a conversation between the Queen and air-raid warden William Waller. 'Are you an old soldier?' the Queen asked. Upon learning about his service during the First World War and his current role, the Queen praised Waller for his renewed and long-standing commitment of service: 'It is most creditable of you to come forward and help your country again.'

Representatives from the hospitals also briefed the King and Queen about how they managed to attend to their normal caseload while providing intensive care for victims of air raids. For example, Miss Waterhouse, matron of the City Hospital, led the contingent of nurses taking part in the parade. The Queen inquired about how the hospital functioned while facing war conditions.

The services provided by various women's organisations likewise captured the royal attention. The King and Queen learned about how women were supporting the war effort by providing new clothing to sailors or supplying books and refreshment to members of the armed services. 'I think the work you in Plymouth are doing is splendid,' the Queen commended. The King concurred: 'You women are doing a very fine work.'

Reports of the afternoon's events took note of the royal couple's relaxed demeanour among members of the military who were on hand for the festivities. Major Frederick Ricketts noted that the King and Queen 'spent several minutes laughing and chatting with him'. Ricketts, who went by the pen name Kenneth J. Alford, was a British Army bandmaster and the director of music for the Royal Marines at Plymouth. During the First World War, he composed the march *Colonel Bogey*, which was instantly adopted by the British military at the outset of the Second World War. In some circles, the song was parodied with irreverent lyrics that derided Hitler and his inner circle of cronies.

As the royal walkabout came to its close, spectators on the perimeter of Guildhall Square were eager to seize their chance to connect with the Crown. Magnetised by the regal presence, they could not contain their excitement. 'During this part of the tour a section of the crowd, including mothers with babies in arms, impulsively surged forward to meet the Queen.' The onlookers were not to be disappointed because once Lady Astor pointed the group out to her, the Queen gave them 'a special wave of her hand'.[29] This interaction underscored the visit's celebratory atmosphere.

As the royal entourage prepared to depart Guildhall Square, the Queen caught sight of Edward Leatherby, who had previously served Plymouth as mayor and was credited with transforming the city into a popular holiday destination. He seemed to skirt the media restrictions imposed on journalists in that he had a cine camera and was capturing footage of the parade and walkabout. As the King and Queen conversed with him, Leatherby shared that he was serving as the chair of the Education Committee and hoped to show the schoolchildren some pictures from the momentous day. The King and Queen smiled for Leatherby's camera and then made their way to their waiting vehicle to continue with the afternoon's programme.[30]

Surveying the bomb damage

Next, the entourage was driven through the Barbican and Cattedown districts to view the aftermath of the recent bombing raids and meet some local people. The *Western Morning News* indicated that these actions further earned the esteem of Plymouth's citizens: 'That the King and Queen could find the time to visit the humblest subjects in the homes many of them scarred by German savagery, was a fact that won the hearts of all.'[31]

While in the Cattedown district, the King and Queen visited Mrs Violet Burring, Plymouth's first war widow. Her husband William had been the chief stoker on board HMS *Forth* and was the victim of a tragic drowning accident at the Earl Grey Basin in Dundee shortly after the war broke out.[32] Violet was now a widowed mother of four. Her youngest, Maureen, had been born shortly after William's death.

Maureen buried her face in her mother's neck, shying away from the Queen, while Mrs Burring spoke with the King about her efforts to raise and provide for her four young children.[33]

The royal couple also spoke with those whose homes had been destroyed or rendered uninhabitable. Following the pattern of the Queen's morning tour in Devonport, these representative conversations served as moments in which others might recognise their own experiences.

One elderly woman, Mrs Rachel Barry, shared that the Council had relocated her to a flat and that she was determined to remain in Plymouth, no matter the risk.

When meeting with the Harkcom family of Elliott Road, the Queen entertained the children. This moment captured the hearts of the spectators, who commented, 'Isn't that lovely. She's a mother, just like us.' Meanwhile, the King spoke with Mrs Muriel Harkcom, commenting on her cheerfulness despite her situation. The *Western Morning News* correspondent captured the housewife's resolve: 'Snatching a Union Flag from one of her children, she waved it and said: "Oh, yes, sir, we can stick it; we are British all right."'[34] Mrs Harkcom's words were emblematic of the 'carry on' and 'the British can bear it' mentality that characterised the home front response to the challenges of war.

Another exchange with an air-raid warden yielded a sound bite that was repeated in contemporary news coverage about the day. When asked how he was faring, the man stated, 'We are keeping our chins up.' To this, the Queen replied, 'It is only by keeping our chins up, as we are doing, that we shall win the war.'[35] Resilience, embodied in the simple phrase 'chins up', was critical to civilian morale and was the essential weapon needed in each citizen's mental arsenal. It would be both the sword and shield that ultimately promised to deliver victory, and the royal visit seemed to have the power to galvanise it.

Visiting Virginia House

The programme continued at Virginia House Settlement. The inclusion of the Astors' charity on the itinerary represented an endorsement and approval of their efforts from the highest level of society. Established by the Astors during the First World War, the centre had evolved into a community hub. Throughout the 1920s, the facility expanded to accommodate an array of clubs and social organisations. Now, in response to the winter air raids, it served as a relief centre where displaced families could find assistance and support.[36] Within the Settlement, each stop revealed a different facet of community life, thus allowing the royal couple to publicly demonstrate their interest in the welfare of citizens of all ages and stations.

As was seen throughout the day, the atmosphere at Virginia House was charged with anticipation of the royal visitors. When the car bearing their insignia came in sight, the crowd erupted with a thunderous roar. The crowd surged forward with such excitement that 'the police had some difficulty in keeping back the crowd at the entrance to the Settlement'.[37]

Moments later, the children assembled in front of Virginia House echoed this tribute: 'They made a pretty picture, for each child had a small Union Flag, which was waved frantically as the King and Queen passed.'

The visit began in the men's clubroom, where the pair spoke with volunteers. Lady Astor introduced several men to the royal couple, including a Mr Clouad who notably gifted them a nine-pound crab.

The royal pair were then treated to a short concert. Lady Astor sat with the King and Queen as the women sang and danced accompanied by a lively piano. The repertoire included 'All the Nice Girls Love a Sailor', 'The Navy, the British Navy', and 'Three Cheers for the Red, White, and Blue'. In honour of the Queen's family heritage, the group also performed a Scottish tune.[38] During the programme, one of the women invited the King and Queen to join in the dancing. The King politely declined: 'We should love to, but we haven't time.'[39]

The pair also spent a few moments with a Sea Scouts Troop. The King asked them several questions about projects, and Scout Scot Symons was eager to speak about the troop's efforts to build a canoe. At the end of the exchange, the youths asked the King and Queen to sign their visitors' log, a simple request that the pair readily agreed to.[40]

Later, the pair visited the nursery. They knelt at the toddlers' eye level, engaging in playful conversations with them—and the media captured these endearing moments. 'The King laughed heartily when he asked a small boy "What is your daddy?" and the little fellow replied "Freddie." Despite encouragement, the child would not utter another word.' Another toddler, absorbed in play, inadvertently placed his toy wheelbarrow in the path of the Queen. The King, displaying a quick reflex, extended his hands to prevent any mishap. 'It's dangerous here,' he joked.[41]

No truer words could have been uttered. In France, Luftwaffe pilots were completing final checks in preparation for their evening raid on Plymouth. If only a stray toy was the worst danger that loomed.

Teatime

The royal entourage was then chauffeured to 3 Elliot Terrace on Plymouth Hoe, the elegant constituency residence of Lord and Lady Astor. The house looked out over Plymouth Sound and provided a picturesque setting for that most British of institutions: afternoon tea.

Among those invited to the 4.30 gathering were the deputy mayor, town clerk, and members of the Emergency Committee and their wives as well as Admiral Dunbar-Nasmith and his wife Beatrix.[42]

Dorothy West's family home backed onto the Astors'. Upon learning that the King and Queen were but steps away, the excited 16 year old hurried outside to attempt to see the royal pair. 'News travelled very quickly, and by the time I got on to the grass opposite their house several hundred other people had arrived.' The crowd was rewarded when the pair made a brief appearance to greet them: 'The King and Queen came on to the balcony to wave to us all.'[43]

The moment was short-lived as the cheers were drowned out by the piercing wail of an air-raid warning.[44] The sudden alarm echoed through the air, and the crowd's eyes looked up to the sky. Dorothy saw a German surveillance plane circling high overhead on reconnaissance: 'almost simultaneously a German "spotter" plane flew over. Obviously they could tell that someone important was there and it left very quickly to go back to its base to report that fact.'[45] Unknown to Dorothy, of course, was that enemy planes were already stationed on runways throughout occupied France where they were waiting for the signal to begin their mission to Plymouth within the next few hours.

By this point in the war, Plymouth had endured eight months of air-raid threats. There were hundreds many more alerts than actual incidents. There had been several notable raids that had resulted in around a dozen casualties each. These occurred in the evening, not in the middle of the afternoon. Thus, despite some rumoured intelligence that 'Plymouth was due to catch a packet tonight', the siren was ultimately deemed to be nothing more than a cautionary alarm.[46]

The tension that momentarily gripped the scene subsided. Indeed, so accustomed to air-raid sirens were the people of Plymouth that those assembled remained in position for the chance of one more sighting of the King and Queen.

The royal party enjoyed their tea, and then proceeded to the final stop on their itinerary 'as if nothing had happened'.[47]

The visit concludes

The day's final engagement was at the Servicemen's YMCA on Union Street shortly after 5 p.m. The visit began with expected formalities and quickly shifted to more relaxed interactions. Once again, these intimate conversations provided citizens with examples of the Crown's personal warmth and concern. Immersing themselves in the lively atmosphere, the royal couple engaged in cheerful conversations with staff about their work. Though they were approaching the conclusion of their busy day, their attention did not wane: 'All the while the King and Queen were surrounded by their admirers, and never for a moment did their Majesties cease to smile at what they heard and saw.'[48]

As with the visit to Virginia House, this was meant to highlight services that were aimed at helping others. For example, the Queen's interest in the food available for servicemen was made evident as she perused the offerings. Her attention was particularly drawn to a tray of treats that the supervisor, Mrs Netten, placed the tray on the counter for the Queen's inspection. The Queen pondered the sourcing of ingredients with the added challenge of wartime rationing.

The *Western Evening Herald* also reported on the King and Queen's conversation with a Mr Endle, a veteran member of the paper's editorial staff. Lady Astor beckoned Endle over and presented him to the Queen: 'Your Majesty, I must present to you one of the oldest journalists in the city. He is an old friend of mine, but sometimes I say stronger things about him.'[49]

The Queen extended her hand to Endle, and as he bowed in response, her Majesty, with a hint of jocular curiosity, inquired, 'What did Lady Astor say then?'

Endle, perhaps still taken aback by the encounter with royalty but nevertheless able to engage with the Queen's playful banter, responded with a touch of self-deprecating humour: 'Sometimes I have heard her describe me as one of the worst people in Plymouth but I don't believe it. I hope you don't, your Majesty.'

Next, Lady Astor presented Endle to the King. Endle shared that during his half-century of reporting he had met and interviewed every president of the United States since Grover Cleveland. He could now add the King and Queen to that esteemed list.

When the entourage returned to Millbay Station for their train's 5.45 p.m. departure to Windsor Castle, the day's theme of unity was reflected in the crowds lining the route. Citizens waved flags in appreciation, the afternoon air charged with a sense of renewed pride and purpose.

As the King and Queen boarded the Royal Train, the air-raid sirens sounded for the second time.[50] The gathered crowd was unperturbed and remained to bid the royal pair a safe return journey. At six o'clock, the train pulled away from the platform and began its easterly voyage. Having seen the King and Queen off, citizens dispersed, buoyed with memories of the day.

A crowning achievement

By all accounts, the visit was a triumph. The Astors had hoped that the magic of monarchy would cast its spell, and it seemed to have done just that.

While the royal visit lifted spirits, it was perhaps the Crown itself that emerged as the day's greatest victor—its presence not only praised but also portrayed as a unifying symbol of shared sacrifice strength. The next day's *Western Morning News* celebrated the positive impact of the visit. An editorial entitled 'Throne and People' highlighted the familial relationship between the King and his subjects:

> Yesterday's Royal visit brought comfort and cheer to many Plymouth victims of Nazi savagery and barbarism. It also served useful purpose in renewing and adding to the zeal and self-sacrificing earnestness with which multitudes of

> citizens are contributing to the war effort. All with whom they came in contact realized that the King and Queen were genuinely interested in what they saw and heard and not making merely perfunctory calls to satisfy a sense of duty. As everybody realized, it was a case of genuine human sympathy.
>
> The visit to Plymouth was one of many their Majesties have paid to bombed areas up and down the country. In all of them they have found evidence of the courage with which men and women of all degrees endure the heavy trials to which they are subjected. Neither personal suffering, bereavement, nor loss of home and property can subdue their spirit. 'We are keeping our chins up,' was said to the Queen by one with whom she expressed sympathy, and it was a typical expression of the general sentiment.
>
> Germany has so little understanding of British character as to be utterly incapable of realising and appreciating the relations of the Royal house and the people. If he only knew it Hitler is strengthening our will to resist by the indiscriminate way in which his terroristic acts are distributed. When common people learn that Buckingham Palace has been bombed and partly destroyed they see in the fact a fresh bond between the Throne and themselves. Those who have lost their homes or are in daily fear of losing them feel that the Royal Family are in no better case. And as rank and power bring no immunity, there is all the more reason for a quiet exercise of the native spirit of endurance.
>
> Probably there never was a time when the wearer of the Crown was held in higher regard by his people. Circumstances have temporarily robbed the highest office in the State and Empire of much of its ceremonial glamour. But what is missing in spectacular attraction is more than made up by the way in which all classes are drawn together in the knowledge of their real kinship.
>
> The feeling is peculiar to the war, or at least is strengthened by it. It may or may not survive the return of peace and the new world we are led to expect will be reared on the ruins of the old one now being destroyed. But so long as it survives England will be unbeatable. Dictators, like mules, leave no progeny, and long after Hitler and Mussolini have passed away and their aberrations been forgotten, this sceptred isle and its dependencies will be held together by the homage they owe to the House of Windsor.[51]

Though citizens had gathered to see the spectacle of the Sovereign, the impression of the day was that the King and Queen had come to see them. The impact of the visit lay not only in the ceremonial pageantry but also in more intimate exchanges. While pre-war royal protocol emphasised separation between Crown and commoner, the circumstances of war demanded a more immediate and personal royal presence. In Plymouth's devastated neighbourhoods, the King and Queen had demonstrated that the Crown's capacity to inspire resilience came not from standing away from and above the people, but rather from standing among them.[52]

The King and Queen's many individual interactions with ordinary subjects, described as having a 'warm friendliness', contributed to the day's success.[53] The mutual exchange of recognition—both the royal acknowledgement of civilian suffering and the public's appreciation of royal concern—seems to have deepened a sense of cohesion. It was not just King: it was kinship. The *Western Morning News* captured this sentiment in quoting a working-class woman's assessment of the day: 'They might just be the head of a big family come to see how we are getting on.'[54]

Yet, as momentous as the royal visit was, it was not the only headline when the Plymouth papers went to press that night. Indeed, the royal visit would not even be the lead story.

10

The Plymouth Blitz Begins

From party to pandemonium

The officials who orchestrated the day's royal programme gathered to revel in the success of their endeavours after the Royal Train departed. The venue for this celebration was the Royal Naval Engineering College at Keyham. Against a backdrop of jubilant chatter and clinking glasses, the King's cousin Lord Louis Mountbatten circulated among the assembled naval brass and municipal politicians.

At her home on Elliot Terrace, Lady Astor sat down to a private dinner party, pleased with how the day had generated the enthusiasm she and Lord Astor had predicted.

At 8.30 p.m., just twenty minutes into the nightly blackout, the air-raid warning sirens sounded for the third time that day. The streets, which only hours before had been the setting of joyful crowds waving Union flags as they cheered for their King, now echoed to the ominous sound.

Lady Astor put down her coffee and hurried outside. She looked up to the sky to scan the horizon over Plymouth Sound. An air-raid warden approached her and directed her to seek cover.[1]

At Keyham, Lord Mountbatten was about to enjoy a glass of wine when a 'dreadful rumbling noise' drowned out conversations between the guests. The mirth of the evening was replaced with unease. To break the tension, one of the servers jokingly called out that an officer had taken a tumble down the stairs.[2] The attempt at levity was short-lived.

Moments later, a naval officer interrupted the soirée and relayed the sobering news that Plymouth faced the imminent threat of aerial attack. The weight of the officer's announcement sank into the gathering. The party ended abruptly. Congratulatory conversations quickly gave way to sharp orders. The revelry was replaced by urgency as partygoers scattered for the safety of shelters or reported to duty stations. The guests hurriedly made their way out of the building and into the darkened streets.

Outside Plymouth, the Royal Train had taken refuge. During the visit, a Home Office Intelligence Unit dispatch had warned of possible enemy action in the south-west.[3] As a precaution, the train had burrowed itself into a tunnel siding near Totnes after departing Plymouth. The King's private diary recorded his memory of spending the night on the train and his concern: 'We heard German bombers overhead, who were on their way to bomb Plymouth.'[4]

Back in Plymouth, the crisp night air, thick with tension, was soon filled with a sinister sound that sent shivers down spines: the unmistakable drone of the incoming Luftwaffe. The disconcerting symphony built in a crescendo. The first wave of the attack force flew over the Plymouth Sound on the approach to their targets.

At 8.39 p.m., a high-pitched shrieking sound sliced through the air.[5] In the next moment, the sound of an exploding bomb reverberated throughout the city as the device struck central Plymouth. The opening shot was followed by a barrage of bombs and incendiaries that ignited the city's core. The night sky was illuminated with an eerie, hellish glow. Minutes later, formations of German Heinkel bombers broke through the smoke and descended menacingly towards the inferno to unleash their payloads.

On Elliot Terrace, the warden had persuaded Lady Astor to return inside her home for safety. Moments after she entered, a bomb hit close to where she had been standing: the impact shattered the glass of the front door. Collecting her dinner guests, Lady Astor made her way to her basement shelter. Her maid and personal companion, Rosina Harrison, was with the party, and she recalled Lady Astor's calm demeanour as the crisis unfolded: 'she seemed utterly serene as she sat there, repeating verses from the Psalms. There were no theatricals, just confidence and strength.'[6]

Only hours after the momentous royal visit, the city was under attack. The Nazi blitzkrieg on Plymouth had begun.

20 March 1941

The German aircrews of Kampfgeschwader (KG) 27 had no need of sophisticated navigational equipment to find their target. With the British disrupting Luftwaffe radio navigational systems over inland targets, the Luftwaffe had shifted its focus to coastal cities in southern England where visual navigation proved far more reliable. Plymouth's geography, which had made it such a vital naval base for centuries, also made it highly vulnerable to aerial attack. On a moonlit night such as 20 March, Plymouth's natural harbour and distinctive coastline were clearly visible to the enemy pilots. The deep inlet of Plymouth Sound, the prominent breakwater, and the unmistakable outline of the Hoe provided perfect visual references.

The specialised KGr100 pathfinder force was among the first to arrive. The squadron transformed the night sky into a hellish festival of light. A firewatcher observing the scene described the showering incendiary devices: 'The scene was grimly beautiful. In one area so many fire-bombs were released that as they burst into flames it looked like a torchlight procession.'[7] Blue, green, red, and crimson flares bloomed against the darkness. Over 12,500 incendiary devices rained down, descending like malevolent stars and igniting buildings throughout the commercial district.

This was a tried and tested strategy from the Luftwaffe campaign playbook. The aim of the advance force was to unleash a torrent of incendiary devices to ignite fires. These were meant to tax emergency personnel resources, thereby reducing the efficacy of their response, and were also intended to serve as signalling beacons for the later waves of Luftwaffe bombers.

The fires were visible miles inland too: neighbouring communities watched the horizon turn red and knew that Plymouth was burning.[8]

The night air over Plymouth filled with the distinctive drone of more bomber squadrons. Among them was the infamous Death Head's Squadron, KG54, with their loads of high explosives. The Edelweiss Squadron, KG51, carried massive 1-tonne bombs that could level entire city blocks. The Luftwaffe commanders had

Pat Twyford, *Western Morning News* war correspondent whose recollections and reporting are captured in *It Came to Our Door*, a vital primary source of the Plymouth Blitz. [*Plymouth Herald* and Chris Robinson, used with permission from Pat Twyford, *It Came to Our Door*, revised edition, 2005]

directed bombers to approach the target zone in a continuous procession, spaced two to three minutes apart, ensuring that the attack would stretch deep into the night.[9] Over the next four hours, 125 Luftwaffe planes took part in the raid. At this unprecedented scale, Plymouth's heart wasn't just being targeted—it was, in the words of the journalist Pat Twyford, being 'torn out and mauled'.[10]

Spooners' Department Store became the night's first major fire. The ornate five-storey emporium dated back to the early days of Queen Victoria's reign. Referred to as Spooners' Corner, the shopping complex ran from its original storefront on Bedford Street around the bend to Old Town Street. Across its five storeys of display cases and merchandise floors, shoppers could find clothing and furnishings for their homes. Now, where shoppers had browsed in elegance, flames consumed everything.

Those sheltering across the street witnessed the store's destruction first hand. As Stanley Goodman recalled,

> Nobody wanted to move much because the noise outside was hellish, but we did file out through the broken front … to find that the whole of Spooners on the opposite side of the road was alight. It was burning steadily and evenly … with a great crackle and roar, and the heat was so great that we could not look at it … it was lighter than day.[11]

'The fate of this imposing block was soon apparent,' Twyford recorded. 'It was a furnace, with the entire shops and vast showrooms blazing from roof to floor. The whole island site was doomed.'[12] What began as a single fire quickly became an unstoppable firestorm that raced through the rest of the commercial district, leaping from one building to the next with terrifying speed. Frank Booker, assistant editor of the *Western Morning News,* witnessed the otherworldly scene and described the wreckage: 'plate glass from shop windows flowing out into the road like lava, of molten gold and silver running from jewellers' shop windows.'[13]

The Royal Hotel was also consumed by fire after a direct hit. *The Times* reported how the disaster escalated and affected surrounding buildings:

> When the hotel caught fire it was occupied, not only by guests and customers in the bar and public rooms but by others who had taken refuge there from the streets. A bomb fell through the roof and many of the occupants ran for cover to a public shelter in the locality. Meanwhile a nearby cinema containing several hundred people was evacuated just in time, as large fragments of masonry were hurled from the roof of the burning hotel into the auditorium.[14]

Against this unfolding terror, Plymouth's citizens mounted a desperate defence of their city. 'Through it all thousands of men and women worked heroically to save their beloved city,' wrote Twyford. 'Tired, begrimed, and soaked, they toiled on. They were beyond fear. It was a grim desperation which carried them on.'[15]

Throughout the night, Plymouth's emergency responders and civil defence personnel fought to contain the spreading blaze. With no way to know when or where the next bombs might fall, these men and women raced between burning buildings and rubble-strewn streets. The arrival of Navy and Army servicemen from Devonport proved a crucial reinforcement and expanded the city's emergency response capacity at its moment of greatest need. Soldiers and sailors worked shoulder to shoulder at the height of the bombardment: 'they were where the danger was greatest, gallantly assisting rescue works either in properly-organised parties under their own officers or with the police and civil defence forces'.[16] This relationship between citizens and service personnel exemplified Plymouth's identity as both a naval port and civilian city, where the lines between service life and city life had always blurred, and never more so than in their combined defence against the Nazi aerial attack.

Heroism alone, however, could not overcome the night's challenges. Plymouth's firefighting forces found themselves critically short of both equipment and personnel. As urgent calls for assistance went out to surrounding communities, the flaws in infrastructure became apparent. Responding units arrived to find a scene of uncoordinated chaos: their equipment incompatible with Plymouth's systems, water mains broken, and the communications systems in disarray. Without a unified command structure, efforts to combat and contain the growing inferno proved tragically ineffectual.[17]

As the night wore on, Plymouth descended into pandemonium. The fires burned with ferocity as the bombardment intensified. While the *Western Morning News* characterised the German strikes as 'indiscriminate' and 'scattered in a blind and vain attempt to spread panic and confusion among civilians', there was intentionality and strategy behind the manoeuvres.[18] Over the course of the night, the Luftwaffe unleashed over 30,000 incendiary devices and delivered 159 tonnes of high explosives, including seventeen 1000-kg bombs, into a concentrated target zone at the centre of Plymouth.[19]

A terrifying chorus of destruction engulfed the city. Twyford recalled the haunting noises of Plymouth's plight: 'Throughout the four hours the noise of crackling fire, the terrifying rush of aircraft and falling bombs, the crash of explosives, the bark of anti-aircraft guns, the crack of bursting shells was incessant.'[20] The soundscape of terror penetrated every shelter and basement where families huddled together, each explosion bringing the possibility that their place of refuge might be next.

Anthony Cornelius, then aged 13, sheltered with his mother Maggie and younger brother Basil at 42 Portland Square, north of the embattled commercial district. The boarded-up windows of their home offered little protection against the deadly onslaught raining down from the sky.[21] His neighbours Barbara Cundy and Stanley Hollett were sheltering across the road in the Portland Square Air-Raid Shelter.

A tremendous explosion rocked the neighbourhood. Stanley recalled the moment that a bomb crashed into the street nearby and detonated:

> There was an almighty bang and I'm sure the shelter we were in rose a foot in the air and down again as the lights went out and the air was full of dust. We were told things were alright, and after a while the lights came back on again, but the crowded shelter occupants lost their singing voices and to say the least they were feeling nervy.[22]

Barbara Cundy remembered the terrifying moment vividly: 'We could feel the blast of that one when it came down it was like a gust of wind going through the shelter and a lot of people were screaming.'[23]

When the 'All Clear' finally sounded, Anthony, Barbara, and Stanley ventured from where they had taken refuge and witnessed the destruction. Anthony recalled that a bomb had struck in the middle of Portland Place East close to Roper's Chemist. The blast obliterated several houses and a small shop that sold sweets. 'I remember going out after the All Clear and seeing this big crater. A water main had broken and there was a smell of gas. I had quite a story to tell at school the next day.'[24] Barbara also recalled the devastation: 'a lot of houses opposite our house were demolished'.[25] Making his way home on the south side of the Square, Stanley considered how narrowly those in the shelter had avoided harm: 'about nine three storey houses only sixty feet away had been flattened by direct hits, just the width of the road away from the shelter'.[26]

At 1 Portland Place East, the Walters family's story was a tragic one. While their neighbours emerged to survey the damage to property, Ernest and Evelyn Walters faced the devastating loss of their son Ronald, aged 13. The boy had been one of Anthony's neighbourhood playmates. One lived to tell his story, while the other became one of the night's many civilian casualties.

The sun rises on Plymouth

When dawn broke on 21 March, Plymouth's citizens emerged to find their city centre transformed into an apocalyptic landscape. 'Many places, so long familiar, had gone in a night; nothing left but a shambles, smouldering ruins, blackened walls, and twisted steelwork,' Twyford recorded.[27]

Among the most striking losses was the neo-Gothic GPO that fronted Westwell Street and was part of the stately architectural backdrop that framed Guildhall Square. It was here where Plymouth had conducted the grand ceremonial parade for King George VI and Queen Elizabeth the previous afternoon. The GPO's grand stone entrance tower, crowned with 6-foot lions at each corner, had been reduced to rubble. The elegant maple wood floors of the sorting room, the modern telegraphists' chamber, and the ornate inlaid art with proud depictions of Drake's ships and the *Mayflower* were all destroyed.

For GPO Home Guard members such as Lang Cornelius, who had likely stood as part of the fire watch that night, the building's destruction would have represented more than just the loss of a workplace. This was where he had built a career, sharing meals in the second-floor dining room with colleagues discussing his stamp collection, and recruiting employees to join the TA and, more recently, the Home Guard. Now, the GPO was a scorched ruin of undelivered letters, tangled telegraph wires, and crumbling masonry.

Nearby, Plymouth's oldest church, St Andrew's, was still standing but severely damaged. The *Western Evening Herald* captured the catastrophic scene:

> The beautiful stained-glass windows have been blasted to shreds, the main body of the church is swimming with water from the hoses which still lead snake-like through the ancient doorways. Parts of the interior are piled high with blacked charred debris from portions of the roof which fell in following the fire. Some of the pipes of the organ sprawl at grotesque angles – in short, the once beautiful interior is a pathetic pile of debris.[28]

From his vantage point near St Andrew's, Twyford surveyed the aftermath of the calculated attack on the city centre. 'It was a sad, forlorn spectacle to gaze across those once bright and colourful gardens to Spooners' Corner,' he wrote. 'Some of the municipal offices were badly damaged, but the Guildhall stood foursquare, to all intents undamaged. At the other end of the Square, however, there was a scene of destruction, for the new Post Office, the County Court offices, and other buildings were completely destroyed.' His eyes took in the scope of the damage, leading him to a stark conclusion: 'Everywhere one looked there was the evidence of insatiable hate wrecked on a civil population.'[29]

Receiving incomplete intelligence from the Home Security Intelligence Unit in Plymouth, the Air Ministry and Ministry of Home Security in London mischaracterised the severity of the attack. Describing the Luftwaffe's activity as of 'much smaller scale', the communiqué inaccurately reported that the raid was 'not of long duration'. While it noted a number of fires and the use of high explosives, the report posited that the casualties from the raid would not be heavy.[30] This preliminary and erroneous assessment would be handed to the press and reported as fact.

The German News Agency, on the other hand, more accurately documented the situation that Plymouth's citizens encountered:

> The explosions of the German bombs caused many fires to break out which looked like a sea of flame over a large area [...] as a total result of this last heavy

> attack on England, it can be stated already now that the damage caused in the harbour of Plymouth and on works of military importance in the rest of the town was extremely serious.[31]

If Plymouth's citizens were not already demoralised by the devastating reality they faced in their streets, the salt in their wounds came from reports of the raid. The enemy's triumphant and eerily accurate assessment of the damage stood in stark contrast to their own government's muted response. It left residents to wonder if authorities in Whitehall and Westminster truly grasped the magnitude of the raid.

Meanwhile, outside London, the train carrying King George and Queen Elizabeth had safely returned to Windsor Castle. Having spent the previous night concealed outside Plymouth, the pair were acutely aware of the city's fate. From their darkened train, they had heard the incessant drone of the squadrons of German bombers.

After being briefed about the attack, Queen Elizabeth sent a letter to her mother-in-law, the Queen Mother. Queen Elizabeth's reflections to Queen Mary revealed how the attack impacted her and her genuine concern for those impacted:

> This morning we returned from Plymouth, and alas! an hour or two after we left last night, the foul Germans made a very heavy attack on the town & dockyard. What brutes they are – I am certain that they first go for the working class houses, hoping to break the spirit of our people. It was such a lovely day yesterday, and the sun shone, and the Hoe looked so picturesque, and one hates to think of the devastation and human misery that these wicked people are bringing to innocent civilians.[32]

King George VI shared his wife's distress. Later that evening, he sent a telegram to the Astors, expressing his faith in the resilience of Plymouth's people: 'AFTER OUR HAPPY DAY YESTERDAY THE QUEEN AND I ARE DEEPLY DISTRESSED TO HEAR WHAT YOU HAVE ALL BEEN THROUGH LAST NIGHT WHATEVER THE PEOPLE OF PLYMOUTH MAY BE CALLED UPON TO SUFFER WE FEEL QUITE CERTAIN THE SPIRIT OF THE WEST COUNTRY WILL RISE ABOVE IT ALL GOD BLESS YOU ALL. GEORGE R.'[33]

Yet before anyone in Plymouth or back in London could fully comprehend the scale of the Luftwaffe's attack, Plymouth would face another, even more severe, night of terror.

A signature Luftwaffe strategy was to conduct multi-night raids. After a lull of a day or even just a few hours, planes would return to a locale and repeat their mission, erasing the progress of any recovery efforts and compounding the crisis. These heavy raids in quick succession, referred to as *doppelgänger* attacks, characterised the pattern used in Sheffield, Merseyside, and Manchester in December 1940 and Swansea in February 1941.[34] The Nazi plan for Plymouth was to deploy this proven tactic from its campaign playbook.

Indeed, by the time King George VI sent his telegram to the Astors, the second raid on Plymouth was already well under way.

11

'It was again hell let loose'

21 March 1941

The Luftwaffe resumed its assault on Plymouth at 8.50 p.m.[1] The pathfinders of KGr100 took extra care in marking their targets, circling for some twenty minutes to ensure their flares would direct the following waves of bombers with deadly accuracy.[2] The goal was to strike the first night's target zone again and expand that perimeter.

The squadron struck with cold precision, unleashing a devastating initial barrage of 7,000 incendiary devices and sixty-four high-explosive bombs to the still smouldering ruins. This was merely the opening volley of what would be a relentless four-hour bombardment.

The scale of the Luftwaffe's commitment to Plymouth's destruction was staggering. It was evident that the Nazi attackers were hell-bent on inflicting carnage. Of the 178 aircraft dispatched to England that night, 171 were assigned to Plymouth, with the balance serving as decoys. Through the rain and low cloud cover, 168 crews successfully reached their targets, dropping their payloads over the city's core in an 'almost identical plan' to the previous night's assault.[3]

Following its tried and practised plan of attack, the Luftwaffe initiated the onslaught with a shower of incendiaries and followed the firestorm with heavy calibre, high-explosive ordnance. By night's end, more than 36,000 incendiary bombs and 197 tonnes of explosives would have rained down on the target zone, amplifying the impact and effecting obliteration.[4] The Luftwaffe's objective was clear: the annihilation of central Plymouth.

The second night of the attack finished off what remained of Plymouth's commercial core. The intense battery unleashed on such a concentrated area was described as 'the most fearful spectacle that Plymouth has ever seen'.[5] From Dingles' Corner to the already-destroyed Spooners' Corner, the popular shopping thoroughfare of Bedford Street crumbled into ruins. Frankfort Street suffered the same fate, while sections of Union Street were blasted and burnt beyond recognition.

Plymouth's civic infrastructure met the same paralyzing fate. Guildhall Square was the beating heart of its governance. When bombs struck the Guildhall, the city's emergency control centre, housed in its basement, had to be evacuated. By night's end, the building was reduced to a burnt-out shell. The entire northern side of the Square, home to administrative and municipal offices, was ablaze. The Town Clerk's Department, Council Chamber, Lord Mayor's Parlour, and Committee Rooms were all gutted in the ensuing inferno.

Nearby, the beloved St Andrew's Church, which had been heavily damaged during the previous night's onslaught, succumbed. The bombardment left the fourteenth-century medieval structure roofless and windowless, yet its tower remained, a defiant sentinel standing over the ruins.

The following morning, Miss Margaret Smith, headmistress of Western College Preparatory School, made her way through the ruins to survey what remained of the church. Unable to approach closer than the Central Library at first, she eventually reached the site and resolved to make a statement of hope—and to do so anonymously. She arranged for a builder to paint a single word on a wooden board and hang it above the north porch. The sign read 'RESURGAM'.[6] Translated from Latin as 'I shall rise again', this watchword expressed the prayer that Plymouth would, like a mythical phoenix, one day arise from the ashes reborn.

Like the tower that stood over the ruins, the plaque famously became a symbol of Plymouth's unconquerable spirit. When a friend revealed Smith's role after the war ended, the educator was rightly praised as 'that person of unconquerable spirit whose inspired actions did so much to keep alive our native pride during those dreadful days'.[7]

'Havoc was widespread'

Yet, on the morning of 22 March, Plymouth did not look like a city capable of resurrection.[8] The statistics painted a grim picture: as many as 20,000 properties, including thousands of homes, were damaged or destroyed. One contemporary estimate for the financial toll of the attack was a staggering £100 million.[9]

The physical destruction seemed endless. Twyford tallied the extent of the loss: 'Almost whole streets of old and imposing houses in the Hoe district, many churches, schools, clubs, revered public buildings, and business premises whose firms had for years been household names, were swallowed in that welter of senseless destruction.'[10] His appraisal was echoed by *The Times*, which reported that the very fabric of Plymouth's urban life had been torn apart with businesses and homes across the city severely damaged or completely destroyed.[11]

The list of destroyed properties read like a roll call of Plymouth's landmark businesses and institutions: the Athenaeum, Promenade Pier, Dingles', Spooners', Costers', the Royal Hotel, the Palladium Cinema, the City Hospital, St Andrew's Church, and Charles Church. Tragically, premises that were meant to provide relief services were themselves casualties of the bombing. It was a cruel irony. The

Virginia House Settlement, where Lady Astor had proudly escorted the King and Queen during their visit, lay among the ruins.[12]

The Cornelius family of Portland Square would learn that their connections to Plymouth's commercial life had been severed as well. Percy Hill, the father of Maggie Cornelius, had established his pawnbroker's shop in Prince Rock on the corner of Alma Street and St John's Road. After Percy's death in April 1940, his wife Emma had run the establishment. Though the shop was located away from the most intense bombing, Prince Rock was also hit. Blast damage wrecked the business and forced its closure, one of countless family enterprises erased during the raids.[13]

In central Plymouth, barely a building remained intact within a 600-yard radius of the Guildhall's blackened skeleton.[14] The smoking ruins of the civic quarter and the commercial district presented not just a scene of devastation, but the collapse of the very administrative and economic systems needed to coordinate the city's recovery. Citizens faced the daunting task of restoring daily life without much of the infrastructure that made those routines possible.

The Germans had indeed brought their worst to Plymouth's doorstep. *The Times* reported that, comparatively, the situation in Plymouth was 'as widespread and severe as any seen in the provinces'.[15] Mass Observation characterised the scene soberly: 'the damage is more serious, in its concentration on the heart of the city, than anything we have seen elsewhere'.[16] As she surveyed the wreckage of her beloved city, Lady Astor delivered her verdict with grim certainty: 'Plymouth knows the meaning of total war.'[17]

From Windsor Castle, Queen Elizabeth found herself haunted by the latest news about the dire situation in Plymouth. The stark contrast between her memories of a vibrant Plymouth and reports of its obliteration moved her to write to Lady Astor. Her letter, penned on 23 March, revealed her personal anguish and her prayers for the people of Plymouth:

> Dearest Lady Astor
> Since early yesterday morning when I first heard of the savage attack on dear Plymouth, I have been thinking of you all without ceasing. I have been praying that the people may be helped to find courage, and ability to face such a terrible ordeal, and I am certain that they have all this spirit already.
>
> Words are not invented to say even mildly what one feels, but having just left you after such a happy and inspiring day, one feels it all so bitterly, and so personally. My heart does truly ache for those good mothers and children and all the splendid workers.
>
> That is one of the hard things about being King and Queen of a country that one loves so much. Every time this sort of murderous attack is made, we feel it, as if our own children were being hurt. All we can do, is to do our very best, and leave the rest in God's hand.

I know how much you love the people, and how much you have striven to better their lives in Plymouth, and my sympathy is very deep and sincere.

I long to hear how Virginia House fared, also the Club and Toc H, as I fear they were in the shopping centre.

Oh, curse the Germans,

With love and thanks for your devoted service to humanity,

Yours affect.

Elizabeth R.[18]

The Queen's letter captured a truth about the British home front experience during the blitz: every level of society, from castle to council house, felt its impact.

Managing the dead: processing Plymouth's losses

The true human cost of the raid was still being tallied as rescue parties worked through the rubble of wrecked buildings. Over the course of the two nights, there were 336 fatalities, more than double the casualty count of all the previous raids on Plymouth combined.

The Hallwell Street Mortuary was a purpose-built facility meant to serve as Plymouth's principal wartime mortuary. While it had managed to handle the casualties during previous attacks, mortuary staff were overwhelmed by the scale of the March raids; nothing had prepared the staff for the task of accommodating such large numbers—between sixty and seventy victims from the first night—in such a short window of time.[19]

The mortuary's location near the city centre proved both a blessing and a curse. While this proximity allowed emergency personnel to quickly transport the deceased to the facility, it also meant the mortuary and its auxiliary support spaces were vulnerable when the Germans returned. Indeed, the second night's attack destroyed many of the deceased's personal effects and duplicate mortuary intake forms, key to identifying the victims, when the municipal buildings where these items were being stored went up in flames. A nearby bomb explosion on 22 March, reports of other unexploded bombs, the compromised structural integrity of the mortuary's roof, and the loss of a steady water supply resulted in the mortuary being shuttered until 24 March.[20]

Once staff finally regained access, they were faced with the grotesque task of processing a backlog of bodies that had been putrefying for several days. Those corpses needed to be prioritised. The processing of other victims was delayed, and some were rerouted to other facilities. As a result, confusion and frustration reigned as surviving family members sought information about the missing and deceased.[21]

After accounting for the dead, Plymouth then faced the task of laying those victims to rest. While most victims were claimed for private burial, 112—including forty-six unidentified individuals—were buried as part of communal burial services organised by Plymouth Corporation at Efford Cemetery.[22]

The scene of the 27 March funeral was both solemn and stark. Coffins lay draped in the red, white, and blue of the Union flag beside a vast burial pit adorned with spring flowers.

Grieving families mourned as religious leaders conducted the multifaith service. 'We are gathered here as a united family', declared Anglican Bishop of Plymouth Francis Daukes, 'without distinction of class, party, profession, occupation, or creed, to offer our deepest and most loving sympathy and our comfort to those who mourn.'

The gravity of the moment was amplified by the presence of numerous dignitaries. Among the civic officials attending were Lady Astor, the Deputy Lord Mayor and Mayoress Modley, and a host of civil servants including Town Clerk and ARP Chief Colin Campbell, the city engineer, the city treasurer, members of the Emergency Committee, aldermen, and past mayors. The presence of top naval brass from HMNB *Devonport* and senior officers of the Army and RAF further imbued the ceremony with a sense of heroic patriotism. Bishop Daukes captured the collective anguish of the assembled, his words reflecting the raw emotion of a city struggling to make sense of such a catastrophe: 'We grieve over their loss, and we ask ourselves to what purpose is all this waste, this sacrifice, this destruction.'

Just steps away, a second communal burial service took place, one that particularly embodied the tragic results of the raids. Here, Plymouth laid to rest three teenage nurses and their infant charges. All were victims of a strike on the maternity ward of the City Hospital. Conducted by the hospital chaplain, the service mirrored the larger communal burial with its use of Union flags, the presence of dignitaries, the tableau of nurse representatives 'in their snowy-white uniforms and navy and scarlet capes', and sprays of spring flowers.[23] In particular, the scene highlighted the indiscriminate nature of the raids and the particular cruelty of lives taken before they had even begun.

'And so Plymouth carries on'

Once the dead were laid to rest, the living had to get on with life. There was no other choice.[24]

In the aftermath of the attacks, Plymouth faced the monumental task of caring for survivors by restoring essential services and commerce. As the *Western Morning News* observed, 'Wreckage is cleared away, the stricken are helped, the intricate jigsaw pattern of a big city's life and services is being fitted together again, and more independent than ever is the spirit of the people who mean to win.' Plymouth's civic institutions and merchants rapidly adapted to meet the urgent needs of a population that seemed determined to carry on. Together, they would demonstrate that while bombs could destroy buildings, they could not break Plymouth's resolve. Like the watchword *Resurgam* defiantly affixed on St Andrew's Church, Plymouth would prove that life could, and would, continue.

The city faced a range of challenges that required immediate attention. The homeless needed to be housed. Buildings needed to be stabilised or razed. The population needed to be provisioned and fed. Businesses, schools, and churches needed to find temporary locations to continue their vital work.

The Emergency Committee led the charge of Plymouth's recovery efforts. Meeting daily, and with naval and military authorities from Devonport present, the committee brought together key municipal decision-makers who could implement critical measures without bureaucratic delays. Lady Astor was a frequent, and vocal, attendee at these meetings. The Committee would define the contours of Plymouth's new normal.

To provide timely communication with the public, the Committee issued daily emergency bulletins that provided essential updates about city services and safety measures. Issued in the week after the raid by ARP Controller and Town Clerk Colin Campbell, the documents intended to inform and encourage citizens as Plymouth authorities worked to gain control of the situation. The bulletins outlined important changes to services and how to access resources, which included amended transportation routes, provisions for schools, the suspension of certain businesses and restrictions on others, the location of and arrangements for food and rest shelters, and a directory listing the premises where municipal services and offices were relocated.[25] Perhaps most importantly, the bulletins were meant to reassure citizens by illustrating that Plymouth's leadership had matters well in hand and was implementing solutions step by step.

The bulletins also encouraged citizens to do their part to economise and help others. The bulletins made an appeal for housing, clothing, and furniture to assist those who had lost their homes and belongings. The Good Neighbour Scheme encouraged families to plan proactively to anticipate how they would manage a loss to property from possible future raids:

> Families are urged to make arrangements now for their accommodation with friends or relatives in other parts of the City, so that, in the event of their houses being rendered uninhabitable, they will be able to proceed to the alternative premises without delay. The arrangements might well be mutual, where circumstances permit, and should be notified to the Warden's Post.[26]

The bulletins also prescribed behaviour by addressing public safety and behavioural expectations in the wake of the attack. The bulletins advised citizens to temper their curiosity and not make a habit of sightseeing in the disaster zone: 'The public are particularly requested not to go into the damaged areas unless they have urgent business.'[27] It discouraged the dissemination of misinformation: 'The public should be warned against the spreading of rumours. These are likely to cause unnecessary alarm and distress.'[28] Mindful of the continued German threat and the persistent belief, contrary to all instances in Plymouth and elsewhere, that a gas attack was a possibility, the bulletins reminded citizens of their 'individual and general interests to carry their Gas Masks – always.'[29] Through these direct communications, the Emergency Committee worked to maintain public safety and social order.

Women's Volunteer Service members helped disseminate this information. Personnel distributed printed pamphlets and used loudspeaker vans throughout Plymouth.[30]

The daily updates ended after a week. After the seventh bulletin on 30 March, the next one was not released until 3 April. There was a further hiatus until 8 April. That bulletin included an important notice that signalled a change in the city's emergency status: 'It is not anticipated that any further bulletins will be issued for the time being.'[31] Notably, that bulletin reversed many of the closures made previously, indicating that while the situation was still far from ideal, the public emergency was at last under sufficient control and citizens could carry on with some of the normal activities of life.

While the Emergency Committee hammered out the overall recovery strategy, it fell to civil servants to implement these plans, often under extraordinary circumstances. These dedicated workers maintained essential operations even as their usual facilities lay in ruins, finding creative solutions to serve Plymouth's citizens by adapting to the circumstances and available resources.

The Post Office's relocation, for example, typified Plymouth's determination to restore a sense of normality. Postal employees and its Home Guard detachment demonstrated remarkable dedication both during the raids and in the challenging days that followed as they worked to re-establish vital services. With the destruction of the GPO building on Guildhall Square, operations shifted to Mutley Plain to ensure that the flow of mail and telegrams continued. The intensity of the destruction of the original location was captured by Anthony Cornelius, who recalled visiting the new site with his father: 'He took me one day to the post office on Mutley Plain where the Home Guard had rescued a number of Home Guard revolvers from the General Post Office which had burned down a couple of nights ago. Because of the heat of the fire the guns had melted into great blocks of metal.'[32]

As part of a series of cabinet-level visits to bombed cities, Postmaster General William S. Morrison came to Plymouth to inspect the bomb damage to the GPO and review the new arrangements. During his visit, he reviewed a guard of honour formed by the GPO Home Guard, including Lang Cornelius, and commended their efforts: 'I congratulate you on your smartness and conduct. Thank you all for the devoted service you rendered in the recent "blitz."'[33] His inspection marked one of many departmental reviews by Whitehall officials which were aimed at learning from Plymouth's experience in anticipation of further attacks elsewhere.

Individual departments assessed their own response to the crisis. Officials identified key issues and worked to develop plans to improve coordination and efficiency in the event of future emergencies. For example, learning from its experience of what was effectively a mass fatality event, Plymouth's War Deaths Department developed several recommendations to enhance mortuary operations. All casualties from a particular raid would be processed at one mortuary site, with Hallwell Street designated as the site to handle larger-scale incidents. Reception racks and stretchers would be numbered for better organisation and the tracking of bodies. Rather than staff being on-call, an official would instead be stationed on-site around the clock to manage paperwork and liaise with those delivering bodies to the mortuary, ensuring crucial identification details would be captured in future incidents.[34]

Plymouth's business community also demonstrated remarkable adaptability and determination. Local merchants refused to let their enterprises falter or citizens go without basic needs. Hence began an unprecedented migration to outlying wards of Plymouth, particularly Mutley Plain and Mannamead. Here, bombed-out businesses set up operations in any available space—from small shops to private homes. The *Western Morning News* captured this spirit of ingenuity, reporting that within two days of the raids, many firms were already 'in full swing' and ensured a steady flow of goods into the city.[35]

This swift commercial reorganisation was crucial in helping Plymouth find its footing and begin the recovery process. When one supply chain was disrupted, merchants established alternative routes. When shops were destroyed, others stepped in to fill the void.[36] This tenacity meant that despite the extensive damage to buildings and infrastructure, Plymouth's citizens were able to access the necessities to carry on.

The dispersal of commerce meant that citizens had to adjust shopping routines. Instead of the convenient centralised shopping district they had known, residents had to navigate a patchwork of relocated businesses, tracking down which merchants had moved where. While goods were still available, the simple task of daily shopping had become a more complex endeavour.

As March ended, some residents dared to hope that Plymouth had truly endured its worst of the Luftwaffe's plans and were thus no longer in its scopes. Such comprehensive destruction in Plymouth surely meant that the Nazi strategists would focus their attention elsewhere. Yet others acknowledged that the docks of HMNB *Devonport* and other areas of the city had escaped with minimal damage, making them prime targets for a future raid.[37]

Any hope that Plymouth's blitz ordeal was over, born perhaps from desperation as much as reason, would prove tragically misplaced. The sobering reality was that Plymouth's immediate future held not relief but further trials. Unknown to Plymouth's weary citizens, Nazi military strategists were preparing to renew the assault on Plymouth with an even more sustained series of attacks in late April. The March blitz, those 'two nights of veritable hell', would only be the beginning of Plymouth's crucible.[38]

12

The Blitz Resumes: 21 April

The heart of Plymouth was a flattened landscape. What more could the Luftwaffe destroy and for what end? The prospect of another all-out attack from the sky was unlikely. Yet the Luftwaffe continued to keep Plymouth in its scopes, if only to be a nuisance. Over the Easter holidays, four minor disturbances consisting of a plane or two pestered the city. It seemed that the worst of the Nazi assault was over.

Perhaps less assured than others, Emma Hill wrestled with departing from her home on Maple Grove for the safety and tranquillity of her cottage in the Devon countryside. Personal matters factored into the calculus of Emma's decision. On 3 April, she grieved the one-year anniversary of the death of her beloved husband Percy. This came on the heels of her own loss during the March blitz. The successful business that they had built together at Prince Rock was one of the commercial casualties of the March raids—the shop and its contents burned to the ground. The destruction she experienced ultimately became too much for her to endure.

Emma implored her daughter Maggie Cornelius to join her in leaving Plymouth. Heavily pregnant, Maggie opted to remain at her Portland Square home as she was due to enter a nursing home to deliver the baby any day. Weighing on her decision was the fact that her husband Lang was recognised as a leader in their circle. He had served as a major in the TA at the beginning of the war and then as part of the Home Guard. Lang planned to stay put and do his part—and Maggie would do her part in supporting him.

The pair decided that their sons, Anthony and Basil, could accompany Emma instead. Anthony, like other boys, initially found the war to be exhilarating; however, more recent events had brought the realities of war too close to home. The March attack included a bomb that detonated just outside the Corneliuses' home. One of Anthony's friends was killed as a result.

Anthony and Basil were all too happy to venture to Restormel for a brief post-Easter holiday of sorts with their grandmother. As it was, lessons at school were in disarray. The absenteeism of pupils who had evacuated to the countryside and the tardiness of those who arrived exhausted, if at all, after spending nights in Plymouth's air-raid shelters did not make for the best environment for robust instruction.[1]

With the young boys out of the house, Lang and Maggie might find a moment of privacy together before the birth of their third child.

The attack

German Air Situation Reports for 21 April note that no daytime operations took place anywhere over Britain owing to a strong haze.[2] The Luftwaffe decided to direct all resources to a single large-scale night offensive instead. Of the 133 aircraft deployed for missions that night, 120 were destined for Plymouth.

The city's month-long reprieve came to an abrupt end and plummeted Plymouth back into chaos.

Plymouth's air-raid warning system alerted citizens to incoming danger. Each stage of an alert was assigned a different colour. Officials had specific responsibilities at each stage. A confidential yellow alert signified 'Preliminary Caution'. With planes an estimated twenty-two minutes away, this warning signal triggered public safety officials to initiate crisis management response protocols. If the planes continued on a trajectory towards the city, the yellow warning status was elevated to red. Meaning 'Action Warning', this message indicated that planes were approximately twelve minutes away. This escalated threat assessment activated Plymouth's central alarm system to warn the public to take shelter immediately.[3]

Victor Saundercock lived close to the Mount Wise signal tower. He recalled the first indicators of the attack: 'At about 9.19 pm on the Monday night the red and green warning light went on, on the tower a warning to ships, this was followed by the red which meant a raid was about to start.'[4]

Next, the warbling note of the siren would have pierced the quiet night. Police officers and dutiful ARP wardens would have echoed the signal on their whistles while shepherding neighbours to the nearest shelter.[5]

The German strategy for 21 April was nearly identical to the March raid. Indeed, reporters instantly drew parallels to the earlier attacks: 'It was a raid which compared in intensity with that of March 20 and 21.'[6] Twyford described the Luftwaffe's tactics: 'a vanguard of planes dropping thousands of flares and incendiaries, which turned night into day and set the beacon fires to illuminate a target area into which successive waves of bombers dived and released their loads of destruction'.[7] The pathfinder group initiated the attack with an opening volley of firebombing. As incoming aircraft approached the city, the fires delineated the target zone and ensured the mission's success.

One objective for the night's attack was to cripple the operations at the Royal Dockyard. HMNB *Devonport* was a critical cog in the British war machine. The port served to repair and outfit ships destined for the Atlantic Theatre. Luftwaffe Target Folders created from a series of reconnaissance flights provided coordinates and landmarks to direct the pilots' bearings.

The Luftwaffe Air Situation Report assessed the preliminary results and detailed the extent of the fires:

> Several large and numerous smaller fires were observed in the facilities of the state dockyards on the east bank of the Hamoaze River and its immediate surroundings, as well as in the harbour and shipyard facilities on the southern edge of the city between the mouth of the Hamoaze River and the harbour facilities at Sutton Pool, and in the adjacent urban areas. Numerous bomb hits could be observed in the harbour facilities, in addition to larger explosions, two of them in the area of the state dockyards. A particularly powerful explosion followed by fire broke out in the gasworks of the state dockyards.[8]

The report echoes British source material detailing that the Luftwaffe segmented attacks into distinct fire and bombing phases.

In addition to the naval base, the Luftwaffe again targeted Plymouth proper. Now, the Nazi fleet unleashed its malice on the thickly settled residential areas that radiated north from the city's ruined administrative and commercial centre. The sector bounded by the markets on the east, Cornwall, Frankfort, and King Streets to the south and Mill Street to the north, became consumed in fire. There were also concentrated bombardments of Alma Road, Embankment Road, Laira Bridge, and the Coxside district.[9] Twyford feared that the goal of this latest attack was Plymouth's total annihilation: 'It now seemed that the Nazis were determined to finish their fiendish work.'[10]

Civil defence organisations, medical professionals, and emergency personnel responded valiantly to the villainy. The first line of defence was the ARP wardens. Often recruited from the community they served, these 'watchful wardens' were prepared for whatever task was required 'from soothing frightened children to handling incendiaries and taking part in rescue work'. Female ambulance drivers, 'grim and with their steel hats jerked a bit more firmly on their heads', sped through Plymouth to respond to calls for assistance.[11] Doctors and nurses treated patients in the city's hospitals.

Despite *Devonport* itself being under attack, the military contributed to the immediate response in Plymouth. Just as they had done in March, servicemen assisted in many capacities and earned the gratitude and admiration of their neighbours: 'All were out in the streets regardless of danger, assisting civilians, collecting the injured, and fire-fighting.'[12]

Fire and police units reacted to critical situations:

> Flames obtained a hold in several business premises. But the firefighters were ready. Before the high explosives came crashing earthwards the fire-fighters

> were on the job. What is more, they stuck to it. Several outbreaks that threatened to become serious conflagrations were dowsed. […] The fire-fighters grimly watched flames licking across the tumbled woodwork that had been crashed previously, but these of course they extinguished lest they provide a target.[13]

Ordinary Plymothians sprang into action to assist too. The Ministry of Home Security's guidance on air raids had stressed that all community members had a part to play in responding to an attack. For example, the pamphlet *Air Raids: What You Must Know, What You Must Do* included instructions about how to smother incendiaries and flares to prevent larger fires.[14] In that regard, men, women, and children 'pounced on many fire-bombs which rained down'.[15] 'Armed with bags of sand, shovels, and stirrup-pumps' these citizens extinguished many smaller fires throughout Plymouth but, ultimately, could not stem the tide.[16]

Indeed, the Nazis' strategy was designed to overwhelm these noble efforts and render them inconsequential. In sum, the Luftwaffe released 35,996 incendiary devices over the city, once more igniting Plymouth into an inferno. 'The worst conflagration was', Twyford wrote, 'again in the centre of the city, where premises which had escaped the desolation of the March "blitz" became just raging furnaces.'[17]

Over the course of the six-hour attack, the Luftwaffe barraged Plymouth. The bombers magnified the fire damage. Correspondents detailed the intensity of this second phase of the strike: 'Raiders jettisoned numerous high-explosive bombs of the heaviest calibre on the fires.'[18] The ordnance included 704 bombs; 31 were 1,000-kilogram bombs, among the largest in the Luftwaffe arsenal.[19]

Twyford detailed the apocalyptic soundscape of this butchery: 'the heavy detonations of the bombs', 'the nerve-wracking dive of the bombers, and the shriek of the falling missile, the crackle of fire', 'the crash of the anti-aircraft guns', 'the sinister whine of shell splinters', and 'the falling of destroyed buildings'.[20] If Plymouth had lulled itself into a dream that the March nightmare was over, the din of war and destruction in April jarred the port city from its slumber.

Plymouth and Devonport mounted a military defence to the attack. The RAF scrambled assets to harass their Luftwaffe counterparts while searchlights criss-crossed the sky. From the ground, anti-aircraft gunners aimed to deter the Heinkels and Junkers from diving to lower altitudes to release their payloads with greater accuracy. The sheer scale of the attack, however, limited the efficacy of these measures.

Across the River Tamar in Cornwall, people witnessed the onslaught in disbelief. They looked with 'cold anger and compassion' as their neighbouring city once more received the brunt of the Nazi war machine. A profound sadness swept over those who watched in exasperation as the tragedy unfolded: 'instead of being able to flock eastward and do something useful, it was our lot only to stand and stare'.

'Wanton destruction'

The next morning on 22 April, Plymouth awoke to a smouldering urban landscape.[21]

Lilian Chapman of 6 Victoria Buildings wanted to send word to her sister-in-law in Scotland that her family had survived the ordeal. At about 8.20 a.m., she sent a brief telegram to her husband's younger sister Nell stating the essential message: 'Everybody ok love Lil.'[22]

Germany did not hesitate to declare the mission a military triumph. The official German News Agency bragged that 'strong German bomber formations successfully attacked Plymouth'. It also reported on some of the damage to military targets: 'Large fires were observed in the harbour and town and explosions were seen in the Dockyard.'[23]

The extent of the damage inflicted on the naval base was not widely reported owing to security measures concerning military installations. Structures throughout the base were impacted including the Royal Dockyard, Mount Wise, the Royal Naval Hospital, and the Royal William Victualing Yard. Barracks were also hit. The assault tragically included a direct strike on Boscawen Block, part of the HMS *Drake* training complex, killing ninety-six.

Whitehall, on the other hand, again seemed to downplay the severity of the situation. Regional newspapers, including Plymouth's local papers, transcribed a communiqué from the Air Ministry and Ministry of Home Security that had been based on partial intelligence:

> Enemy aircraft attacked the South-West of England last night. The raid did not last long, but in one town, which was the main target, a number of fires were started, some of them large. The fire situation was under control before daylight and reports indicate that although the raid was severe neither damage nor casualties were as serious as previous attacks on this area.[24]

Beyond not naming Plymouth outright, the memorandum missed the mark. The raid was a six-hour ordeal which included the loss of public buildings and private properties throughout the city. Plymouth had sustained another mass casualty event, and the death toll was still being tallied.

Echoing the memorandum, the BBC characterised the raid as 'short and sharp'.[25] As happened in March, this misinformation earned incredulous irritation from those on the ground.

Subsequent reporting reframed the story. By nightfall, regional reporters had obtained additional information and sombrely noted, 'it is feared that the list of killed and wounded may be serious'.[26] Indeed, it was serious: at least 113 were killed.[27] Likewise, *The Times*, which had initially relayed the Ministries' communiqué, later detailed that Plymouth had suffered a two-part raid: a fire storm followed by intense bombardment. A full news cycle removed from the incident, the paper was able to sort out the facts and indicated that casualties were likely to be significant.[28]

The damage, however, had already been done. The initial inaccurate reporting shaped the narrative for the nation and undermined Plymouth's confidence in the media as well as in the various ministries in London. Lady Astor seized on these sentiments in the days that followed as she took charge of responding to the city's latest crisis.

A reckoning at daybreak

Regional Civil Defence Commissioner Sir Hugh Elles arrived at Plymouth at five in the morning. He reported, 'Dawn was beginning to break and a number of fires were still visible over Plymouth.' Throughout the rest of the morning, Elles assessed the situation—both in terms of Plymouth's needs and the leadership's ability to address them.[29]

A month past the March blitz, Plymouth had started the recovery process. This latest attack, however, reversed any progress and set the city back even further. 'It reopened many healing wounds, and created new vicious gashes in the city's body, for there was again a high concentration on the commercial life.'[30] Many of the businesses that had relocated operations found themselves bombed out again.[31]

Heavier bombs had finished off city-centre properties. Correspondents documented the destruction: 'Plymouth, in parts, was a flaming cauldron into which murderous high-explosives were to be poured, another ghastly illustration of the hideous meaning of Hitler's "total war."'[32] Two churches and three cinemas were among the buildings destroyed. The destruction of homes and tenement buildings exacerbated an already critical housing shortage.

Indeed, most troubling in the aftermath of the 21 April raid was that 'clearly-defined residential areas' were not spared from the attack.[33] The local morning paper was filled with sorrowful accounts of families killed in their homes or taking refuge in their Anderson shelters.[34]

Plymouth's Emergency Committee was scheduled to meet at 11 a.m. Commissioner Elles was present for this meeting. Unfortunately, it began half an hour late, an uninspiring start that set the tone of the day. In his assessment, Elles found that the Emergency Committee was overwhelmed by the magnitude of the crisis and the urgency of developing a strategic response. 'I am afraid that my impression of the Committee', he reported, 'was complete lack of any system or procedure.' Town Clerk Colin Campbell read out situation reports to provide an overview of the attack but did not appear to have a grasp on all the data. Elles characterised further discussion about the incident and how to respond to it as 'haphazard'.[35]

Ultimately, Elles was not convinced of the capacity of the Emergency Committee to comprehend, much less manage, the crisis:

> I feel I must add that, even making due allowances for the fact that everybody was tired, the Emergency Committee did not strike me as being very effective. The Chairman was anxious to fulfil his functions but seemed incapable of taking charge or of introducing any order into the proceedings. The other members when they spoke at all seemed more anxious to argue about the past than to settle the urgent problems of the present.[36]

Indeed, much of the morning's meeting concerned the reorganisation of Plymouth's Fire Brigade. The Committee concluded that the Fire Service needed to operate separately from the Police and that an experienced professional should be appointed to take the helm. They also deliberated the allocation of further financial resources to increase the strength of the force and equip personnel with the tools they needed.[37] In the face of the Luftwaffe's firebombing, this restructuring was a needed measure but one that, in Plymouth's case, perhaps came too late to be of real benefit and had little bearing on addressing the exigencies of the moment.

Elles took matters into his own hands. He anticipated the possibility of the Germans returning for another strike that evening and urged officials to prepare for that scenario. By the afternoon, 'sufficient resources' had been mobilised to be on standby as a precautionary measure, largely at Elles's insistence.[38]

During the day, ARP wardens prepared for the possibility of another attack. In addition to their vital public safety work during an alert, wardens' duties also included making sure that the area they were responsible for was prepared for whatever may lay ahead. Wardens' posts contained necessities such as first aid equipment that would need to be checked and replenished. The communal shelters would need to be inspected for cleanliness in anticipation of residents seeking shelter in a subsequent alert. Twyford wrote admiringly of the wardens' efforts: 'during the intensive raids of 1941 many of them went days with only snatches of rest, during their wardens duty and carrying on with their work in a spirit which tested their endurance but never knew defeat'.[39]

The Emergency Committee reconvened at 4 p.m. The group appeared no better informed about the status of rescue operations or of other details pertaining to questions raised during the morning meeting. To Elles, the group did not seem 'to take any great interest' in some of the logistics of these matters until he raised them himself.[40] Even then, the Committee failed to demonstrate the urgency that the situation demanded and showed little initiative in preparing for what might come next.

Instead of focusing on strategy, the Committee coped with the stress of the crisis by busying itself with minutiae. The Committee muddled its way through the afternoon, despite Commissioner Elles's efforts to guide them. Indeed, and to Elles's dismay, members deliberated the provisioning of meals for rescue and reinforcement parties for an hour and a half. Elles detected 'resentment' from the membership about his presence. Yet in his assessment, Plymouth—or any community for that matter—was ill-equipped to handle a crisis of this magnitude on its own and would have devolved into 'little but chaos' without an outside expert's perspective.[41] Elles resolved to remain in Plymouth in the event that his prediction came true and the Luftwaffe launched another attack after nightfall.

Decisions at dusk

As the day wore on, residents grew worried that the Luftwaffe might return as had happened in March and in attacks on other cities. Fear is a powerful motivator, and by the middle of the afternoon, residents began to leave the city. Emergency Committee Bulletins officially discouraged this behaviour. One of the first Emergency Bulletins after the March attacks implored citizens to remain in Plymouth: 'Every effort should be made to discourage persons leaving the City for the night, as this, apart from a bad effect on public morale, increases the danger to property from incendiary bombs.'[42] Mass evacuation signalled a defeatist attitude and was potentially detrimental to the morale of those required to remain. Further, from a public safety perspective, vacant properties were a fire hazard because there would be a delay in detecting or extinguishing incendiaries. Yet the Emergency Committee also implicitly sanctioned these evacuations. The city provisioned rest centres and directed additional transportation resources to those locations. If there were to be a retreat, it would at least be orderly.

Stanley Hollett recalled watching the droves of people making an exodus each afternoon: 'In Tavistock Road opposite the Museum there would be hundreds of people, men, women + children queuing up where lorries and any form of transport would take them out of the city, as long as it was out of the nightmare.'[43]

Cathi Hunt also witnessed the daily egress, though she never felt it necessary to join the crowd: 'We never dreamed either of joining the hordes trekking out to the Moors every night with every means of transport including carts and barrows. They used to pass us in their hundreds, perhaps thousands. They were taking their children to safety,' she reflected, noting parents' protective instincts. 'If my children had been born then, I think we would have been among them.'[44]

At Glanville Place a couple of blocks south of Portland Square, Jack and Nellie Temlett and their mother Gladys prepared to vacate the city. Jack was insistent on leaving town, and Gladys acceded to his request. They packed up some necessities for the night and left their flat to check in on family members who lived at Victoria Buildings.

Gladys and Jack called in at the Chapmans' flat to pick up Gladys's favourite nephew Leslie. She attempted to persuade her sister-in-law Lilian to make the trek

Bella Gill, left, and Lilian Chapman, right. Lilian lived at 6 Victoria Buildings and sent her sons Peter and Leslie with her sister-in-law out of Plymouth on the night of 22/23 April. [Peter Chapman]

with them. Lilian opted not to leave the city. She had found sanctuary in the solidarity of neighbours gathering in the Portland Square Shelter in the past. She would do so again that evening.

Gladys made a similar plea to her friend, and Lilian's neighbour, Florence 'Win' Davies. With the prospect of packing up and transporting her six children, including her infant Kenneth who was only three months old, Win similarly decided to stay put in Plymouth. If she needed to, she could always head to the shelter at Portland Square as her family had done many times before with the help of relatives, neighbours, and friends on Victoria Street.

Young Peter Chapman, on the other hand, saw the opportunity to tag along for the night with his brother and cousins. He asked his mother to allow him to go away with Aunt Glad. Time was ticking, and a few miles lay ahead of them before nightfall. Lilian consented. Peter recalled how his mother bade him farewell that afternoon and sent him off to the countryside with his aunt: 'My mother gave me a street wash – which was a face wipe with her apron.'[45]

From there, the group departed, and Lilian prepared for the possibility of spending another night in the Portland Square Air-Raid Shelter with neighbours from Victoria Buildings such as Mrs Mary Sherlock, a woman her children affectionately referred to as Gran.

John MacGregor and his elderly mother Jane decided to walk the perimeter of Portland Square for some fresh air in anticipation of another night in the communal shelter. John's daughter Ena and her boyfriend would meet them inside the shelter later at their usual spot. 'We had written up on the wall: "Reserved for No. 9," the number of the house in which we lived,' recalled Ena.[46]

Meanwhile, at 4 Portland Square, the Hollett family was planning to shelter in place at home. Stanley Hollett, however, heard that his neighbourhood friends were planning to spend the night in the air-raid shelter across the road. He considered his own plans for the night ahead, perhaps motivated by the allure of an opportunity to socialise with friends. Indeed, just like the park above it, the shelter was a place of community where camaraderie thrived: 'we enjoyed singing and all sorts of things helping people keep their spirits high.'[47]

Stanley asked his mother for permission to join his friends in the shelter—just as he had done in the March raids. She felt uneasy about the plan and preferred for the family to remain at home together. As any teenager might, Stanley persisted over the course of the afternoon in his quest. Eventually, his mother caved in to his request: 'she relented and just before dark I went to the shelter with some friends and the families from around us.'[48]

13
The Incident at Portland Square: 22–23 April

The sun set over Plymouth at 8.22 p.m. on 22 April. Theatres and other public gathering places closed at 8.30, effectively compelling people to return home. Shortly afterwards, at 8.52, the nightly blackout ordinance went into effect. By this time the previous evening, the city was already under attack. Tonight, it was quiet—and the skies were clear.

At 42 Portland Square, Maggie Cornelius set the table. She and her husband Lang prepared to enjoy a late, quiet dinner. They were thankful that their sons Anthony and Basil were safely out of town with their grandmother Emma and had been spared the events of the previous evening.

Across the Square at No. 27, William 'Bill' Cundy was preparing his uniform for the following day's work. Bill was a bus conductor employed by Plymouth Corporation. His daughter Barbara recalled him taking great pride in the appearance of his uniform and how he fastidiously polished the silver buttons on his coat.[1]

Plymouth's nightmare, however, was far from over. The Nazi command had orchestrated another *doppelgänger* raid. German Air Situation Reports detailed the mission objective: 'The attack was directed against the parts of the city located in the harbour area with facilities, power plants and dockyards, with a focus on the state dockyards, gasworks and main supply depot.'[2] The Germans would also be searching for new targets. Drake's Ward, which had been spared substantive damage in previous attacks, presented a largely blank canvas on which the Luftwaffe might demonstrate their destructive power. Reservoirs in the area were likely infrastructure targets.

Generalfeldmarschall Hugo Sperrle's Luftflotte 3 wing was responsible for the night-time strike. Squadrons of Heinkel 111s from Chartres, Dreux, Rennes, Tours, Vannes, and Villacoublay would rendezvous in a coordinated assault on Plymouth. These were among the largest bombers in the Nazi air fleet. They could each carry a payload of 10,000 kilograms. These seventy-seven planes would be joined by an additional forty-eight aircraft from Luftflotte 2, including forty of the versatile and swift Junker 88s. In sum, 125 planes were allocated for the night's mission. Before the embers of the previous night had cooled, Plymouth would once again endure the full force of the Luftwaffe.

Plymouth's alert status changed to yellow at 9.34 p.m. At 9.35, a special purple alert indicated that any external lighting on buildings that had been granted an exemption from the black-out regulations was to be extinguished. At 9.44, the air-raid sirens sounded, but by this time the first planes were already over the city.[3] *The Times* later recounted: 'Aircraft were first heard over the city early in the night, and it was evident that another major raid was developing.'[4]

This first wave included the specialist pathfinder force based at Vannes. Another twenty aircraft from Tours and Rennes rounded out the first battle group.

This was, once more, a moment that residents feared but had also prepared for. The Ministry of Home Security's pamphlet *Air Raids: What You Must Know, What You Must Do* reminded citizens of the importance of staying calm and following a plan. 'During a raid and, indeed, at all times in an emergency, it is necessary to keep calm, and to act swiftly, with the knowledge of the right course which must be gained beforehand.'[5] This now played out in the environs of Drake's Ward as residents of Portland Square and Victoria Street hurriedly emptied out of their homes and made their way to the air-raid shelter under the park.

The Woodfin family lived on Portland Place East. During the March raids, a bomb had struck near their home, killing neighbour Ronald Walters. The memory still fresh, the family made for the eastern entrance to the Portland Square Air-Raid Shelter. Philip Woodfin was one of the ARP wardens responsible for keeping order and enforcing regulations. As they made their way to the bunker, his wife Winifred looked after their young sons Kenny and Jimmy.

At 42 Portland Square, Maggie and Lang Cornelius exchanged a glance as they decided to abandon their dinner. Instead of remaining in their home, they would make their way across the street to the sanctuary of the communal shelter. After all, Maggie was heavily pregnant with their third child, and the company of neighbours might calm her nerves. They quickly executed their family action plan. Families would ordinarily bring a box of emergency provisions into the shelter with them; essential items often included candles and matches, toilet paper, a first aid kit, water, and a few rations to nibble on.[6] Lang gathered several belongings, documents, and valuables into a valise as a precaution. Maggie bundled herself in a grey tweed coat to confront the brisk evening and the damp conditions that awaited them in the shelter. She affixed a brooch of St Christopher to her ensemble. Leaving their cat and half-eaten pasties behind, the pair closed the door, crossed the street, and descended into the communal shelter.[7] Once inside, they found a space to the left. There were several bunk beds fitted into the walls in this sector to accommodate families and provide a place for children to sleep. As such, the section was not ordinarily as tightly packed nor as noisy as other sections of the shelter.

John Allison lived at 27 Portland Square. [Deborah Horton]

On the other side of Portland Square, Winifred 'Win' Cundy implored her father John Allison to join her and her daughters, Barbara and Betty, in the public shelter. During earlier alerts, the whole family had taken refuge in the Anderson shelter in their garden. The Cundys' home had sustained some damage during a previous raid, and so the family adapted and became accustomed to joining their neighbours in the communal shelter.[8] John, however, preferred to stay in the Anderson shelter and often spent the duration of an entire alert by himself. There, he could keep an eye on his shoe repair shop, which backed onto their property from the adjoining street. He insisted on doing so again.

Tonight, would be different. Win had been unnerved by the previous night's bombing and was adamant that the entire family should endure the raid together.

William and Winnie Cundy's wedding, 26 December 1927. The Cundy family lived at 27 Portland Square. [Deborah Horton]

Barbara recalled her mother saying, 'Come into the Portland Square shelter tonight, dad.'[9] John relented to Win's plea.

Win bade farewell to her husband Bill who was on-call that night. John led his granddaughters Barbara and Betty out of the house and across the street to the park. From the porch of their home, Bill watched the family disappear into the dark as they hurried along to the bunker's entrance. He promised to look in on them and bring them a hot tin of tea as he had done during prior alerts. [10]

Barbara was surprised not to see the Borokrof family present when her family settled onto the wooden benches in the shelter's east wing. They lived on the opposite side of Tavistock Road and were ordinarily among the first to arrive at the

Betty and Barbara Cundy, 1940. Betty died at Portland Square. Barbara survived and was the last living survivor of the incident. [Deborah Horton]

shelter. Unknown to Barbara, Mrs Borokrof had gone into labour and given birth to a baby boy.[11]

Like John Allison, newlyweds Harry and Cathi Hunt also required a bit of persuasion to take refuge in the public shelter. During previous raids, the couple had sheltered in their basement; tonight, air-raid wardens knocked on the door of their Portland Square home and encouraged the couple to join their neighbours. The Hunts knew that many of their neighbours found solace in the strength of the concrete structure and were comforted by the convivial atmosphere of singing, stories, and shared snacks in the shelter; the Hunts, though, preferred to keep their distance:

'Somehow it seemed undignified to use the public shelter.'[12] Thus, they decided to remain at home, but promised they would give the wardens' recommendation some additional consideration if the situation spiralled.

At 82, Eleanor Boynes of 6 Endsleigh Place was averse to going to the shelter. Just five feet four inches tall, she was known to shake her fist at the sky, cursing the Luftwaffe. Tonight, she was finally persuaded to shelter below ground.[13]

With the attack already under way, other neighbours had far less hesitation. Those residing on the square's eastern side entered the nearest access point and found seats near each other: Mr and Mrs Harry Andrews of 37 Portland Square; Mr and Mrs Ernest Harris of No. 38; and the Rendle family of George, Elsie, and Anthony—with their toddler nephew Robert in tow—from No. 39.

Families from nearby Victoria Street also flooded into the shelter. Located south of Portland Square, Victoria Street consisted mainly of multi-family dwellings.

Kenny Allen lived at 3 Victoria Buildings. [Frances Payne]

Portland Square's shelter was the designated refuge for the people who lived there. The nearest entry point was on the east end of the park.

Teenagers Phyllis Pepper and her best friend Barbara Allen quickened their steps from Victoria Street. Usually, the pair would have kept some of the elderly women in their flats company, but tonight they made for the shelter. Unbeknownst to Barbara, her father William and brothers Kenny and Gordon were already there.

Though the shelter could accommodate a large number, it seemed that more people than usual were seeking a space to sit out the raid. Barbara Allen recalled the large crowd: 'The shelter was packed, hundreds of people in the four sections. We were in the eastern section. Some people were sitting on the stairs, it was so busy.'[14] She and Phyllis opted to share a bunk. The friends would support each other through the stressful ordeal.[15]

Back on Victoria Street, Barbara's cousin Win Davies hastened out of her flat and up the block to Portland Square, shepherding her six young children: Winifred, Albert, Patricia, Iris, Dennis, and Kenneth, aged 3 months to 14 years. Her husband Albert Davies was a soldier and away from Plymouth on active duty with his unit. Thankfully, Win's aunt and uncle Florence and Claude Chubb were on hand to help manage the brood. So too were neighbours such as Lilian Chapman and Mary Sherlock. The familial relationships between those who lived on Victoria Street were such that all were willing to lend a helping hand to those who needed one.[16]

Young Albert wanted to remain above ground as he had done during other alerts and attacks. His mother won out, and the teenager joined his siblings underground.[17] As they had done on previous raids, the Davies family found space across from where the Cundy family sat.[18] Albert's sister Winifred was both deaf and mute.[19] An institute to support these individuals and their families was based at one of the buildings on Portland Square. This support extended to helping the deaf during air raids. Tonight, however, overcrowding meant that members from the Institute were not able to enter the same section of the shelter that they normally used—where the Davies family now sat. Instead, they found a space in another section.[20]

Members of Phyllis Pepper's extended family also rushed to the shelter. Phyllis's grandmother Lavinia Luxton was the matriarch. Lavinia's widowed sister-in-law Emma Reeve was staying with the family and had been adopted into the community with the nickname 'Aunt Em'. Lavinia's two daughters, Amelia Pepper and Lavinia Surgeoner, lived on Victoria Street with their families. The Surgeoner family—William, Lavinia, and their daughter Eileen—and Aunt Em found space in the section of the shelter where Phyllis and her friend Barbara were sitting. Phyllis's parents—William and Amelia Pepper—found a space elsewhere with Grandmother Lavinia.

Arthur Davis also lived on Victoria Street. He looked up at the sky as he came out into the street: 'It was as clear as day that night, a lovely moonlit night.'[21] Just a boy, he and his siblings were directed into the shelter by their mother. They were relieved to be inside. 'I thought it was the safest place in England – a monument of strength,' Arthur recalled.[22]

Larry Stevens and his family lived in nearby James Place. Like most who lived on Victoria Street, his family relied on the communal shelter. He noted their habit of taking refuge at Portland Square: 'As soon as the air-raid warning sounded we gathered up some warm clothes/blankets etc., and made a dash through the streets to reach the shelter before the "fireworks" began.'[23] This evening, his family found a place in the western half of the shelter.

A group of teenagers referred to as the James Street Gang also routinely took refuge at Portland Square. The group seemed to take the danger from the skies in their stride. Ben Bennett, one of the members, recalled that he and his friends kept each other's spirits up through music: 'It was our want to have a good time really I suppose by playing ukuleles, singing songs, and such things and head towards the shelter most nights.'[24] The shelter provided an outlet for socialisation and for the friends to support one another.

Tonight, a girl called Sylvia Birch was at the front of the pack. She recalled, 'Furious with the enemy but thinking it gave me more time to stay out later that evening, as my father was a very strict disciplinarian when it came to time! we met up – Stan Wills with his banjo, Fernley [?] with a mouth-organ, and dear Ben.' Though the attack was under way, the party entered the shelter singing. Although the teenagers were in violation of the Public Shelter Rules, to 'not sing or play a musical instrument in a shelter', nobody seemed to mind.[25] Someone shouted to the group to turn to the left where they would ordinarily pass the night. Bennett recalled that Sylvia heard the instructions but chose to ignore them. Instead, he said, she mischievously 'turned around over her shoulder, and cocked a snook, and went to the right.'[26] The rest of the group followed suit and found seats several feet inside the start of the shelter's western tunnel.

Noreen Wise, only 8 at the time, also remembered joining her family in the shelter's western section after leaving their flat. Like others, she recalled the 'cold, slatted benches' and feeling 'cold, tired, and frightened' as she bunkered underground while the Luftwaffe fleet descended on Plymouth.[27] The Rich family which lived in a flat at No. 12 was in this section too. Only 3 at the time, Craig Rich recalled being wrapped in a blanket and sleeping on his parents' laps once they found a space for the night.[28]

Though primarily intended to be a haven for citizens who lived nearby, especially for those who did not have access to a private shelter, the public shelter opened its doors to accommodate others passing through the area when the raid unfolded. Reginald and Ivy Morgan had been visiting friends in the eastern end of Drake's Ward. Rather than chancing a perilous journey to the shelter nearer their home on Patna Place, they entered the Portland Square shelter.

Buses abandoned service. At least one busload of passengers evacuated into the safety of the bunker.[29]

Reg and Ivy Morgan lived at 10 Patna Place and were visiting friends in the vicinity of Portland Square on the night of 22/23 April. [Pete Joll]

Lillian Saunders and her dog Blackie had been out for an early evening walk when the sirens sounded. When they attempted to enter the shelter, they were prevented from doing so. Though Lillian was heavily pregnant, and in spite of the active raid, they were denied entry. Her cocker spaniel would have contravened Plymouth's Public Shelter Rules. These were clear: 'A person shall not take into a shelter any animal or bird.'[30] Signs on the shelter walls likewise reminded those inside the structure about these expectations. Refusing to part company with Blackie, whom she considered 'her best friend' and constant companion, Lillian returned home instead.[31] Two weeks later, she gave birth to a son.

On many nights, Charles Palmer worked as a firewatcher at a factory outside Plymouth. He was responsible for extinguishing incendiary bombs that landed on the roof, thereby preventing larger fires. This night, he was off duty. Palmer had been visiting relatives earlier in the day: their home had recently been hit by a bomb, and his sister was among the dead.[32] Palmer's route home to Lockyer Road took him through Portland Square. With the Luftwaffe closing in and bombs already falling, he recognised the danger and took refuge: 'As the raid seemed to be going to be a heavy one and shrapnel was beginning to fall. I took cover in the Portland Air Raid shelter; I stood by the entrance on the top of the Western side of the Square.'[33]

Similarly, newlyweds Ted and Pauline Hempkins were also caught out in the open. Married only days before, they had spent the early evening visiting Pauline's parents James and Ellen on Amity Place and were returning to their home closer to the seafront. When the warning sirens sounded, Portland Square was the closest shelter where they could take cover.

The first German aircraft descended at 9.43 p.m.—nine minutes after the city's alert status was escalated. A minute later, air-raid sirens sounded. The eight Heinkel 111s from Tours released their payloads from a height of 3,400 to 4,000 metres. Over the span of the next half-hour, they released seven 500-kilogram, fourteen 250-kilogram, and fifty-six 50-kilogram thin-cased bombs as well as three 250-kilogram long-delay fuse bombs. The planes also dropped almost 600 1-kilogram incendiary devices.

Two minutes later, the Tours contingent was reinforced with a complement of a dozen Heinkel 111s from Rennes. Barrelling low over Plymouth at heights of 2,800 to 3,200 metres, they contributed a ferocious bombardment to the night's opening salvo. Over the course of the next hour, these planes released forty 250-kilogram and eighty-two 50-kilogram thin-cased bombs as well as eight 250-kilogram long-delay fuse bombs. They also released more than 1,000 incendiaries, helping to kindle what would become a fierce firestorm.

At 9.50 p.m., the pathfinder group from Vannes arrived on the scene several minutes behind schedule. Charged with outlining the target area, the planes released 8,064 incendiaries. This amounted to approximately a quarter of the total number of incendiary devices that would be dropped over Plymouth that night.

Fire services could not cope with the onslaught. 'Firemen fought bravely', the *Western Morning News* opined, 'but they were confronted with a herculean task.'[34] The incendiaries sparked fires throughout Plymouth, including at the site where the furniture of those affected by the March raids was being stored: 'The devouring appetite of the flames could not be satiated.'[35] The firefighters battled the blaze, but to no avail. 'Some areas presented a solid wall of flame, which pushed the fire-fighters back step by step.'[36] Twyford assessed the severity of the situation: 'with the fire-fighting services utterly unable to cope with such a major task, the flames spread with terrible fury, devouring everything in their course.'[37]

The conflagrations would serve as homing signals for the successive waves of bombardiers that were due to arrive within the half-hour. 'The glare was so bright', the *Western Morning News* reported, 'that incoming raiders had an easily-found beacon.'[38] Indeed, such was the intensity of these fires that German crews were able to see the light from over the horizon line.[39]

This was just the opening volley. The *Western Morning News* documented the progress of the night's attack:

> German planes flew in from the South-East in waves, and made low level attacks on many burning objectives. Incendiary and high explosive bombs were showered unceasingly on thickly-populated commercial and residential parts of the city. Buildings collapsed in blazing ruins. Hot ash and sparks drifted high over the city as if from a volcano. Not content with the roaring inferno they had caused the raiders continued to shower down fire bombs into the red glare and smoke.[40]

Lilian Northwood lived on Alexandra Road and witnessed the attack: 'There was such a red glow in the sky it was like being in the middle of an inferno,' she remembered. 'The droning of the German bombers, bombs continually raining down, the anti-aircraft gun fire, the sky lit up with searchlights.'[41]

Regional Commissioner Hugh Elles had remained in Plymouth and was stationed at the Group Control Command Centre. While he had little confidence in the political leadership he observed earlier in the day, Elles was impressed with how the rank-and-file emergency response staff responded during the onslaught: 'Colonel Collet took charge of the Control efficiently and was seldom at a loss during the very intensive period of the raid.' Over the evening, the command centre became overwhelmed with coordinating the response to the crisis, never mind also keeping officials outside Plymouth apprised as the situation deteriorated. Elles observed: 'Neither his staff nor his accommodation was sufficient to ensure that Regional Headquarters could be kept in constant touch with the situation as it developed. There would have been no time for him to have made any detailed situation reports.'[42]

The scope and scale of the attack had its intended effect of collapsing Plymouth's emergency response infrastructure. Adding to the chaos, an auxiliary command centre under the market in Devonport was hit, and telephone communications were interrupted. This hampered efforts to coordinate efforts and deploy resources appropriately as the attack continued.[43]

In Berlin, the German News Agency shared updates about the raid as the first wave of pilots made their way back across the Channel to France. The Luftwaffe felt confident enough in the results of its initial manoeuvres to declare the entire operation a success: 'Strong forces of the German Air Force took off late this evening in successive waves to attack important military objectives in the British Isles. The first wireless messages from the bomber crews report that the targets had already been effectively hit by high-explosive and incendiary bombs. Many large fires were observed among harbour installations.'[44]

Over the next hour, the ferocity of the raid would increase. A contingent of forty-eight aircraft from the Luftwaffe's 55th battle wing arrived on the scene carrying some of the largest explosives in the German arsenal, including twenty 1,000-kilogram bombs and a 1,800-kilogram bomb. Units within this detachment flew as low as 2,000 metres, bringing the frightening ferocity of the attack closer to the civilians huddling in shelters across the city. The formation also released an additional 19,380 incendiaries, effectively nullifying any efforts to contain the fires.

Twyford described this phase of the raid as 'showers of incendiaries, followed by wave after wave of bombers diving down on the flaming city'.[45]

The Times chronicled the relentless character of the attack: 'Apart from one lull there was a continuous procession of bombers [...] in the later stages the raiders bombed indiscriminately and the tale of wanton destruction includes the bombing of a complete terrace of houses.'[46] While the initial wave of bombers appeared to have defined mission objectives, the *Western Evening Herald* reported that later detachments jettisoned their payloads wherever they saw fit: 'In later stages the raiders indulged in indiscriminate bombing, but at the outset they carried out a set plan.'[47]

Barbara Cundy was frightened. Though she knew the families seated around her, the brutality of the bombardment above was terrifying. When she began to cry, her mother spoke firmly: 'If you don't stop that noise, I am going to take you home.' With that, Barbara buried her head into her mother's lap, closed her eyes, and lulled herself to sleep.[48]

Outside, on Portland Square, Cathi and Harry Hunt reasoned that they might be better off in the shelter after all. As midnight approached, they hurried across the street and found a place in the western half of the shelter. Cathi described it as 'their first and only visit'.[49]

While the Hunts made their way into the bunker, Stanley Hollett was extracted from it. During the course of the bombardment, Mrs Hollett rethought her decision to permit Stanley to spend the night in the shelter with his friends. She insisted that her husband go to the shelter and bring their son home. In the middle of the bombardment and with other ARP responsibilities demanding his attention, Mr Hollett descended into the shelter and located his son in the eastern tunnel. Stanley was upset that his social time was cut short and begged his father to allow him to remain with his friends. His petition was to no avail: 'I pleaded with him to let me stay but he said no and walked me home.'[50]

Another family—a mother, her son, and her nephew—was passing by the Holletts' house when they observed incendiaries on the roof. The two boys stopped to help extinguish the flames and sent the woman along to the shelter.[51]

The clock ticked closer to midnight—23 April, St George's Day. Bill Cundy arrived at the shelter to bring his family their promised warm kettle of tea. Gordon Allen stepped away from his brother and father to peek outside the entrance and see what was happening outside for himself.[52] Finding the shelter chilly, Ena MacGregor and her boyfriend left John and Jane in their place and found new seats nearer to the entrance where there were more people.[53]

In the aerial battleground above Drake's Ward, one of the Luftwaffe bombers released a heavy calibre, high-explosive bomb. Perhaps the intended target was the expansive Drake's Reservoir, an important water supply for the city located close to Portland Square. If this was the case, the bomb missed its mark. It sliced a path through the crisp night sky. Moments later, it crashed through the reinforced ceiling of the eastern wing of the Portland Square Air-Raid Shelter. The bomb took only a fraction of second to pass through the tunnel, break through the floor, and bury itself beneath the bunker.

Then it detonated. 'There was a massive shudder, and I felt myself being lifted into the air. It was as if the whole room had jumped,' recalled Barbara Allen.[54]

At the epicentre of the blast, the force of the explosion propelled concrete, earth, and bodies into the night sky and left a gaping 30-foot by 40-foot crater in Portland Square Park.

Those sheltering in other parts of the complex recalled the violent shockwaves that reverberated through the underground labyrinth. Larry Stevens 'felt the terrific

The FARMERS MEET
FARMERS HOME
DRAKE ST. PLYMOUTH

Western Evening Herald
EXTRA FINAL

And Western Evening News
WEDNESDAY, APRIL 23, 1941.
ONE PENNY.

THE CHANCELLOR OF THE EXCHEQUER
PLYMOUTH & S.D. SAVINGS BANK
VICTORY ... FORCES ... NEW ...

Grim Rescue Work Today After Plymouth's Second Successive Blitz.

MANY KILLED WHEN HEAVY BOMB HITS COMMUNAL SHELTER.

R.A.F. AGAIN BOMB BREST.

Man Dug Out Alive Sings "Tipperary."

IN LAST NIGHT'S BLITZ ON PLYMOUTH A LARGE CALIBRE HIGH-EXPLOSIVE BOMB FELL ON THE CORNER OF A COMMUNAL SHELTER.

Casualties here were heavy, and many bodies have already been recovered. Two injured people were rescued alive this afternoon. Digging for the dead goes on.

FOR HELP AND ADVICE.

CITY BUREAU FOR BLITZ VICTIMS.

R.P. CHIEF BURIED IN DEBRIS, RESCUED ALIVE IN S.W.

"PREP." SCHOOL HIT.

"FRONT PAGE NEWS" ON BACK.

ITALIANS CLAIM SURRENDER OF A GREEK ARMY.
BRITISH DID THEIR JOB AT BARDIA.
NEW DEPUTY C.-IN-C. IN THE MIDDLE EAST.
IRAQ WILL KEEP PLEDGES TO BRITAIN.

GREEK KING IN CRETE.
"Hard Destinies Of War."

LATEST

YUGOSLAVIA WILL FIGHT ON.

MATSUOKA NOT INVITED.

AT HISTORIC PASS.

BLOW TO GREEKS.

Western Evening Herald, 23 April 1941. The headline story references the strike on Portland Square. [*Plymouth Herald*]

blast and heard the screams'. Lilian Crocker recalled the intensity of the sound: 'I remember the awful noise and vibrations, it was similar to a huge thunderbolt.' Ben Bennett recalled nothing but 'air rushing past us'.[55] Noreen Wise described the horrific moment: 'The world turned upside down. The noise, the dust and complete darkness cannot be described.'[56]

Sylvia Birch remembered the moment of impact. 'Suddenly the BOMB dropped – a violent roar and a blast. Then an Erie silence temporarily. Everything went black. My ears felt as if long needles were piercing my head. Thick dust and dirt filled the air. I could not breathe. All I can remember are the screams and shrieks, and Betty W. hysterical, clutching me around the throat in fear.'[57]

On the southern side of Portland Square, Mr Hollett and his son Stanley had just made it back home when they were knocked off their feet by the explosion behind them:

> I remember we went through the front door and were halfway through the passage, when the biggest explosion I had ever heard took place, and we were thrown to the floor with everything coming down on top of us. Through the noise I could hear timber breaking which went on for about 5–6 seconds. The ceilings had come down on top of us and you couldn't see for dust and we thought either side of us had had a direct hit in the commotion. We managed to get downstairs amongst all the debris where the others were.[58]

Meanwhile, in the shelter that the Stanley and his father had departed only minutes before, acrid smoke and dust thick with debris filled the air. Her head still burrowed into the folds of her mother's flower-patterned apron, young Barbara Cundy 'heard glass breaking and everything went black'.[59]

14
Response and Rescue

Bernard Chapman, 13, stood on the roof of the Public Secondary School in Glanville Street with Jim Brown, one of the air-raid wardens for the sector of Drake's Ward that included Portland Square. They surveyed the surrounding area while Luftwaffe planes flew menacingly overhead unleashing their bombs on the neighbourhood below.

Though only a boy, Bernard had a significant responsibility on the evening of Tuesday 22 April. He was a fire watcher. His nightly role was to survey the surrounding area for any fires from the incendiary bombs that were part of the Nazi assault. It was also his duty to extinguish any incendiaries that might drop on the school where he was posted. It was dangerous work and placed those who performed it directly in harm's way.

A fierce explosion sounded to the north just after midnight. A debris cloud erupted over nearby buildings. It rose into the atmosphere like a volcanic plume and propelled fiery fragments into the night sky.

Bernard did not realise exactly where the bomb struck, but his colleague seemed to know instantly. The pair quickly descended from their sentry point and sprinted the couple of blocks north to Portland Square. A pall of smoke rose from the centre of the park. The veil lifted and revealed a horrific scene. 'I had never seen such devastation,' Brown recalled. 'The crater was at least 30 ft deep and 40 ft across.'[1]

Brown rapidly assessed the damage. He saw that the warden's post had been blasted off its concrete footings and now stood askew amid the carnage. A section of the underground air-raid shelter had suffered a direct hit.

When others arrived at Portland Square, the size and scale of the blast zone struck them too. William Johns was, like Bernard, another teenager fulfilling a role in various emergency services. Upon his arrival at the scene, he witnessed rescue efforts already underway:

> When I arrived at the scene it was to find a pit of hell, a hole I imagined as deep as the houses were tall. To look up was to see a sky alight with the reflection of a thousand fires; to look about was to see a twilight where only the branches of

> trees that had been scythed down like match sticks, moved; to look down was to see a black abyss, where a Rescue Unit in which, the dustmen of the day, the heavy brigade of the night, laboured like black beetles in a disturbed nest to rescue the survivors, help the injured, and recover the dead.[2]

Doreen Jessop, a 17-year-old ambulance driver, encountered a similar site when she arrived to help transport any critically injured survivors to the hospital: 'When I arrived the scene looked just like a deep glen with lanterns at the side, like hills. It turned out to be soldiers with lights digging people out at the sides of the crater.'[3]

As teams of rescue and emergency personnel arrived, Cathi and Harry Hunt were among those making the exodus from intact sections. Cathi remembered an atmosphere of shock, 'The rest of us stumbled out over the rubble. We must have been stunned because there was no panic.'[4]

The boys who were atop the Holletts' house raced to the entrance. Their mother and aunt had survived the blast, and she set the boys to assisting in the search for any survivors.[5]

Sylvia Birch described her relief at being found and rescued by a friend: 'From the darkness I heard Stan's voice calling me "Sylv, Sylvia!" And then he was there in his ARP uniform carrying a lantern. He found us and oh how I remember that hug! Next thing I recall are ARP volunteers and Firemen digging above us, and we were lucky enough to be near the steps that had been cleared away for us to get through.' The scale of the disaster became apparent when she emerged from the shelter. 'Stan went back to help others as I stood between two wardens, gazing in horror at the devastation before me. Huge trees torn out from their roots, railings crushed and the gracious houses that had towered around the garden square in flames, flattened and crashing around us.'[6]

When the rest of the James Street Gang evacuated, Ben Bennett realised how narrowly he had escaped the bomb and almost certain death. 'The wing where we would've gone, there was just the end of the crater of the rubble down there and people were dashing around obviously excitedly, Air Raid Wardens and such.'[7]

Emergency personnel arrive

On the evening of 22–23 April, there was a full complement of emergency personnel stationed on duty across the city. The staff included 330 full-time and 1495 part-time ARP wardens and 355 full-time medical personnel with an additional 161 part-time medics.[8] Contingents of these first responders rapidly mobilised to the scene at Portland Square.

The teenage courier boys of Plymouth's Civil Defence Corps were among the first to arrive. Teenager Frank Phillips was at the wardens' post on Portland Square when 'we heard a bomb coming, we dived to the ground, but were lifted a few feet in the air by the blast.' Phillips was sent on a perilous journey to the ARP Control Centre to relay the news and rally the emergency response.[9] With phone lines unreliable, if functional at all, during an attack, these boys acted as a conduit between central command, rescue parties, and incident sites.

Kenneth Searle, 14, was another one of the messengers on duty. 'If people were trapped it was my job to run and find a rescue team. But ultimately, I ended up doing a lot of the rescuing myself. I will never forget the horrors I saw.'[10] He was drafted into the early attempts to descend into the bomb crater as part of the search and rescue effort. 'I was lowered on a rope into the shelter. There was a small gap in the rubble which I crawled down and I could hear a whistling sound.' The sound he heard promised the hope of life, a flickering flame of optimism while the German attack continued to rage. Yet before Kenneth could make it through the debris to the person trapped beneath, the rescue party was recalled from its work to take shelter. 'Then the raids started again and I was told we had to abandon it.'[11]

William Johns was also on duty as a courier. Earlier in the evening, he had been dispatched to verify staffing levels at several posts. The ferocity of the night slowed his movements. He frequently paused to take shelter, scurrying from one refuge to the next during the brief lulls between the bombs. When he eventually returned to his home base, he found the post abandoned. As William searched for his team, he encountered a woman who told him where everyone had gone:

> Then when making my way back to the street I was almost knocked down by the publican's wife emerging from the cupboard beneath the stairs, 'Where is everyone?' I asked. 'Portland Square. The underground shelter there has been hit. There are thousands dead.' The lady's estimate of the casualties was rather exaggerated. I doubt if five hundred people could have got into it had they been packed as the proverbial sardines in a tin. Nevertheless, the incident was butchery on a grand scale. Seventy two dead, alone!

For the personnel in William's detachment, Portland Square was out of their jurisdiction. 'As far as 3F2 personnel were concerned, Portland Place was not in their Sector, Group or Division,' he stated. News—and, as evidenced by William's encounter, rumours—about the extent of the disaster spread quickly. The scale of the situation spurred emergency personnel to attend.

William's next course of action was to follow, intending to aid in whatever capacity might be needed. The air-raid shelter had been a sanctuary. It was now a sepulchre for those entombed beneath twisted metal and concrete slabs. 'Those who had been sheltering there died the instant the earth had erupted in a blood red fissure of soil, stone, earth, flesh and bone. Their fate of no immediate concern,' William later reflected.[12] The deceased would be recovered later.

For now, personnel engaged in an urgent search and rescue mission. There was the chance that some individuals had survived the blast; alive but trapped beneath the wreckage. It would be a race against the clock to locate them and bring about their salvation.

The rescue of Barbara Cundy

Underneath the rubble, a frantic fight for life unfolded. Several people had indeed survived the blast but now faced another frightening prospect: being buried alive. If the rescue parties could not get to these individuals in time, the survivors would succumb to death from serious injuries or from suffocating beneath the debris in a state of extreme physical and emotional distress.

Barbara Cundy, 11, had entered the shelter with her grandfather, mother, and sister earlier that evening. Around midnight, she buried her head in her mother's lap to sleep.[13] The position ultimately saved her because her mother's body shielded her from the debris when the bomb detonated—a final protective act.

Barbara's first impulse upon realising that she was alive—but buried beneath tons of rubble—was to scream. Frightened by her fate, she yelled for help. 'When I came round I started shouting,' she recalled. 'I could not move so I started to scream and then found I could move my hands so I tried to get out.'[14] Survival instincts kicked in. Knowing that her best chance of survival was to make it to the surface, Barbara clawed her way through the rubble. 'I wasn't buried very far down. I was trying to dig my way out with my hands.'[15] The task must have been exhausting and took a physical and psychological toll on the young girl. 'I seemed to be there a long time,' she recalled, 'and it was getting hard to breathe.'[16] At last, she made it close enough to the surface that a member of a rescue party detected her movements. 'Suddenly I heard a man's voice shouting all right my love I am coming.' The man moved pieces of the jagged wreckage and created a passage to liberate her. 'It wasn't long before I was taken out of the tomb as I called it and was laid for a while on the earth, I can remember there was a man lying beside me still as anything.'[17]

Remarkably, Barbara's injuries were not serious and amounted to only minor cuts and bruises. Eventually, she was moved to St Matthias's Church on North Hill for the rest of the night. The next morning, she was taken to Mutley Plain. Authorities asked for her name and worked to locate her family. It was then that Barbara learned that she lost her mother, father, sister, and grandfather.[18]

Others who survived but who were buried deeper down had to wait for their rescuers to operate safely. The ongoing blitz and raging fires throughout Plymouth hampered efforts and limited the personnel and equipment that were deployed to respond to any singular incident. The rescue parties could only do so much in the darkness of the night and had to work with the tools they had at their disposal.

Neighbours assist

Stanley Hollett's family returned to the shelter complex soon after the bombing. The family was in their home at 4 Portland Square when the bomb detonated. Indeed, Stanley and his father had walked through their front door only seconds before. Mr Albert Hollett quickly assessed the damage to their home and was worried about a possible gas leak. Thus, while others were exiting the shelter, Albert escorted his family back to the park and placed them in an intact wing of the shelter at about 12.15 a.m.

He then rapidly switched gears from taking care of his family to supporting the rescue efforts already under way. As a warden, Albert had local knowledge that would support the emergency response personnel arriving from other parts of the city. He was keenly aware of the extent of the crisis and that more volunteers would be needed in the race to rescue those trapped in the wreckage.

Stanley recalled his father returning to the shelter later that night to recruit additional assistance: 'It was about an hour later he came into the shelter to ask for male volunteers to help with a rescue operation, and he said to us to stay put and we could see coat + waistcoat + trousers of his were covered in blood.'[19] For Stanley, the sight of his father's blood-soaked clothing and appeal for help signalled the magnitude of the situation. 'He was covered in blood from his chest to his knees and his heart was broken,' he remembered.[20]

Ordinary citizens made a difference in the rescue efforts. While some were asked to help, others joined on their own initiative. Indeed, the Ministry of Home Security had hoped people would take it upon themselves to assist in a moment of need. A pamphlet encouraged citizens to do their part: 'When it is safe to do so after a raid, it is better to go out and help others than to stay at home and fret.'[21] What the Ministry did not, perhaps, anticipate were the heroics that ordinary people would undertake in the midst of the assault to come to the aid of their fellow citizens.

For example, Bertie Andrews, a labourer in Plymouth's Engineering Department, was among the brigade of citizens who attended the scene. His wife Mabel and their three daughters, Iris, Muriel, and Barbara, had all sought refuge in the Portland Square complex. Upon realising that his family might be among those in peril, Bert raced to the disaster zone: 'In the pitch darkness he worked like a madman to get them. A huge tree had been uprooted and had fallen across the shelter, and in one corner where the shelter had been was a huge crater and under tons of debris were human beings.'[22]

Bert eventually learned that his family was unharmed, but recognised that others were in distress. He was in a position to make a difference and decided to help despite the risk to his own safety. Throughout the rest of the evening and into the next day, he contributed his expertise and energies to the rescue efforts. Having helped to build the shelters in Plymouth, Bert was intimately familiar with how they were constructed and how precarious the situation was. 'There was only room for one small man to crawl into the enclosed space, and Andrews, by improvisation shored up the dangerous concrete.'[23] As he dug into the debris, Bert simultaneously stabilised his area of the site: 'lanterns, timber, ropes, and tools were brought, and that part of the shelter which could be was shored up.'[24]

Just as Bert braced the faltering shelter walls, he bolstered survivors' morale as they waited for medical aid. One of the men cried out in thanksgiving, 'God bless you; I know you won't leave me.' His resolve unfaltering, Bert promised, 'No, I won't leave you.'[25] When doctors arrived on the scene, they began to distribute medication to relieve the pain of those still trapped. True to his word, Bert remained by the man's side, working tirelessly until, at last, he freed him from the debris. As the injured man was whisked away to the hospital, Bert turned back to the task at hand, knowing there were still others counting on him.

Over eight hours, amid raging fires and the ongoing bombardment, Bert focused on tunnelling through the wreckage. Thanks to these efforts, he was responsible for the rescue and survival of fourteen strangers, and was later celebrated and honoured for his contribution.[26]

A singular mission: Charles Palmer and Nelson Eyres

Nelson Eyres, a clerk with the Great Western Railway Company, rented rooms at 38 Portland Square where Ernest and Emma Harris lived. The deafening explosion and force of the bomb incapacitated him: 'I was rendered unconscious.'[27]

Eventually, he regained his senses, finding himself alive but trapped: 'upon coming to, [I] found I was completely buried underneath and concrete some distance down and unable to move any part of my body. I had a small space around my face with a supply of air, although I cannot say how long this would have lasted.'[28] Twisted ribbons of reinforcing wire pressed down on his head and were wrapped tightly around his neck. 'I was in the shelter and completely buried alive, well down in the crater, unable to move hand or foot.'[29] Nelson's situation was dire, and there was little he could do to extricate himself without making matters more precarious. He cried out for help, his screams muffled by the dirt and debris that enveloped him.

Charles Palmer was among those who had sheltered in the western end of the complex. He experienced the direct hit on the shelter and recalled the immediate recruitment of volunteers: 'After I had been there for some time, I heard a loud explosion and I thought a bomb had dropped very close but I did not realise that it had struck the shelter until a man came over the top of the shelters and shouted for men.' Palmer immediately sprang into action. 'I asked him why he required them and he told me that their help was needed at once. I said I was prepared to do anything and he told me to follow him over the top of the shelters toward [the] east side of the Square.' They crossed a landscape torn apart by the bomb's destructive force.

> I followed for a short distance and then lost him in the darkness. As I was walking through the trees, I found myself treading on something soft and, when I stopped to find out what it was, I felt a woman's hand. I then found several other bodies lying around and came upon the large crater which had been caused by a high explosive bomb hitting the shelter on the east side of the Square.

A group of men was already at work attempting to clear away concrete and rubble. Palmer joined the crew. 'I got up on the raised edge of the crater and saw some men working so I asked them where I could be of most use. They told me to help them, so I got a pick and shovel from one and started to dig.'[30]

'Someone said he had heard a noise,' Palmer later recounted to the *Western Morning News*. 'And when I listened carefully I heard a man groan: "Oh, my head."'[31] Palmer began to burrow his way through the debris to the voice crying out for deliverance. The man trapped beneath was Nelson Eyres.

Charles worked furiously to dig towards the voice:

> After I had dug for a bit, I felt the pick strike something soft so I used the shovel and my hands and eventually found the lapel of a coat and then a woman's body. She was apparently dead. I managed to get one arm loose and then the top part of her body which allowed me to pass a rope under her arm, and the men higher up tried to pull her out. They failed to do this because the lower part of her body was jammed by slabs of concrete. When the woman's body was partly raised, the man's voice referred to above said, 'you've taken a weight off my head.' I then knew exactly where he was buried. I found that the only way I could get near the buried man was to sit on the woman's body and shovel away the rubble between the body and the place where the voice was coming from.[32]

Eyres recalled his harrowing ordeal, the details of the night seared into his memory:

> My calls for help were eventually heard and Mr. Palmer worked continuously for a considerable time during the height of the severe raid to rescue me, and of course, any others that might have been alive, which unfortunately were only one or two. He had great difficulty in locating me exactly, as I was well under, but kept at it under dangerous conditions, working in the crater with bombs continually falling, danger from concrete and earth falling down the crater, and the gruesome business of removing the dead in an endeavour to get at me.[33]

Palmer worked with urgency and purpose. The air was thick with dust and the smouldering embers of destruction. He dug through a mass of concrete, rebar, and rubble. The weight of the concrete fragments and mangled mess of reinforcing wire presented obstacles at every inch that separated him from Eyres:

> I endeavoured to keep the man cheerful by speaking to him and he told me his name was Bill Eyres of 39 Portland Square, a clerk on the railway. I continued to dig and occasionally tapped the concrete wall to see if I was getting nearer to Eyres. At first, I got no answer but afterwards I heard him say, 'I can hear you very faintly.' Each time I tapped afterwards he said it was getting louder. He kept on saying, 'My poor head, my poor head. I'm not complaining and

> whoever you are you must be a bloody hero.' I continued to work and joked with him to keep him happy.[34]

Palmer made steady progress, but additional tools were needed to complete the job. As the night wore on, teams of professional personnel arrived. One of the ARP wardens overseeing the rescue efforts determined that the work of freeing Nelson was so perilous that it could only be addressed by one person working at a time. 'Several efforts were made to get Palmer to take a rest for a bit or to allow someone else to carry on with the work, but he kept on stubbornly refusing to allow anyone to take his place.'[35]

Instead, Palmer requested their assistance with procuring the tools needed for him to finish his mission:

> While I was in the midst of this work some Police Officers arrived and shouted up to them to come down and get me a hammer and chisel. I heard one of the officers, I think he was the Superintendent say, 'We must get a hammer and chisel for him if I have to go and get it myself.' Soon afterwards a hammer and chisel were passed down to me and I was able to cut through some concrete which was pinning the man's head down.

Finally, Charles reached Nelson and set his focus on freeing the man from his predicament.

> I then found the man's head and I covered it over with a sack to keep the debris from hurting him. I continued to work with my hands until I had cleared the man's head altogether and cleaned his face and mouth. He told me he could breathe. I then cut away another piece of concrete which was resting on the back of his neck, and put a piece of board under his chin and a pad and a cushion at the back of his head to make him as comfortable as possible.[36]

Nelson credited his survival to Charles's singular determination and unflagging focus to reach him:

> He eventually found a way to my head, which was held down with reinforcing wire round my neck, he obtained improvised tools to cut through this and then got my head free, thereby saving my life, as although I had some air there was the possibility this would soon have given out. He was unable to do more, the rest of my body being wedged in with heavy blocks of concrete, which could not be removed until the military arrived with suitable tackle and daylight to work.[37]

Charles remained at Nelson's side through the predawn hours while they waited for additional assistance. 'Palmer refused all offers of relief,' reported Plymouth's Chief

Constable George Lowe. 'and insisted on staying by the side of this man until he was relieved 5 hours later because of exhaustion. Bombs fell for considerable time after the discovery of this man but Palmer remained at his post throughout the whole period of the raid.'

Nelson remembered Charles's endurance and kind demeanour.

> All the time Mr. Palmer worked he kept up my spirits by continuously encouraging me with cheerful talk, although it at the time must have seemed somewhat hopeless to get at me. So far as I am aware he had little assistance, he seemed to me to be there the whole time and must have shewn great qualities of courage, resource and perseverance.

Palmer at last left the scene and made his way home. Emergency personnel extracted Eyres when specialised equipment arrived on site later that morning.

Several months later, in August, Charles Palmer was included among a small group of Plymothians who received letters of commendation for their brave deeds during the blitz. His deeds were detailed in the *Western Morning News*: 'He worked for hours to extricate a man who was trapped under the wreckage.'[38] Upon reading this account in the paper, Nelson Eyres put pen to paper to record his memories of the night. Recuperating with friends from Portland Square in the village of Noss Mayo, Nelson appealed to Plymouth Town Clerk and Air Raid Precautions Controller Colin Campbell to confer a higher honour on Charles Palmer so as to more appropriately recognise his extraordinary efforts: 'It is perhaps natural for the rescued to praise his rescuer, but I do feel that Mr. Palmer deserves more than a letter of commendation, particularly having regard to other awards that have been made for gallantry during air raids on the City.'[39]

Against all odds: Barbara Allen's rescue from the rubble

Teenager Barbara Allen experienced a similar ordeal to Nelson Eyres. She recalled the immediate aftermath of the bombing. Both of her legs and feet were crushed under the weight of two dead women and debris from the shelter. Unable to move, she listened: 'I don't know who they were but I heard one of them dying. I kept calling for Phyllis, but no-one answered.'[40] Her best friend had died in the explosion beside her.

Amid the wreckage, Barbara thought she heard her father calling her name and asking if she was all right. She held onto the sound. Later, she learned that he had been caught in the collapse and died while being removed from the rubble.[41] She also learned the tragic news that one of her brothers, Kenny, as well as many neighbours from Victoria Buildings whom she regarded as family, had also been killed in the blast. Her brother Gordon, on the other hand, had been at the shelter's entrance when the bomb hit and was blown into a tree by the force of the explosion. He was later found by a doctor who cared for him until he could be reunited with his family.

Barbara Allen, one of the few survivors of the incident. [Frances Payne]

Barbara waited alone in the darkness for more than twelve hours surrounded by death and debris and in excruciating pain. She feared that the rescue workers were going to administer a sleeping draught to sedate her until they could safely remove her the next day.[42] Thankfully, as evening approached, a party managed to tunnel its way through the wreckage to extract her.

After her rescue, Barbara faced a long and painful journey through multiple hospitals as she began to recover. She was first taken to the Prince of Wales Hospital on Greenbank Road before being moved to St Lawrence Hospital in Bodmin, Cornwall, which had opened a ward specifically to care for the injured. She was later transferred to Hollymoor Emergency Hospital in Northfield, Birmingham, where she remained from 1 May to 3 July. There, she received treatment for the injuries to her lower body and underwent rehabilitation.

Two other individuals were extracted and transported to hospitals but had sustained fatal injuries. Eric Farrant, aged 11, succumbed to his injuries at City Hospital. His parents Samuel and Mabel died in the shelter. John MacGregor, aged 54, died soon after arriving at the Prince of Wales Hospital, Greenbank.

It took some time before Ena MacGregor was able to learn the fate of her father and grandmother. She had survived her own ordeal in the bombing. 'I was unconscious for some time, but recovered consciousness to find that I was buried. I thought at first that a water main had broken and that I would drown while I was buried, as what appeared to be water was gushing over me. Later, I found it was blood.' Ena's boyfriend worked to rescue her. 'The pitch darkness was full of screams. My friend dug me out with his bare hands, and I was uninjured.' That night and again the next day as bodies were being recovered from the site, Ena could not find her family. 'I walked for two days trying to find out where my family were. I went to every hospital and mortuary, but to no avail.' By chance, Ena read an account in the *Herald* that a man had been dug out alive and immediately asked for a cigarette before being transported to the hospital. Intuiting that this was her father, Ena went to the hospital. She was correct, but discovered that John had died only minutes after reaching the facility. Ena later saw Jane's name on a casualty list. 'I have never understood how it came about that all three of us in my family were sitting shoulder to shoulder and should have died together, yet I came out of it physically uninjured,' she reflected. 'The best part of my life ended at the age of 20 in Portland Square shelter.'[43]

The power of positivity

An account of an unidentified survivor underscored the arduous labour that rescue workers shouldered, and how a sense of optimism was as critical as physical efforts to help the few survivors of the tragedy.

One rescue party was tasked with clearing a path to an elderly man trapped in the crater. In spite of his predicament, the man was in high spirits and conversed with the rescuers as they tunnelled their way to him. As the rescuers got closer, he broke out in song: 'This man upheld the true tradition of the British and sang the most famous song of the last war, in which he probably served in the Army – "Tipperary."'

At last, the rescuers were able to move the debris and pull him to the surface. Exhausted from the distress and relieved at his deliverance, the man passed out: 'On being dragged into the open air he collapsed, and it was impossible to question him as to his identity.'[44] Like Barbara Allen, the man was taken by ambulance to hospital to receive medical attention.

Plymouth's rescue workers continued to labour with unrelenting urgency, driven by the hope that others might yet be found alive and pulled from the rubble. Each shout, each clatter of shifting masonry, carried with it the possibility of survival. The city's newspapers made note of these sustained efforts: 'At least one big communal shelter was hit, and there were casualties. The shelter was in a square in a residential district, and the work of rescuing people buried was continued today.'[45] Yet removing someone from the wreckage was only the beginning; the challenge to save them continued once they were in their rescuers' arms.

15
Recovery and Retrieval

As the night progressed, the mission evolved from extracting survivors to providing medical attention. The scene resembled a battlefield: the injured were laid out wherever space could be found, lanterns and flashlights casting harsh light on broken bodies. Trained professionals and volunteers alike were forced to make difficult decisions and triage the wounded amid exhaustion and chaos. Those who stood the best chance of survival were treated first; those most gravely hurt received attention only if there was still hope of saving them.

Sylvia Birch was ushered towards an ambulance so she could be transported for further evaluation. She thought, 'No, I must get home. My father will kill me for being late!' She succeeded in convincing the aide party that she was not badly injured and could make her way home. Sylvia kept her ordeal a secret, 'No-one was home and my father never ever knew I was in Portland Square that night.'[1]

While the living cried out for aid, the silence of those beyond help was equally inescapable; side by side, the work of healing and recovery unfolded.

The efforts of William Johns

When teenage messenger William Johns arrived on the scene, he was assigned to assist with transporting the injured to a nearby staging area for further assessment.[2] William recalled that all available personnel were drafted into this vital work: 'all spare hands were conscripted to help for it was immediately apparent that there were not sufficient "First Aiders" or Nursing Auxiliaries to meet their immediate needs'. Indeed, the ARP Controller's Report for the Air Raids of 21, 22, and 23 April praised the conduct and efforts of the emergency personnel, including messengers such as William, for going beyond expectations and doing their part to respond to the crises: 'The work and behaviour of the personnel was excellent. No cases have been reported of personnel hesitating to proceed to an incident during the height of the raids. Special mention has been made by several Unit Commanders of the excellent behaviour and courage shown by messengers attached to their Units.'[3]

ARP Messenger Service William P. Johns, who wrote an account of the night of 22/23 April 1941, is at centre front [W.P. Johns family]

William and his pal Danny MacKay were put to the task of finding or improvising materials that could be used to stabilise the injured during transport. William recalled being sent on a 'foraging expedition' into the homes that bordered the Square. Personal property and even homes' architectural elements were requisitioned. He searched for blankets and bedding that could be used to dress wounds or keep survivors warm. William also acquired a collection of wooden railings to use for bracing broken bones, 'I soon learnt that a good kick at banister rails would provide excellent splints.'

William and Danny were soon called from this task to help move the injured to the triage station and ambulance staging area. The Royal Army Medical Corps had established a medical station at the Sherwell Congregational Church Hall, and a fleet of ambulances was positioned on Tavistock Road. It was up to individuals such as William to move individuals who 'had been laid out in the passageways or back ground floor rooms of adjoining houses' to this auxiliary location to receive treatment and aid.

The number of able-bodied emergency personnel who were able to respond to the Portland Square situation was insufficient to meet the needs that the disaster demanded. In ordinary circumstances, a stretcher party might have included four grown men—one at each corner of the stretcher. Instead, William found himself paired with Danny—and only Danny. Assessing his own strength, William questioned whether he would be physically capable of carrying out his assignment: 'For two to carry a laden stretcher any distance, under the most favourable of conditions, required the brawn of not only grown men, but those of some physical stature.'

The pair was tasked with moving an unconscious woman who had sustained a head wound. Determined to assist in the efforts, William convinced himself that the short distance around the perimeter of the Square and down Portland Place East to the grounds of the churchyard would be manageable and resolved to take up the quest. Though the task seemed straightforward, the realities of the night presented a series of challenges.

Resources were limited, and stretchers, William learned, were hard to come by. He recalled: 'Our first dilemma was to procure some means of conveyance for her.' A fireman unhelpfully first suggested that they use a door requisitioned from the home. The idea was quickly rejected. The door and the woman together were too heavy for the boys to lift, much less carry all the way to the staging area. The fireman devised an alternative plan:

> He was full of initiative and quickly assured us he had the right thing on his fire appliance, a light weight ladder. This he fetched, and with a few hefty strokes of his hatchet reduced it to the length of about six feet. Then having accomplished his crude handiwork he gave the assurance. 'It's quite light. Grab an overlay or a couple of blankets from a bedroom upstairs and stick a pillow under her head and she should be all right. You haven't far to go.'

A makeshift stretcher now at their disposal, William and Danny surveyed their route to the church hall. Though they did not have far to travel, the pavement was 'strewn with wreckage from the shelter and the facades of fronting houses', requiring the pair to 'weave our way through a street blocked with various Civil Defence vehicles, besides those pavements and carriageways still in existence being strewn with debris and glass.'

With the Luftwaffe still circling overhead, the pair waited for a window of relative calm. At last, the moment came. The boys' confidence grew as other people also began to make use of the lull in the attack: 'The blinded and walking casualties being led by women and the broken limbed carried by men on stretchers as novel in construction as ours.' They followed suit. 'It all seemed so heroic at that moment,' William recalled, 'and I felt very noble when MacKay called, "Right Billie."'

The task of moving the unconscious woman immediately taxed the pair. As William later reflected, 'the heroics became hysterics, reality becoming a tragic farce'. They hoisted the stretcher and hurriedly descended the stairs. When Danny reached the bottom of the steps, he stopped to collect himself. William, carrying the rear of the stretcher, was carried forward by the momentum and had to side-step to avoid pushing Danny over. While Danny remained upright, the woman slipped from the stretcher and fell onto the ground.

The pair set down their makeshift stretcher and hoisted the unconscious woman back onto it. Danny ran back into the house and emerged with a large curtain. They tore the fabric into strips and used it to secure the woman to the ladder. 'I was to reflect later, on our buccaneering attitude of trespass and the purloining of other people's property,' William explained, 'but at the time we considered it not only expedient but right.' With that, the pair lifted the stretcher and resumed their journey.

Fuelled by adrenaline, the pair sprinted along the Square. 'We ran as fast as we were able, hugging the walls, for their shelter, slipping and slithering over broken glass and slates that were everywhere, deviating only when our path was blocked.' This initial sprint only covered 20 yards. After resting, the pair continued their efforts, but found that each successive try had a diminishing return: 'The distance covered each time becoming less, the time for recovery longer.'

At last, the pair ducked into the passageway of a house to assess their prospect of success. Danny asked William whether he thought he could complete the mission. 'I must have looked the picture of dejection,' William reflected, 'and with tears of irritation running down my face I shook my head in reply.'

Yet, feeling compelled to help, the pair resolved that if they could not lift the stretcher, then they would drag it instead. It was perhaps fortunate for the woman that she was unconscious. William and Danny each grabbed a handle and towed the ladder behind them down Portland Place East. 'Although this manner of locomotion was not as easy as we had hoped, nevertheless we at last reached Tavistock Road,' William remembered.

No sooner had the pair arrived at the intersection that the strafing of anti-aircraft machine gun fire aimed at the Luftwaffe bombers forced them to take refuge. The entrance of a chemist's shop provided them with shelter. Based on maps of the area, this was most likely Roper's Chemist. The timing, approximately 12.30 a.m., indicates that the planes overhead were likely sorties of Junker 88s that comprised the tail-end of the German assault.

William's memories of the scene were mostly about the colourful language Danny used to steel himself in this climatic moment:

> However whilst we were huddled in the doorway, it was time not wasted, for I acquired innumerable new swear words to add to the Lexicon of Blasphemy and Sacrilege I was acquiring. MacKay's vocabulary, which included every

> profanity acquired in his lifetime, on the barbaric action of German airmen machine gunning stretcher bearers was to say the least extensive, although in this particular instance misdirected. On reflection it was then that I perceived that MacKay was not quite the gentleman I had first thought.

Finally, the pair reached their destination, the Army's Casualty Reception Centre. 'The place was awash with blood and gore,' William remembered. 'My first impression of the hall, lit by several hissing naphthalene lamps, its walls draped with white sheets, was that of a gun deck of a French man-o-war that had been raked again and again by one of Nelson's Three Decker's.' Indeed, Plymouth was a war zone, and the hall's atmosphere was that of front-line field hospital.

The centre was staffed by two men—a sergeant and a private of the Royal Army Medical Corps. When the boys entered, the private gestured for them to put the stretcher down so he could examine the woman. He untied the curtain straps, removed the blanket, and unwrapped the bandage from around the woman's head. He felt for a pulse but could not locate one. Protocol required that the sergeant should confirm what the private had already determined: the woman was dead.

The sergeant was busy attending to a burn victim. William described the grotesque severity of the individual's condition: 'like a freshly cooked lobster except that his flesh was peeling from his body, but nevertheless smelt like newly boiled ham. He made no noise so mercifully he was unconscious, but his eyes fluttered beneath bulging purple and yellow eyelids.' Determining that nothing could be done for the man except to relieve his pain with morphine and wait for him to die, the sergeant made his way across the hall to assess the woman.

William described the sergeant's attire as strangely comical, like something from a farce rather than the macabre reality of the evening. 'In his own good time "Sarge" came across the hall, looking to me somewhat ludicrous in a tent like surgical gown that covered him from neck to ankles, a steel helmet on his head and the largest pair of scissors I had ever seen in his right hand.'

The sergeant made a quick study of the woman. First, he felt for her pulse. When he could not find one, he pulled her eyelids open. There was no reaction. Next, he removed his helmet and placed his head on the woman's chest to listen for a heartbeat. Hearing none, he used his scissors to cut through her clothing to continue his examination. Speaking to the private, the sergeant pointed to a tiny blue bruise on the woman's chest and provided an appraisal of her injuries: '"If what hit her in the head didn't do for her, that would have, she's been hit by shrapnel. Must have been red hot when it hit her. Look it sealed the blood vessels as it entered," tapping the wound with his scissors as he spoke.'

Having concluded his diagnosis, the sergeant proceeded to evaluate the next case. He directed the boys to carry the woman to one of the idling mortuary vans:

'Still that's the way it goes. She's dead all right, outside, down the road your people have a removal van. Stick her in it as you go by.'

Incredulous, Danny asked if a medical professional should be called. The sergeant, who, of course, was one, had little patience for this query, and argued that his suggestion was pointless:

> 'What bloody good would a doctor be?' challenged the sergeant indignantly. 'All that can be done here is to try to keep the living alive long enough to reach proper medical aid. Mister, you can take it from me, when I say they're dead, they're dead.' This he quickly followed with the order. 'Look at her heels, her calves, her buttocks, her elbows, they're black, that's blood starting to "pond," her heart stopped some time ago.'

To further make his point, the sergeant brandished his scissors and made an incision on the woman's chest. He then repeated his order for the pair to remove the body. William was spent from his labours and traumatised by what he had just witnessed. Realising this, the sergeant swiftly softened and advised the pair to place the woman in the corner until another party could finish the task. William eventually returned home and collapsed in exhaustion.

The clock ticks: from rescue to retrieval

In time, as silence settled over the wreckage, the grim truth became unavoidable. The work of saving the living had given way to the equally harrowing duty of retrieving the dead.

Frank Davey was among the emergency personnel who had been dispatched to Portland Square. He managed a squadron of three ten-man teams which were responsible for razing or stabilising buildings that had been blown out by bombs or charred by fires. Given his responsibility for overseeing structural integrity, Davey descended into the bomb crater and entered the ruined air-raid shelter to conduct a safety assessment. The terrible tableau he encountered was that of the single-worst civilian incident that Plymouth experienced in the entirety of the blitz:

> I shall never forget the sight which greeted us when we arrived on the scene. Every one of them had been killed in exactly the position they were occupying when the bombs fell. It was like being at Madame Tussaud's, looking at waxwork figures, only these had been alive and well only minutes before. They had all been blackened by that blast and when you touched them they just fell over.[4]

Though horrific and haunting, the sight did not deter Davey from his duty and the sombre task that now confronted him and the other personnel: 'I'm afraid that by that time we had become somewhat hardened to similar sights, albeit on a smaller scale. If we had allowed ourselves to be caught up in the full horror of it all we might have cracked. We had a job to do and we got on and did it.'[5] Indeed, Davey's attitude and approach was characteristic of that most British of war slogans: to 'keep calm and carry on'.

Ambulance driver Doreen Jessop was assigned to a crew tasked with entering the shelter to carry out the deceased. The scene she encountered was, as it was for Davey, a moment frozen in time: 'We then went into the shelter, and there were all the people just sitting, some with children still on their laps, people with glasses on, and the glass still intact, and they were all dead, killed by the blast. The thing I saw, which was different, their hair, looked like wigs, sort of lifeless, and dusty.'[6]

After delivering his report to ARP Control Centre, courier Frank Phillips returned to Portland Square to assist. 'The square was full of men and women trying to save people from the shelter. I went down a hole with a rescue team, where I saw a dead person for the first time in my life, there appeared to be rows of dead people.'[7] Eleanor Boynes's grandson Roy was also in the courier service and reported to Portland Square. Later, he learned that his grandmother was among the dead.[8]

The horrors of war

These events brought the nightmarish horrors of modern war to the home front. The carnage made tabulating the exact number of causalities imprecise. Elizabeth Searle, who lived on Portland Square, recalled the horror with grim clarity: 'It was impossible to know how many died as some were blown to pieces.'[9]

Part of Doreen Jessop's assignment was to tag dismembered body parts. 'Some were just parts of bodies and, where it was possible, we had to attach a label to the body or parts, with my name, and the name of the first aid post and whether it was male or female.'[10]

There were several reports of limbs being blown apart from torsos and scattered across the blast zone.[11] Catherine Hunt of 16 Portland Square remembered her husband Harry attempting to retrieve some items from their flat. Several wardens attempted to stop him from entering, but he persisted and prevailed; the wardens may had been trying to shield him from the grotesque scene he encountered inside. Catherine recalled Harry sharing that 'he found a child's head in our kitchen and a sailor's body draped over a tree in our back garden'.[12]

Body parts were also reported as being found on the tops of trees and on the roofs of nearby buildings such as Sherwell Congregational Church.[13] The day after the incident, a corpse was seen on the roof of the church hall. Doug Barretto, who resided in the area, described the nauseating image: 'I well remember during the next day or two following the tragedy, seeing a stain of blood spreading down from the top of a hall where the man had been found. The wall is near the pavement in Tavistock Road.'[14]

Even emergency personnel struggled to stomach the sites they faced in their work. William Johns remembered an encounter with a First Aid Unit leader who had been among the first on site and had descended into the shelter. William recalled the man's description of what he saw: 'We found a lot of them huddled together like little black birds, their bodies intact, just a little blood from the mouth, but when we tried to pick them up – they were just pulp, we had to pour them into sacks!' The scene traumatised the man, and William recalled the physical signs of the man's state of shock: 'He was involuntarily shaking with the experience, his face gaunt, his eyes dull and lifeless, and spoke with an effort and with uncertain pauses as if having difficulty expressing the horror he had found.'

Naval ratings hardened by combat were enlisted to assist with the gut-wrenching collection and cataloguing of remains. William witnessed this work in the aftermath of the incident, 'In the morning a squad of men, with strong stomachs would collect what pieces were left. The oft used cliché "We scraped them off the wall" was here a literal truth.'

These gruesome details were often not reported in contemporary newspapers in the interest of maintaining public morale.[15]

***

Jim Brown, who had sprinted to the Square in the immediate aftermath of the bombing to search for survivors, helped to shift pieces of the concrete slabs as he and others manoeuvred through the crater to extract the dead. He was profoundly affected by the task of removing the corpses of men, women, and small children. 'Time after time the bodies were those of neighbours and friends—people he had known well. Many could only be identified by their clothing.'[16] The bodies were transferred to the city's wartime mortuary on Halwell Street just a block away from the shelter. As one of the sector's air-raid wardens, Jim remained at the crater throughout the day and into the following evening. Then, he went to the mortuary to aid in the task of identifying the deceased. 'You see,' he reflected years later, 'I knew most of them.'[17]

16

'They had gone home'

On Maggie Cornelius's grey coat was a small silver brooch of St Christopher, the patron saint of travellers and, as tradition held, protector against sudden death.[1] When her body was lifted from the wreckage of the Portland Square Air-Raid Shelter around dusk on 23 April, the saint's image was dulled by dust.

Crews had been working since midnight to search for survivors, treat the injured, and retrieve the deceased. As personnel worked through the rubble, they braced the collapsed concrete masonry and the twisted iron of the shelter's superstructure. By dusk, the pace had slowed; exhaustion hung over the site as the last of the day's discoveries were made. Maggie's body was recovered alongside her husband Lang's at seven o'clock in the evening, marking the close of a long day's labour among the ruins.

At eight o'clock, the Corneliuses' bodies were brought a short distance to the city's provisional mortuary a block south on Halwell Street. Inside, the staff worked under the eye of the mortuary superintendent to navigate the monumental task before them: processing not only the over seventy victims of the Portland Square incident but also dozens of casualties being transported from other sites across Plymouth.

Every death left a paper trail. Even amid the height of the Blitz, the British state insisted that local authorities follow a process: forms filled out, bodies numbered, effects listed, names confirmed. The 'Civilian War Death Due to War Operations' (C.W.D.) form was how authorities maintained a sense of order after the crisis. Forms were filled out carefully, noting the condition of each body and the personal effects recovered.

Maggie's record quietly captures the detail of two lives cut tragically short. She was described as 'stout', a bureaucratic understatement that did not capture the deeper tragedy: that she had been heavily pregnant when she was killed. The mortuary attendants catalogued her clothing as a blue dress and a grey tweed coat. Her possessions included three items of value: a pendant, a plain gold wedding ring, and a silver brooch of St Christopher. These pieces of jewellery were bagged for safekeeping with the same record number as Maggie's body: 167.

The objects found with Lang Cornelius offer a window into the life he led and the world he navigated. His inventory included a purse containing £10; a case with glass and comb; personal letters and papers; a gold wristlet watch; two gold rings; a whistle; a cigarette lighter; another watch; three fountain pens; five pencils; two cigarette cases, one gilt and one silver; a tin of lozenges; scissors in a case; two pocket diaries; snapshots; a Lloyds Bank cheque book; spectacles in a case; three pocket knives; two pencil sharpeners; three identity discs; formamint lozenges; three pieces of rubber; and driving licence A46745.

This meticulous accounting of victims' belongings was not mere administration. Each object would help friends and family confirm the identity of the deceased. In a space filled with dust and rubble, these items often facilitated recognition while also providing surviving relations a measure of comfort in their hour of loss.

The following day, 24 April, and after enduring a third consecutive night of the Luftwaffe's bombing campaign, the Rev. Roger Welchman joined the queue of relatives and neighbours at the doors of the Halwell Street Mortuary. It fell to him as both priest and friend to identify the Corneliuses. As the vicar of St Matthias's Church on North Hill, he had enjoyed a close relationship with Lang Cornelius in the administration of the parish. Now, just as the vicar had ministered to Lang and Maggie in life, he stood among the silent rows of the dead to call out their names once more.

On the official forms, Welchman's signature appears twice, recording that he had identified 'Major William Cornelius' and 'Marjorie Cornelius'. He gave their particulars: name, address, occupation, and age. For Maggie, Welchman relied on her 'personal effects'. In Lang's case, he made the identification by inspecting the body and confirming details through Lang's 'uniform' and 'driving licence'.

Lang and Maggie's son Anthony Cornelius's recollections from the week suggest why Welchman may have taken care to examine these belongings as further evidence. 'According to my aunt Kitty Hill "when Maggie was found she was just covered with dust. Lang was badly knocked around." Her husband, my Uncle Pat, was the person who claimed the bodies from the Halwell Street morgue and had them removed for burial so he obviously knew the condition they were in.'[2]

It was from the Rev. Welchman that Anthony soon learned the tragic news that would divide his childhood into before and after. The vicar's words were quiet but final, carrying the weight of both pastoral care and the irrevocable truth of death. Anthony recalled that day vividly:

> One morning I was told by my grandmother that we were going into Plymouth. She did not give me a reason. There was a lodger staying at Restormel who was working on the new RAF airfield of Harrowbeer. My Uncle Pat was at Restormel at the time, presumably on leave from the Army. He accompanied us into Plymouth. On the way into Plymouth I can remember thinking 'why

> are we going into Plymouth?' 'Something must have happened.' 'Maybe my cat had died?' I really couldn't imagine what had happened. Entering town we stopped outside the vicarage in St. Lawrence Road, the home of Roger Welchman, the vicar of St. Matthias church where we all used to go. I remember going into the house and being shown into the sitting room. After we were seated Roger Welchman said that my parents 'had gone home.' I do remember those were the words he used.[3]

Patrick Hill, Maggie's brother and Lang's brother-in-law, went to the mortuary separately. He arranged for the retrieval of the bodies for a private funeral service and interment in the Hill family plot at Ford Park Cemetery.

In time, the family received the official notice of condolence from the government. It was a standard, printed message sent to thousands of bereaved families across the blitzed British home front: 'The Minister of Health asks me to express the deep sympathy of His Majesty's Government with you in your loss.'[4] The words were formal and measured, offering an expression of sympathy in print, yet could scarcely fill the void left behind at 42 Portland Square or in the memories of the Corneliuses' young sons.

Across Plymouth and throughout Britain, countless families faced the same sudden rupture, the same quiet negotiation between official procedure and personal grief. The Corneliuses' story offers a window into this world and the systems that rose in response; where the work of remembrance began not in monuments or memoirs, but in the mortuaries. On Halwell Street in Plymouth—and in every blitzed city—this was how order returned: one name, one entry at a time.

17
Civilian Casualty Management

The sun rose at 6.08 a.m. on 23 April. The dawn of St George's Day revealed the harrowing reality of the latest Luftwaffe bombing raid. The first rays of sunlight refracted off the smoke and ash clouds that shrouded Plymouth in a dark pall. The smouldering embers from the incendiary bombs illuminated the frenetic movement around the bomb crater at Portland Square as the rescue mission firmly pivoted its focus from the search for survivors to the retrieval of the dead.

The City Diary for Plymouth made note of the situation and recorded it in bold, capitalised letters, the sentence bordered by thickly weighted lines: 'Very large no. of people killed in Portland Square Public Shelter which received a direct hit.'[1]

Stanley Hollett and his family surveyed the damage. Their idyllic neighbourhood was now a scene of complete devastation. Portland Square looked apocalyptic:

> Every house in the Square had all the windows blown out and curtains hanging in shreds and front doors hanging off. The street was full of stones + earth and branches of trees and we made our way back to our home about 30 yards away, and with daylight we could see the damage to the house but inside was far worse. All windows back and front were gone, doors were hanging off, every ceiling in the house had come down on top of the furniture smashing a lot of it. Words could never explain the feelings or the sadness shown in people's faces.[2]

Stanley looked out across the Square. From his vantage point, he observed emergency personnel like his father at work. 'We could see a lot of activity at the top right hand corner or Portland Square where several large trees had come down, and we could also see lots of white sheets covering an area of the ground around it.'

He watched as the dead were extracted from the ruined shelter and prepared for transport to the mortuary nearby. 'The bodies of most of the victims from the shelter were brought down opposite our house only about 30 feet away and were covered in white sheets which were heavily stained in blood.' How narrowly, he realised, had he avoided that fate. The night before, he had been sitting with friends in the very section of the air-raid shelter that had been hit before his father brought him home only minutes before the bomb strike. Stanley recalled his father checking in on the family later on that morning. That conversation confirmed the thoughts that haunted his mind: 'My father looked in to us a little later to tell us that a land mine had a direct hit on the shelter that he took me from only ten minutes before, and that everyone there had been killed with lots just blown to bits.'

Throughout the morning, Stanley witnessed a nauseating scene unfold as not just bodies but dismembered limbs were collected from the bomb site and delivered to the mortuary. 'There were large linen baskets with arms + legs etc from some who were blown apart, and some of these people were our neighbours and were aged from babies to grandparents.'

Ben Bennett encountered a similar scene when he and his James Street friends emerged from the shelter: 'After it calmed down a bit we tried to head out of the shelter again to see what we could do to help. But, of course, being young people, 16–17, we were told "Oh, no, you sit back and wait."' The James Street Gang had also narrowly avoided the tragedy. Ben waited and watched the emergency teams at work. The result from the blast was grim. 'A little later on I noticed that they were on top of the grass part there, they were laying out sheet-covered bodies, I didn't know how many there were, of course, we knew there was a tragedy.'

The site seared into the memory of Noreen Wise as her family departed for safety elsewhere: 'I remember the scene the next morning as we left the city – the air-raid patrol workers, the devastation, the acrid smell and the covered stretchers.'

Per protocol, vehicles arrived on the scene to transport the deceased from the bomb site to the mortuary. Though the mortuary facility was located only a block away on Halwell Street, teams of men positioned the lifeless bodies on stretchers and makeshift cots and conveyed them to the waiting vehicles for delivery.

Stanley remembered the scene that played out before his front door: 'The bodies were then put into refuse vehicles and taken to the mortuary, which was the large warehouse that had been the timber importers in the street at the rear of our house, where the Army Medical Corps had the job of cleaning them up for relatives to identify them.'

The aftermath of the Portland Square bombing also became a moment when years of behind-the-scenes planning for this very crisis was put into practice. For those managing the dead, it marked the grim activation of a system designed years earlier, one built on forecasts, committee meetings, and government circulars. The white sheets, the refuse vehicles, the warehouse-turned-mortuary: little of it was improvised. To understand how Plymouth came to have the systems and protocols to manage such horror, we must turn back to the years before war broke out.

Preparing for the unthinkable

In the early 1930s, the British government predicted that another global war would yield high civilian causalities because such a conflict would undoubtedly include aerial attacks on civilians on the home front. Officials had to envision scenarios they hoped would never materialise. The most daunting disasters to anticipate were concentrated and prolonged attacks. Estimates forecasted an extraordinary death toll, one that would overwhelm resources dedicated to the 'disposal' of the dead.

Such catastrophes would cripple a city's funerary infrastructure. How would communities cope when large numbers were killed, when churches and civic organisations were called upon to conduct multiple services simultaneously, or when cemeteries faced the challenge of preparing numerous burial plots in rapid succession? What impact would this have on the morale of those who survived?

The Home Office studied the problem and regularly convened the interdepartmental Burials Committee in 1936 and 1937 to discuss it. Ultimately, civil servants developed a series of recommendations about the necessary infrastructure needed to manage these anticipated scenarios. The Committee drafted a directive that advised local councils about how to implement those measures. The Home Office transferred oversight of burials to the Ministry of Health at the start of 1939.

Under an emergency modification to the Poor Law Act, the Ministry delegated responsibility for civilian casualty management resulting from war operations to local authorities. The Poor Law was Victorian-era legislation created to care for the destitute, including making provisions for basic funerals. Rooting wartime burial policy in this law, however, would later cause difficulties. Though civilian death was a consequence of the war, the social stigma about state-funded burials endured: such services were viewed as a 'pauper's burial'—and carried a sense of inferiority borne by the deceased's family. Local officials would need to approach the issue with sensitivity and finesse.

In February 1939, the Ministry of Health released two foundational documents to guide the creation of war deaths preparedness schemes: *Circular 1779* and its accompanying *Memorandum 222.*

Circular 1779 affirmed that the management of civilian war dead would fall to local authorities. Indeed, its purpose was to outline these responsibilities: 'to acquaint Local Authorities with the nature of the duties which they would have to perform in time of war, and to enable them to consider beforehand the necessary arrangements'.[3] This included the administration of mortuaries and oversight of cemeteries and burial services.

While the Ministry emphasised preparedness, it also assumed that, except in a mass fatality incident, most burials would resemble peacetime norms: families, when possible, would claim their loved ones and arrange for private funerals: 'It may be expected that, in the majority of areas, the bodies of any persons who might be killed as a result of war operations would be taken directly to their own homes—or, if taken to a mortuary, removed therefrom—by relatives or friends, who would make arrangements for burial.'[4]

Memorandum 222 supplemented this directive with step-by-step instructions on record-keeping, identification, and the registration of deaths. In routine cases, families completed Part B of the Civilian War Death Form—'Body Claimed and Removed for Burial by Relatives or Friends'—and took possession of the remains. A designated informant, typically a family member, would register the death and receive official permission to 'dispose of the body' through a private funeral.[5]

Grants were later offered to offset the cost of private funerals for certain individuals, such as Civil Defence personnel; these were exceptions. [6]

If no one came forward or the family lacked the capacity to claim and bury the body, the local authority, drawing on precedents established under the Poor Law, had the responsibility for doing so.

The Ministry proactively worked to equip local authorities with the knowledge to adapt and operationalise protocols for civilian war death and burial. These policies required careful handling, and the pre-war preparatory work was not meant to be conducted publicly. In June 1939, a conference at Portsmouth and Southsea brought together public health officials to encourage conversation around this topic.

Dr A.B. Williamson, medical officer for Portsmouth, was the principal speaker at the event, and he addressed the practical challenges of translating national directives into local practice. In his remarks, published as 'The Problem of the Disposal of the Dead After Air Raids', Williamson unpacked *Circular 1779* and *Memorandum 222*, highlighting how national guidelines established broad expectations while leaving local officials with discretion about how to interpret and implement them. The topics for authorities to investigate and contemplate further included a redefinition the responsibilities of civil officials, such as the town clerk, medical officer, and coroner; the method for handling a mass casualty incident; and logistics pertaining to the staffing, design, and location of both mortuary and burial facilities.

Echoing the government guidance, Williamson assumed that wartime burials would follow traditional, family-directed burial customs, though at elevated rates. To that end, he emphasised that mortuary facilities needed to be prepared to process remains efficiently to expedite the sensitive task of returning the deceased to their families.

Adopting a solutions-centred approach, he noted the most urgent steps that local authorities should prioritise were to prepare for their role in supporting bereaved families. Readiness, he contended, was less about the burial of the dead and more about supporting the living. Staff had to be hired and trained; facilities needed to be secured and equipped; responsibilities had to be clearly defined and delegated—and all before the bombs began to fall.[7]

Ministry of Health guidance and instructions evolved once the blitz began. Procedures for identification and record-keeping were issued piecemeal through supplementary circulars and memoranda. A comprehensive reference manual was eventually compiled in 1942, but by then the worst raids were long past.[8]

From directives to deployment: planning in Plymouth

One of the most pressing items for local authorities was to assemble the property portfolio needed to conduct the business of civilian casualty management. *Circular 1779* outlined this process. First, officials were to conduct a review of existing municipal buildings. This assessment would identify needs and thus serve as the basis for developing a strategic plan for how to rectify those deficiencies.[9] Additional inventory identified as being essential for carrying out the plan could then be acquired through emergency requisitions of private property, including cemeteries, chapels, and sites that could be repurposed as mortuaries. *Circular 1949* formalised this process, indicating that expenditures connected with the purchase, maintenance, and administration of these facilities would be reimbursed, provided they adhered to government regulations.[10]

In Plymouth, the lumber yard on Halwell Street was identified as the location for the city's principal provisional wartime mortuary. The site was spacious enough to accommodate the site requirements and recommended facility schematic from the Ministry of Health. This included a preparation space, rows for three-tiered storage racks, a private family viewing area, offices, and accommodation for bodies contaminated from gas attacks. Located in Drake's Ward, the site's location made it centrally positioned to respond to crises and convenient to other municipal resources with which it might need to liaise such as the police, emergency food organisations, and other offices.[11]

Stanley Hollett witnessed the appropriation of the warehouse before the war broke out: 'In Halwell St behind our house there used to be a large warehouse owned by Coles Timber Importers that used to be stacked high with new joinery and all sorts of timber, all of which was cleared out and the building taken over by the Civil Defence? Then locked up.'[12]

Likewise, a site for the city's publicly funded burials was secured at Efford Cemetery. Chief Mortuary Superintendent Leslie Martin described the plot as a 'pleasant position in the Church of England Ground. The Grave is 63 ft. long by 20 ft. wide by 10 ft. deep.'[13] The *Western Evening Herald* would later describe the site as a tranquil place of repose for the dead and reflection for the living: 'a setting of beauty and peace, which looks out over a wonderful panorama of the Devon hills.'[14]

While property requisitions and adaptions to facilities provided the physical framework for Plymouth's casualty management scheme, these sites were only as effective as the people tasked with running them. The success of the system hinged on the ability to identify, train, and coordinate a staff capable of responding swiftly, and compassionately, under extraordinary pressure.

Staffing the system: organising the mortuary response

Behind the bricks and mortar of Plymouth's mortuary response was a team of public servants tasked with turning planning into action. Several municipal officials took on expanded responsibilities as a part of this scheme. Their roles drew on transferable civil service skills—record-keeping, chain of command, and communicating with the public—but they now had to be applied under the most difficult of circumstances.

The Ministry of Health recommended deputising sanitary inspectors and other officials to fulfil leadership roles connected with civilian war deaths. Throughout the war, official guidance characterised the role of mortuary superintendent as 'one of trust and responsibility' that 'demands organizing ability'.[15]

William Griffin Bickford was the superintendent of parks and open spaces for Plymouth. He was made the superintendent of Halwell Street Mortuary. Likewise, Percy Cole, Plymouth's entertainments manager, was deputised as the War Deaths Officer and managed the War Deaths Department. This role gave Cole oversight of mortuary and cemetery facilities and staff. Town Clerk Colin Campbell coordinated all efforts in Plymouth as the municipality's chief Air Raid Precautions Controller.

Circular 1779 stressed the value of being proactive in assigning staff and familiarising them with operations: 'Each mortuary would need to be placed in charge of a superintendent, and one or more competent persons should be provisionally selected for this work, which would be a task of substantial responsibility, and should make themselves acquainted with the proposed procedure.'[16]

The role of the superintendent was to oversee the efficient operation of the facility, not necessarily to be engaged in clerical tasks or technical procedures. It was advised that these administrators be 'as free as possible for supervision and control'.[17] Bickford's work would thus have included overseeing the attendants and coordinating a team of administrative clerks to file records and handle enquiries. Undertakers and funeral home employees were intended to share their professional training with the staff. Reserve personnel were recruited from these ranks to assist in an emergency. Mutual aid agreements with other localities, such as those organised for the city's fire services, would further augment staffing in the event of a large-scale incident.

As mortuary leadership was primarily drawn from other fields, training in job-specific duties was vital. Dr Williamson emphasised that maintaining the public's trust hinged on competence and efficiency: 'A provisional selection of staff should be made with a view to their becoming familiar with their duties. Nothing would shock the public more than delay and careless method in handling the dead.'[18]

Informative Ministry of Health pamphlets and circulars provided foundational texts on procedures. These documents provide a sense of the processes that local authorities in Plymouth would have followed. For example, *Memorandum 222* outlined the steps that officials were to follow for the reception and identification of a deceased person as well as the maintenance of records pertaining to a civilian death that resulted from enemy action.[19] Throughout the war, staff were reminded of the expectation that they be familiar with the procedures outlined in these documents.[20]

Staff also participated in exercises to practise the routines necessary for the mortuary to function efficiently. Official guidance suggested that there be opportunities for staff to 'know each other, and to work as a team'.[21] It was deemed important for personnel to have some practical experience and understand one another's roles and how they functioned within the larger whole.

Once the war began, it was possible to learn from the experience of other locales. Mass Observation contended that local authorities could—and should—use affected cities as case studies that could inform future best practices. 'It is idle to go on making these reports on individual towns as if each one was a separate problem. Most of the problems of each town are common to all.'[22] After Plymouth's own blitz ordeal in 1941, it organised a conference for other communities in December 1942 which included lectures, tours, and demonstrations of valuable knowledge for personnel across the south.[23]

***

All the planning, paperwork, and preparation had been aimed at being ready for moments such as navigating the aftermath of the Portland Square incident. Now, the systems devised in committee rooms before the war collided with the raw reality of grief and destruction. The extent of what unfolded behind the doors of the mortuary on Halwell Street revealed the stress that those systems and the people working within them had to bear.

As Stanley Hollett later recalled of the atmosphere: 'The smell of death was everywhere and wouldn't go away.'[24]

18
Halwell Street Mortuary

The bombing of Portland Square shattered Stanley Hollett's home, his neighbourhood, and his sense of safety. But it was what lay just behind his house, inside the converted warehouse on Halwell Street, that truly unsettled him.

Drawn by an adolescent urge to understand the unthinkable, he and a friend crept around the side yard and peered through the mortuary's open doors. What they saw would linger in Stanley's memory for the rest of his life: 'Being inquisitive we (a friend and I), went into the yard area in front of the mortuary and looked through the doors to see the corpses on what looked like wire bunks three high and it frightened the life out of us.'[1]

What Stanley glimpsed was grim order: the impact of the blitz had activated Plymouth's system for managing a high number of civilian casualties. Inside the former lumber yard, mortuary attendants moved with quiet efficiency, carrying out procedures honed through civil defence manuals and emergency trainings. This was work which few discussed but which was necessary to moving forward.

Mortuary operations: reception

The Halwell Street Mortuary was a hive of activity when the first victims from Portland Square started to be transported to the site on the morning of 23 April. As the site was Plymouth's principal mortuary facility, it was responsible not only for processing the casualties of the nearby Portland Square disaster but also of other incidents from across the city. Of the 404 civilian casualties from 21–24 April, 317 came through Halwell Street. The Emergency Committee Minutes for 23 April noted that there were several communal shelters that received a direct hit during the air raid: '6 public shelters had been hit, the one in Portland Square being the worst incident of this kind.'[2]

Resources were quickly stretched to their breaking point. Just as the Luftwaffe attack strategy was essentially a replay of its March blitz, so too were the challenges that the mortuary staff faced in their work. On the morning of 23 April, staff faced a backlog of bodies from the first night of the raid. Complicating matters, the information bureau set up at the public library on Tavistock Road became engulfed in flames during the raid. That fire destroyed vital documents and data about the first wave of victims, resulting in many more casualties being placed on the unidentified list and slowing down operations. The staff scrambled to set up a provisional information bureau and to complete their work pertaining to the first night's victims while additional bodies began to arrive from bomb sites, such as Portland Square, from the second night's attack. The reserve personnel of local undertakers and their employees were unable to assist the Halwell Street staff because funeral facilities themselves became overwhelmed with families arranging private burials for their beloved.

The Ministry of Health provided guidance as to the processes that staff were to follow as they received the bodies into the mortuary. Standardised paperwork, Form C.W.D., 'Civilian War Death Due to War Operations', ensured that appropriate information about the victims would be recorded. Later in the war, an amended copy of *Memorandum 222* implored officials to familiarise themselves with the form to maximise efficiency: 'Mortuary Superintendents, Mortuary Clerks, and other responsible officers are earnestly requested to study Form C.W.D. and this Memorandum carefully. Inaccurate details not only impose unnecessary work on other people but may also cause hardship to the relatives of the deceased.'[3]

The sixty-six Form C.W.D. for the Portland Square incident document particulars about each victim.[4] Collectively, the records not only reveal information about the dead but also provide a means to reconstruct how the Halwell Street Mortuary functioned on the morning of 23 April.

The first task that confronted officials pertained to the collection and delivery of the victims. After the bodies were extracted from the shelter complex at Portland Square, they were initially laid out on the ground and shielded from view with sheets. Even though the disaster zone was only one block away, victims were still transported to the mortuary facility by vehicle. The explosion dismembered several victims; body parts were collected and delivered to Halwell Street. The Army Medical Corps and staff from HMNB *Devonport* augmented emergency personnel who responded, particularly those completing this macabre task.

Mortuary records reveal that bodies were received at the mortuary approximately one hour after they were recorded as being removed from the shelter site. Hubert Wright was the first victim delivered to Halwell Street. His body arrived at 4.00 a.m. Another nineteen were recorded an hour later. There was then a pause in documented activity for several hours. During this time, the recovery operations would have continued to excavate the bunker to retrieve the remaining bodies while the mortuary prepared to receive them.

The lull was likely tied to resetting the rhythm of the mortuary site and staff—taking stock of how they would navigate the magnitude of the situation that they now faced.

The next significant wave of bodies arrived mid-afternoon, with the bodies of twelve victims being delivered at 4.00 p.m. and another seventeen at 5.00 p.m. As the evening progressed, two more victims were delivered at 6.00 p.m. and another two at 7.00 p.m. Another group of eight was transported at 8.00 p.m. The last victim delivered to the mortuary on 23 April was identified as 10-year-old Margaret Watson at 9.00 p.m. By this late hour, mortuary officials were approaching their twentieth hour of work—and the menacing roar of yet another wave of German planes was thundering in the distance as the Luftwaffe returned to strike Plymouth for a third consecutive night.

Upon receiving a body, officials assigned a sequential serial number to it. Halwell Street used a disc system for this purpose. At the pre-war conference of cemetery and crematoria officials to discuss how to handle a large casualty event, Dr A.B. Williamson recommended such 'identification discs' as being on the list of necessary mortuary supplies. Indeed, instructions from the Ministry of Health advised that 'a metal or bakelite disc bearing the identity serial number should be securely affixed to the body'.

Next, officials were directed to complete Part A of Form C.W.D. *Memorandum 222* dictated that this step should be completed 'at once' and that 'wherever possible, be signed by the officer or other person who brings the body to the mortuary'. Officials recorded the date and time that the body was received at the facility and then addressed five questions about the deceased: where the death occurred or where the body was found; the date and hour of either the death or the discovery of the body; the sex of the victim; an estimate of the victim's age; and the cause of death.

The sixty-six Form C.W.D. for the Portland Square Air-Raid Shelter incident all list 'Bomb Explosion' as the cause of death. Greater precision was evidently not needed. Rather, operating in the midst of a wartime emergency, it was enough to paint in broad strokes and simply characterise the death as the result of enemy action.

If individual autopsies had been completed, an even more harrowing picture of the tragedy would probably have emerged. Some victims would likely have been found to have died from shrapnel wounds or debris projectiles. Other deaths could have been characterised as blunt trauma from being crushed under the rubble. Asphyxiation from fumes or ingesting particles while buried beneath the collapsed structure was also a possibility. Another cause could have been bomb blast. The dual pressure waves released by the bomb's explosion and vacuum effect would have created extreme force on internal body cavities. This pressure would have caused gas-filled organs to rupture and haemorrhage, resulting in instant death without visible external injuries.

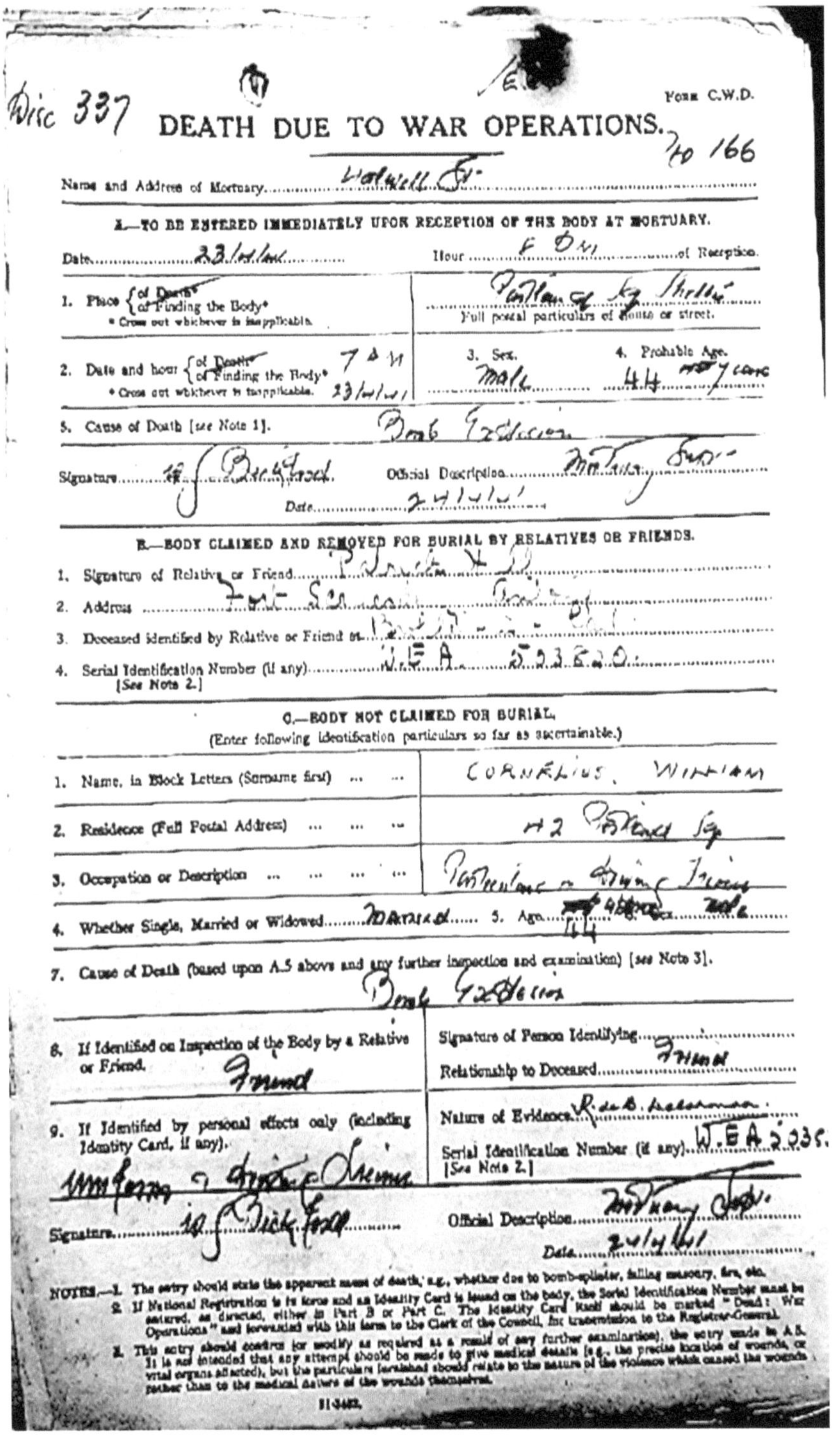

Disc 337

Form C.W.D.

DEATH DUE TO WAR OPERATIONS.

7/0 166

Name and Address of Mortuary .... Halwell St.

A.—TO BE ENTERED IMMEDIATELY UPON RECEPTION OF THE BODY AT MORTUARY.

Date .... 23/4/41 .... Hour .... 8 Pm .... of Reception.

1. Place {of Death* / of Finding the Body*} *Cross out whichever is inapplicable. .... Portland Sq Shelter .... Full postal particulars of house or street.

2. Date and hour {of Death* / of Finding the Body*} *Cross out whichever is inapplicable. .... 7 PM 23/4/41

3. Sex. .... Male

4. Probable Age. .... 44 years

5. Cause of Death [see Note 1]. .... Bomb Explosion

Signature .... W. J. Bickford .... Official Description .... Mortuary Supt. .... Date 24/4/41

B.—BODY CLAIMED AND REMOVED FOR BURIAL BY RELATIVES OR FRIENDS.

1. Signature of Relative or Friend ....
2. Address ....
3. Deceased identified by Relative or Friend as ....
4. Serial Identification Number (if any) .... W.E.A. 503520. [See Note 2.]

C.—BODY NOT CLAIMED FOR BURIAL.

(Enter following identification particulars so far as ascertainable.)

1. Name, in Block Letters (Surname first) ... ... CORNELIUS, WILLIAM
2. Residence (Full Postal Address) ... ... 42 Portland Sq
3. Occupation or Description ... ... Parliament & Drying Dress
4. Whether Single, Married or Widowed .... Married .... 5. Age .... 44 .... 6. Sex .... Male
7. Cause of Death (based upon A.5 above and any further inspection and examination) [see Note 3]. .... Bomb Explosion
8. If Identified on Inspection of the Body by a Relative or Friend. .... Friend .... Signature of Person Identifying .... Relationship to Deceased .... Friend
9. If Identified by personal effects only (including Identity Card, if any). .... Nature of Evidence .... Serial Identification Number (if any) .... W.E.A. 5035 [See Note 2.]

Signature .... W. J. Bickford .... Official Description .... Mortuary Supt. .... Date 24/4/41

NOTES.—1. The entry should state the apparent cause of death, e.g., whether due to bomb-splinter, falling masonry, fire, etc.

2. If National Registration is in force and an Identity Card is found on the body, the Serial Identification Number must be entered, as directed, either in Part B or Part C. The Identity Card should be marked "Dead: War Operations" and forwarded with this form to the Clerk of the Council, for transmission to the Registrar-General.

3. This entry should confirm (or modify as required as a result of any further examination), the entry made in A.5. It is not intended that any attempt should be made to give medical details (e.g., the precise location of wounds, or vital organs affected), but the particulars furnished should relate to the nature of the violence which caused the wounds rather than to the medical nature of the wounds themselves.

51-3462.

Civilian War Death Form, side 1, William 'Lang' Cornelius. [Dunham family and The Box]

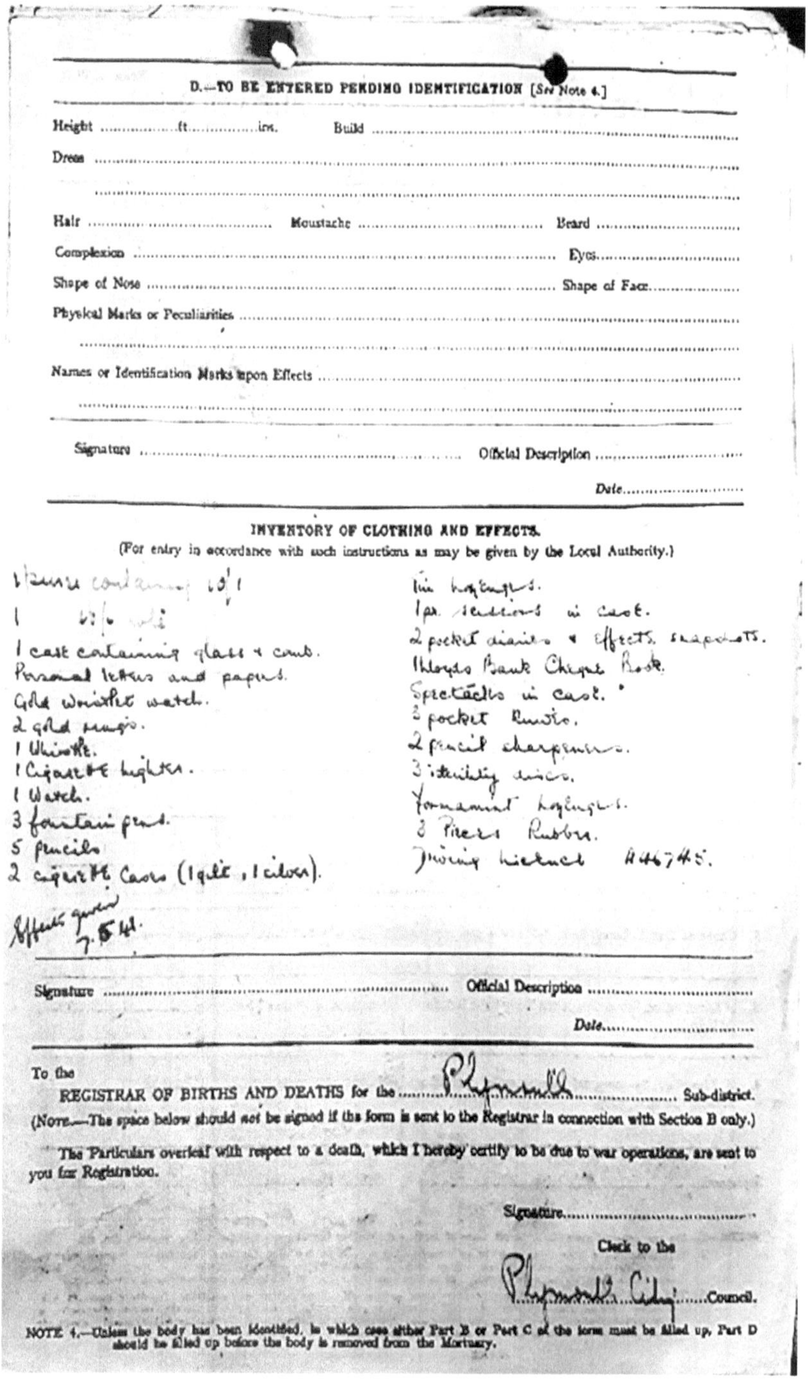

D.—TO BE ENTERED PENDING IDENTIFICATION [See Note 4.]

Height ....ft..................ins. Build ....

Dress ....

....

Hair .... Moustache .... Beard ....

Complexion .... Eyes..............................

Shape of Nose .... Shape of Face..........................

Physical Marks or Peculiarities ....

....

Names or Identification Marks upon Effects ....

....

Signature .... Official Description ....

Date..............................

INVENTORY OF CLOTHING AND EFFECTS.

(For entry in accordance with such instructions as may be given by the Local Authority.)

1 Purse containing 10/1
1 [illegible] 4/6 [illegible]
1 case containing glass & comb.
Personal letters and papers.
Gold wristlet watch.
2 gold rings.
1 Whistle.
1 Cigarette lighter.
1 Watch.
3 fountain pens.
5 pencils
2 cigarette cases (1 gilt, 1 silver).

Tin lozenges.
1 pr. scissors in case.
2 pocket diaries & effects, snapshots.
Lloyds Bank Cheque Book.
Spectacles in case.
2 pocket knives.
2 pencil sharpeners.
3 identity discs.
Formamint lozenges.
3 Pieces Rubber.
Driving licence A44745.

Effects given 7.5.41.

Signature .... Official Description ....

Date..............................

To the

REGISTRAR OF BIRTHS AND DEATHS for the ....Plymouth.......... Sub-district.

(Note.—The space below should not be signed if the form is sent to the Registrar in connection with Section B only.)

The Particulars overleaf with respect to a death, which I hereby certify to be due to war operations, are sent to you for Registration.

Signature..............................

Clerk to the

Plymouth City......Council.

NOTE 4.—Unless the body has been identified, in which case either Part B or Part C of the form must be filled up, Part D should be filled up before the body is removed from the Mortuary.

Civilian War Death Form, side 2, William 'Lang' Cornelius. The inventory of belongings found with him were part of the 'corroborative evidence' used in the identification process. [Dunham family and The Box]

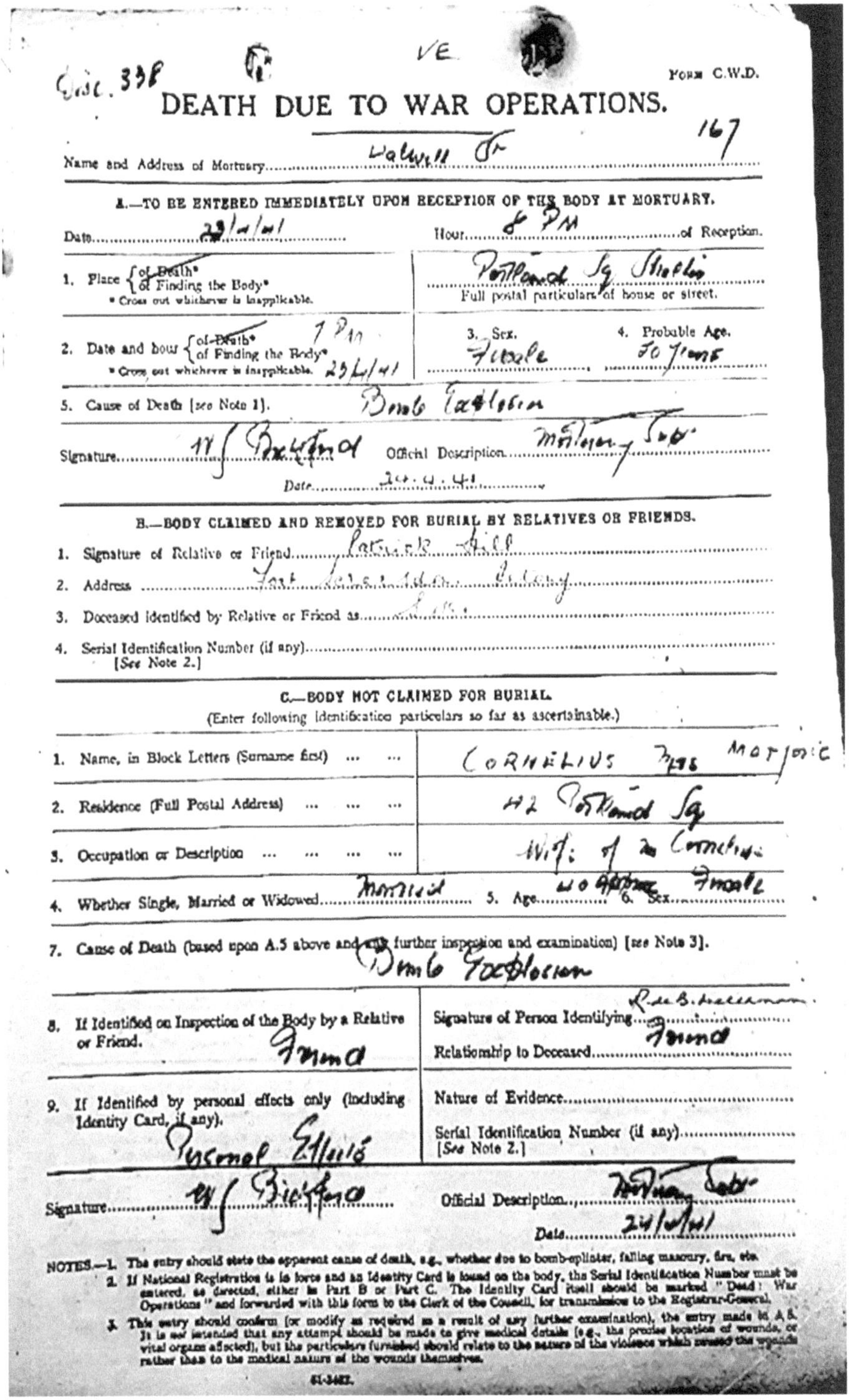

Circ. 338 VE FORM C.W.D.

DEATH DUE TO WAR OPERATIONS.

167

Name and Address of Mortuary........ Halwell St

A.—TO BE ENTERED IMMEDIATELY UPON RECEPTION OF THE BODY AT MORTUARY.

Date........ 23/4/41 .... Hour........ 8 PM ....of Reception.

1. Place { ~~of Death*~~ / of Finding the Body* } .... Portland Sq Shelter .... Full postal particulars of house or street.
* Cross out whichever is inapplicable.

2. Date and hour { ~~of Death*~~ / of Finding the Body* } 7 Pm 23/4/41
* Cross out whichever is inapplicable.

3. Sex. Female 4. Probable Age. 50 years

5. Cause of Death [see Note 1]. Bomb Explosion

Signature........ W J Bickford .... Official Description........ Mortuary Supt ....
Date........ 24.4.41 ....

B.—BODY CLAIMED AND REMOVED FOR BURIAL BY RELATIVES OR FRIENDS.

1. Signature of Relative or Friend........ Patrick Hill ....
2. Address ....
3. Deceased identified by Relative or Friend as........
4. Serial Identification Number (if any)........ [See Note 2.]

C.—BODY NOT CLAIMED FOR BURIAL.
(Enter following identification particulars so far as ascertainable.)

1. Name, in Block Letters (Surname first)	CORNELIUS Mrs Marjorie
2. Residence (Full Postal Address)	42 Portland Sq
3. Occupation or Description	Wife of ... Cornelius
4. Whether Single, Married or Widowed........ Married	5. Age........ 40 approx 6. Sex........ Female

7. Cause of Death (based upon A.5 above and any further inspection and examination) [see Note 3]. Bomb Explosion

8. If Identified on Inspection of the Body by a Relative or Friend. Friend	Signature of Person Identifying........ R. de B. Hallaman .... Relationship to Deceased........ Friend ....
9. If Identified by personal effects only (including Identity Card, if any). Personal Effects	Nature of Evidence........ Serial Identification Number (if any)........ [See Note 2.]

Signature........ W J Bickford .... Official Description........ Mortuary Supt ....
Date........ 24/4/41 ....

NOTES.—1. The entry should state the apparent cause of death, e.g., whether due to bomb-splinter, falling masonry, fire, etc.
2. If National Registration is in force and an Identity Card is found on the body, the Serial Identification Number must be entered, as directed, either in Part B or Part C. The Identity Card itself should be marked "Dead: War Operations" and forwarded with this form to the Clerk of the Council, for transmission to the Registrar-General.
3. This entry should conform (or modify as required as a result of any further examination), the entry made in A.5. It is not intended that any attempt should be made to give medical details (e.g., the precise location of wounds, or vital organs affected), but the particulars furnished should relate to the nature of the violence which caused the wounds rather than to the medical nature of the wounds themselves.

51-3482.

Civilian War Death Form, side 1, Marjorie 'Maggie' Cornelius. [Dunham family and The Box]

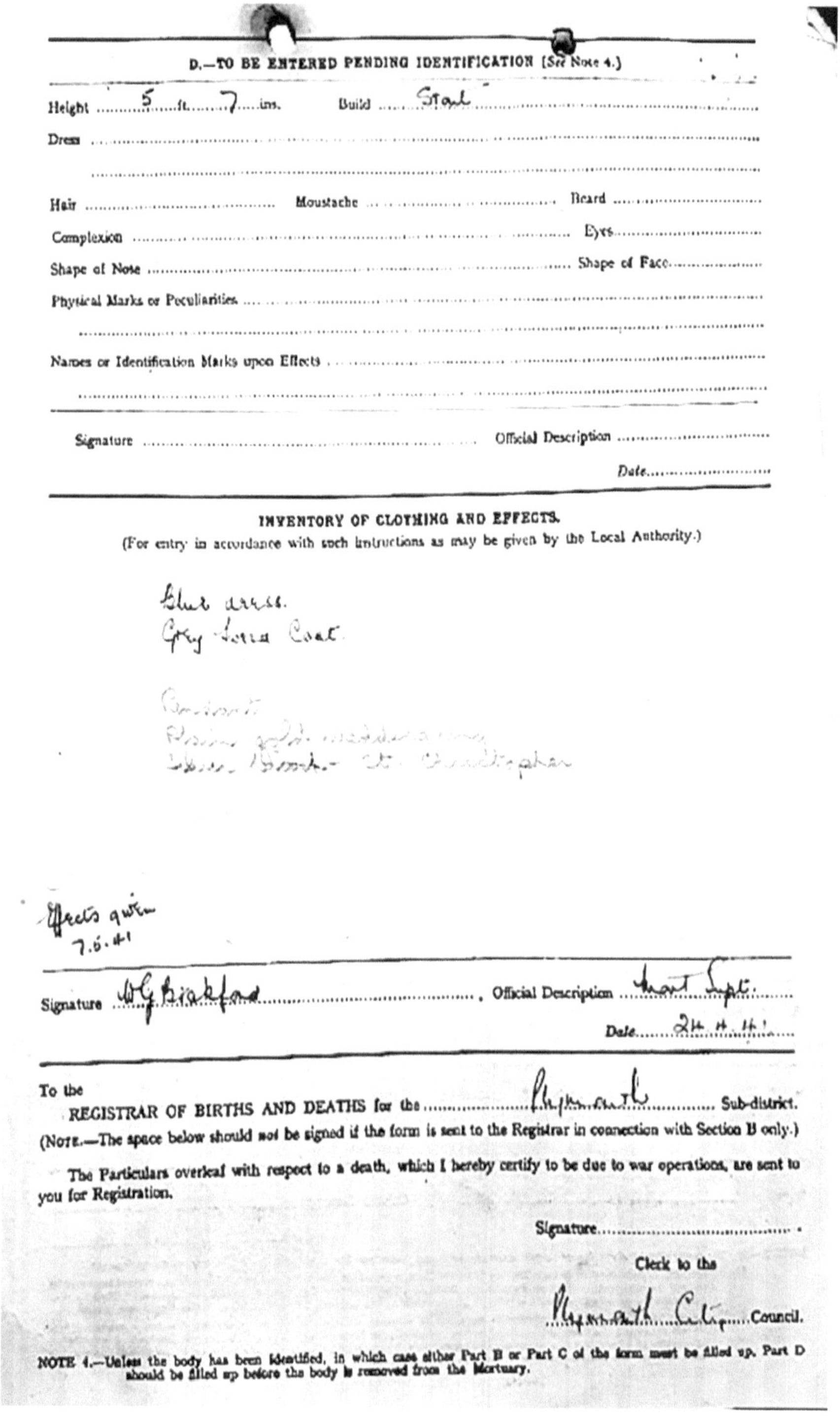

D.—TO BE ENTERED PENDING IDENTIFICATION [See Note 4.]

Height ....5....ft.....7....ins. Build ....Stout....

Dress ....

Hair .... Moustache .... Beard ....

Complexion .... Eyes....

Shape of Nose .... Shape of Face....

Physical Marks or Peculiarities ....

Names or Identification Marks upon Effects ....

Signature .... Official Description ....

Date....

INVENTORY OF CLOTHING AND EFFECTS.

(For entry in accordance with such instructions as may be given by the Local Authority.)

Blue dress.
Grey Lorna Coat.

Contents
Plain gold wedding ring
Silver Brooch - St. Christopher

Effects given
7.6.41

Signature W G Bickford.... Official Description ....Mort. Supt....

Date....24.4.41....

To the

REGISTRAR OF BIRTHS AND DEATHS for the ....Plymouth.... Sub-district.

(Note.—The space below should not be signed if the form is sent to the Registrar in connection with Section B only.)

The Particulars overleaf with respect to a death, which I hereby certify to be due to war operations, are sent to you for Registration.

Signature....

Clerk to the

....Plymouth City....Council.

NOTE 4.—Unless the body has been identified, in which case either Part B or Part C of the form must be filled up, Part D should be filled up before the body is removed from the Mortuary.

Civilian War Death Form, side 2, Marjorie 'Maggie' Cornelius. [Dunham family and The Box]

Discrepancies in the records: numbering the bodies

Much of the paperwork pertaining to the Portland Square incident was verified by Superintendent William Bickford. His signature is recorded at least once on sixty of the sixty-six forms connected with Portland Square. Indeed, his signature was the only one on forty-nine of the forms. This indicates that for most of the victims of this incident it was Bickford who ultimately affirmed the work of the clerks: details pertaining to the receipt of the body, the identification of the deceased, the cataloguing of clothing and effects, and the paperwork necessary for burial. Leslie Martin, the Superintendent of Efford Cemetery, was the other official who had oversight. He seems to have been brought in to assist Bickford given the scale of the work that was necessary.

Despite the meticulous attention to paperwork and much of that work being verified by one individual, several discrepancies were found in the mortuary records. These errors concern the identification number assigned to several victims. As noted, the Halwell Street Mortuary made use of a disc system. While this organisational system functioned well in earlier raids with smaller casualty counts, it was not as effective in a mass fatality event. The disc number was, like the number written atop the Form C.W.D., issued chronologically. Problematically, these two numbers were not necessarily the same. Therefore, most bodies had two, often different, numbers assigned to it.

Several victims were assigned identical numbers. Iris Davies and Robert Hakenjos were both assigned no. 112 on their respective Form C.W.D. and disc 420. Iris was processed by Leslie Martin, and Robert was processed by William Bickford. Was this, perhaps, a case of administrators working in isolation under extreme pressure, issuing numbers as quickly as possible without the chance to cross-check with one another, so that duplication crept in amid the chaos?

William Bickford gave both Betty Cundy and Kathleen Hanlon no. 156 on their Form C.W.D. but assigned different disc numbers: 327 and 454, respectively.

Leslie Martin made several redundancy errors. He marked the paperwork for Susan Pearn and Florence Davies with both no. 115 on their Form C.W.D. and disc 423, and labelled the documentation for Anthony Rendle and Albert Davies with both no. 127 on the boys' Form C.W.D. and disc 435. Although Martin handled proportionally far less paperwork than Bickford, his records contain a disproportionate share of these mistakes, suggesting either a lapse in his own procedure or the strain of the circumstances in which he was working.

The confusion caused by the numbering of the deceased was brought up in the official assessment of mortuary operations after the raids of 21, 22, and 23 April. It was recommended to replace the disc system with a system of printed labels. Henceforth, a body would not be assigned any identification number until it was received at the mortuary. From that point onwards, that singular number would be

Susan, Gwendoline, and William Pearn, *c*.1914. The family lived at 9 Kirkby Place. Susan and William were among the casualties. [Chris Roberts]

used for every aspect of the process: the paperwork, identification tags on the body, the cataloguing and storage of inventoried personal effects, and the stretcher rack location.

This new labelling system promised to enhance functional efficiency. In practice, the revised process meant that administrative staff would be more likely to liaise directly with the rescue parties delivering the bodies and could verify information while completing the Form C.W.D. paperwork. The new processes were instituted in time for the raids on 28 and 29 April and had the intended result of improving operations.[5]

Other discrepancies concerned the dates listed on the mortuary paperwork. Both William Allen and Phyllis Pepper were recorded as having been found at the bomb site around 8 p.m. on 22 April but as having been received at the mortuary at 9 p.m. on 23 April. Their death date was erroneous: the air-raid shelter was not hit on 21–22 April. Both individuals were alive on 22 April and in the shelter when the bomb struck on the evening of 22–23 April. Phyllis went to the shelter with her friend Barbara Allen, and William was in the shelter with his sons—and Barbara's brothers—Kenneth and Gordon. Further, in examining the body identification numbers at the top of each individual's Form C.W.D., both Phyllis's and William's numbers, 173, disc 344, and 174, disc 345, respectively, fall chronologically after the numbers recorded for other victims, not before them.

An inventory of the incident

After reception, the staff's next task was to attempt to identify the victim. The process of putting a name to the deceased was the fundamental purpose of the mortuary and was critical to local authorities' management of the civilian war dead. The identification process not only allowed for accurate record-keeping but also enabled relatives to begin to seek closure. Indeed, as it was assumed that many victims would be buried privately by their families, it was vital that bodies be correctly identified so that they could be released. Identification was also essential for legal and administrative purposes, including the registration of the death, the settlement of estates, and the processing of any pension and insurance claims.

Some documents found on the deceased enabled officials to identify victims almost immediately. Purses or small valises often contained identity-bearing documents such as bank books, pension plans, ration cards, cheque books, diaries, letters, and personal papers. For example, Susan Pearn wore her identity bracelet; Claude Chubb had a form noting his military service and honours; William Allen was found with hospital membership cards, ambulance cards, a naval permit and his army pension book; John Norton had his civil defence identification card; Ivy Morgan held two ration books; and Samuel Farrant carried a diary and letters addressed to him. The Ministry of Health recommended that attending staff record these pieces of 'corroborative evidence' on the mortuary records to expedite the identification process for attending families.[6]

The officials' next task was to prepare each body for viewing by the deceased's relatives, neighbours, or friends for the purposes of confirming the deceased's identity. As a part of this step, officials were instructed to inventory the clothing and personal effects found on or near the deceased as additional corroborative evidence in Part D of the form.[7] Of the sixty-six records for the Portland Square incident, fifty-seven have at least some notation in Part D. Of the nine records in which Part D is blank, six of those individuals were youths aged 15 or younger.

The details noted on the records provide insight about these individuals.

The descriptions of patterned dresses and colourful jumpers add a sense of life and realism to the black-and-white images of the past. Margaret Blake, 30, wore a Scotch plaid scarf and red, green, and yellow jumper. Elsie Rendle, 41, sported a green and white spotted scarf with a brown astrakhan collar. Mabel Farrant, 52, wore a blue flowered frock and a flower-patterned pinafore.

It must have been a brisk spring evening, or at least chilly in the subterranean shelter, as many of the victims are recorded as wearing coats or layers of clothing. Adelaide Watson, 52, wore a wool-skin coat over a black woollen dress. Florence Chubb, 50, had a green pin-striped coat. At 82, Eleanor Boynes wore a blue dress and brown scarf with her brown fur coat. Jane MacGreggor, 77, kept warm with a black dress and black coat as well as a navy cardigan with red trimming. Sarah Jane Ledden, 73, wore a yellow jumper underneath a white-spotted black jumper, a flower-patterned apron, and a black astrakhan coat. Florence Harris, 54, layered a red dressing gown over her black dress and orange jumper. Lavinia Surgeoner, 35, wore a printed frock, blue overall, and a black coat.

Children were likewise dressed for cooler conditions. Kenneth Allen, 14, wore a brown checkered coat over a blue waistcoat, brown shirt, green and white tie, and grey flannel trousers. Kathleen Hanlon, 13, wore her dark blue school overall, a light blue jumper, and a blue coat; two 'fancy' handkerchiefs and a brown scarf with white spots completed her outfit. Winifred Davies, 14, wore a double layer with both a brown coat and an orange jumper. Her younger sister Patricia, 7, wore a blue and white print dress under her blue coat. A red scarf and a pair of brown and green striped socks completed Patricia's ensemble.

Whole families entered the shelter bundled for warmth. William Cundy, 38, who spent the night between his home on Portland Square and the shelter was described as wearing three pullovers—one each of brown, purple, and fawn—with blue trousers, a leather belt, and braces. His wife Winifred, 35, wore a mauve dress with a flower-patterned apron underneath a blue coat. Their daughter Betty May, 10, wore a bright red velveteen dress with a pink cardigan and a light green coat. We might imagine that Barbara Cundy, the sole survivor of the family, was similarly dressed, and can visualise how she buried her tired face into her mother's patterned apron or clutched her blue coat when the bomb ricocheted through the air-raid shelter.

The attending staff filled out this paperwork meticulously. Pens scratching across the pages, they also catalogued the range of personal effects that were found with the victims—keys, fountain pens, spectacles, and smoking accessories such as pipes or engraved cigarette cases and lighters. Each item was another clue in the important task of identifying the deceased. Personal effects were placed in numbered paper parcels that corresponded with the victim's identification number.

Given their financial and sentimental value, rings, watches, and other jewellery seemed to be recorded with extra precision. They would likely be among the prized keepsakes and heirlooms that surviving family members would treasure in memory of their loved ones. For example, Sarah Jane Ledden wore black jet beads, a plain gold wedding ring, a brilliant brooch, and a small shamrock brooch, while her daughter Irene had a gold watch and gold expansion bracelet as well as a brilliant brooch and gold engagement ring. Lavina Surgeoner's collection included a plain gold wedding ring, a gold ring with a flower design, a gold wishbone brooch, a pair of gold earrings, and a three-stone engagement ring.

These and similarly distinctive items might have been a key to identifying a victim. Indeed, they were frequently used as a part of the identification process because officials found that the bereaved felt more confident in making their identification when they were able to reference the deceased's personal effects.[8]

Once a victim's belongings were inventoried, family and friends could complete the heart-wrenching but necessary task of making a positive identification of the deceased.

Identifying the deceased

In addition to the administrative tasks associated with record-keeping and operating the facility, officials such as Superintendent Bickford would also interact with individuals seeking information about missing and deceased relations and friends. Taking on the role of counsellor and consoler, they conversed with the bereaved and helped families to identify loved ones and decide on burial arrangements. Plymouth War Deaths Officer Percy Cole, recognising the emotional weight of these moments, emphasised that staff interacting with the bereaved needed to exhibit 'considerable care'.[9]

***

Their eyes swollen from their tears and the exhaustion of yet another sleepless night, individuals checked in on the homes and apartment buildings surrounding Portland Square in the search for their loved ones.

Stanley Hollett's home gave him a front-row seat to what transpired in the immediate aftermath of the bombing. 'It was very sad seeing relations/sons/daughters at the end of the road being held back by police some screaming to be allowed to go to the very large crater where the body search was going on, having previously gone to the damaged homes of the dead and finding no one there.'[10] Stanley was, of course, a neighbour and friend of many of the victims and would have known members of their families.

Failing to locate their relations and friends, individuals experienced the realisation that their loved one was either wounded or likely among the dead laid out in the nearby mortuary—which given its proximity had the potential to become crowded with relatives seeking information. Officials followed Ministry of Health guidance that family and friends would only be admitted to the mortuary in the afternoon.[11] By segmenting the work in this way, a degree of operational efficiency was able to be maintained for the benefit of staff and bereaved alike.

'Hysteria was rife,' Stanley reflected, 'as the body search lasted for several days and apparently some victims were never found.'[12]

Over the next couple of days, the scene at Halwell Street was sombre and heart-wrenching. Stanley recalled the week vividly. People came to the mortuary to identify not only the victims of the Portland Square tragedy but also casualties from other incidents from the three-night German assault: 'I can remember the queue of relatives consisting of several hundred people outside the mortuary awaiting their turn to identify parents—brothers—sisters who had been brought there from all over the city. This lasted for several days with no let up.'[13]

It must have been a heart-wrenching experience. Brothers were tasked with identifying the remains of sisters and their families. Sons and daughters confirmed the corpse of their mother or father by a familiar pocket watch or piece of jewellery. Aunts and uncles identified nieces and nephews. Friends and neighbours stepped in to do the same.

The deceased were laid out in orderly rows, their belongings neatly arranged nearby. 'There were between 400 and 600 bodies there at that time,' estimated Stanley, 'and as soon as they were made presentable, they were taken away for burial and more would take their place.'[14]

Amid the rows of makeshift cots and the chilling silence of the mortuary, a poignant scene unfolded. Soft sobs and hushed prayers echoed through the air. Officials carried out the solemn task of working with grief-stricken families to show them their deceased and record additional information about them on the Form C.W.D.: name, age, address, and occupation. The standardised questions helped Bickford and his assistants navigate the process.

Identification occurred in a dedicated viewing space, consistent with the efforts to surround the entire process with the proper degree of 'reverence and respect'.[15] Family and friends made their way from a waiting area into a sequestered space to which a trolley had delivered the body and belongings for identification. Corroborative evidence from personal effects often made this a formality and a quick step in the process.

Expediency was the order of the day. The mortuary was governed by the Ministry of Health's maxim of 'speedy identification and rapid clearance' in order to make the site and its staff available to confront the next crisis.[16] Leslie Martin echoed this in his remarks at the conference Plymouth hosted in 1942: 'speed and efficiency, coupled with consideration for the feelings of the bereaved relatives, will do much to maintain [public morale]'.[17] Victims with identifying documents were thus prioritised. Ordinarily, staff removed a deceased person's clothing and cleaned the body prior to storing it on the stretcher racks. Given that time and space were limited, this step was bypassed.

Though focused on efficiency, compassion was expected to temper procedure. Small gestures of humanity were not forgotten. The Ministry of Health suggested that mortuary staff might make efforts to sympathise with the bereaved by offering tea and, of course, by being considerate of their feelings.[18] Superintendent Martin detailed the role of mortuary staff in these moments and the emotional toll this important work exacted: 'Of all the varied procedures, the thing I dreaded most was identification. The scenes are too sad to be mentioned. These people need all our help and sympathy, and one had to call on all their reserve of tact in dealing with them.'[19]

The weight of these moments left an indelible mark. William Chapman confirmed the death of his wife, and mother to their four boys, Lilian. Beatrice Denning identified her husband Frederick Denning, a fitter at the Dockyard. She also identified her father-in-law, the tailor William Denning. Albert 'George' Peeke was granted compassionate leave from his unit in Kent after news of the incident reached him. Accompanied by his mother, Lucy, he entered the mortuary to identify his father and namesake. Though he could not look upon his father's face, the distinctive pattern of two crowns in Albert's hair left no doubt. Among Albert's possessions was a letter, written in his own hand, addressed to his son. George's

Albert George Peeke lived at 2 Victoria Buildings. [Maggie Pugh]

wedding, planned for just two months later, would take place without the presence of a father who had hoped to see his son settled and with whom he enjoyed a close friendship. Lucy attested to Albert's identity and claimed him for private burial.[20]

Phyllis Hakenjos was the younger sister of Elsie Rendle. The Rendle family lived at 39 Portland Square and had taken in Phyllis's young son Robert to live with them. Thus, in addition to identifying her sister, her brother-in-law George, and her 8-year-old nephew Anthony, Phyllis also claimed her son, Robert Hakenjos, aged 2. Wearing a brown coat, fawn jersey, and green trousers, Robert was one of the youngest victims of the tragedy.

For Reginald Hanlon, the bombing compounded a grief he already knew too well. Already widowed after his wife Primrose was killed by enemy action in London in 1940, he was now faced with identifying the bodies of his two teenage daughters, Vera, 19, and Kathleen, just 13. After Primrose's death, Reginald had moved his family to Plymouth, drawn by familial connections in Devon and Cornwall and by the hope that the city would be safer than the capital. The family lived at Tavistock Terrace, a short walk from Portland Square. The sisters had taken refuge together. Vera was among the first casualties to be discovered and delivered to the mortuary. Kathleen was found twelve hours later. In time, her scarf and handkerchiefs were returned to her father, heartbreaking tokens by which to remember her.[21]

In several cases, the victims were severely disfigured, complicating the identification process. Nine of the sixty-six records for Portland Square included a notation that the corpse was 'not to be seen'. Presumably, they were so badly disfigured that an effort was made to spare family and friends from further distress. Indeed, guidance described such cases as 'an ordeal which relatives should, if possible, be spared'.[22] The nine victims who received this designation were Henry Andrews, Margaret Blake, Frank Budge, Claude Chubb, Winifred Cundy, Samuel Farrant, Charles Horn, William Pickard, and the body that would later be identified as Phyllis Strong.

In these circumstances, officials were directed to dissuade relations from making a physical inspection and to instead establish identity through other means, such as their clothing or other items found on their person. The form for Frank Budge indicates that his brother confirmed his identity by inspecting his identity card. Margaret Blake was identified by a friend by the 'cloth of coat & button'. In William Pickard's case, his widow Edith confirmed the identity of her late husband by the receipts from radio rentals found among his personal effects.

The Nortons

Rita Boswell's account of her parents' experience at the mortuary illustrated the process of identifying the dead and retrieving their belongings. The tragic loss and finality of the experience left an enduring scar of sorrow.[23]

John and Violet Norton lived at 37 Portland Square. [Rita Boswell]

Rita's maternal grandparents John and Violet Norton were avid musicians who lived at 37 Portland Square. Violet played piano and occasionally provided accompaniment to silent films. John, who in 1941 was working as an Assistance Board investigation clerk, was a keen ham radio enthusiast and, for a time, operated a shop called Norton's in Torquay that sold Murphy radios. A friend, R. Clarke, identified John and another friend, D. Brown, identified Violet.

The Nortons' son-in-law Alec was serving in the RAF at the time and was recalled to Plymouth after the incident. He and his wife Lilian were living in Newark-on-Trent, a Nottinghamshire market town, hours from Plymouth. The couple made the lengthy journey to visit the mortuary and collect the Nortons' personal possessions. These included Violet's two rings and a gold wristlet watch as well as a watch, pocket diary, and personal papers found on John. The grief Lilian felt at the sudden loss of her parents was tremendous. She was close to her mother, and the horrific nature of what had happened triggered a lasting depression. Lilian was pregnant at the time, but soon after lost the baby. Throughout her life, Lilian went into mourning for several weeks every year on the anniversary of the incident.

A soldier's loss: the tragedy of the Davies family

Some stories from the mortuary were marked not just by death but by the void left in its wake: entire families killed in an instant. For the Davies family, the loss was absolute: six children and their mother were killed, leaving behind a single figure to carry their names and memory, the family patriarch Albert Davies.

Corporal Davies was stationed away from Plymouth with the Devon Regiment. His family lived on Victoria Street next to the Victoria Buildings. When the air-raid sirens went off, his wife Florence took refuge in the Portland Square shelter with their six children: Winifred, 14; Albert, 11; Patricia, 7; Iris, 5; Dennis, 2; and Kenneth, 3 months.

Davies received a telegram indicating 'bad news' at home.[24] Comrades took up a collection to fund his train ticket to Plymouth. When he arrived, he made his way to his sister's home in the Mount Gould district. En route, he stopped at Portland Square as he knew that his family would have taken refuge there. The massive crater confirmed what Davies suspected in his heart. When he arrived at his sister's home, she told him what he already knew: his entire family had been killed.[25]

Davies held out hope that his oldest son and namesake Albert, nearly 12, had survived the attack because the boy was averse to taking shelter in Portland Square and had spent other raids above ground. Neighbours shared, however, that they had seen the young Albert go into the shelter with his mother, siblings, and extended family. Another recalled that Mrs Davies had all six of her 'kiddos – three boys and three girls' with her.[26]

In this atmosphere of grief and despair, Davies, dressed in his uniform, made his way to the Halwell Street Mortuary to identify his family. His weathered face betrayed a mixture of exhaustion, disbelief, and a feeling of deep sorrow that must have penetrated his very being. Davies identified his wife and children. The oldest, Winifred, wore a brown coat and orange jumper. The baby, Kenneth, was swaddled in a blue and yellow frock. A City Corporation official who assisted with the identification of the victims at Halwell Street was assigned to facilitate Davies's unique case. The unnamed civil servant praised his demeanour in confronting this personal tragedy: 'Mr. Davies is one of the bravest chaps I have seen. He has been a hero in one of the most tragic cases we have had to handle.'[27]

A vignette about Davies is singularly accorded space in Pat Twyford's memoir about the war. The account conveys Davies's patriotic sense of duty even as he grappled with an unimaginable personal loss:

> One of the most heart-throbbing scenes was that which followed the raid when so many lives were lost in the Portland Square shelter. Among the victims were the wife and six children of a soldier. He was serving away from Plymouth, and was the sole survivor of the family. He came to Plymouth on special leave for the melancholy task of identifying his wife and children. In the mortuary he stood for a few minutes looking at his sleeping family. But only for a few minutes. There was no scene; just a grim tightening of the lips. He was a soldier. Suddenly he pulled himself upright, put on his cap, clicked his heels to

> attention- and saluted. Then he about-turned. 'Come on', he said to the attendant. 'I've got a job to do.' He went back to his regiment, and forthwith asked to be sent to the battle-front.[28]

Indeed, after laying his family to rest as a part of the communal burial service later in the week, Davies determined he could no longer reside in Plymouth, such was his grief.[29] He gave use of his home to his wife's relations because they had lost their own home during the raids.[30]

The identification of Phyllis Strong

Initially, Phyllis Strong, 15, was reported as missing. And yet her body lay near her deceased mother at the Halwell Street Mortuary. Tagged as Form C.W.D. 162, disc no. 333, Phyllis's body was unidentified—perhaps in part because it was in such a state that it was flagged with the designation 'not to be seen'.

On both the unidentified person's list and the subsequently completed Form C.W.D. itself, Phyllis was described as a 5-foot 3-inch female adolescent of a 'stout' build and 'fair' hair. Among the notations about personal effects, a blue jumper and blue slacks with a zip fastener are listed. So too is a note about a coloured stone ring worn on the left hand. The mortuary official who inventoried the effects catalogued it as a piece of costume jewellery with 'no value'.[31]

The process of clearing individuals off the unidentified persons list from the April raids was an administrative challenge. The situation was exacerbated by the catastrophic destruction of records connected to the 21 April raid victims when the library that housed the mortuary files caught alight during the 22 April attack. This was a devastating setback, and the situation worsened when additional bodies and remains from the Portland Square bombing began to be delivered to the mortuary.[32]

Unidentified bodies were buried as part of the communal burial at Efford on 28 April.

It was not until 27 May, a month after the burial, that Phyllis's brother identified his sister by her personal effects, repeating the same process their father George followed on 24 April when he identified Ivy, the family matriarch.

Phyllis's case was complex because it was atypical. It required confirming Phyllis's identity after interment and without the benefit of a physical inspection of the corpse. As such, this instance seemed to necessitate the involvement of a more senior official. With oversight of every aspect of Plymouth's civilian casualty management, Percy Cole fitted the bill. His signature is found on Phyllis's Form C.W.D.

After the dust settled: the discovery of Emma Reeve

Another unique case also necessitated Cole's oversight. This concerned the discovery of a corpse some three weeks after the raid.

Stanley Hollett and some friends were cutting up some of the felled trees in Portland Square. Stanley recalled that he threw his axe to the ground and that it 'bounced'. Curious, he investigated further. He 'crouched down and saw a piece of red cloth sticking out of the ground'. He pulled, but the cloth was lodged underneath the earth. 'As I uncovered more of the cloth,' he remembered, 'I tore at it and some came away exposing a white surface, and it took a little while for it to sink in that it was skin.'[33]

The teenage boy sprinted home and alerted his father to his morbid discovery. In his capacity as an ARP warden, Mr Albert Hollett rounded up a crew and immediately set to work to exhume the body.

Stanley theorised about how the body managed to be buried at some distance from the blast site and therefore was not recovered in the initial efforts on 23 April. 'What had happened was when the explosion took place, her body had been blown up from below ground in the shelter and had landed about 60 feet away on the ground after which all the shillet [shale] + earth that went skywards came down and buried her just deep enough so she wasn't found.'[34]

After the body was uncovered, a secondary search was made of the site for additional victims.

And so Emma Reeve's body was retrieved from the bomb crater on 10 May, a fortnight after the incident. With the extent of time that had elapsed since the incident, it was logical that a senior administrator such as Percy Cole would be involved in navigating the paperwork and processing.

Emma had been presumed dead but missing. The discovery of her body brought added closure to her family and spared them of going through the legal system to declare her as dead. She was identified by her daughter Eva Amelia Reeve of Keyham. Emma's effects included her wedding ring and another ring as well as a purple dress, a blue cardigan, and a blue-red checked scarf—the garment that Stanley had unearthed in the park. She was buried several days later.

In Stanley's recollections, he described Emma as 'Grandmother Pepper who had lived in Victoria Lane behind Portland Square'.[35] Emma was indeed related to the Pepper family and spent time at the family's Victoria Street home; however, Emma Reeve was Phyllis Pepper's widowed great-aunt rather than her grandmother. Phyllis's maternal grandmother, Mrs Lavinia Luxton, on the other hand, survived but lost several family members to the 23 April bombing: her granddaughter Phyllis Pepper, her daughter Lavinia Surgeoner, her son-in-law William Surgeoner, her granddaughter Eileen Surgeoner, and her sister-in-law Emma Reeve.

Declared dead: the case of Pauline Hempkins

Despite a thorough search of the bomb site, not every person who was presumed dead was found. How would the local authorities account for those individuals?

Edward and Pauline Hempkins were married just days before the April raids and had been visiting Pauline's parents in the vicinity of Portland Square on the night of 22/23 April. [Plymouth: The People's Blitz]

With the home front now a battle zone, the government made provisions in the regulatory code to process and resolve instances where there were no tangible remains. Under the Wartime Defence Regulations, the coroner was accorded the extraordinary ability to issue a death certificate without a corpse.

The *Western Morning News* reported on these new regulations on 25 March 1941, just days after the March raids. In ordinary times, a coroner would appeal to the High Court for permission to rule someone as dead in a situation when a body was not found or was not definitively identifiable. Given the extreme number of casualties and the critical situation in Plymouth, the Coroner's Office was granted the autonomy to adjudicate these cases itself. The powers were limited to situations in which there was 'reasonable cause to believe that a death has occurred in consequence of war operations'.[36]

To pursue this course, the body would need to have either not been found, found in a state beyond recognition, not been able to be recovered, or initially buried incorrectly as someone else. Once this claim had been made, the coroner would then publicise an inquiry and invite those with knowledge of the case to send information or attend the hearing. The coroner would hold a public inquest during which time they would review the relevant documents and testimony without a jury. At the end of this process, the coroner had the discretion to pronounce an individual as deceased and direct the registrar to issue a death certificate. This final step allowed processes such as wills, probate, and insurance claims to move forward.

The process to declare Pauline Hempkins as one of the casualties of Portland Square illustrates these administrative and legal steps in action.[37] Pauline, 19, and Ted Hempkins, 24, were married at the Plymouth Register Office on 14 April 1941. Ted took two weeks of shore leave for their wedding and the couple's honeymoon. They both took refuge in the Portland Square Air-Raid Shelter when the raid sirens signalled the incoming Nazi aerial attack as they were making their way home from Pauline's parents' home.

In the aftermath of the incident, Pauline's husband Ted's body was identified by Pauline's father. As Ted was on active service with the Royal Navy, documentation about his death did not fall under the same jurisdiction as that of civilians and is not catalogued with the civilian casualty paperwork from the evening. Pauline's body was not found nor were partial bodily remains able to be identified as hers. She was missing, yet the circumstances left little doubt that she had perished in the blast.

On 6 May, Town Clerk Colin Campbell sent a note to the Registrar of Births and Deaths detailing Pauline's death and initiating the process of issuing a death certificate under the provisions of the Defence Regulations: 'I hereby certify that there does not appear to be sufficient evidence to establish the identity of Pauline Madge Louvain Hempkins (who is understood to be missing) as being one of the persons buried by the Local Authority as "unidentified" as a result of an Air Raid on the 22nd April, 1941.'

With this documentation, the registrar, Walter Naylor, submitted a letter to William Edward John Major, a solicitor deputised to review such cases, to advance the inquiry process:

> Application was made to me by Mrs. E. Hoskins of 8, Amity Place, Plymouth, for the registration of the death of her daughter, Mrs. Pauline Madge Louvain Hempkins, who was presumed to have been killed in the Portland Square shelter during the air raid on the 22nd April, 1941, and whose body has not been recovered. In accordance with regulations, statements made by Mrs. Hoskins and the Town Clerk, were submitted to the Registrar-General. He has now written instructing me to refer the case to you with a view to an enquiry being held should you deem fit, as provided under Regulation 30A of the Defence Regulations, 1939. For your information, I enclose herewith the statements made by Mrs. Hoskins and the Town Clerk. I have today informed

> Mrs. Hoskins, at the Registrar-General's request, that the application has been referred to you.

A statement from Pauline's mother Ellen was submitted with the letter as a part of the application. Ellen's letter imagines Pauline and Ted's final moments and emphasises their bond as newlyweds, their marriage cut short through tragedy:

> I live at 8 Amity Place. Pauline Madge Louvain Hempkins was my daughter. This occurred on 22 April 1941. They [Pauline and husband Ted] left my home – she and her husband at about 9.20 or 9.30 pm to go to their home at West Hoe – no. 5 Pier Street. The raid started at about 9.35 or 9.40 pm. They would have been together at the time of the raid shortly afterwards. The body of Mr. Hempkins, the husband has been found in the Portland Square Air Raid Shelter. It was identified by my husband. This shelter had a direct hit on the night of 22 April.
>
> The Town Clerk can't identify the body of any other person found as my daughter. I have never seen her since. She would have communicated with me. They left a note saying 'Love from Pauley and Ted' on the mantle. They were only 9 days married. They wouldn't separate in a raid.
>
> I certify that my daughter Mrs. Pauline Madge Louvain Hempkins and her husband Mr. Edward Hempkins was on their way home after being at my house at 8 Amity Place, off Tavistock Road.
>
> And was caught in the air raid and ran to Portland Square shelter. Her husband has been found. Dead at the Shelter.

The inquest was held at the court at Greenbank in Plymouth to review the details on 23 May. At the conclusion, Major confirmed Pauline's death 'as a result of enemy action'. Pauline was added to the roll of the dead, now officially deemed a casualty of the direct hit on Portland Square.

***

In the wake of the tragedy and as the blitz continued to rain down on Plymouth throughout the rest of April, the Halwell Street Mortuary was a custodian of the lives lost and tallied the tragedy in its paperwork. Here, the routine of filling out forms offered a semblance of order amid chaos. Grieving family and friends navigated the painful process of identifying those whom they held dear, cementing the reality of the situation, and preparing to bid their final farewells.

19
Burial of the Dead

The morning of 23 April was a sunny yet cool spring morning. Peter Chapman made his way back into Plymouth with his cousin Nell and older brother Leslie. As they approached the drinking fountain on Tavistock Road, the trio was met by Mrs Eastlake, one of Nell's neighbours from Glanville Terrace. Mrs Eastlake was in tears and called out to Nell. She whispered into the teenager's ear. Nell remained calm and composed as she took in the news. Her face did not betray the heart-breaking reality that would forever change the lives of her cousins. Peter and Leslie's mother Lilian was among the dead at Portland Square.

The trio continued their walk back to Victoria Street through Portland Square, where they saw the scene of the devastation. The boys were taken to their relatives while the rest of the family decided what to do next.[1]

Mr Chapman's sister Florence sent an urgent telegram to their sister in Scotland: 'Regret Lil killed. Everybody else is safe.'[2]

The next day, Mr Chapman's sister Gladys, who had taken Leslie and Peter out of Plymouth, sent a letter with the names of another thirty friends and neighbours who perished alongside Lilian in the shelter:

> I am writing to tell you of the great loss we have suffered here. It is a miracle that my Nellie little Peter + Leslie + myself were not killed (I took them with me). My Jack made me go out of the town where we went before or else we would have been among them in Portland Square shelter a hit where we sat. So you can guess Nell how many are gone. Poor Win + her six children. You know about our Lil. She + Win would not go with me. Ivy is gone + they do not know about Phylis. Win's aunt Mabel + Uncle Bert. Mrs. And Mr. Farrant + Eric. Mr. Allen + Kenny. Mr. Harris Mrs. Harris + Jackeline. Mr. And Mrs. Sturgeoners [*sic*] and Eileen. Phyllis Pepper + Aunt Em. Mrs. Woodfin Mr. Woodfin. Little Kenny + Jimmy. You know Nell all those down our side who need to go.[3]

Gladys's daughter Nell added a postscript. 'Poor old Frank Budge + Mrs. Blake are gone. We could write a book of it.'[4]

For the Chapman family, the letter was a catalogue of familiar faces and daily relationships, all extinguished in a single night. In total, at least thirty-one victims were known directly to them, an almost incomprehensible share of the tragedy.

To shield Peter from the gravity of the situation, his family kept him away from the funeral and the private burial at Ford Park Cemetery. Eventually, they made arrangements for him to relocate to the Cornish countryside with their neighbour Beatrice Cook as he had done when he was recuperating from an illness some months earlier. Beatrice would be like a second mother to Peter and would ultimately raise the boy into adolescence.

Peter's story was not unique. Across Plymouth, grieving families were ushered into new routines while facing the heartbreaking task of burying their beloved dead. In the midst of the continued wail of air-raid sirens and the thunder of bombs, some found comfort in rituals of farewell.

Who decides? Civilian burial and the question of control

Far from a solely administrative task, the implementation of a burial policy for the civilian war dead became one of the most emotionally and socially charged issues on the British home front.

Private, family-led funerals remained the ideal. The government anticipated that this would be how most families would honour their dead. Yet *Circular 1779* also recognised these private arrangements might not always be possible. Young adults might be killed with no burial plans in place, or a single household might lose multiple members at once, an unbearable tragedy compounded by an insurmountable financial burden. Some form of burial would, however, be needed, and the local authority would have to step in.

The most urgent concern centred on how to manage burial after mass fatality events. Funeral staff, cemetery space, and coffins might all be in short supply in these situations. If dozens, or even hundreds, were killed in a single attack, individual arrangements, however much they might be desired, might prove logistically impossible.

To bring closure, the Ministry of Health strongly recommended that authorities consider publicly funded communal burials. These services offered a practical solution to the challenge of scale by conserving resources and capturing organisational efficiency. A shared ceremony could also serve a psychological function. One communal service could spare communities the exhaustion of repeated individual funerals, and the use of ritual on a grand scale might uplift the grieving.

The Ministry directed local authorities to develop plans for burial arrangements and submit proposals for review and feedback. Whitehall underwrote the implementation of approved plans that complied with government guidance.

Circular 1779 presented communal funerals as a dignified solution in extraordinary times, but the public's perceptions of this option were already tainted. Whitehall effectively undermined confidence in the communal option by associating publicly funded burials for civilian war dead with the Victorian Poor Law. In Plymouth, War Deaths Officer Percy Cole later observed that 'there seems to be an impression that a "Pauper's" funeral is indicated if you suggest that the burial be carried out by the Local Authority'. Fuelling these anxieties, the Ministry advised that public services should avoid 'any unnecessary display or expense.' Further discussions about possible cost-saving measures such as cremation, shrouds instead of coffins, and unmarked mass graves intensified hesitation about the public option.[5]

The real test of policy, however, lay not just in its drafting but in its delivery. How would officials translate national directives into action on the ground?

Plymouth meets the moment

In Plymouth, the implementation of burial policy reflected a careful negotiation between civic messaging and individual agency. Despite the scale of civilian fatalities in March and April, Plymouth, unlike some other blitzed cities, did not invoke the emergency powers to mandate public communal burials. Under wartime provisions, local authorities had the power to exercise total control over burial decisions. In cities such as Coventry and Hull, public funerals after the most intense raids were not a suggestion, they were the only option. Private funerals were suspended to ensure speed, efficiency, and public order.[6] Plymouth, by contrast, sought to preserve family choice. After the blitz, victims could either be collected for private burial at the family's sole expense or could be buried in a publicly funded, communal service.

Officials designed these communal funeral services as tableaux of national unity and sacrifice. In this regard, a public funeral served a dual purpose—honouring the dead and underscoring the state's narrative.[7] Yet for this symbolic work to succeed, it was not enough for the state to stage the message; the bereaved also had to recognise it as meaningful.[8] Efforts were made to convey it as such.

Pageantry and military trappings would evoke the honours typically reserved for fallen soldiers. Indeed, public services were promoted as 'no less honourable than the burial of a solider by his comrades on the battlefield'.[9] Authorities were even granted explicit permission to elevate funerary arrangements through employing the national flag: 'the use of the Union Jack as a pall at the funeral of any civilian whose death is due to enemy action is appropriate and would be a fitting tribute, and those responsible for the funeral arrangements are fully at liberty to use the flag in this manner as in the case of Service funerals'.[10] The expenditure of social capital through the presence of religious, military, and civic dignitaries would lend ceremonial gravitas and further underscore that the deceased were important and had died for King and country.[11]

In Plymouth, a blueprint of sorts was established after the March raids. That service had been detailed in the *Western Morning News* and was a point of reference about what April's public services, planned for 28 April, might look like. After the March raids, victims were interred in wooden coffins that were draped with the national flag. The service was a large-scale, ticketed event celebrated by the Bishop of Plymouth and attended by a host of civic officials, military brass, and interdenominational religious leaders. The burial site at Efford Cemetery was described as one of Plymouth's 'greatest memorials' to those who died in the blitz.[12]

As families came to the Halwell Street Mortuary to identify their deceased, local officials were expected to educate the bereaved about burial options.[13] The state would cover the cost of the communal option, but in doing so, the family would have to relinquish control over the arrangements. Staff were trained to reassure grieving families that these state-funded funerals would not be conducted on the cheap but would be 'decent and seemly' events that would honour the dignity of the deceased.[14]

While the city took deliberate steps to elevate public funerals and dispel the negative attitudes about the state's involvement, many families still chose to pursue private burial rites. Though coffins would be used, a promise of a future memorial was made, and the blueprint of the overall communal service from March was shared, the families of thirty-five victims from the Portland Square disaster would instead claim their relations for private burial. Indeed, there was such a large number of private funerals after the April raids—224 in total—that the mortuary became short-staffed because undertaker and cemetery resources had to be directed towards private services.[15]

It was not just about where a person was buried; it was about how they were remembered. In a wartime culture that encouraged unity over individuality, private burial was unmistakably countercultural. These services pushed back against the idea that mourning could or should be scripted by the state. Although communal services had tremendous power and dignity, private funerals gave families space to grieve in their own language, with prayers, familiar hymns, and stories only they could tell: a way to the celebrate the individual's life rather than, as the state service seemed to do, memorialise their death.

A number of factors impacted burial type including the age of the victim, economic status, and the scale of loss within a household. Working-class families, especially those who lost multiple members, were more likely to select, whether by choice or out of necessity, the publicly funded communal option. By contrast, middle-class families, such as those who lived on Portland Square and Portland Place, even if multiple members of the household were killed, were generally able to bury their dead privately.[16]

The final farewell: personal stories from private burials

In the days that followed the April raids, many families gathered quietly to bury their loved ones on their own terms.

Anthony Cornelius recalled the moment he realised the finality of his parents' passing after hearing the news from the Rev. Roger Welchman, vicar of St Matthias's Church.

> The full impact of what he was telling me didn't hit until we left the vicarage and went down into Portland Square. I remember seeing people working around where the entrance to the shelter had been. We went to my house to collect clothing etc. I distinctly remember going into the living room and seeing on a tray table the remains of two suppers – pasties. It was then that I knew that I would never see my mum and dad again.[17]

Seeking comfort, Anthony searched for his pet, the family cat. The poor creature was so traumatised by the noise and chaos of the bombings that it had gone into hiding. Anthony's efforts to coax the creature from its hiding space were met with fearful hisses and frantic dashes.

> I remember looking for my cat. He wasn't in the house but I eventually found him cowering in the outside toilet. Poor pet, he must have been in the garden and when the raid got close he must have got in through the toilet window because no one was home to let him in the house. Uncle Pat took him to a vet. to be destroyed.[18]

The weight of this decision was a crushing blow that compounded the grief Anthony was already grappling with. Indeed, throughout the rest of his life, the death of a pet would be an emotional trigger that stirred up memories of late April 1941. The loss of his parents had left a void, and now the loss of his cat, a symbol of familiarity and comfort, felt like another cruel twist of fate as Anthony readied himself for his parents' funeral.

Anthony recalled the preparations for the services. On the eve of the funeral, a local undertaker, Westlake, arranged for the wake to be held at 5 Maple Grove, the home of Lang's parents. 'The two coffins were placed in the front room,'[19] Anthony recalled. 'I was taken in to see them. They were plain wooden coffins with a bunch of flowers on each.'[20]

The next day, the Anglican funeral service was held at St Matthias's on North Hill. St Matthias's was a parish with deep significance to the Cornelius family as the centre of their sacramental life. Lang and Maggie had married there in 1923 and baptised their sons there. Lang had served the parish community in several leadership roles over time: a member of the Parochial Church Council, treasurer, people's warden, and ultimately the vicar's warden, the most senior lay leadership position. Now, the couple was brought once more before the altar, united in their love, even in death.

The Rev. Roger Welchman presided over the funeral service. That he celebrated at the funeral was just not a matter of protocol, but of friendship. Welchman had supported the family in the aftermath of the bombing, notably identifying the bodies at the Halwell Street Mortuary and delivering the grievous news to young Anthony that his parents had died.

The venue, religious ritual, and celebrant all contributed to grounding the Corneliuses' funeral in personal meaning.

Those in attendance included not only family but also a retinue of uniformed service personnel. The inclusion of these groups reflected traditional peacetime funeral honours that would have been accorded someone of Major Cornelius's rank and standing in the community. This ceremonial presence personalised the service through referencing his professional and military affiliations. 'I think there must have been a funeral party of the Post Office Home Guard and probably some of the Signal Corps,' Anthony remembered of the entourage. [21] Major Cornelius, a veteran of the First World War, had also served in the TA at the outbreak of the Second World War and, after being medically discharged, in a division of the Home Guard.

Anthony recalled the solemn moments at the end of the service as he stood in the doorway under the church's massive stone tower: 'I do remember following the two coffins down the nave of the church and standing on the steps waiting for the hearses to load.'[22] The funeral retinue then made its way to Ford Park Cemetery. The Hill family held a private plot located in the southeastern quadrant of the 34-acre cemetery. There, Lang's and Maggie's coffins would be interred with Maggie's father Percy and her paternal grandparents. An engraved headstone would mark their final resting place.

Anthony recalled making a small gesture of personal farewell to his parents. He closed his eyes, offering a prayer of remembrance. As the final words of the interment blessing were spoken, in a mixture of reverence and sorrow, Anthony released the flowers from his grasp. 'I also remember standing beside the open grave in Ford Park cemetery and tossing a bunch of primroses on the top coffin.'[23]

Anthony turned away from the gravesite, stepping back into the embrace of his relatives. With the continued threat of air raids and in light of the family tragedy, Anthony and his younger brother returned to his grandmother Emma's cottage outside the city. 'During the next few days, my brother and I stayed at Crapstone. I think Basil knew something was up, and eventually, I told him. I don't think he really understood for a long time. He was only 6 years old.'[24]

Later, Anthony and Basil's family worked out arrangements about who would care for the boys. Emma, their maternal grandmother, was made their guardian.

Ford Park Cemetery was also the setting for the funeral of the Corneliuses' neighbours: the Allison and Cundy families. The *Western Morning News* reported on the services held for patriarch John Allison, his daughter Winnie and her husband William Cundy, and the Cundy's daughter Betty May.

Like the Corneliuses' service, the Allison-Cundy committal included deeply personal elements. William Cundy had worked as a conductor for Plymouth Corporation's bus service. In tribute, twenty drivers and conductors from the depot acted as pallbearers and carried the coffins of their fallen colleague and his family. Floral tributes adorned the site. Tokens from John Allison's trade associations were interspersed among these remembrances, commemorating his professional work as a bootmaker and his leadership in various associated business organisations.[25]

In addition to Lilian Chapman, the Corneliuses, and the Allison and Cundy families, other victims buried at Ford Park included Eleanor Boynes, Frank Budge, Ann Bunker, Claude and Florence Chubb, Kathleen and Vera Hanlon, Emma and Ernest Harris, Sarah and Irene Ledden, Jane and John MacGregor, Susan and William Pearn, Albert Peeke, and the entire Woodfin family. Florence and Harry Andrews, Richard Coombe, William Denning, the William Harris family, and Hubert Wright were buried privately elsewhere.[26]

Collective remembrance: Plymouth's communal funeral

On 28 April, Plymouth conducted a communal burial service at Efford Cemetery for victims of the 21–24 April raids. Of the 148 buried, there were thirty-five victims from the Portland Square incident, including eighteen of the twenty-six victims who lived in the working-class housing on Victoria Street. Seventeen of those victims came from families that experienced more than one fatality, including one household, that of the Davieses, that lost seven members.[27]

Bishop of Exeter Charles Curzon was the principal celebrant at a service held in All Saints' Church on the eve of the burial. He used the opportunity to preach about human dignity and how the blitz's indiscriminate bombing and wanton destruction assaulted this tenet of Christianity. 'We speak of the value of the individual and the sacredness of personality, and we say these are the foundation of democracy. That is the issue between us and our enemy; he despises the common man who, to him, is a mere chattel to be blasted to death,' he declared.

Assuming his ordained role as shepherd of his flock and a representative of the entire diocese, the bishop expressed solidarity with the people of Plymouth: 'I trust my presence here may be taken as a symbol of the sympathy and remembrance of the whole diocese to those at this city now mourning the loss of many whom they loved, those who have lost their homes, and in particular those congregations who have lost what has been their spiritual homes from childhood.'

One of the communal burial services at Efford Cemetery. These ceremonies were intentionally imbued with pageantry including the use of the Union flag and the presence of civic, military, and religious dignitaries to elevate the service and communicate the state's message that the victims had died a hero's death. [*Plymouth Herald* and Chris Robinson, used with permission from Pat Twyford, *It Came To Our Door*, revised edition, 2005]

With humility, Curzon acknowledged the limitations of his prayers in expressing his sympathy or offering comfort; but he hoped the service, with its setting and the solidarity of others, would transcend and heal: 'Words are very poor things to convey what is in our hearts, the deepest things cannot be spoken. It is a law of life that the deepest things require some other kind of expression, and this service is ordained for that very purpose.'

Bishop Curzon enjoined the faithful not to lose hope. He remained steadfast in placing trust in both humanity's capacity for love and the transformative power of God: 'No one could doubt that God's intention for the race of man is that they should be a family of brothers. There is no loss that God cannot turn into gain.'[28]

The following day, hundreds of mourners gathered at Efford Cemetery to attend the committal service.[29] This read as a near carbon-copy of the March memorial service.[30] The *Western Evening Herald* complimented the thoughtful planning and execution by the municipal officials and religious leaders to commemorate the lives lost: 'There is no more tragic task than the organization of a communal funeral such as this, but the reverence and consideration which were shown by all concerned were striking indications of a city's deep sympathy with those who bear the heavy burden of sorrow.'[31]

Once more, the scene evoked a military service. The bodies were placed in wooden coffins. These and the vast burial trench were shrouded in the red, white, and blue bunting of the Union flag, signalling that the civilians who perished had indeed died a hero's death. The presence of representatives of the military services further underscored this message.

Grieving relations were joined by civic dignitaries. The attendance of political officials such as Lady Nancy Astor, Town Clerk Colin Campbell, and members of the Emergency Committee demonstrated support. Indeed, their presence signalled that the victims' deaths were a matter of public, not just private, concern.

The *Western Morning News* detailed the touching moments of relatives and friends offering prayers for the departed amid the floral tributes that adorned the gravesite: 'There were hundreds of wreaths, some expensive, others just humble posies. Some people put these posies to their lips before depositing them at the side of the grave.'[32] The *Western Evening Herald* also made note of 'beautifully-arranged wreaths and crosses' as well as 'humble posies of primroses and violets gathered from hedges.'[33] The variety of tributes reflected the diverse backgrounds of the victims and highlighted the reality that the blitz affected all of Plymouth. The *Western Evening Herald* commended the service's inclusivity: 'As the victims came from all classes and creeds of the community, it was fitting that the graveside service should be representative of all denominations.'[34] In addition to Bishop Curzon, other religious leaders present included the Bishop of Plymouth Francis Whitfield Daukes, the Roman Catholic Bishop of Plymouth John Barrett, and Rev. W.D. Campbell, President of the Free Church Council.

In his remarks, Bishop Curzon praised the courage of those who perished in the raids: 'They are of the same stuff as their fellow-citizens, who in these last few days have by their collective heroism written new pages in the glorious history of this city.'[35]

As he continued his eulogy, the bishop consecrated the deceased's place of final repose as holy ground, intoning words aimed to bolster the spirit of those assembled to mourn their deceased neighbours, family, and friends.

> There are many sacred spots in this city which are dedicated to the memory of great men whose names are known in English history, and to those sacred spots there has been added today this spot, no less sacred; indeed, perhaps more sacred, because it is dedicated to the memory of ordinary men and women. Known only by name to those who love them, but who, like the great ones, faced the danger and met death in the cause which England has always fought and will always fight until victory is won.[36]

The patriotic encouragement of the bishop must have resonated with Corporal Albert Davies who was burying his wife Florence and their six children. Davies's brother-in-law characterised Albert as a loving husband and father: 'He adored his wife and children.'[37] The *Western Morning News* took note of Davies's presence at the funeral and detailed how Lady Astor personally extended her condolences to him: 'As the mourners walked away Lady Astor moved alongside the corporal, and, holding his hand, walked some distance along the cemetery path with him, offering words of sympathy and comfort.'[38]

These scenes of public mourning made an impression. Plymouth's War Death Officer Percy Cole later intimated that bereaved citizens who witnessed a communal funeral such as this later wished that they had participated in the Plymouth-led services instead of private burials: 'I have known cases where people have undertaken a private burial and then, having later experienced a funeral undertaken by the Local Authority, expressed their regret that they did not allow their relatives to be buried by the Local Authority.'[39]

Plymouth faces the next storm

As families came together to inter the dead, rumours that the Luftwaffe campaign on Plymouth was still not complete cast a looming shadow on the horizon. Would Plymouth's Nazi nightmare ever end?

Indeed, as the sun set after the burials on 28 April, waves of Luftwaffe pathfinders and bombers once again departed the airfields of France to conduct further raids. Plymouth braced itself for another onslaught of incendiary and high-explosive bombs. Once again, the city experienced a *doppelgänger* raid. For two consecutive nights, the unrelenting storm of war rained down once more, this time battering the western wards of the city that abutted the naval facilities at HMNB *Devonport*.

At the end of the assault, the volunteer researchers of the Mass Observation project reported on the incomparably dire situation in the battered port city:

> The civil and domestic devastation in Plymouth exceeds anything we have seen elsewhere, both as regards concentration throughout the heart of the town, and as regards the random shattering of homes all over the town. The dislocation of every day life also exceeds anything we have seen elsewhere, and an enormous burden is being placed upon the determined spirits of the people.[40]

The courage of Plymouth's citizens in the face of this unrelenting attack drew the attention of the British Bulldog himself, Prime Minister Winston Churchill. He would come to see the damage with his own eyes, but also to stand with the people in their darkest hour, to acknowledge all they had lost, and to help steady them for the long road to recovery ahead.

20

A Day in the Life of Winston Churchill: 2 May 1941

Will he come?

The editors of the *Western Evening Herald* opined that the reason behind the continuous Luftwaffe attacks on Plymouth and elsewhere was to undermine Britain's confidence in its leaders. 'The German aim, in short, is to ensure that where indignation is inevitable it shall be directed not against the enemy but against the government of the country concerned.' In essence, Hitler hoped that the raids would force a change in leadership in Whitehall. A new government might do what the current one adamantly would not: surrender.

Political leadership in Britain was embodied in the nation's masterful orator, Prime Minister Winston Churchill. He famously asserted that Britain would never yield to Nazi aggression. The Germans knew, however, that it was the ordinary citizens who were bearing the brunt of the blitzkrieg. How much longer would those same individuals endure hardship?

On 27 April, people across Britain turned on their radios to listen to Churchill. The prime minister provided a briefing on the war and made a direct appeal to the United States for assistance. In Plymouth, those taking shelter in rest centres homed in on Churchill's words about the impact of the Luftwaffe bombing raids:

> I thought it would be a good thing to go and see for myself what this 'uneasiness' amounted to, and I went to some of our great cities and seaports which have been most heavily bombed, and to some of the places where the poorest people have got it worst.
>
> I have come back not only reassured, but refreshed. To leave the offices in Whitehall with their ceaseless hum of activity and stress, and to go out to the front, by which I mean the streets and wharves of London, or Liverpool, Manchester, Cardiff, Swansea or Bristol, is like going out of a hot house on to the bridge of a fighting ship. It is a tonic which I should recommend any who are suffering from fretfulness to take in strong doses when they have need of it.

Churchill concluded his address with a rousing invocation of hope. The *Evening Herald* reported that listeners were inspired by Churchill's words, particularly by the poetic ending of his speech. Indeed, one listener expressed: 'The speech was very touching at the end. It made you feel things would be alright after all.'[1]

But what of Plymouth? Churchill had, of course, visited Plymouth to be a part of the celebrated return of *Exeter* earlier in the war.[2] But now, there seemed little indication that Plymouth was on his radar—six other blitzed cities were named in his speech—or on anyone else's. In the wake of such stirring oratory, some began to question if the prime minister himself should now appear in their bomb-shattered city: if he might turn those words of hope into visible solidarity and seek a 'strong dose' of the 'tonic' that Plymouth offered. After all, visiting a disaster zone such as war-ravaged Plymouth was well within the expected scope of his duties.

The omission seemed part of a broader pattern. While London and Coventry were regularly cited in national speeches and press coverage—London as the capital under siege, Coventry as a symbol of civilian sacrifice—other cities such as Plymouth were left unnamed, their destruction obscured by wartime censorship and a tightly controlled media narrative. National reporting was often intentionally vague about the location and severity of the attacks. The details of Plymouth's blitz experience—not just the attack, but the aftermath—were largely confined to the local press. The relative absence of national attention about the situation in Plymouth frustrated residents.

In the immediacy of the blitz, Lady Astor criticised the skewed reporting and directed her ire towards the national government. She lambasted the Ministry of Information as the 'Ministry of Inflammation', contending that the limited details in official broadcasts 'inflamed and drove people mad'.[3] While additional disclosures could have combated rumours and misinformation, wartime reporting needed to balance important security considerations. The role of the censor was to limit Germany's intelligence about the impact of the raids; however, the information embargo meant that the British public was also in the dark.

An opinion piece that ran in the *Western Morning News* on 1 May 1941 commended Lady Astor for her efforts to shed light on the plight of Plymouth—and elsewhere—in Parliament and her righteous dismay about the scant coverage in the press.

> Not only her own constituents but the inhabitants of every severely bombed town will endorse Lady Astor's spirited protest against the way in which news of their experiences is officially disseminated. People who have had death and destruction rained upon them from the sky, who have to mourn the loss of relatives and friends, and whose life work is laid in ruins may be forgiven for feeling they are trifled with when some mincing announcement dismisses

> the whole thing in a sentence or two and leaves the impression that nothing important happened.
>
> Suppressing the truth is something worse than actual lying. It will be felt to be so in these cases. For besides doing less than justice to the thousands of men and women who suffer and endure it without complaint, it entirely fails of its purpose. It certainly does not deceive the enemy. The Germans know well enough the main effects of their 'frightfulness' excursions, for there are the fires and ruins to tell them. Moreover, in the suggestion that little damage has been done there is an invitation to the Luftwaffe to come over and finish its evil work.
>
> We sincerely hope Lady Astor will raise the question in the House of Commons. She should there be assured of the support of Mr. Churchill, who by example and precept shows his trust in the people. She should also be able to call to her side another Minister in the person of Mr. Alexander, who from actual observation knows what Plymouth is like and on the occasion of his visit bore the testimony to the courage and fortitude of Dockyard workers who after a night of bombing in their homes were found at their benches in the morning. Men who do this do not seek praise, but they have a right to be honestly and sympathetically dealt with.[4]

With opinion pieces like this now swirling following the blitz on 28–30 April, there was speculation as to whether Churchill might now visit Plymouth as he had visited other affected locales. A visit would be an astute public relations move. His presence would convey an alternative narrative that could remedy those feelings of alienation and abandonment—and quiet the formidable Lady Astor.

The press pursued this lead but were met with evasive replies. City and regional officials alike seemed tight-lipped when it came to disclosing information, perhaps taking to heart the critique about how they shared too much information about the royal visit in March. The police declined to comment on the rumours, while officials at the Ministry of Information were, ironically, uninformed. The local deputy claimed to 'know nothing about the visit at all'.[5] This lack of clear information 'infuriated' journalists.[6]

Lady Astor scored points with those frustrated members of the press at a private meeting she held on the evening of 1 May. Speaking to a press pool of eleven journalists, she laid speculation and rumours to rest by providing confirmation that Plymouth was indeed on Churchill's calendar. In fact, the prime minister would arrive in Plymouth the very next morning.[7]

Churchill arrives

In London, Churchill departed the war rooms of Whitehall and boarded his train for Plymouth. The overnight journey was filled with activity. En route, the prime

Winston Churchill surveys the damage from the blitz in Plymouth, 2 May 1941. [*Plymouth Herald* and Chris Robinson, used with permission from Pat Twyford, *It Came To Our Door*, revised edition, 2005]

minister reviewed the assignment of various officials connected with aircraft production. Britain needed to close the gap between the crews available to fly planes and the shortage of aircraft available for them to carry out those missions. He also discussed war strategy and the perilous situation in the Atlantic with German submarines threatening vital convoys of supplies.[8]

Churchill arrived in Plymouth mid-morning on 2 May. Since Lord Mayor Waldorf Astor was again ill and recuperating out of town, it was the responsibility of his wife, Lady Astor, to welcome Churchill and serve as the official host for his visit. Wearing a tailored navy suit and matching hat with a tip-tilted brim and bedecked with a double row of pearls, Astor was prepared to use the visit to assert the needs of her Plymouth Sutton constituents—and to make sure that they knew she was doing so.[9] She waited on the platform of Plymouth's railway station with another American-born politician, Beatrice Rathbone, MP for Bodmin. At 9.30, the train arrived, and Churchill emerged to begin his visit.

Churchill wore one of his iconic wartime looks: the Trinity House Uniform. This ensemble consisted of a navy blue double-breasted coat and a coordinating hat. It was important for him to see Plymouth—and for residents to see him, hence his decision to don a familiar costume. The *Western Morning News* alluded to this in describing Churchill's progress through the city: 'there was quick recognition of the familiar figure standing up in the car, with his peaked cap at a jaunty angle, his tightly-buttoned reefer coat, and the inevitable cigar'.[10] He dispensed with his trademark cigar for the official photograph that ran in the *Western Morning News* on 5 May. Indeed, the caption specifically pointed out that Churchill could be seen 'wearing his famous Trinity House cap, but minus his cigar'.[11] As HMNB *Devonport* was part of the morning's programme, Churchill's attire also signalled his commitment to the naval forces and his solidarity with the men.

The entourage for the visit included Mrs Churchill and American president Franklin D. Roosevelt's personal envoy W. Averell Harriman.[12] Harriman had helped to coordinate the Lend-Lease programme which provided food, fuel, and military ordnance. Harriman's visits to devastated cities such as Plymouth provided him with unfiltered insights about how the British bore the brunt of the Nazi attacks, a perspective that he would consequently relay to Washington.

To Lady Astor's surprise, that morning she learned that Mrs Churchill was not just in town but would also accompany the prime minister in all his official engagements. He dismissed Lady Astor's claim that the logistics of the day could not be amended at the last minute and walked off in a huff. After a brief exchange, she acquiesced to the prime minister's firm stance, and Mrs Churchill, it was decided, would join in throughout the visit.[13]

Winston Churchill at Elliot Terrace, 2 May 1941. Mrs Churchill is seen wearing the 'This is London Wall' scarf from Jacqmar of London. [*Plymouth Herald* and Chris Robinson, used with permission from Pat Twyford, *It Came To Our Door*, revised edition, 2005]

Mrs Churchill unquestionably stole some of the spotlight from Lady Astor with her metropolitan ensemble. The *Western Morning News* detailed her tailored brown dress and full-length snow leopard fur coat. But what gave her attire a distinct look was the scarf draped in turban style on her head. This particular piece was the 'London Wall' print from the Mayfair fashion house Jacqmar of London. Mrs Churchill described her colourful accessory to a reporter: 'They call them London Wall scarves. They are embroidered with quotations, among them some of which my husband has made.'[14] It depicted a brick wall covered with posters. A turquoise poster read 'careless talk costs lives' while an orange one quoted the prime minister himself: 'we shall not flag or fail, we shall go on to the end'. With additional phrases such as 'Go to it' and 'Save for victory' emblazoned on her head, she expressed encouragement to the British people.[15] Mrs Churchill's use of clothing, like her husband's uniform, was a form of political language. Even fashion could be a canvas for encouraging morale.

A military morning at HMNB *Devonport*

Like the royal visit a month earlier, Churchill's visit began in the dockyards of HMNB *Devonport*. After a welcome at Admiralty House, the prime minister began his inspection of servicemen and naval facilities. British Movietone footage of the day captured Churchill walking through the complex with a pipe in his mouth and a cane in his hand.[16] Plymouth's newly minted Commander-in-Chief, Admiral of the Fleet Sir Charles Forbes, and First Sea Lord, Admiral of the Fleet Sir Dudley Pound, were among the naval brass who followed in his wake.[17] Progressing along the quays and through the workshops, Churchill was able to inspect warships and maximise his visibility among the sailors and civilian workers critical to the war effort.[18]

Churchill passed the ruins of Boscawen Block, part of the HMS *Drake* barracks and training centre for cadets. In April, it took a direct hit that resulted in the death of nearly 100. Only seventy-eight bodies were recovered; another eighteen were presumed to have been incinerated in the resulting inferno. The destruction from the Nazi raids was so widespread that the naval gymnasium was the only available place to house the large number of injured and deceased servicemen. A curtain divided the hall, with the wounded on one side and, on the other, the bodies retrieved from the barracks. Those recovering in their beds could hear the sound of coffins being hammered shut just a few feet away.[19] After this sobering stop, Churchill proceeded to his lunch engagement with Devonport brass.

The itinerary then included a sacrosanct feature of the Prime Minister's daily routine: his afternoon nap.[20] Non-negotiable throughout the war, Churchill's nap was critical to his stamina and focus. Following this brief respite at Admiralty House, Churchill began the next phase of his visit: a brief tour of Plymouth, slated to start at 3.40 p.m.

Surveying the damage

Over the course of the day, news that Churchill was in the city spread. The *Western Morning News* reported that the prime minister had been at the naval base for 'many hours' before the general public caught on to his presence.[21]

While the public was undoubtedly satisfied that Churchill had come to Plymouth, the mid-afternoon timing for his tour of the city proper meant that smaller crowds were on hand to welcome him. Many citizens had become accustomed to seeking refuge outside the city every evening. With many homes destroyed or rendered uninhabitable from the raids, even more people were joining the nightly exodus to the outskirts. As a result, when Churchill finally began his tour at 4 p.m., nearly half an hour behind schedule, the streets were not as populated as they might otherwise have been.[22] Indeed, a police car was to travel at the head of the motorcade to announce the prime minister's arrival with the goal of encouraging those who remained in the city to line the streets.[23]

The chroniclers from Mass Observation estimated that only a fraction of Plymouth's citizens were able to see Churchill during his visit: 'On a necessarily rough but careful estimate, we suggest that about 500 people saw him closely enough to feel in personal contact, that another 1,500 saw him clearly passing, and that another 2,000 glimpsed him as he passed, often not taking in who it was until after he had passed.'[24] The newsreel documenting the visit, however, painted a different picture. The film depicted streets packed with citizens, the crowd one or two deep as Churchill's car drove through Plymouth. Through the artful use of selective camera angles and editing, this created an illusion of a larger turnout. The voiceover triumphantly reported that 'in the midst of it all, the cry goes up, "Here comes Winston." Accompanied by Mrs. Churchill, the Prime Minister and his wife come to be with the indomitable people of Devon.'[25] This was a masterful propaganda manoeuvre: utilising the media to produce the desired narrative.

Nevertheless, those who had the opportunity to see Churchill were grateful for his presence. It had been a great honour for Plymouth to host King George VI and Queen Elizabeth in March. The prime minister's visit was likewise significant: it was an acknowledgement that carnage inflicted upon the city in March and April had been seen by the nation's leaders.

Churchill's tour was 'extensive and rapid'.[26] The 10-mile route took his entourage through the battered Barbican, the ruined commercial core, and bombed-out residential neighbourhoods. The Plymouth he surveyed was a smouldering shell of the vibrant place the Windsors had visited several weeks earlier. Lady Astor accompanied him to provide perspective and continue to advocate for her constituency. The journey thus provided Churchill with first-hand knowledge of the extent of the raids and how the people of Plymouth were coping.

Among the casualties of the recent raids, the communal air-raid shelter at Portland Square would have been a likely topic of conversation given the sheer number of casualties. Minnie Weeks, the Astors' Plymouth-based cook and housekeeper, had lived at 38 Portland Square and would have known many of the victims. Lady Astor herself had comforted the bereaved Albert Davies on the loss of his wife and six children at the communal burial at Efford Cemetery shortly before Churchill's visit.[27] Might this have been one of the vignettes she shared?

The prime minister's Daimler limousine continued to drive through the devastated streets. The roads were lined with broken glass and debris. Buildings lay in ruins. They passed homes that were now nothing more than steps leading up to piles of bricks and charred wood. 'In street after street he found houses uninhabitable,' reported the *Western Morning News*. 'And in others he saw little knots of people still endeavouring to salvage possessions in their battered homes.'[28] 'Deeply moved by the scene of wanton destruction he saw, the prime minister was frequently heard to express his horror. He told a *Western Morning News* reporter before he left the city: "I think it is absolutely marvellous the way Plymouth has taken it; indeed, it is thrilling."'[29] Churchill's reaction and comments echo his 27 April speech about the unconquerable spirit of the British people and the 'tonic' that such encounters provided.

Over the course of his one-hour drive, Churchill's entourage only stopped on two occasions. He did not leave his car to walk among the people as he did during similar visits to London's East End and elsewhere.[30] Instead, people approached him to share their stories and express their gratitude for his presence: 'At one point the crowd was so great right across the street at a point where homes were wrecked that Mr. Churchill's car had to come to a standstill. Many pressed around the car to shake the Premier by the hand.'[31]

Churchill's presence fortified the people's patriotic spirit. 'Above the cheers there came a voice: "We are British, and we can take it," to which the Prime Minister replied: "Yes, thank God."'[32] The people's brave-faced outlook masked their anger and grief. Mass Observation researchers ascribed this attitude to the city's naval heritage: 'Strong local pride and a tradition of toughness connected with the sea, makes people determined to show that they can take it just as well and better than anywhere else.'[33]

As the tour continued, Churchill witnessed the ongoing recovery efforts. Some residents were clearing debris; others were providing aid to those in need. Indeed, it was this 'carry on' mentality that would ultimately allow life to adapt to the new normal and continue in the face of such devastation. 'Mr. Churchill had a ready greeting for the men of the Services, especially the working parties engaged in clearing the debris and removing dangerous buildings,' detailed the *Western Morning News*.[34] 'These men gave him a grand welcome, waving their steel hats, picks, and shovels, while here and there amid the ruins they had brightened things by hoisting Union Flags.'[35]

Crews of municipal workers and servicemen could be found throughout Plymouth. These demolition teams featured prominently in the *Pathé* newsreel documenting the tour.[36] At the time of Churchill's visit, crews were prioritising crucial public safety tasks such as clearing streets and razing unstable buildings in the heart of Plymouth. A crowd of about 120 workers greeted him outside the remains of the Guildhall:

> At the Guildhall he saw a begrimed naval working party, who stopped the task of clearing the debris for a few moments and surged around his car. His familiar cry of 'Are we downhearted?' was answered by an echoing shout of 'No,' followed by three lusty cheers, led by a stoker. When someone shouted 'What about Berlin?' Mr. Churchill replied: 'We are giving it them more every day.'

At one point, the motorcade approached Old Town Street close to the gutted remains of St Andrew's Church. It was at this location, in the aftermath of the March attack, where Margaret Smith had nailed a wooden sign bearing the defiant message *Resurgam* above the charred door. As the prime minister's car slowed, a young girl emerged from a florist's shop and presented a red carnation to Mrs Churchill, which she pinned to her ensemble.

A reporter for Mass Observation summarised the sentiments of the crowd:

> It was impossible even for the most objective observer not to be deeply moved by the sight of this great man, fierce faced, firmly balanced on the back of the car, with great tears of angry sorrow in his eyes. He was so visibly moved by the suffering that he saw, yet so visibly determined to see that it spelt not defeat but victory. A man overflowing with human sympathy, an epic figure riding through this epic of destruction.[37]

After the journey through Plymouth, Lady Astor hosted a tea at 3 Elliot Terrace. This too had been damaged in the raids, resulting in the household, like so many of Plymouth's residents, departing the city in the evenings.[38] A number of city officials were on hand for the reception. They included Town Clerk Colin Campbell, City Engineer James Paton Watson, and Chief Constable George Sydney Lowe. Also in attendance were aldermen and past mayors Lovell Dunstan, James Churchward, and Solomon Stephens who continued to contribute their administrative experience as members of Plymouth's Emergency Committee.

Journalists were also present for this gathering. Pat Twyford of the *Western Morning News* reflected on his personal encounter with Churchill:

> As I write I recall the words which the Prime Minister himself said to me when I was introduced to him at Lord Astor's residence on the occasion of his visit to Plymouth after the particularly heavy raids in 1941. I asked him for a message

Winston Churchill at Plymouth, 2 May 1941 [*Plymouth Herald* and Chris Robinson, used with permission from Pat Twyford, *It Came To Our Door*, revised edition, 2005]

> of encouragement to the citizens. 'What can I say?' he asked, adding, 'Your homes are low, but your heads are high.'[39]

These words were soon recrafted as the soundbite headline for the *Western Morning News* chronicle of the visit, 'Their houses are low, but their hearts are high.'[40]

An impactful visit

After tea, Churchill and his party departed in the same manner they arrived, by train. There were queues of citizens gathered at the station making their way out of Plymouth for the evening. When the prime minister arrived, the people erupted in enthusiastic applause. Churchill boarded his special carriage and was reported to pick up a copy of the *Western Evening Herald*, put on his spectacles, and settle into a chair to read the paper.[41]

The conductor whistled on the platform, and as the train rolled out of the station, the crowd again cheered for the prime minister. A spectator said to a journalist covering the day's events, 'I hope you have got a good photo of that great guy.'[42] A portrait of Churchill duly ran in the *Western Morning News* on 5 May.[43]

The prime minister's visit to Plymouth seemed to have the intended effect of keeping citizens' sentiments of frustration or abandonment at bay. As one observer reflected, 'For Mr. Churchill to make the long journey was as unexpected as it was appreciated. His cheery smile, his affable manner, and his air of confident optimism were infectious, and many a puckered brow was cleared when he had passed.'[44] The visit provided a balm, however temporary, to a community devastated by the brutality of aerial warfare.

Churchill was deeply affected by both the ruined buildings and the resolute spirit of the people. On several instances, he was moved to tears. Lady Astor, known for her quips, especially those directed towards Churchill, provoked him to take action: '"It's all very well to cry, Winston," said Lady Astor tartly. "You've got to do something."'[45]

Yet the very act of Churchill travelling to Plymouth to assess the damage himself was doing something. Indeed, he was profoundly impacted by his visit. As Jock Colville, his assistant private secretary, noted in his diary upon returning to the prime minister's weekend retreat at Chequers, 'It is largely Plymouth that has caused him such melancholy; he keeps repeating, "I've never seen the like."'[46]

Churchill's visit underscored an important message vital to morale and the recovery process: Plymouth was neither alone nor forgotten. The *Western Morning News* praised the prime minister's hands-on approach: 'Mr. Churchill's visit to Plymouth was characteristic of his desire to see things for himself.'[47]

As with the royal visit in March, the people needed to experience Churchill bearing witness to their reality. In the estimation of the Mass Observation researchers, Churchill's visit achieved this:

> They are in need of stimulation, direction, revitalisation, local and national leadership. That is why they are encouraged and moved by the sight of a Prime Minister, to whom they confidently look for help and sustenance. Part of their pleasure at seeing him is pleasure at some sign, any sign, that the whole thing is real, that it is being dealt with, and dealt with by an aggressive character.[48]

It could no longer be said that those in power did not know of the harsh reality that the people of Plymouth faced.

In the editorial section of the *Western Evening Herald*, one resident positively opined that Churchill's visit was not made out of political necessity or performative obligation but rather, like the King and Queen in March, from a genuine care for the people and a desire to stand with them: 'That the Prime Minister, amid all the cares of State and the tremendous demands upon his time and energy should pay Plymouth a visit was a courtesy and tribute which heartened the city.'[49]

Just as Churchill achieved through his rousing speeches and inspirational writings, the prime minister's visit kindled hope. Onlookers described him as 'like a lighthouse', a beacon amid some of the darkest days of the war.[50] Mass Observation concluded that the citizens of Plymouth were ultimately encouraged by Churchill's visit: 'they feel that as a result of his visit something more will be done to deal with the local and national problems which are deeply felt, though not resented, by those who have been blitzed'.[51] After experiencing the hell of war, relief, if not salvation, was coming.

Plymouth Police Constable Lowe echoed the prime minister's own word, 'tonic', in his fortnightly report to Whitehall about the situation in Plymouth: 'Although seen only by a comparatively small number of people, his visit provided a tonic to the suffering community.'[52]

Mass Observation evaluated the transformative impact of Churchill's visit. 'For those who really got a see and sniff of him, the experience was profoundly moving and stimulating. He brought a breathe of real aggression and initiative into an atmosphere of negative devastation.'[53]

Writing after the war, Twyford reached a similar conclusion: 'His presence had an enormous effect on the morale of the people, and the way in which they everywhere flocked around and greeted him, and his response with characteristic mannerisms and gestures, were all features which helped to rekindle the flame of hope and grim resolution in the hearts of the citizens.'[54]

The end of the blitz in Plymouth

On the heels of Churchill's visit, Mass Observation outlined the new reality that Plymouth and, indeed, all of England would face if the Nazi offence continued to rain down:

> The Plymouth situation is, from a long term point of view, the most serious yet. It opens up a new vista of civilian war. It possibly indicates a new policy for enemy air attacks; the incessant blitzing of a town for nights on end, then a lull of weeks, then another series. As we have pointed out in earlier reports, this is much the hardest type of attack to get used to. Many people appear to find it impossible to condition themselves to this rhythm. And in any town of much under a million inhabitants, it is very doubtful if people can condition themselves to more than three nights of intensive attack in a week. That is to say, people cannot condition themselves if it is left to themselves to do the conditioning as it is now. If they are left passive, relatively defenceless, and without any alternative outlets from the emotions and repressions which inevitably follow upon nights of random death and a destruction which is far more amazing and terrible to the ordinary people who have lived all their lives in the

> town and perhaps in the same street – that they have no answer to their local disaster. They are not defeatist – far from it. But they are defeated. Their town has suffered a major military defeat; and they, the untrained and undisciplined soldiers of the Home Front, can (at present) do nothing much about it.[55]

The government would need to provide not just care but also direction and education. As part of a 'psychological rescue party', officials would need to help ordinary citizens to reframe their personal tragedy from a purely local incident to seeing their loss within the context of the larger war.[56] The people of Plymouth may have suffered defeat and borne a terrible price for the kingdom, but victory itself was still possible.

The Luftwaffe launched sixteen additional attacks on Plymouth between 3 May 1941 and 30 April 1944. Half of those were conducted in May 1941; however, these were significantly smaller sorties with most of them dropping fewer than ten bombs rather than the massive payloads of thousands of incendiary devices and bombs that rained down throughout the blitz in March and April.

As the war dragged on, other German military priorities forced the Luftwaffe High Command to deploy its aerial fleet towards other strategic objectives, thereby reducing the frequency and intensity of the air raids across all of England. The Allied liberation of the airfields in France in 1944 and the eventual march towards Berlin further reduced the threat of aerial attack.

Plymouth and her people were resilient. As Churchill witnessed during his visit, the beleaguered city would not surrender in the fight for its survival. The resilience of Plymouth's people would eventually empower the port city to rise from the ashes of destruction to forge a new path forward to the future—and to remember.

21

'An episode that should not be forgotten'

On a busy weekday morning in 2026, students and faculty hurry across the University of Plymouth campus.[1] Many pass by a 10-foot stone sculpture of a parent lifting a child skyward. Some pause briefly, perhaps noting how the sunlight plays across the Portland stone or catching their own reflection in the curved stainless-steel panel behind the figures. Perhaps few realise they are walking near the site of Plymouth's single greatest civilian tragedy of the Second World War.

The university buildings that now dominate the landscape bear little resemblance to the uniform rows of homes that once bordered the leafy-green oasis of Portland Square. This transformation was part of Plymouth's post-war journey: from devastation to renewal, from a site of tragedy to place of future promise. Yet, amid this rebirth and growth, the imperative to remember has persisted.

Rising from the ashes: Portland Square in Plymouth's post-war reconstruction

The physical toll of the blitz on Plymouth was staggering. The Luftwaffe's bombing campaign left the city centre in ruins: two main shopping centres, the Guildhall and administrative complex, a theatre, six hotels, and eight cinemas were among the structures reduced to rubble. The destruction reached deep into every aspect of city life: twenty-six schools lay in ruins, forty-one churches bore the scars of bombing, and nearly 2,000 public houses were destroyed by bombs or fire. Perhaps most devastating was the impact on housing: 3,754 homes were deemed unsalvageable and another 18,389 required major repairs.

As the smoke rose from Plymouth's ruins, the seeds of rebirth were being planted. Not even ten days after the devastating March blitz, city engineer James Patton Watson was already imagining ambitious plans to rebuild and replan the city. Like the mythical phoenix rising from its ashes, Plymouth, Watson envisioned, would emerge from the trials of war and be reborn to rival some of the grand cities of Europe.[2]

This early vision of straighter roads to replace congested medieval lanes in the Barbican and new amenities for Plymouth's citizens would soon evolve into something far more expansive. The unprecedented obliteration from the blitz created an equally unprecedented opportunity for framing the future of the city. Civic leaders pursued a path not to simply rebuild what was lost but to fundamentally reimagine and boldly realise a new Plymouth.

In 1943, Watson joined forces with renowned architect and urban planner Patrick Abercrombie to develop *A Plan for Plymouth*. Crafted under their joint guidance, this plan approached the city as a blank canvas for putting modern urban planning into practice. Their innovative design would entail not just the 'plotting of the streets' but thinking strategically about housing, commerce, industry, and the needs and social patterns of the city's citizens.[3]

Officially presented to Plymouth City Council on 25 April 1944, *A Plan* was comprehensive in its scope and ambition. It proposed an almost complete removal of what remained of the decimated city centre. In its place would rise a grand north–south axis, originally called Phoenix Way, later renamed Armada Way, intersected by a grid of streets that delineated distinct commercial, business, and civic precincts. A major east–west thoroughfare, Royal Parade, would separate the civic and commercial areas.

Within this framework, there were specific plans for the future of Portland Square. Given that 'the buildings, especially around Portland Square, have suffered to a considerable extent by enemy action; most of what is left is of a considerable age, being at least from 75 to 100 years old', the planners saw an opportunity to redevelop the site into an educational quarter.[4]

Plymouth Corporation's expanding property portfolio, which already included properties on the Square, coupled with the large number of buildings slated for demolition, created favourable conditions for rapid implementation. To ensure that the vision became reality, *A Plan* proposed that any rebuilding in the district be strictly limited to educational and cultural institutions.[5] Portland Square's original design as a residential area would be phased out. This new vision would prove transformative, launching decades of academic expansion that would reshape the character of what had once been one of Plymouth's most desirable neighbourhoods.

The post-war plan for Portland Square as an educational hub would be realised through the gradual evolution of what would become the University of Plymouth. Plymouth's Technical College had established its presence adjacent to the Square before the war. The institution evolved into Plymouth College of Technology in 1962, and its academic ambitions were further recognised with the granting of polytechnic status in 1970. As the institution grew, it gradually acquired and repurposed buildings around Portland Square to accommodate its expanding needs for facilities. The 1980s saw further growth as several smaller institutions, notably Rolle College of Education in Exmouth, Exeter College of Art and Design, and Seale-Hayne

Agricultural College, came under the umbrella. The conglomeration was renamed Polytechnic Southwest in 1989. The government granted the institution university status in 1992. The newly christened University of Plymouth then initiated an ambitious programme of centralisation and capital improvements in Plymouth proper, at last manifesting Watson's post-war zoning plans for Portland Square from half a century earlier.

This transformation profoundly reshaped the physical landscape of Portland Square. The Victorian homes that had survived the war gave way to modern academic facilities. The last of the original structures were demolished in the early 2000s. An ambitious capital project launched in 2001 resulted in the construction of state-of-the-art medical, science, and technology facilities. Today, the campus boasts over twenty academic buildings as well as student housing and facilities integral to the support of students. Portland Square lives on only in name, lending its identity to the Portland Square Building, a modern hub for teaching and learning across multiple disciplines.

While the neighbourhood's physical transformation reflected Plymouth's post-war aspirations for the future, the wartime tragedy of the devastating loss of civilian life in Portland Square's air-raid shelter demanded recognition and, in time, for the episode to be reclaimed as part of the city's history and the university's heritage.

The first step: a quest for recognition

When Arthur Davis retired and moved back to Plymouth in 1979, he found a city transformed—and one where the tragedy he had witnessed and survived as a 10-year-old boy had been largely forgotten. On the night of 22–23 April, Arthur, his sister, and their mother ran from Victoria Street to the Portland Square shelter: 'I thought it was the safest place in England – a monument of strength,' he recalled. Arthur's section escaped the ferocity of the bomb blast that took the lives of so many of his neighbours and friends. [6]

On 21 March 1981, Arthur placed a notice in the *Western Evening Herald* seeking information about that fateful April night. Forty years after the tragedy, he was among the first in post-war Plymouth to investigate the circumstances of the bombing of the shelter. This desire to learn more about his past would launch a nine-month campaign for remembrance.[7]

A month later, a column summarised the results of his research. The article included the memories of Bernard Chapman, a firewatcher, and Jim Brown, chief air-raid warden for the ARP sector that included Portland Square. These men were some of the first rescue personnel to arrive on the scene of the tragedy in 1941. Arthur felt that the Portland Square incident was a story that had yet to be told but needed to be remembered—not only to honour the dead, but also to pay tribute to the heroic efforts of the rescue workers such as Bernard and Jim.[8]

Inspired by his conversations and determined that there should be a physical reminder of the incident, Arthur submitted a petition to the City Council asking for a plaque to be installed, 'so people will know what happened'.[9]

Plymouth already had a substantial memorial in the form of the ruins of Charles Church. This had been rededicated as a memorial to all those who died in the blitz.[10] Located in the heart of the redeveloped city-centre, the structure was a prominent feature of the cityscape, standing in stark contrast with the modern buildings that were a hallmark of Abercrombie and Watson's designs.

Further, Plymouth had dedicated a memorial in Efford Cemetery to those who had been buried communally. The octagonal limestone monument, inscribed with the names of the nearly 400 interred in the communal grave, was a record of loss. Like the headstones that marked the gravesites of those privately buried, the presence of names offered a tribute that reclaimed and preserved the individual identity of the raids' victims.

Where others saw remembrance in names carved in stone, Arthur believed the commemoration had to be rooted in location, in the very place where the lives were lost. He viewed the Portland Square incident as a distinct tragedy with its own victims and story: 'it just wasn't right that people should walk past the site every day and not know what happened there'.[11] By marking the exact location of the bombing, people could understand the blitz not only as a citywide event, but also as moments of localised catastrophes that forever altered individual lives and neighbourhoods.

Politicians were initially hesitant to support Arthur's request for even a small, self-funded memorial. The Public Services Committee of the Plymouth City Council discussed his proposal as part of their 21 April business meeting.[12] Some couched their reluctance in terms of fairness and precedent. Connie Pasco raised concerns about it appearing as if the Portland Square Air-Raid Shelter bombing were receiving privileged recognition over other sites: 'Some people's immediate reaction would be, "are our dead of less value?"'[13] For Pasco, it was a matter of equity that had the potential to open the floodgates of requests for other memorials. In essence, if every incident could not be memorialised individually, then the City Council was not inclined to support any.

Perry Washbourn took the stance that Plymouth needed to focus on its future instead of dwelling on its past: 'the best memorial Plymouth could have to its dead was its commitment to build a better city'.[14] In his mind, Plymouth's continued recovery and rebirth called for forward momentum to continue realising the grand plans imagined for the city. But for citizens who lived through the blitz, healing required remembrance, not just rebuilding.

After some debate, the committee agreed to defer their vote. They instructed Arthur to collect additional information and resubmit his request for future review. In delaying the decision and putting the onus on Arthur, city officials created conditions where initial public interest—and perhaps even Arthur Davis's passion—might fade without requiring their direct opposition and potentially upsetting constituents. The Council calculated incorrectly.[15]

The next evening, 22 April, Arthur led a memorial service that he organised to mark the fortieth anniversary of the bombing.[16] More than sixty people joined him. The group gathered outside the School of Maritime Studies which was built on the grounds of the former Portland Square Park. The crowd included survivors such as Barbara Allen, relatives of victims such as Nell Temlett, friends such as Norman Crocker, and rescue personnel such as ARP messenger Ken Searle and ARP warden Jim Brown. Doug Barretto, who had lived on James Street and had taken refuge in a separate section of the shelter on 22 April with his mother and his brother Gordon, was also present. In reflecting on the service, Doug observed, 'the sadness of the occasion is reflected in the faces of everyone'.[17] The ceremonial firing of a single gunshot initiated two minutes of silence in tribute to the dead. The assembly continued to stand in solemn remembrance as a Royal Marine cadet played *The Last Post*.[18]

While the Public Services Committee had, perhaps, hoped that stalling further conversations about the memorial would effectively extinguish interest around the initiative, the service instead generated a contingent of supporters. The gathering on such a significant anniversary offered an opportunity for survivors and others to bear witness to what had happened and reflect. They came to the realisation that the tragedy and the dead needed to be commemorated.

Jim Brown was among those who affirmed the importance of honouring the past. 'All those who sacrificed their lives should be remembered,' he insisted. 'It doesn't matter how small the plaque is. This is an episode that should not be forgotten.' He expressed his disappointment with the City Council for not yet endorsing the memorial petition. Jim indicated that he—and others—would raise any necessary funding.

City Councillor Tom Jones was among the next to add his voice and public support. He penned an editorial that ran on 9 May in which he drew on his own lived experiences of taking refuge in the shelters during the blitz. Councillor Jones argued that the Portland Square Air-Raid Shelter tragedy deserved specific recognition precisely because it occurred in a place meant to protect civilians. Arthur now had an ally on the Council who championed his aim and encouraged his campaign. 'It is right in the circumstances that a memorial plaque should be fixed to a suitable point in the vicinity of the Portland Square disaster,' Jones wrote. 'I trust that the survivors will pursue this point with appropriate authority.'[19]

Another breakthrough came in June. Arthur submitted the appeal for the committee to reconsider his petition. The committee deliberated, revisiting the same concerns that had previously stalled the proposal. Members again expressed apprehension about setting a precedent that might lead to requests for every incident of similar or smaller magnitude. Despite these reservations, the Council granted permission for a bench with a commemorative plaque to be situated outside the School of Maritime Studies.[20] Plymouth Polytechnical College agreed to the proposal. Arthur and his supporters would be responsible for raising the funds to design, purchase, and install the plaque.[21]

In order to fit on one of the planks of the wooden bench's backrest, the dedication plaque was to be sized at about 2 inches by 6 inches. The wording was simple: 'In remembrance of the 72 victims who died in the Portland Square air raid shelter, which was located at this site and which received a direct hit from a high explosive bomb during the night of the 22nd–23rd April, 1941.'[22]

Yet even this modest memorial faced further bureaucratic hurdles. Days before the planned installation in November, the College of Further Education objected. The college asserted that the proposed site fell on their property, not on polytechnic land as had been previously assumed. College administrators felt that they had not been properly consulted and did not have the appropriate information nor context to make an informed decision.[23] This last-minute injunction threatened to derail the entire project.

The site for the bench was ultimately relocated elsewhere on the campus of Plymouth Polytechnical College. On 21 December 1981, Arthur Davis and Betty Easton, chair of the Public Services Committee for the City Council, jointly unveiled the memorial bench.[24]

While there was now a physical tribute to the deceased of the largest single civilian incident of the Plymouth blitz, it was located some distance from the actual site of the tragedy, diluting Arthur's goal in marking the location of the incident for posterity. Nevertheless, the memorial bench served as a crucial first step in acknowledging the events of the past. The silence and collective amnesia that had shrouded the city's blitz experiences was beginning to lift. In time, Arthur Davis's modest act of remembrance would catalyse a movement for a more substantiative memorial.

The weight of memory

John Cornelius emigrated to the United States after the Second World War. He lost both of his parents—Maggie and Lang—in the Portland Square incident. As a child, he was affectionately known as 'Anthony'; after that unspeakable tragedy he was 'John'. The boxes of family photographs and documents about his past had been tucked away in his Connecticut home for years.

According to family lore, John had an ancestor who served under Vice-Admiral Horatio Nelson at the famous Battle of Trafalgar. It was not until the 1980s that John began to investigate this claim. While reading through his late father's diary, John came across a note dated in 1923: 'Cornelius, Wm, LM, Royal George, 1st June, Trafalgar, 23 June 1795.' His curiosity piqued, he immediately contacted the Royal Naval Museum and the Public Records Office at Kew.[25] The Museum confirmed the family legend as reality. There was indeed a William Cornelius who was a landsman on the battleship HMS *Royal George* and who served as an able seaman on HMS *Prince* at Trafalgar. This discovery fulfilled John's quest for a connection to his ancestral heritage. With his forebear's naval service confirmed, he was satisfied—for the moment.

Almost a decade later, finding himself with time on his hands after retiring from his engineering job and with an interest in further researching his family's story, John picked up genealogy as a hobby to fill in the gaps between himself and his naval ancestor.

The conventional advice for genealogists is to start with the most recent generations and work backwards. John, however, stalled as soon as he reached his parents. His focus shifted from his naval ancestor to the larger, unspoken tragedy that had shaped his own life—his parents' death in the blitz. While his naval ancestor represented a distant glory, his parents represented an immediate, unresolved loss.

There was so much about their story that he didn't know. Lang and Maggie were among those who died in Portland Square on 23 April 1941; but by chance, John and his younger brother were in the Devon countryside with their maternal grandmother and escaped their parents' terrible fate. While his own memories of the immediate aftermath were seared in his mind, the story of what happened that fateful night was never discussed, leaving a void in his understanding of this critical moment in his life.

The same impulse that drove John to confirm his connection to William Cornelius now compelled him to honour his parents by investigating the night of 22 April 1941 further. For nearly fifty years, the story surrounding their deaths had hung over him. Now, half a century later, John was determined to uncover the details of the tragedy that had altered his life's trajectory. The skills he had developed researching his naval ancestor—scouring archives, connecting with institutions, piecing together evidence—would serve him in this even more personal quest.

In the late 1980s, John visited Plymouth and the site of his childhood home. The city was still rebuilding, continuing to realise the urban designs that Abercrombie and Watson had proposed decades earlier. The familiar landscape of his youth had changed dramatically. John found that many of Portland Square's buildings, his own former home included, had been demolished.

No. 42 Portland Square was now a grassy plot of land waiting to be redeveloped. He saw an opportunity to reclaim a piece of his past and to do the same for others. John envisioned that the site might be transformed into a memorial to those who died in the air-raid shelter: 'I think that it would have been an ideal spot for some small remembrance. Maybe I can still do something about it.'[26] With that statement, John initiated his ambition to appropriately recognise the lives, like his parents', that were lost at Portland Square during the height of the Plymouth Blitz.

In time, John learned that a memorial to the Portland Square victims already existed. He heard about the memorial bench and plaque that Arthur Davis had campaigned to install in 1981. During a later visit to Plymouth in 1995, John went searching for it: 'One September morning, I spent about an hour trying to find it. Eventually I went to the University security people and they directed me to the bench. It was tucked away behind a concrete wall opposite some pre-fab. buildings near the University Library.'[27]

When he finally found the bench, John was surprised by its seeming insignificance—a weather-beaten wooden bench with a small metal plate seemed to whisper, rather than declare, the magnitude of the tragic event that had occurred. He was disappointed with what he encountered. Not realising the compromises made in 1981 to install the memorial in the first place, to John, the bench's placement seemed arbitrary, disconnected from the epicentre of the tragedy: 'The present memorial seat is in a terrible location that has no relevance to the shelter.'[28] Though the memorial was well intentioned, John believed it now needed a reimagining, not only to honour those who died but also so that the living could pay their respects and learn from the past.[29]

When he revisited the grounds of 42 Portland Square, John found that the plot was now home to a memorial garden dedicated to the students of the university. This spot seemed like a more appropriate location for Davis's bench. By relocating the bench to this reflective space, by placing it where two of the victims—his parents—had once made their home, John felt that the memorial bench might better fulfil its intended purpose, and that the university could honour the heritage of the area.

John dedicated himself to spearheading this initiative. Driven by a desire to comprehend a more complete picture of the bombing, he set out to locate survivors and individuals who might provide insights into the incident, hoping to build support for relocating the memorial bench in the process. While leafing through documents at the West Devon Record Office, John met James Mildren, a reporter for the *Evening Herald*. Mildren wrote about their encounter in the paper's 'Seen and Heard' column, detailing John's research efforts and his desire to see a more fitting placement for Arthur Davis's memorial bench.[30]

The response to John's appeal was almost immediate. Former neighbours reached out to share their experiences and memories. As tight-knit a community as Portland Square was, John was only now meeting some of these people for the first time; individuals such as Doug Barretto, Noreen Wise, and Barbara Mills (née Cundy). 'Originally, I had planned to campaign for the memorial bench to be relocated to the memorial garden which is on the site of No. 42 Portland Square,' John explained in a letter to Doug Barretto. 'Please understand that I do not in any way want to detract from Mr. Davis's efforts to get the memorial bench installed. However, it is in the wrong place to begin with, and it is inaccessible to the vast majority of the public who pass through Portland Square each day.'[31]

As John collected more stories and built relationships with survivors and stakeholders, relocating the memorial bench no longer seemed adequate given the magnitude of the tragedy. The worn bench with its small, generic inscription did not capture what had happened or who had been lost. What had once been a modest proposal for a simple relocation soon evolved into a grander plan. Conversations with Gerard Wasley, a local researcher and author of one of the few books detailing Plymouth's blitz experience, sparked a more ambitious idea. John now envisioned an entirely new memorial. He thought that it might take the form of a plaque listing all of the victims' names, ensuring each person lost that night would be individually acknowledged and collectively remembered. The plaque could be installed in the university's memorial garden.

The broader cultural moment was ripe for conversations about a new memorial project. The world was commemorating the fiftieth anniversary of the Second World War. Historians, journalists, and community leaders were increasingly aware that the window for capturing first-hand accounts of the events of the 1940s was beginning to close. Those who had lived through the war were aging, their memories beginning to fade, their personal archives gradually disappearing.

In 1997, John took his proposal directly to the university. He invited the institution to take on the mantle as the 'custodian of a memorial to a tragic but important part of Plymouth's heritage'. He wrote to Vice-Chancellor R.J. Bull to share his idea, his personal connection to the incident, and his commitment to supporting it:

> The University has a memorial garden on the corner of Portland Place East. I was born in the house which stood here – No. 42 Portland Square [...] I would like to propose that a plaque be designed, showing the names of all those who died in the shelter, and that this plaque be installed in this garden. Further, I think it would be appropriate that the plaque be designed [and fabricated?] within the University's Faculty of Arts. I am prepared to share in the cost of such a plaque.[32]

The process to execute the project, however, was far from straightforward. Having absorbed several colleges and looking to centralise resources, the university was undergoing a master site plan for the campus. The redevelopment presented an opportunity for John's memorial to potentially take on an even more substantial form. 'Evidently the University is undergoing a complete review of its Plymouth campus,' John wrote of his correspondence with the chancellor, 'and he has asked the consultant doing the review to consider what form such a memorial should take and where it might be located.'[33] The plan would need to come first, and the memorial project was not the only priority in the plan. For the time being, John—and his vision—would need to wait.

Remembrance: the memorial sculpture

Nearly a decade later, in 2005, John received an unexpected letter from Dr Tony Rees, a senior lecturer at the University of Plymouth. The professor had attended a series of lectures on campus that were part of the commemoration of the sixtieth anniversary of the end of the Second World War. One speaker mentioned the Portland Square shelter tragedy and the absence of a fitting memorial to honour the victims on the university grounds.

Intrigued, Tony began researching the disaster. He collected details about the victims and reviewed accounts of the night. Determined to learn more, he located and reached out to some of the same individuals that John had connected with over the previous decade—people such as survivor Barbara Mills and former Portland Square residents such as Cathi Hunt. Through this process, Tony discovered John's personal connection to the tragedy and learned of his previous attempts to establish a memorial on campus.

For John, the connection with Tony Rees represented a significant development: an ally within the institution. Their shared interest in commemorating the Portland Square incident developed into a meaningful friendship and an effective partnership. This new alliance had barely taken root when, in July 2005, a newspaper article caught John's attention. Scanning the *Evening Herald*, he spotted a brief detail buried within a report on the university's ongoing campus restructuring initiatives. The article indicated, almost in passing, that a memorial was in the works: 'The Rolle Building will be created next to a new public square in honour of those who died in Portland Square during the Blitz.'[34] After years of correspondence, this single printed sentence suggested his goal might finally materialise. John, who had all but abandoned his campaign, immediately wrote to the university's vice-chancellor, Roland Levinsky. John's letter balanced his personal investment in the memorial project with his frustration about how progress on the project stalled over the last decade: 'A hiatus ensued and I had resigned myself to believe that this matter had either been shelved or forgotten.'[35]

Tony, also enthusiastic about the newspaper article, contacted John. In Tony's view, the public announcement, however small, was a 'breakthrough' because it would be difficult for the university to reverse course.[36] He viewed the announcement as an opportunity to help shape plans for the memorial. He believed that something more substantial than even the plaque John had envisioned was necessary to appropriately mark the gravity of the tragedy.[37]

Developments accelerated later that summer and throughout early autumn. Tony worked with fellow administrators to build institutional support. He envisioned using the memorial installation as a learning opportunity for students that would engage various academic departments, and also liaised with the *Evening Herald* to galvanise broader community support. On 26 November, the paper shared the personal account of survivor Barbara Mills and presented a case for a more appropriate memorial for the victims: 'There should be something more [...] a proper memorial, something that all those young people would see and make them think about the history,' Barbara implored.[38] The article appeared next to a notice about the university's commitment to honouring the victims of the tragedy with a memorial and academic programming.[39] Thanks to Tony's continued advocacy, the memorial would indeed take on a more substantial form.

By late autumn, these behind-the-scenes efforts began to bear tangible results. On 9 December, an optimistic Tony sent John an encouraging update: 'Things definitely on a roll now.'[40] The memorial plans now included the commission of a sculpture by artist Frances Favata. The future unveiling ceremony would be complemented by an arts festival featuring a lecture about Portland Square and the premiere of a new choral work to be performed at St Andrew's Church.[41] The university estimated a total cost of £40,000 for the sculpture, and the vice chancellor committed £10,000.[42] Just as one hurdle had been cleared, a new challenge now emerged: the need to bridge the funding gap.

The sixty-fifth anniversary of the Portland Square incident in April 2006 provided the moment for the soft launch of the fundraising campaign. The *Evening Herald* would play a key role in rallying community support. The paper detailed the university's memorial plans and officially announced its partnership to assist in the endeavour:

> The initiative, backed by the *Evening Herald* and the University of Plymouth, aims to find funds for this fitting memorial, which will help keep alive the memories of the men, women and children who died. And we are confident that it will find favour with the modern-day population of our city, which still recognize the importance of honouring our war dead.
>
> 'We believe that many people will share that feeling, and will dig deep to finance this wonderfully worthwhile and significant project,' remarked Vice Chancellor Levinsky. 'Those who died deserve to be remembered, and this would be a perfect way to honour and respect them.'[43]

Frances Favata's designs for the commission were profiled as part of the appeal. Fittingly, she would sculpt the memorial from Portland stone. The work would depict an adult raising a child to the sky. Favata drew inspiration from an account that Tony Rees shared with her about a young couple sending their child to the countryside during the blitz. She intended for her stone figures to communicate themes of 'rebirth', 'the tenacity of the people of Plymouth', and the 'special effort to preserve the next generation'. The installation would also include reflective steel panels, inviting viewers to interact with the piece while distorting their image, a way to symbolise the destructive impact of war on communities.[44]

The fundraising campaign took shape around a powerful yet simple advancement strategy: to connect potential donors to the human story behind the tragedy through a series of personal narratives. The first testimony employed was that of the last living survivor of the incident, Barbara Mills. The article captured her first visit to her family's grave in Ford Park Cemetery. After recounting her memories of the tragic night and the pain of loss that she endured throughout her life, the article shared Barbara's support of the memorial: 'Our generation is going slowly and the descendants of the people who were killed, and those who survived, need something that honours what happened. It'll make people think about what happens in war, with so many innocent people getting killed.' She appealed for the public to make a modest contribution to help make the memorial a reality: 'Even if people in the city just give £1 each it would gradually mount up.'[45]

After the initial announcement, the paper profiled Tony Rees as the driving force behind the project. The piece highlighted his dedication to researching the tragedy and making sure that the story of Portland Square was not forgotten. A memorial would serve to preserve the history and honour the victims of the tragedy. 'This was a community disaster and it's right that Plymouth has a memorial the whole community can share,' Tony commented. 'It'll make the students aware of what happened on the site where they studied and hopefully bring members of the public on campus when they might previously have shied away.'[46]

The paper then facilitated drip-coverage to bring further attention to the memorial project and grow support by keeping the initiative at the forefront of people's minds. For example, there were a succession of human-interest stories about people who had a connection to Portland Square and were now supporting the fund for the memorial. One account told the story of Fred Saunders' mother Lillian. Though heavily pregnant and with the attack already under way, she was refused entry into the Portland Square Shelter because she insisted on taking her dog inside with her. She returned to her home and thus escaped the bombing. The account concluded with noting the family's pledge to support the memorial project.[47]

A couple of days later, the paper relayed the memories of Norman Crocker. Crocker lost several classmates in the bombing, including Barbara Mills's sister Betty. 'I remember going to school at North Road Primary and realising a lot of my school friends hadn't turned up to class,' he remembered, noting the importance of a more permanent memorial: 'I think that site needed more than a plaque on a bench which could rot away with all the memories. The sculpture will remind people of the terrible catastrophe that happened beneath their feet.' Contributing £10 to the appeal, Crocker's modest donation demonstrated that the campaign welcomed—and benefited from—contributions of all sizes.[48]

The fund received a significant boost when John Cornelius made a donation of £1,500. The *Evening Herald* featured his personal connection and support for the memorial project a couple of days later: 'I wanted their sacrifice recognised. There are a lot of war memorials in Plymouth but they are all military related.' His donation represented more than just financial support; it symbolised his decade-long commitment to seeking to commemorate the lives of his parents and the other civilian victims. 'I had been pushing for a memorial and I thought I'd better put my money where my mouth is,' he added, demonstrating the sincerity behind his advocacy.[49]

The next week broadened the appeal to the business community. Chairman of the Plymouth Chamber of Commerce Charles Howeson and his family made a corporate contribution of £500 and challenged the business community to commit to join them and together raise a quarter of the necessary funds: 'I look forward to my colleagues also placing on record their support for this permanent mark of civic respect that represents perhaps the most painful moment in recent memory, in our city's long history.'[50]

Each story built upon the previous ones, creating momentum that culminated in an official fundraising event at the university on 11 May. The evening's programme included a lecture on the history of Portland Square and unveiled a model of the proposed sculpture. With the campaign already having secured pledges towards its funding goal, the event served as both celebration of progress and a catalyst for the next phase of fundraising.

That same month, the Portland stone for the sculpture arrived on site. While it seemed as if the project was on track, progress on the memorial was still dependent on other campus construction projects. The delay, coupled with the need to secure the remaining funds, necessitated adjustments to the timeline that Tony had initially shared.

The next anniversary of the incident was again used to cultivate community engagement and make progress towards the fundraising goal. 'This will be a fitting memorial to those who died in the disaster and the funds so far raised are testimony to the great sense of loss it continues to evoke in the city,' shared the university's head of fundraising Helen Pearson. The public was invited to observe Frances Favata at work on the sculpture and speak with her about the creative process. 'We are deeply indebted to the public of Plymouth for helping fund this memorial, so it's only right they have an opportunity to view it as it starts to take shape and talk to the artist.' It was hoped that this programme would increase the public's personal and financial investment in the project.[51]

In October 2007, John visited Plymouth with his wife Rosemary and their daughter Rosanne and had the opportunity to view progress on the memorial for himself. 'This is the first time I have seen the sculpture. I have only ever seen models of how the work will look before. It is fantastic; it is sort of overwhelming. To see it in the flesh, or in the stone as it were, is just so powerful,' he commented.[52] John's visit was leveraged to reinvigorate interest in the project. Tony Rees praised him for his persistent advocacy and partnership: 'Without people like John, this memorial

John Anthony Cornelius, Frances Favata, and the in-progress Portland Square memorial. [*Plymouth Herald*]

may never have happened and it is particularly satisfying for me that after all the hard work and negotiation, it is now all coming to fruition.'[53]

The culmination of these efforts came when the memorial was formally unveiled on 23 April 2009. The sunny day marked the sixty-eighth anniversary of the blitz. Approximately 250 people gathered for the ceremony, which included speeches from university leaders and faculty, Frances Favata, and Barbara Mills.

As the last living survivor of the tragedy, Barbara was accorded the honour of unveiling the memorial sculpture, which was entitled 'Hope': 'I feel very proud and honoured to be asked to do this. I had to do it for those that are gone,' Barbara remarked. Her role for the day carried the weight of both her personal loss and the community's collective remembrance.[54]

'Hope', Frances Favata, 2009. This sculpture serves as the memorial to the victims of the Portland Square Air-Raid Shelter bombing and is located on the campus of the University of Plymouth. [Author].

John 'Anthony' Cornelius in his study in Connecticut. It was here that he wrote his memoir, corresponded with people associated with the bombing, researched his family history, and spearheaded the campaign for the Portland Square memorial. [*Plymouth Herald*]

The efforts of the previous two decades had been about more than just creating a physical monument; they had been about honouring the memory of those lost and giving the community a place to come together. Through loss, there could be renewal; through tragedy, there could be healing.

John followed the press about the dedication from his home in the United States. A sense of accomplishment filled him as he read coverage about the ceremony. He sat quietly in his Connecticut study, his eyes lingering on the images of the new memorial and the photographs of his parents Maggie and Lang. The memory of their tragic death had been a heavy weight on his heart his entire life. Though he could not be in Plymouth himself for the unveiling, he knew that the ceremony had been a pivotal moment both for his beloved city in reclaiming a part of its past and for his own life's journey.

John at last achieved what he set out to do: to help reclaim the story of Portland Square and ensure that the lives lost on that tragic April night would not be forgotten.

Afterword

John 'Anthony' Cornelius's own hope in initiating the memorial project had always been personal and motivated by his family: 'I'm doing this mainly for my two grandchildren, so they will get to understand, in some small way, what happened to their great-grandparents,' he wrote.[1] My own journey began in much the same way, driven by the desire to know and honour the family I had married into and to understand someone my wife Jessica loved so deeply: her late grandfather.

Visiting Plymouth in the summer of 2023 with Jessica felt like stepping into a story both intimate and vast. Part research trip, part pilgrimage, it was a journey filled with reflection. The visit was a chance to connect with the history of the Cornelius family. We walked through the streets, allowing ourselves to be anchored to the space and the past. We laid flowers at the family plot at Ford Park Cemetery. I spent an afternoon at the Plymouth archives, examining records associated with Portland Square and the tragedy of 23 April 1941.

When we visited the Portland Square Memorial at the University of Plymouth to read the seventy-one names inscribed behind the statue, it occurred to me that my project was not just about our family. The Cornelius story was one thread in a larger tapestry. Each name represented a life interrupted, a story that had almost been lost to time, and a community of families and neighbours forever altered by the events of that night. By tracing our family's story, I could also illuminate the wider impact of the blitz in Plymouth.

The project soon expanded beyond our family. Throughout my research, I've met people connected with the tragedy who have entrusted me with their memories and those of their loved ones. I interviewed Peter Chapman, who as a little boy stood in Victoria Street only hours before the bombing as his mother kissed him goodbye and sent him off to the countryside for the night. Through their memoirs, I encountered William Johns, one of the courier messenger boys, as well as Noreen Wise and Stanley Hollett, both witnesses to the Portland Square tragedy. As the circle expanded, relatives of victims shared pictures and accounts of their loved ones. Though I did not meet the last living survivor of the night, Barbara (Cundy) Mills, her daughter shared many memories and photographs of her mother with me.

It was a humbling responsibility: to tell a story that mattered beyond our family. Through letters and interviews, I could give voice to those who had not survived, to those whose memories might otherwise fade, and to those who still carried the echoes of that horrific April night in Plymouth.

Just as the Cornelius family became a lens through which the blitz could be seen not only as a historical event but also as a human experience, bringing this account to light also grew into a reckoning with the larger historiography. Too often, the story of the blitz is told through a London-centric lens that dominates the national collective memory, leaving cities such as Plymouth relegated to the margins.

To begin to pivot that historical narrative, my scholarship needed to be as robust as the personal memories were fragile. My research took me into archives across the country, from local collections in Plymouth to the Royal Archives at Windsor.[2] I drilled into primary source documents—official reports, civil defence records, and local media coverage—seeking to understand how the tragedy at Portland Square was documented, interpreted, and sometimes overlooked.

Throughout, I aimed to meet scholarly standards, subjecting the work to peer review and academic scrutiny, but I was never writing for scholars alone. This book is meant equally for those who still feel the echoes of that night, for descendants and readers who recognise in these stories something of their own families and communities. Only through that balance of rigour and empathy could I hope to tell the story with accuracy, fairness, and respect for those whose lives it seeks to honour.

In the course of this work, I've endeavoured to recover the stories beneath the statistics: to restore faces, voices, and moments of humanity that time had nearly erased. This was, in the end, the fulfilment of what John Cornelius had first hoped for when he began gathering his family's story: that future generations might come to understand. However modestly, I hope this book contributes to the ongoing legacy of memory: ensuring that the ordinary people of Portland Square, and all those lost in Britain's darkest days, are not remembered as numbers or names alone, but as lives once lived in full.

In Memoriam: The Seventy-One Lost

Portland Square Air-Raid Shelter, 23 April 1941

Kenneth Victor Allen, age 14, 3 Victoria Buildings
William Thomas Allen, age 56, 3 Victoria Buildings
John Thomas Allison, age 68, 27 Portland Square
Florence Andrews, age 55, 37 Portland Square
Henry Andrews, age 56, 37 Portland Square
Margaret Blake, age 30, 3 Portland Place East
Eleanor Julia Boynes, age 82, 6 Endsleigh Place
Frank Prout Budge, age 42, 6 Victoria Street
Ann Gidley Bunker, age 72, 13 Endsleigh Place
Lilian Elizabeth Chapman, age 36, 6 Victoria Buildings
Claude Leonard Chubb, age 47, 24 Victoria Street
Florence Mabel Chubb, age 50, 24 Victoria Street
Richard Henry Coombe, age 45, New Carlyon, Carclaze, St Austell, Cornwall
Marjorie Clarissa Cornelius, age 39, 42 Portland Square
William John Lang Cornelius, age 44, 42 Portland Square
Betty May Cundy, age 10, 27 Portland Square
William Cundy, age 38, 27 Portland Square
Winifred Cundy, age 35, 27 Portland Square
Albert Davies, age 11, 9 Victoria Street
Dennis Davies, age 2, 9 Victoria Street
Florence Davies, age 32, 9 Victoria Street
Iris Davies, age 5, 9 Victoria Street
Kenneth Davies, age 3 months, 9 Victoria Street
Patricia Davies, age 7, 9 Victoria Street
Winifred Davies, age 14, 9 Victoria Street
Frederick Denning, age 42, 29 Tavistock Road
William Alfred Denning, age 75, 6 Ferndale, Victoria Road, Dartmouth
Eric Farrant, age 11, 1 Victoria Buildings

Mabel Farrant, age 52, 1 Victoria Buildings
Samuel Farrant, age 52, 1 Victoria Buildings
George Thomas Gorvin, age 51, 39 Portland Square
Robert Hakenjos, age 2, 39 Portland Square
Kathleen Maria Hanlon, age 13, 4 Tavistock Road
Vera Blanche Primrose Hanlon, age 19, 4 Tavistock Road
Emma May Harris, age 60, 38 Portland Square
Ernest Thomas Gibbs Harris, age 71, 38 Portland Square
Florence Harris, age 54, 5 Victoria Street
Jacqueline Harris, age 12, 5 Victoria Street
William Harris, age 52, 5 Victoria Street
Edward Hempkins, age 24, 5 Pier Street
Pauline Hempkins, age 19, 5 Pier Street
Charles Herbert Corindon Horn, age 57, 57 Gibbon Street
Irene Harriet May Ledden, age 40, 23 Portland Square
Sarah Jane Ledden, age 73 23 Portland Square
John MacGreggor, age 52, 9 Kirkby Place
Jane MacGreggor, age 77, 9 Kirkby Place
Ivy Morgan, age 35, 10 Patna Place
Reginald Morgan, age 39, 10 Patna Place
John Norton, age 48, 37 Portland Square
Violet Norton, age 46, 37 Portland Square
Susan Pearn, age 51, 9 Kirkby Place, North Road
William Pearn, age 57, 9 Kirkby Place, North Road
Albert George Peeke, age 60, 2 Victoria Buildings
Phyllis B. Pepper, age 15, 4 Victoria Street
William Stanley Pickard, age 45, 19 Collins Close, St Budeaux
Emma Reeve, age 63, Willow Cottages, Willow Street
Anthony Rendle, age 8, 39 Portland Square
Elsie Rendle, age 41, 39 Portland Square
George Rendle, age 39, 39 Portland Square
Ivy Strong, age 39, 5 Victoria Buildings
Phyllis Strong, age 14, 5 Victoria Buildings
Eileen Surgeoner, age 20, 4 Victoria Street
Lavinia Grist Surgeoner, age 35, 4 Victoria Street
William John Surgeoner, age 44, 4 Victoria Street
Adelaide Watson, age 52, 72 Houndiscombe Place
Margaret Watson, age 10, 72 Houndiscombe Place
James Woodfin, age 6, 5 Portland Place East
Kenneth Woodfin, age 8, 5 Portland Place East
Philip Woodfin, age 33, 5 Portland Place East

Winifred Woodfin, age 35, 5 Portland Place East
Hubert Alfred Wright, age 42, 33 Salisbury Road, St Judes

This list is derived from the list of seventy-one names noted at the Portland Square Memorial on the University of Plymouth campus and which is reflective of the research completed for this book. The number reflects those victims who were identified in 1941 and confirmed thereafter, though the historical record suggests that the toll of the tragedy was most likely greater.

Notes

Preface

1. Henry Patrick Twyford, *It Came to Our Door* (Plymouth: Underhill, 1946).
2. Rachael Dodd, 'Devastating Air Raid Claimed Dozens of Civilians', *Plymouth Herald*, 21 April 2018, 24. Dodd makes note of seventy-six victims, but does not provide a list. Of those referenced, there are several errors—including Violet Chowne, William and Lavinia Surgeoner, and Joseph Coombes. I use the number seventy-one, which aligns with the listing of the individuals identified on the Portland Square Memorial panels and in historical records.
3. Michael Charleston, 'The Prophetic Notices for Rebirth of a City', *Western Morning News*, 21 March 1991, 4.
4. John Cornelius, 'John Cornelius to Noreen Wise', 13 March 1996.
5. Twyford, *It Came to Our Door*, 99–112.

Chapter 2: Portland Square

1. Richard Nicholls Worth, *History of Plymouth: From the Earliest Period to the Present Time* (Plymouth: William Brendon & Son, 1890), 370.
2. Borough of Plymouth, Engraved by John Cooke, 1820; Plans of the Towns and Harbour of Plymouth, Stonehouse, Dock, Morice-Town, Stoke and the Environs in the County of Devon, 1820.
3. Plymouth, Devonport, and Stonehouse, John Tallis & Company, London, 1851.
4. The Box, Plymouth, retains an extensive collection of materials concerning the development of the city such as permits for construction at Portland Square.
5. *Eyre's Post Office Plymouth & Devonport Directory, 1895* (J.G. Hammond & Co. Ltd, 1895). Available at the University of Leicester, <https://leicester.contentdm.oclc.org/digital/collection/p16445coll4/id/64277/>.
6. Gerald Wasley, *Blitz: An Account of Hitler's Aerial War Over Plymouth in March 1941, and the Events that Followed* (Exeter: Halsgrove, 1991), 35.
7. W.P. Johns, *Days of Destiny*, unpublished manuscript (2001). The Box, Plymouth (4263/293), 47.
8. Stanley Charles Hollett, 'Looking Back', unpublished memoir (n.d.).
9. John Cornelius, *My Journey to the New World*, unpublished memoir (n.d.), 1.
10. Hollett, 'Looking Back'.
11. Noreen Wise, 'Noreen Wise to John Cornelius' (1996).
12. Hollett, 'Looking Back'.
13. John Cornelius, 'John Cornelius to Barbara Mills', 5 January 1996.
14. Barbara Mills, 'Barbara Mills to John Cornelius', 1 January 1996.
15. Johns, *Days of Destiny*, 47. A 'panel patient' refers to someone who received medical attention under the National Health Insurance scheme. In this regard, Johns concluded that the physicians with practices in Portland Square office spaces were operating private surgeries.
16. Cornelius, 'Mills'.

17. Johns, *Days of Destiny*, 47.
18. *1939 England and Wales Register*. Lehi, UT, USA: Ancestry.com Operations, Inc., 2018.
19. Johns, *Days of Destiny*, 47.
20. Wise, 'Cornelius'.
21. Classified listing: 42 Portland Square, *Western Morning News*, 5 November 1940, 4.
22. Cornelius, *My Journey*, 1.
23. Ibid., 2.
24. Ibid.
25. Wise, 'Cornelius'.
26. Cornelius, *My Journey*, 1.
27. Hollett, 'Looking Back'.
28. Cornelius, *My Journey*, 1.
29. Ibid., 3.
30. Michael McLaughlin, 'Interview with Peter Chapman', 10 April 2024.
31. Ibid.
32. Ibid.
33. Ibid.
34. Cornelius, *My Journey*, 3.
35. Cornelius, 'Mills'.
36. Hollett, 'Looking Back'.

Chapter 3: The Cornelius Family of 42 Portland Square

1. John Cornelius, *Two Journeys*, unpublished genealogy (n.d.).
2. British Army Form B199A for William John Lang Cornelius.
3. Classified listing: Nurse-General, *Western Morning News*, 19 August 1903, 1; Classified listing: General, *Western Morning News*, 10 June 1904, 1; Classified listing: Nurse, *Western Morning News*, 29 October 1904, 1; Classified listing: General, *Western Morning News*, 26 May 1905, 1; Classified listing: Nurse, *Western Morning News*, 13 September 1906, 3.
4. Classified listing: Nursery Governess, *Western Morning News*, 27 August 1910, 2.
5. Classified listing: Nursery Governess, *Western Morning News*, 27 January 1911, 2.
6. Classified listing: Girl, *Western Morning News*, 19 April 1909, 1.
7. Classified listing: Mother's Helper, *Western Morning News*, 13 October 1911, 1.
8. 'Lord Mayor's Ball', *Western Morning News*, 7 October 1936, 4–5.
9. Cornelius, *My Journey*, 3.
10. Cornelius, *Two Journeys*; John Cornelius, 'John Cornelius to Catherine Hunt', 10 September 1993.
11. Ibid.
12. Classified listing: Stable, *Western Morning News*, 11 May 1915, 3.
13. 'Wedding: Cornelius-Hill at Plymouth', *Western Morning News*, 24 November 1923, 5.
14. 'No Licenses', *Western Morning News*, 28 October 1927, 4; 'No Wireless Licence', *Western Morning News*, 28 April 1928, 11; 'Unlicensed Wireless Sets', *Western Morning News*, 18 September 1928, 4; 'Western Police Courts', *Western Morning News*, 15 August 1930, 3; 'Plymouth Wireless Sets Without Licences', *Western Morning News*, 9 May 1931, 13.
15. 'Falkland Islands', *Western Morning News*, 9 May 1936, 7.
16. 'Philatelic Lecture', *Western Morning News*, 10 April 1937, 7.
17. John Cornelius, 'John Cornelius to Noreen Wise', 1 December 1996.
18. 'Vicar Resigns at Plymouth', *Western Morning News*, 7 April 1936, 4.
19. 'Farewell to Parish', *Western Morning News*, 11 January 1939, 5.
20. 'Two Ceremonies Coincide', *Western Morning News*, 25 February 1939, 7.

21. Cornelius, *My Journey*, 3.
22. Ibid.
23. Plymouth College and Mannamead School, Sports Standard Certificates, 1938, 1939.
24. Cornelius, *My Journey*, 3.
25. Ibid., 4.
26. Ibid., 3.
27. Ibid., 2.
28. Cornelius, 'Mills'.
29. Ibid.
30. Ibid.

Chapter 4: Bunkering Down for War: Air-Raid Shelters in Plymouth

1. 'Sir John Anderson Speaks on the Need for Air Raid Precautions (ARP) (1939)', YouTube video, 0.40, posted by British Pathé, 10 November 2020, <https://www.youtube.com/watch?v=Ll5f7X15Mdg>.
2. Lucy Noakes, *Dying for the Nation: Death, Grief, and Bereavement in Second World War Britain* (Manchester: Manchester University Press, 2020). 75.
3. 'Future of Anglo-German Relations', *The Times*, 1 October 1938, 1.
4. 'Country Divided into Three Groups', *Western Morning News*, 10 January 1939, 7.
5. 'Air-Raid Shelter for Every House', *Western Morning News*, 2 February 1939, 7.
6. Ibid.
7. Noakes, *Dying for the Nation*, 86.
8. '30,000 for Plymouth', *Western Morning News*, 6 March 1939, 8.
9. 'Free Shelters Critics', *Western Morning News*, 14 February 1939, 6. With a lengthy estimated waiting period, individuals with means turned to the private sector. Several Plymouth businesses, such as FJ Moore, advertised premium products, including concrete shelters and trench linings that were a grade above the Anderson shelter model. Advertisement: FJ Moore, *Western Morning News*, 28 March 1939, 1; Advertisement: FJ Moore, *Western Morning News*, 22 April 1939, 12.
10. 'Sample Shelter', *Western Morning News*, 12 April 1939, 11.
11. 'Is the West Prepared?', *Western Morning News*, 6 April 1939, 5.
12. 'A.R.P. Parade on the Hoe', *Western Morning News*, 12 August 1939, 7.
13. Larry Stevens, Primary Source Testimony, <www.cyber-heritage.co.uk/history/blitz.htm>.
14. 'Underground Air Raid Shelter', *Western Morning News*, 18 April 1939, 5.
15. 'Government A.R.P. Policy', *Western Morning News*, 7 July 1939, 7.
16. 'Trenches for Civilians', *Western Morning News*, 24 February 1939, 7.
17. 'Shelters at New Schools', *Western Morning News*, 14 January 1939, 7.
18. 'Trenches Dug in Crisis', *Western Morning News*, 21 January 1939, 9.
19. 'Protecting City in Air Raids', *Western Morning News*, 8 February 1939, 5.
20. 'Shelters in All New Buildings', *Western Morning News*, 12 May 1939, 5
21. 'Whitehall is to Blame', *Western Morning News*, 16 May 1939, 7.
22. Hollett, 'Looking Back'.
23. 'City Council to Hear of New Plans', *Western Morning News*, 15 June 1939, 7.
24. 'Trenches and Shelters', *Western Morning News*, 11 February 1939, 10.
25. Hollett, 'Looking Back'.
26. Stephen Johnson, 'Plymouth's World War Two Underground Air Raid Shelters', in K. Ray (ed.), *Archaeological Investigations and Research in Plymouth, Volume 1: 1992–93*. Plymouth Archaeology Occasional Publication No. 2 (Plymouth: Plymouth Archaeology, 1995), 41–46.

27. Ibid.
28. 'Memorial to 72 Dead Unveiled', *Western Evening Herald*, 22 December 1981, 3.
29. Laura Quigley, *Bloody British History: Plymouth* (Stroud: The History Press, 2012).
30. 'Shelter Bomb Killed 72', *Western Evening Herald*, 21 April 1981, 4.
31. Johnson, 'Plymouth's World War Two Underground Air Raid Shelters.'
32. Stephen Wade, *Air Raid Shelters of World War II: Family Stories of Survival in the Blitz* (Barnsley: Pen & Sword Military, 2011).
33. Johnson, 'Plymouth's World War Two Underground Air Raid Shelters.'
34. 'Bigger ARP Bill', *Western Morning News*, 20 April 1939, 5.
35. 'A.R.P. Parade on the Hoe', *Western Morning News*, 12 August 1939, 7.
36. 'Damage to Air Raid Shelters', *Western Morning News*, 23 October 1939, 3.
37. 'Accelerated A.R.P.', *Western Morning News*, 1 September 1939, 3.
38. 'Notes in the West', *Western Morning News*, 28 August 1939, 3.

Chapter 5: 'This country is at war'

1. The heading for this chapter comes from: Neville Chamberlain, *Radio Address by Neville Chamberlain, Prime Minister*, 3 September 1939. Transcript from the BBC Archive.
2. George VI, 'The King's Speech', audio, 3 September 1939. National Archives, Kew.
3. 'No Jingoism in West Determination', *Western Morning News*, 4 September 1939, 3.
4. Wasley, *Blitz*, 55.
5. Cornelius, *My Journey*, 4.
6. Hollett, 'Looking Back'.
7. 'Plymouth Air-Raid Shelters', *Western Morning News*, 30 September 1939, 7.
8. 'Locked Air-Raid Shelters', *Western Morning News*, 3 November 1939, 4.
9. Mills, 'Cornelius', 1 January 1996.
10. 'Trees and Trenches', *Western Morning News*, 19 September 1939, 3.
11. 'Damaged Shelters', *Western Morning News*, 15 September 1939, 3.
12. 'Damage to Air Raid Shelters'.
13. 'Damaged Shelters'.
14. 'Damage to Air Raid Shelters'.
15. 'Trees Have Survived', *Western Morning News*, 20 March 1940, 3.
16. Twyford, *It Came to Our Door*, 100.
17. Wasley, *Blitz*, 26.
18. 'Air-Raid Shelters Wrongly Erected', *Western Morning News*, 20 April 1940, 5.
19. 'Impaired Safety Shelters', *Western Morning News*, 1 April 1940, 3.
20. 'Air-Raid Shelters: Some to be Built in Middle of Road at Plymouth', *Western Morning News*, 4 May 1940, 5.
21. 'To A.R.P. Shelters', *Western Morning News*, 25 July 1940, 2.
22. 'Direction Signs', *Western Morning News*, 29 July 1940, 5.
23. 'Damage to Raid Shelters', *Western Morning News*, 9 May 1940, 5.
24. 'Raid Shelter Key-Keepers', *Western Morning News*, 5 June 1940, 5.
25. 'Air Raid Shelter Wardens', *Western Morning News*, 24 May 1940, 1.
26. 'Shelter Guards', *Western Morning News*, 25 June 1940, 5.

Chapter 6: A Wartime Portrait of a Father and Son

1. Cornelius, *My Journey*, 4.
2. Ibid.
3. 'In Camp at Cornwood', *Western Morning News*, 13 June 1938, 5.

4. 'Army Cable-Laying', *Western Morning News*, 13 August 1938, 10.
5. British Army Form B199A for William John Lang Cornelius.
6. 'Territorial Army Officers', *Western Morning News*, 1 February 1930, 5; 'Territorial Ball at Plymouth', *Western Morning News*, 14 February 1931, 7.
7. 'Troops Who Lined the Route', *Western Morning News*, 14 May 1937, 5.
8. 'Need for More Operators', *Western Morning News*, 5 December 1932, 5.
9. 'Pride in the Forces', *Western Morning News*, 22 January 1934, 6.
10. 'Territorial Specialists', *Western Morning News*, 28 January 1935, 4.
11. 'Territorial Units', *Western Morning News*, 31 March 1937, 11.
12. 'Recruiting for Territorials', *Western Morning News*, 30 April 1937, 5.
13. 'Praised by General', *Western Morning News*, 31 January 1938, 2.
14. 'City Plans New "Drive" for Recruits', *Western Morning News*, 20 April 1939, 5; 'Plymouth Recruiting', *Western Morning News*, 24 April 1939, 5; 'Recruiting Drive', Photograph, *Western Morning News*, 24 April 1939, 10.
15. 'Signal Company's Training Camp', *Western Morning News*, 12 July 1939, 2; '"Warfare" in the Rain', *Western Morning News*, 17 July 1939, 5.
16. 'Wessex Signals', *Western Morning News*, 11 August 1939, 4; 'Employers Thanked', *Western Morning News*, 12 August 1939, 7.
17. Lang Cornelius, 'Lang Cornelius to Anthony Cornelius', 19 November 1939.
18. Lang Cornelius, 'Lang Cornelius to Anthony Cornelius', 18 February 1940.
19. Lang Cornelius, 'Lang Cornelius to Basil Cornelius', 18 February 1940.
20. Cornelius, *My Journey*, 7.
21. 'Traders' Tribute', *Western Morning News*, 8 April 1940, 5.
22. Advertisement: Sale this Day, *Western Morning News*, 6 June 1940, 1.
23. Lang Cornelius, 'Lang Cornelius to Marjorie Cornelius', 30 May 1940.
24. Lang Cornelius, 'Lang Cornelius to Marjorie Cornelius', letter, 1 June 1940.
25. Cornelius, *My Journey*, 8.

Chapter 7: Attacks from the Air

1. 'Target Swilly 1940, 6th July', YouTube video, 25.12, posted by Cyberheritage Steve Johnson, 11 November 2022, <https://www.youtube.com/watch?v=4wcjTgyHON0>.
2. Twyford, *It Came to Our Door*, 9; 'Death-Roll in Raids', *Western Morning News*, 8 July 1940, 6.
3. Henrietta Mould, 'Henrietta Mould to Audrey Mould', 9 July 1940.
4. 'Target Swilly 1940, 6th July'.
5. Mould, 'Mould'.
6. 'Four Killed in Raid in West Town', *Western Morning News*, 8 July 1940, 5–6.
7. Twyford, *It Came to Our Door*, 9–10.
8. Michael McLaughlin, 'The Forgotten Beginning to Plymouth's Blitz', *Plymouth Herald*, 5 July 2025, 15.
9. Twyford, *It Came to Our Door*, 100; 'Four Killed in Raid on West Town'.
10. Twyford, *It Came to Our Door*, 100; 'Bombs Hit Club and Shop', *Western Morning News*, 9 July 1941, 5.
11. Twyford, *It Came to Our Door*, 100.
12. Ibid., 101.
13. Ibid.; 'Girl Safe in Debris of Home', *Western Morning News*, 22 July 1940, 5.
14. 'Black-Out Offenders at Plymouth', *Western Morning News*, August 1940, 5.
15. Cornelius, *My Journey*, 7.
16. Stuart Abel, 'A Tribute to the Shelter Victims', *Evening Herald*, 6 October 2007, 7.

17. J. Cornelius, 'Wise'.
18. Abel, 'A Tribute to the Shelter Victims'.
19. Cornelius, *My Journey*, 4.
20. Ibid.
21. McLaughlin, 'Interview with Peter Chapman'.
22. Abel, 'A Tribute to Shelter Victims'.
23. J. Cornelius, 'Wise'.
24. Wise, 'Cornelius'.
25. 'Shelter Bomb Killed 72'.
26. Wise, 'Cornelius'.
27. Stevens, Primary Source Testimony.
28. 'Shelter Bomb Killed 72'.
29. J. Cornelius, *My Journey*, '4.
30. Twyford, *It Came to Our Door*, 12.
31. 'Shelter Amenities', *Western Morning News*, 21 August 1940, 6.
32. 'Practice to Cease', *Western Morning News*, 24 August 1940, 5.
33. 'Dogs and Smoking', *Western Morning News*, 6 July 1940, 5.
34. 'Eight Rules for Public', *Western Morning News*, 29 August 1940, 5.
35. The Ministry of Health. 'Six Health Hints'. Poster, *c.* July 1941. The Box, Plymouth (1561/127).
36. 'Wardens Have No Powers', *Western Morning News*, 30 August 1940, 6.
37. 'Warden Assaulted During Raid', *Western Morning News*, 12 September 1940, 5.
38. 'In Private Shelters', *Western Morning News*, 17 August 1940, 5.
39. 'Opposed at Plymouth', *Western Morning News*, 14 August 1940, 5.
40. 'Police Help Needed', *Western Morning News*, 3 September 1940, 5.
41. Juliet Gardiner, *The Blitz: The British Under Attack* (London: Harper Press, 2010), 85–87.
42. Ministry of Home Security. *Home Security Circular No 290/1940: Air Raid Shelters*. 11 December 1940. The Box, Plymouth (1561/127).
43. 'Wet Shelters Numerous', *Western Morning News*, 11 November 1940, 5; 'Shelters Are On the Urgent List', *Western Morning News*, 15 November 1940, 5.
44. 'Shelter Amenities', *Western Morning News*, 20 September 1940, 3.
45. 'Bunks for 1,000', *Western Morning News*, 31 January 1941, 5.
46. 'Disinfection of Shelter', *Western Morning News*, 8 October 1940, 5.
47. 'Big Raid Shelters Will Have Sick Bays', *Western Morning News*, 18 October 1940, 3.
48. Twyford, *It Came to Our Door*, 106; ; 'South-West Town Main Nazi Target', *Western Morning News*, 28 November 1940, 5; 'Enemy Planes Over Three S.W. Towns', *Western Morning News*, 29 November 1940, 5.
49. Michael McLaughlin, 'Night the Bombs of the Luftwaffe Blitzed Plymouth', *Plymouth Herald*, 28 November 2025, 4.
50. Twyford, *It Came to Our Door*, 107; 'Many Fires in Town's Most Severe Raid', *Western Morning News*, 30 December 1940, 5.
51. Twyford, *It Came to Our Door*, 110; 'Plymouth Defiant and Carrying On', *Western Morning News*, 15 January 1941, 5.
52. Hollett, 'Looking Back'.
53. Ibid.
54. Twyford, *It Came to Our Door*, 111.
55. Michael McLaughlin, 'The Night the Sirens Were Silent', *Plymouth Herald*, 28 February 2026, 16.
56. Twyford, *It Came to Our Door*, 111.
57. 'Plymouth Is On the Danger List', *Western Morning News*, 7 March 1941, 6.

Chapter 8: Pageantry amid the Peril: The Making of a Royal Visit

1. 'Daphne for the Queen', *Western Morning News*, 7 April 1941, 2.
2. Wasley, *Blitz*, 100.
3. 'Receives D.S.O. from the King', *Western Morning News*, 21 March 1941, 5.
4. 'She Is a Lovely Lady', *Western Morning News*, 21 March 1941, 4.
5. 'Receives D.S.O. from the King'.
6. Wasley, *Blitz*, 103.
7. Nancy Astor, 'Nancy Astor to Plymouth Town Clerk', 13 August 1940. Special Collections, Nancy Astor Archive, University of Reading (MS 1416/1/6/119).
8. Arthur Penn, 'Arthur Penn to Waldorf Astor', 29 September 1940. Special Collections, Nancy Astor Archive, University of Reading (MS 1416/1/6/119).
9. John Ramsden, 'Churchill: A Man Who Believed', *Finest Hour*, 129 (Winter 2005), 30.
10. 'Facing Up to Hitler', *Western Morning News*, 15 January 1941, 5.
11. Mass Observation, *Second Report on Plymouth*, April 1941. File Report No. 626. 1. Reproduced with permission of Curtis Brown, London, on behalf of the Trustees of the Mass Observation Archive. © The Trustees of the Mass Observation Archive.
12. Arthur Penn, 'Arthur Penn to Waldorf Astor', 20 February 1941. Special Collections, Nancy Astor Archive, University of Reading (MS 1416/1/6/119).
13. Nancy Astor, 'Nancy Astor to Arthur Penn', 23 February 1941. Special Collections, Nancy Astor Archive, University of Reading (MS 1416/1/6/119).
14. Arthur Penn, 'Arthur Penn to Waldorf Astor', 28 February 1941. Special Collections, Nancy Astor Archive, University of Reading (MS 1416/1/6/119).
15. Waldorf Astor, 'Waldorf Astor to Arthur Penn', 1 March 1941. Special Collections, Nancy Astor Archive, University of Reading (MS 1416/1/6/119).
16. Baring Gould, 'Notes of Miss Baring Gould', 3 March 1941. Special Collections, Nancy Astor Archive, University of Reading (MS 1416/1/6/119).
17. Nancy Astor, 'Nancy Astor to Arthur Penn', 8 March 1941. Special Collections, Nancy Astor Archive, University of Reading (MS 1416/1/6/119).
18. Great Western Railway, *Notice No. 10*, March 1941. Royal Archives, Windsor (RA PS/PSO/GVI/WARBOMB/04932/234).
19. Alexander Hardinge, 'Alexander Hardinge to Waldorf Astor', 10 March 1941. Royal Archives, Windsor (RA PS/PSO/GVI/WARBOMB/04932/214).
20. Edward Owens, *The Family Firm: Monarchy, Mass Media and the British Public, 1932–53* (London: University of London Press, 2019), 230.
21. Ibid., 233.
22. Office of the Commander-in-Chief, Mount Wise, Devonport, *Memorandum No. P.357/4: Visit of Their Majesties the King and Queen*, 18 March 1941. Special Collections, Nancy Astor Archive, University of Reading (MS 1416/1/6/119).
23. 'Letter from Lord Mayor's Secretary', 18 March 1941. Special Collections, Nancy Astor Archive, University of Reading (MS 1416/1/6/119); 'Visit of Their Majesties the King and Queen, Groups of Women War Workers Invited to Send Representatives', March 1941. Special Collections, Nancy Astor Archive, University of Reading (MS 1416/1/6/119).
24. 'Letter from Colin Campbell', 18 March 1941. Special Collections, Nancy Astor Archive, University of Reading (MS 1416/1/6/119).
25. 'Notes for Lady Astor: Y.M.C.A.', 18 March 1941. Special Collections, Nancy Astor Archive, University of Reading (MS 1416/1/6/119).
26. 'Notes for Lady Astor: Virginia House', 18 March 1941. Special Collections, Nancy Astor Archive, University of Reading (MS 1416/1/6/119).
27. Owens, *The Family Firm*, 231.

28. Andrew Morton, *The Queen: Her Life* (New York: Grand Central Publishing, 2022), 31.
29. Waldorf Astor, 'Waldorf Astor to Alexander Hardinge', 15 March 1941. Royal Archives, Windsor (RA PS/PSO/GVI/WARBOMB/04932/217).
30. Ibid.
31. Mass Observation, *Second Report*, 10.
32. Ibid., 9.
33. Security Control Officer – Plymouth Control. 'Copy of Extract from Fortnightly Intelligence Report', 30 March 1941. Royal Archives, Windsor (RA PS/PSO/GVI/WARBOMB/04932/228).
34. Mass Observation, *Second Report*, 10.
35. Security Control Officer – Plymouth Control.
36. Ibid.
37. 'Household Notes', 18 March 1941. Special Collections, Nancy Astor Archive, University of Reading (1416/1/6/119).
38. Gerald Wasley, *Plymouth: A Shattered City* (Exeter: Halsgrove, 2004), 95.
39. Wasley, *Blitz*, 102.

Chapter 9: The Crown Comes to Town: 20 March 1941

1. 'Court Circular', *The Times*, 21 March 1941, 7.
2. George VI, 'Private Diary of King George VI', 20 March 1941. Royal Archives, Windsor (RA GVI/PRIV/DIARY/WAR/1941: 20 March).
3. 'Royal Visit to City', *Western Evening Herald*, 21 March 1941, 1; 'Visit of their Majesties the King and Queen to Western Approaches Command, Plymouth, 20 March 1941'. Photograph. Imperial War Museum Archive, London (A3483); 'She Is a Lovely Lady'.
4. Norman Hartnell, *Silver and Gold: The Autobiography of Norman Hartnell* (London: V&A Publishing, 2019), 100.
5. 'Royal Visitors at Bombed Plymouth', *Western Morning News*, 21 March 1941, 5.
6. 'Receives D.S.O.'.
7. 'The King and Queen at Plymouth A Crowded Seven Hours', *The Times*, 21 March 1941, 7.
8. 'Receives D.S.O.'.
9. Wasley, *Plymouth*, 90.
10. 'The King and Queen at Plymouth'.
11. 'Receives D.S.O.'.
12. 'Proud Moment in Royal Visit to Devonport', *Western Evening Herald*, 21 March 1941, 4.
13. 'Receives D.S.O.'.
14. 'Royal Visitors at Bombed Plymouth'.
15. Ibid.
16. Ibid.
17. Ibid.
18. Ibid.
19. Owens, *The Family Firm*, 235.
20. Wasley, *Blitz*, 103.
21. 'Royal Visit to City'.
22. 'Receives D.S.O.'.
23. Ministry of Information, *Plymouth Blitz*, 1942.
24. 'The Queen Praises Women of Plymouth', *Western Morning News*, 21 March 1941, 5.
25. Ibid.
26. 'Address of the Lord Mayor', 29 October 1947. Royal Archives, Windsor (RA PS/PSO/GVI/PS/VISUK/ 08717/065).
27. 'The Queen Praises Women of Plymouth'.

28. Ibid.
29. Ibid.
30. 'The Queen Praises Women of Plymouth'.
31. 'Royal Visitors at Bombed Plymouth'.
32. Navy Registers of Seamen's Services, 1848–1939, for William Henry Burring. 'Body Recovered from Dock', *Dundee Evening Telegraph*, 8 September 1939.
33. 'Royal Visitors at Bombed Plymouth'.
34. Ibid.
35. Ibid.
36. Mass Observation, *Third Report on Plymouth*, October 1941. File Report No. 903. 4. Reproduced with permission of Curtis Brown, London, on behalf of the Trustees of the Mass Observation Archive. © The Trustees of the Mass Observation Archive.
37. 'City Mothers Sing', *Western Morning News*, 21 March 1941, 5.
38. Ibid.
39. 'The King and Queen at Plymouth'.
40. 'City Mothers Sing'.
41. Ibid.
42. Wasley, *Plymouth,* 92.
43. Dorothy Stanleick, Untitled Memories (1989).
44. Wasley, *Blitz*, 103.
45. Stanleick, Untitled Memories.
46. John Van der Kiste, *Plymouth: A City at War 1914–1945* (Stroud: The History Press, 2014), 77.
47. 'Royal Visitors at Bombed Plymouth'.
48. 'Cakes Attract Queen', *Western Morning News*, 21 March 1941, 5.
49. 'Herald Man Meets Queen', *Western Evening Herald*, 21 March 1941, 1.
50. Twyford, *It Came to Our Door*, 114.
51. 'Throne and People', *Western Morning News*, 21 March 1941, 2.
52. Owens, *The Family Firm*, 230.
53. 'Royal Visitors at Bombed Plymouth'.
54. Ibid.

Chapter 10: The Plymouth Blitz Begins

1. 'Fortitude and Strength of Astors Came Shining through Dark', *Evening Herald*, Blitz Supplement, 6 March 1991, 11.
2. Wasley, *Blitz*, 111.
3. Ibid., 106.
4. George VI, 'Private Diary'.
5. Twyford, *It Came to Our Door*, 112.
6. 'Fortitude and Strength'.
7. 'Fire Bombs by the Thousand', *Western Morning News*, 21 March 1941, 3.
8. 'Cold Anger in County', *Western Morning News*, 26 April 1941, 2.
9. Gerald Wasley, *Devon at War: 1939–1945* (Devon: Devon Books, 1994). 73.
10. Twyford, *It Came to Our Door*, 113.
11. Crispin Gill, 'Heaps of Rubble Spewed into Road', *Evening Herald*, Blitz Supplement, 6 March 1991, 18.
12. Twyford, *It Came to Our Door*, 113.
13. Gill, 'Heaps of Rubble Spewed into Road'.
14. 'Severe Raid on Plymouth', *The Times*, 22 March 1941, 4.
15. Twyford, *It Came to Our Door*, 113.

16. 'Services Did Fine Work in City Raids', *Western Morning News*, 29 March 1941, 6.
17. Wasley, *Blitz*, 112.
18. 'Fire Bombs'.
19. Winston G. Ramsey (ed.), *The Blitz: Then and Now: Volume 2* (London: Battle of Britain Prints International, 1988), 493; Wasley, *Blitz*, 207.
20. Twyford, *It Came to Our Door*, 113.
21. Hannah Wood, 'Son's Donation to Blitz Tribute', *Evening Herald*, 6 May 2006, 6.
22. Hollett, 'Looking Back'.
23. Mills, 'Cornelius', 1 January 1996.
24. J. Cornelius, 'Mills'.
25. Mills, 'Cornelius', 1 January 1996.
26. Hollett, 'Looking Back'.
27. Twyford, *It Came to Our Door*, 113.
28. 'Ancient Church Is Damaged', *Western Evening Herald*, 21 March 1941, 1.
29. Twyford, *It Came to Our Door*, 114.
30. '100-Planes Raid Starts Plymouth Fires', *Western Evening Herald*, 21 March 1941, 1.
31. Ibid.
32. 'Queen Elizabeth to Queen Mary', 21 March 1941. Royal Archives, Windsor (RA QM/PRIV/CC12/158).
33. George VI. 'George VI to the Astors', 21 March 1941. Royal Archives, Windsor (RA PS 04932/224).
34. Gardiner, *The Blitz*, 13.

Chapter 11: 'It was again hell let loose'

1. The heading for this chapter comes from: Twyford, *It Came to Our Door*, 114.
2. Wasley, *Blitz*, 117.
3. Twyford, *It Came to Our Door*, 114.
4. Ramsey, 494.
5. 'Nazis Dive-bomb Blazing City in Second Plymouth Blitz', *Western Evening Herald*, 22 March 1941, 1.
6. Crispin Gill, *Resurrexi: I Have Risen Again* (Plymouth: Hitchings & Mason Ltd, 1997).
7. Charleston, 'The Prophetic Notices for Rebirth of a City'.
8. The subheading above comes from: Twyford, *It Came to Our Door*, 115.
9. Ibid. 116.
10. Ibid. 115.
11. 'Many Homeless in Plymouth', *The Times*, 24 March 1941, 2.
12. Mass Observation, *Third Report*, 5.
13. John Cornelius, 'John Cornelius to Pamela Selley', 2 July 1996.
14. John Ray, *The Night Blitz, 1940–1941* (London: Arms and Armour Press, 1996), 217.
15. 'Many Homeless in Plymouth'.
16. Mass Observation, *Second Report*, 2.
17. 'Plymouth Shows Its Courage', *Western Morning News*, 24 March 1941, 6.
18. 'Queen Elizabeth to Nancy Astor', 23 March 1941. Special Collections, Nancy Astor Archive, University of Reading (MS 1416/1/4/8).
19. War Deaths Department, 'Air Raids on Plymouth, 20th and 21st March', Notes, 1941. The Box, Plymouth (1564/2/16).
20. Ibid.
21. Ibid.
22. Ibid.

23. 'One Grave for Raid Victims', *Western Morning News*, 28 March 1941, 2.
24. The subheading above comes from: 'City Council is Still in Control', *Western Morning News*, 27 March 1941, 5.
25. City of Plymouth: 'Emergency Bulletin No. 2', 25 March 1941; 'Emergency Bulletin No. 3', 26 March 1941; 'Emergency Bulletin No. 4', 27 March 1941; 'Emergency Bulletin No. 5', 28 March 1941; 'Emergency Bulletin No. 6', 29 March 1941; 'Emergency Bulletin No. 7', 30 March 1941; 'Emergency Bulletin No. 8', 3 April 1941; 'Emergency Bulletin No. 9', 8 April 1941. The Box, Plymouth (1561/194).
26. City of Plymouth. 'Emergency Bulletin No. 8'.
27. City of Plymouth. 'Emergency Bulletin No. 2'.
28. Ibid.
29. City of Plymouth. 'Emergency Bulletin No. 7'.
30. 'Plymouth Goes to Task of Cleaning Up', *Western Morning News*, 24 March 1941, 6; 'They "Jumped To It"', *Western Morning News*, 31 March 1941, 2.
31. City of Plymouth. 'Emergency Bulletin No. 9'.
32. Cornelius, *My Journey*, 8.
33. 'Epic of the "Blitz"', *Western Morning News*, 5 April 1941, 2; 'Handshake for Post Office Hero'. Photograph, *Western Morning News*, 7 April 1941, 2.
34. War Deaths Department, 'Air Raids on Plymouth, 20th and 21st March'.
35. 'Plymouth Has Taken Hard Knock Well', *Western Morning News*, 25 March 1941, 5.
36. *Front Line: 1940–41: The Official Story of the Civil Defence of Britain* (London: His Majesty's Stationery Office, 1942).
37. Mass Observation, *Second Report*, 2.
38. Twyford, *It Came to Our Door*, 115.

Chapter 12: The Blitz Resumes: 21 April

1. 'City Schools After the Blitz', *Western Morning News*, 10 April 1941, 5.
2. 'Air Situation Report, 21 April 1941'. Imperial War Museum Archive, London (Document 8378). Translated.
3. Gardiner, *The Blitz*, 51.
4. Victor Saundercock, 'Devonport Blitz'. 2004. WW2 People's War. A2938421.
5. Ministry of Home Security. *Air Raids: What You Must Know, What You Must Do.* 1940. The Box, Plymouth (1151/46). 8.
6. 'Plymouth Gets New-Type Double Blitz', *Cornish Evening Herald*, 22 April 1941, 1.
7. Twyford, *It Came to Our Door*, 119.
8. 'Air Situation Report, 21 April 1941'.
9. *Plymouth Blitz 'Bomb Book'*. 1941. The Box, Plymouth (1555/40). Air Raid 38, 21 April 1941.
10. Twyford, *It Came to Our Door*, 118.
11. 'Plymouth Gets New-Type Double Blitz', *Cornish Evening Herald*.
12. 'Vicious Raid on South-West Coastal Town', *Western Morning News*, 22 April 1941, 6.
13. Ibid.
14. Ministry of Home Security, *Air Raids: What You Must Know, What You Must Do*, 25–30.
15. 'Bomber Shot Down By A.A. Guns in Plymouth Blitz', *Western Evening Herald*, 22 April 1941, 1.
16. 'Plymouth Gets New-Type Double Blitz', *Cornish Evening Herald*.
17. Twyford, *It Came to Our Door*, 119.
18. 'Vicious Raid on South-West Coastal Town'.
19. Wasley, *Blitz*, 207.
20. Twyford, *It Came to Our Door*, 119.
21. The subheading above comes from: Twyford, *It Came to Our Door*, 118.

22. Lilian Chapman, Telegram, 22 April 1941.
23. 'Plymouth Gets New-Type Double Blitz', *Cornish Evening Herald.*
24. "Plymouth Gets New-Type Double Blitz', *Cornish Evening Herald.* 'Plymouth Gets New-Type Double Blitz', *Western Evening Herald*, 22 April 1941, 1.
25. Twyford, *It Came to Our Door*, 121.
26. 'Plymouth Gets New-Type Double Blitz', *Cornish Evening Herald.*
27. City of Plymouth. *Emergency Committee Minutes.* 23 April 1941, 4.30 p.m. The Box, Plymouth (1561/183).
28. 'Heavy Attack on Plymouth', *Times*, 23 April 1941, 4.
29. 'Raids on Plymouth 21st to 23rd April, 1941. Note on Visit to Plymouth'. National Archives, Kew (HO 186/625).
30. 'Plymouth Gets New-Type Double Blitz', *Cornish Evening Herald.*
31. 'Bomber Shot Down by A.A. Guns in Plymouth Blitz'.
32. 'Plymouth Gets New-Type Double Blitz', *Cornish Evening Herald.*
33. Ibid.
34. 'Bomber Shot Down By A.A. Guns in Plymouth Blitz'.
35. 'Raids on Plymouth 21st to 23rd April, 1941'.
36. 'Raids on Plymouth 21st to 23rd April, 1941'.
37. City of Plymouth. *Emergency Committee Minutes.* 22 April 1941. The Box, Plymouth (1561/183).
38. 'Raids on Plymouth 21st to 23rd April, 1941'.
39. Twyford, *It Came to Our Door*, 91.
40. 'Raids on Plymouth 21st to 23rd April, 1941'.
41. Ibid.
42. City of Plymouth, 'Emergency Bulletin No. 2'.
43. Hollett, 'Looking Back'.
44. Michael Charleston, 'When Pain and Death Poured from the Skies', *Western Morning News*, 23 March 1991, 4.
45. McLaughlin, 'Interview with Peter Chapman'; Michael McLaughlin, 'A Plymouth Boy's Blitz Survival Story', *Plymouth Herald*, 22 April 2025, 4–5.
46 Ena Payne, 'Vain search for family after shelter was bombed,' courtesy Friends of Ford Park Cemetery.
47. Hollett, 'Looking Back'.
48. Ibid.

Chapter 13: The Incident at Portland Square: 22–23 April

1. Mills, 'Cornelius', 1 January 1996.
2. 'Air Situation Report, 22/23 April 1941'. Imperial War Museum Archive, London (Document 8378). Translated.
3. City of Plymouth. *Plymouth City Diary.* 22 April 1941. The Box, Plymouth (773/16).
4. 'Heavy Damage at Plymouth', *The Times*, 24 April 1941, 2.
5. Ministry of Home Security, *Air Raids*, 22.
6. Vicky Norman, *Scattered Homes, Broken Hearts* (Vicky Norman, 2002), 97.
7. Cornelius, *My Journey*, 9.
8. 'Loss to Boot Trade', *Western Evening Herald*, 28 April 1941, 4.
9. Martin Freeman, 'We Must Not Forget the 76 Victims of Portland Square', *Evening Herald*, 26 November 2005, 4.
10. Mills, 'Cornelius', 1 January 1996.
11. Ibid.
12. Charleston, 'When Pain and Death Poured from the Skies'.

13 Michael McLaughlin, 'Book gives voice to the effects of Blitz's toll,' Plymouth Herald, 26 May 2026, 16.
14. Freeman, 'We Must Not Forget the 76 Victims of Portland Square'.
15. Charlie Morton, 'Survivor', *Evening Herald*, 21 April 2001, 1.
16. McLaughlin, 'Interview with Peter Chapman'.
17. 'Soldier Hero of Raid Tragedy', *Western Evening Herald*, 26 April 1941, 1.
18. Mills, 'Cornelius', 1 January 1996.
19. Douglas Barretto, 'Doug Barretto to John Cornelius', 22 September 1996.
20. Cornelius, *Two Journeys*.
21. 'Memorial to 72 Dead Unveiled'.
22. 'Arthur Seeks Air Raid Survivors', *Western Evening Herald*, 12 March 1981, 12.
23. Stevens, Primary Source Testimony.
24. 'Ben Bennett, a Survivor of the Portland Square Air Raid Shelter Disaster Speaks in 1993, Audio Only', Facebook video, 16.21, 2 December 2017, <https://www.facebook.com/stephen.johnson.54379236/videos/1738580232821522>.
25. Ministry of Health. 'Public Shelter Rules', 20 March 1941. The Box, Plymouth (1561/127). I.4.c.
26. 'Ben Bennett'.
27. Wise, 'Cornelius'.
28. 'Plymouth: The Blitz Remembered – Portland Square', regional television news programme, March 2001.
29. Charleston, 'When Pain and Death Poured from the Skies'.
30. Ministry of Health, 'Public Shelter Rules'.
31. Hannah Wood, 'My Family Wouldn't Exist if it Wasn't for Blackie the Spaniel', *Evening Herald*, 29 April 2006, 3.
32. Nelson Eyres, 'N. Eyres to Collin Campbell', 19 September 1941.
33. Charles Palmer, 'Report Made by Charles Palmer', (n.d.), courtesy Anne Corry, 11 October 2024.
34. 'Food Convoys Rushed to Plymouth', *Western Morning News*, 24 April 1941, 5.
35. 'Severe Raid on S.W. Coastal Town', *Western Morning News*, 23 April 1941, 4.
36. 'Food Convoys Rushed to Plymouth'.
37. Twyford, *It Came to Our Door*, 122,
38. 'Food Convoys Rushed to Plymouth'.
39. 'Air Situation Report, 22/23 April 1941'.
40. 'Food Convoys Rushed to Plymouth'.
41. Lilian Northwood, 'The Air Raids on Plymouth', 2 November 2003. WW2 People's War. A1951959.
42. 'Raids on Plymouth 21st to 23rd April, 1941'.
43. Wasley, *Blitz*, 151.
44. 'Severe Raid on S.W. Coastal Town'.
45. Twyford, *It Came to Our Door*, 121.
46. 'Heavy Damage at Plymouth'.
47. 'Many Killed When Heavy Bomb Hits Communal Shelter', *Western Evening Herald*, 23 April 1941, 1.
48. Freeman, 'We Must Not Forget the 76 Victims of Portland Square'.
49. Charleston, 'When Pain and Death Poured from the Skies'.
50. Hollett, 'Looking Back'.
51. 'Fate and Hitler's Firebomb', *Western Evening Herald*, 11 September 1998, 10.
52. Frances McLaughlin, personal correspondence with the author, 18 September 2025.
53. Payne.
54. C. Morton, 'Survivor'.
55. 'Ben Bennett'.

56. 'A Night of Horror that Changed Lives Forever', *Evening Herald*, 21 April 2001, 14.
57. Brock.
58. Hollett, 'Looking Back'.
59. Freeman, 'We Must Not Forget the 76 Victims of Portland Square'.

Chapter 14: Response and Rescue

1. 'Shelter Bomb Killed 72'.
2. Johns, *Days of Destiny*, 47.
3. 'Saddest Duty in Raids', *Evening Herald*, Blitz Supplement, 6 March 1991, 13.
4. Charleston, 'When Pain and Death Poured from the Skies'.
5. 'Fate and Hitler's Firebomb'.
6. Brock.
7. 'Ben Bennett'.
8. Colin Campbell, 'ARP Controller's Report for the Air Rads of the 21st, 22nd, 23rd April and 28th and 29th April, 1941', 16 May 1941. The Box, Plymouth (1495/54). III.C and III.D.
9. Frank Phillips, 'Messenger's memories,' courtesy Friends of Ford Park Cemetery.
10. Charlie Morton, 'I Didn't Want to Die by Being Buried Alive', *Evening Herald*, March 12, 2001, 4.
11. Ibid.
12. Johns, *Days of Destiny*, 46.
13. Freeman, 'We Must Not Forget the 76 Victims of Portland Square'.
14. Mills, 'Cornelius', 1 January 1996.
15. Freeman, 'We Must Not Forget the 76 Victims of Portland Square'.
16. Mills, 'Cornelius', 1 January 1996.
17. Ibid.
18. Freeman, 'We Must Not Forget the 76 Victims of Portland Square'; Barbara Mills, untitled memories, courtesy Friends of Ford Park Cemetery.
19. Hollett, 'Looking Back'.
20. 'A Night of Horror that Changed Lives Forever', *Evening Herald*, 21 April 2001, 14.
21. Ministry of Home Security, *Air Raids*, 22.
22. 'City Labourer is Awarded B.E.M.', *Western Morning News*, 19 July 1941, 6.
23. 'Bert's Endurance', *Western Morning News*, 3 December 1941, 2.
24. 'City Labourer is Awarded B.E.M.'.
25. 'Bert's Endurance'.
26. 'Bert's Endurance'.
27. Nelson Eyres, 'Report made by Nelson Edgar Eyres', (n.d.) courtesy Anne Corry, 11 October 2024.
28. Ibid.
29. Eyres, 'N. Eyres to Collin Campbell'.
30. Palmer, 'Report'.
31. 'Brave Plymothians', *Western Morning News*, 16 August 1941, 2.
32. Palmer, 'Report'.
33. Eyres, 'N. Eyres to Collin Campbell'.
34. Palmer, 'Report'.
35. L. Brickwood, 'Report Made by L. Brickwood', (n.d.) courtesy Anne Corry, 11 October 2024.
36. Palmer, 'Report'.
37. Eyres, 'N. Eyres to Collin Campbell'.
38. 'Brave Plymothians'.
39. Eyres, 'N. Eyres to Collin Campbell'.
40. C. Morton, 'Survivor'.

41. F. McLaughlin, personal correspondence.
42. Ibid.
43. Payne.
44. 'Many Killed when Heavy Bomb Hits Communal Shelter'.
45. 'Another Double Blitz on Plymouth Starts Fires, Wrecks Houses', *Cornish Evening Herald*, 23 April 1941, 1.

Chapter 15: Recovery and Retrieval

1. Brock.
2. Unless otherwise indicated, references in this section are from Johns, *Days of Destiny*, 47–52.
3. Campbell, 'ARP Controller's Report'.
4. 'Whole Families Killed in the Worst Single Disaster of the Blitz', *Evening Herald*, Blitz Supplement, 6 March 1991, 21.
5. Ibid.
6. Jane Waller and Michael Vaughn-Reese, *Blitz: the Civilian War, 1941–45* (London: Macdonald & Co, 1990), 146.
7. Phillips.
8. Michael McLaughlin, 'Book gives blitz.'
9. 'A Night of Horrors Changed Lives Forever', *Evening Herald*, 21 April 2001, 14.
10. Waller and Vaughn-Reese, *Blitz*, 146; 'Saddest Duty in Raids'.
11. Freeman, 'We Must Not Forget the 76 Victims of Portland Square'.
12. Charleston, 'When Pain and Death Poured from the Skies'.
13. Rita Boswell, personal correspondence with author, 10 August 2023; Barbara Mills, 'Barbara Mills to John Cornelius', 19 November 1996; Freeman, 'We Must Not Forget the 76 Victims of Portland Square'.
14. Doug Barretto, 'Doug Barretto to John Cornelius', 9 October 1996.
15. Van der Kiste, *Plymouth*, 101.
16. 'Shelter Bomb Killed 72'.
17. Ibid.

Chapter 16: 'They had gone home'

1 Unless noted, references in this chapter (including the chapter heading above) are derived from the Civilian War Death Forms for William and Marjorie Cornelius, part of 'Mortuary Records: Portland Square Air Raid Shelter', 1941. The Box, Plymouth (773/16). Cornelius, *My Journey*, 8.
2. Cornelius, *Two Journeys*, 1–2.
3. Cornelius, *My Journey*, 8.
4. Ministry of Health. *Circular 1914*, November 1939. The Box, Plymouth (1564/10/1).

Chapter 17: Civilian Casualty Management

1. City of Plymouth, *Plymouth City Diary*.
2. Hollett, 'Looking Back'.
3. A.B. Williamson, 'The Problem of the Disposal of the Dead after Air Raids', *Report of Proceedings Eighth Joint Conference of Cemetery and Crematorium Authorities* (Portsmouth, 26 June 1939).
4. Ministry of Health, *Circular 1779*.
5. Ministry of Health, *Memorandum 222*, 1939.
6. Ministry of Health. *Circular 2470*, 1941. The Box, Plymouth (1564/2/16).
7. Williamson, 'The Problem of the Disposal of the Dead after Air Raids'.

8. Ministry of Health. *War Deaths: Emergency Mortuary and Burial Arrangements*, 1942. The Box, Plymouth (1714/4/5).
9. Ministry of Health, *Circular 1779*.
10. Ministry of Health. *Circular 1949*, January 1940. The Box, Plymouth (1564/10/2).
11. Ministry of Health. *Circular 1846*, August 1939. The Box, Plymouth (1564/10/1).
12. Hollett, 'Looking Back'.
13. Leslie Martin, 'The Duties of a Mortuary Superintendent', 1942. The Box, Plymouth (1714/6/6).
14. 'City's Blitz Victims Are Laid at Rest', *Western Evening Herald*, 28 April 1941, 1.
15. Ministry of Health, *War deaths*.
16. Ministry of Health, *Circular 1779*.
17. Ministry of Health. *Circular 2112*, August 1940. The Box, Plymouth (1564/2/16).
18. Williamson, 'The Problem of the Disposal of the Dead after Air Raids'.
19. Ministry of Health, *Memorandum 222*, 1939.
20. Ministry of Health. *Circular 2398*, 1941. The Box, Plymouth (1564/2/16).
21. Williamson, 'The Problem of the Disposal of the Dead after Air Raids'.
22. Mass Observation, *Third Report*, 3.
23. Percy Cole, Lecture, December 1942. The Box, Plymouth (1714/6/4); Martin, 'The Duties of a Mortuary Superintendent'; Ministry of Health. 'Draft Conference Syllabus', October 1942. The Box, Plymouth (1714/6/3).
24. Hollett, 'Looking Back'.

Chapter 18: Halwell Street Mortuary

1. Unless noted, references to the victims and administration of the incident at the Portland Square Air Raid Shelter are derived from an analysis of 'Mortuary Records: Portland Square Air Raid Shelter', 1941. The Box, Plymouth (773/16). Hollett, 'Looking Back'.
2. City of Plymouth, *Emergency Committee Minutes*, 23 April 1941.
3. Ministry of Health, *Memorandum 222: Civilian Deaths due to War Operations Identification, Records and Registration*', revised July 1941. The Box, Plymouth (1714/6/1).
4. The deaths of five other victims were recorded elsewhere: Eric Farrant and John MacGregor, both of whom survived the blast, were moved to the City and Prince of Wales, Greenbank hospitals, respectively, where they later died; William Surgeoner and Ted Hempkins were active servicemen whose deaths fell under the jurisdiction of the War Department; and the body of Ted's wife Pauline was never found.
5. Ibid.; Campbell, 'ARP Controller's Report'; Cole, Lecture.
6. Ministry of Health, *Circular 2112*.
7. Ministry of Health, *Memorandum 222*, 1939.
8. Cole, Lecture.
9. Ibid.
10. Hollett, 'Looking Back'.
11. Cole, Lecture; Ministry of Health, *War Deaths*.
12. Hollett, 'Looking Back'.
13. Ibid.
14. Ibid.
15. Ministry of Health, *War Deaths*.
16. Ibid.
17. Martin, 'The Duties of a Mortuary Superintendent'.
18. Ministry of Health, *War Deaths*.
19. Martin, 'The Duties of a Mortuary Superintendent'.

20. Maggie Pugh, personal correspondence with author, 20 August 2025.
21. Graham Plant, personal correspondence with author, 10 September 2025.
22. Ministry of Health, *Circular 2112*.
23. Boswell ,personal correspondence.
24. 'Soldier Hero of Raid Tragedy'.
25. Van der Kiste, *Plymouth*, 114.
26. 'Soldier Hero of Raid Tragedy'.
27. Ibid.
28. Twyford, *It Came to Our Door*, 148.
29. Van der Kiste, *Plymouth*, 114; 'Soldier Hero of Raid Tragedy'.
30. 'Soldier Hero of Raid Tragedy'.
31. 'Missing Persons List', April 1941. The Box, Plymouth (1714/5/5).
32. War Deaths Department, 'Air Raids on Plymouth, 21st, 22nd, and 23rd April, and 28th and 29th April, 1941'.
33. Hollett, 'Looking Back'.
34. Ibid.
35. Ibid.
36. 'Can Presume Raid Deaths', *Western Morning News*, 25 March 1941, 2.
37. Plymouth: The People's Blitz. 'Faces of the Blitz: Hempkins', Facebook. <https://m.facebook.com/PlymouthThePeoplesBlitz/photos/faces-of-the-plymouth-blitz-this-lovely-wedding-photo-of-edward-hempkins-and-his/702859976490784/>, 22 April 2015.

Chapter 19: Burial of the Dead

1. McLaughlin, 'Interview with Peter Chapman'.
2. Florence Chapman, 'Telegram, 23 April 1941'.
3. Gladys Temlett, 'Gladys Temlett to Nell', 24 April 1941.
4. Ibid.
5. Julie Rugg, 'Managing "Civilian Deaths due to War Operations": Yorkshire Experiences During World War II', *Twentieth Century British History*, 15(2), 2004, 152–173.
6. Noakes, 'Valuing the Dead'; Rugg, 'Managing "Civilian Deaths due to War Operations"'.
7. Noakes, *Dying for the Nation*.
8. Noakes, 'Valuing the Dead'.
9. Ministry of Health, *War Deaths*.
10. Ministry of Health, *Circular 2470*.
11. Rugg, 'Managing "Civilian Deaths due to War Operations"'.
12. 'One Grave for Raids Victims'.
13. Ministry of Health, *Circular 2470*.
14. Ministry of Health, *War Deaths*.
15. War Deaths Department, 'Air Raids on Plymouth, 21st, 22nd and 23rd April, and 28th and 29th April 1941'.
16. Michael McLaughlin, 'Private and Public Civilian Burial in Second World War Britain: A Case Study of the Plymouth Blitz,' *Journal of Mortality*, 2025 (Dec), epub.
17. Cornelius, *My Journey*, 8.
18. Ibid., 9.
19. Ibid.
20. Cornelius, *Two Journeys*, 1–2.
21. Cornelius, *My Journey*, 9.
22. Ibid.
23. Ibid.

24. Ibid.
25. 'Transport Bearers', *Western Morning News*, 6 May 1941, 5.
26. 'Deaths due to War Operations. Air Raids 21st, 22nd & 23rd April, 1941. Bodies Received and Identified at Halwell Street & Weston Mill. & Efford', 1941. The Box, Plymouth (1714/4/2); Ford Park Cemetery, 'Portland Square Mortuary and Burial List'.
27. War Deaths Department, 'Air Raids on Plymouth, 21st, 22nd and 23rd April, and 28th and 29th April 1941'; 'Deaths due to War Operations'.
28. 'Man a Mere Chattel to the Nazis', *Western Morning News*, 28 April 1941, 3.
29. To preserve order, friends and relatives were able to obtain tickets to the service from the Technical College on Tavistock Road. 'Evacuation Area?', *Western Morning News*, 28 April 1941, 3.
30. 'One Grave for Raids Victims'; 'Their Grave is Sacred', *Western Morning News*, 29 April 1941, 2.
31. 'City's Blitz Victims Are Laid at Rest'.
32. 'Their Grave is Sacred'.
33. 'City's Blitz Victims Are Laid at Rest'.
34. Ibid.
35. 'Their Grave is Sacred'.
36. Ibid.
37. 'Soldier Hero of Raid Tragedy'.
38. 'Their Grave is Sacred'.
39. Cole, Lecture.
40. Mass Observation, *Third Report*, 1.

Chapter 20: A Day in the Life of Winston Churchill: 2 May 1941

1. 'Premier Heartens Homeless in City Centre', *Western Evening Herald*, 28 April, 3. The speech ended with a quote from "Say Not the Struggle Naught Availeth" (1849) by Arthur Hugh Clough.
2. As First Lord of the Admiralty, Winston Churchill visited Plymouth on 14 February 1940 to welcome home the cruiser HMS *Exeter* from the first naval battle of the Second World War, the Battle of the River Plate.
3. 'Lady Astor Indicts "Ministry of Inflammation"', *Western Evening Herald*, 29 April 1941, 1; 'That "Short, Sharp Raid" Bulletin', *Western Morning News*, 30 April 1941, 5.
4. 'Less than the Truth', *Western Morning News*, 1 May 1941, 2.
5. Mass Observation, *Third Report*, 35.
6. Ibid.
7. Wasley, *Blitz*, 178; Mass Observation, *Third Report*, 35.
8. Winston Churchill, 'The Prime Minister's Personal Minutes. May, 1941'. Churchill Archives Centre, Cambridge (Char 20/35/5).
9. 'Premier in Plymouth', *Western Morning News*, 3 May 1941, 3.
10. Ibid.
11. 'Their Hearts are High', Photograph, *Western Morning News*, 5 May 1941, 5.
12. Frank Wintle, *The Plymouth Blitz* (Cornwall: Bossiney Books, 1981), 54.
13. Van der Kiste, *Plymouth*, 110.
14. 'Premier in Plymouth'.
15. 'This is London Wall'. Object. Imperial War Museum Archive, London (EPH 9785).
16. 'Mr Churchill Visits Plymouth – NO SOUND', YouTube video, 6.33, posted by British Movietone, 21 July 2015, <https://www.youtube.com/watch?v=4i49oc0yJ2M>.
17. Admiral Sir Martin Dunbar Nasmith relinquished his command of Plymouth at the end of April. Churchill's visit coincided with Forbes's installation.
18. Wasley, *Blitz*, 182. Van der Kiste, *Plymouth*, 109.

19. Wasley, *Blitz*, 182.
20. Van der Kiste, *Plymouth*, 110.
21. 'Premier in Plymouth'.
22. Mass Observation, *Third Report*, 35.
23. Ibid.
24. Ibid.
25. 'Churchill Visits Plymouth', YouTube video, 1.04, posted by British Pathé, 13 April 2014, <https://www.youtube.com/watch?v=I5Tr-iPL01U>.
26. Mass Observation, *Third Report*, 35.
27. 'Their Grave is Sacred'.
28. 'Premier in Plymouth'.
29. 'Ibid.
30. Wasley, *Blitz*, 182. Van der Kiste, *Plymouth*, 111.
31. 'Premier in Plymouth'.
32. Ibid.
33. Mass Observation, *Third Report*, 6.
34. 'Premier in Plymouth'.
35. 'Mr. Churchill Tours Ten Miles of Blitzed Plymouth', *Western Evening Herald*, 3 May 1941, 3.
36. 'Churchill Visits Plymouth'.
37. Mass Observation, *Third Report*, 36. Reproduced with permission of Curtis Brown, London, on behalf of the Trustees of the Mass Observation Archive. © The Trustees of the Mass Observation Archive.
38. 'Astor Home Hit', *Western Evening Herald*, 23 April 1941, 1.
39. Twyford, *It Came to Our Door*, 2.
40. 'Premier in Plymouth'.
41. 'Mr. Churchill Tours Ten Miles of Blitzed Plymouth'.
42. Ibid.
43. 'Their Hearts are High'.
44. 'Talk of the City', *Western Evening Herald*, 3 May 1941.
45. Wintle, *The Plymouth Blitz*, 54.
46. Wasley, *Blitz*, 182.
47. 'Premier in Plymouth'.
48. Mass Observation, *Third Report*, 37–38.
49. 'Talk of the City'.
50. Mass Observation, *Third Report*, 37.
51. Ibid., 38.
52. George Lowe, *Situation Report for the Fortnight Ending 10 May 1941*, 12 May 1941.
53. Mass Observation, *Third Report*, 36.
54. Twyford, *It Came to Our Door*, 131.
55. Mass Observation, *Third Report*, 2–3.
56. Ibid., 11, 15, 25.

Chapter 21: 'An episode that should not be forgotten'

1. The heading for this chapter comes from the article 'Last Post for Blitz Victims', *Western Evening Herald*, 23 April 1981, 1.
2. 'A Plymouth to Rival Copenhagen', *Western Morning News*, 2 April 1941, 5.
3. J.P. Watson and Patrick Abercrombie. *A Plan for Plymouth: The Report Prepared for the City Council* (Plymouth: Underhill, 1943). 28.
4. Ibid.

5. Ibid.
6. 'Arthur Seeks Air Raid Survivors'.
7. Ibid.
8. 'Shelter Bomb Killed 72'.
9. Ibid.
10. Imperial War Museum, War Memorials Register, 'Plymouth City Blitz', <https://www.iwm.org.uk/memorials/item/memorial/25734>.
11. 'Memorial Battle Victory', *Western Evening Herald*, 10 June 1981, 7.
12. City of Plymouth, *Minutes of the Plymouth City Council Public Services Committee*, 21 April 1981. Plymouth & West Devon Record Office, Plymouth (PWDRO, PCC/1/1).
13. 'Decision on Blitz Plaque Put Off', *Western Evening Herald*, 22 April 1981, 5.
14. Ibid.
15. 'Another Round in Plaque Fight', *Western Evening Herald*, 30 May 1981, 4.
16. 'Shelter Bomb Killed 72'.
17. Douglas Barretto, 'Doug Barretto to John Cornelius', 3 December 1995; Barretto, October 1996.
18. 'They Went and Remembered', *Western Evening Herald*, 23 April 1981, 5.
19. Ibid.
20. City of Plymouth, *Minutes of the Plymouth City Council Public Services Committee*, 9 June 1981. Plymouth & West Devon Record Office, Plymouth (PWDRO, PCC/1/1).
21. 'Memorial Battle Victory'.
22. Imperial War Museum, War Memorials Register, 'Portland Square Air Raid Shelter Victims', <https://www.iwm.org.uk/memorials/item/memorial/46036>.
23. 'Blitz Memorial Plan Delayed', *Western Evening Herald*, 21 November 1981, 1.
24. 'Blitz Disaster Memorial to Go Ahead', *Western Evening Herald*, 11 December 1981, 3.
25. Cornelius, *Two Journeys*.
26. J. Cornelius, 'Letter to Catherine Hunt', September 1993.
27. J. Cornelius, 'Mills'.
28. John Cornelius, 'John Cornelius to Catherine Hunt', 1 December 1996.
29. Charlie Morton, 'Shelter Blast Killed Dozens', *Evening Herald*, 15 March 2001, 4.
30. 'Seen and Heard', *Evening Herald*, 25 September 1995, 6.
31. John Cornelius, 'John Cornelius to Doug Barretto', 31 March 1997.
32. John Cornelius, 'John Cornelius to R. J. Bull', 6 February 1997.
33. J. Cornelius, 'Barretto'.
34. 'Shock at University Plan to Close Campus', *Evening Herald*, 9 July 2005, 9.
35. John Cornelius, 'John Cornelius to Roland Levinsky', 17 July 2005.
36. Tony Rees, 'Tony Rees to John Cornelius', 10 July 2005; Tony Rees, 'Tony Rees to John Cornelius', 16 July 2005.
37. Tony Rees, 'Tony Rees to John Cornelius', 15 July 2005.
38. Freeman, 'We Must Not Forget the 76 Victims of Portland Square'.
39. 'Memorial Soon for Disaster', *Evening Herald*, 26 November 2005, 5.
40. Tony Rees, 'Tony Rees to John Cornelius', 9 December 2005.
41. 'Memorial Plea for Blitz Dead', *Evening Herald*, 9 December 2005, 24.
42. Rees, 9 December 2005.
43. 'They Shall Be Remembered'.
44. Hannah Wood, 'For Those Who Died', *Evening Herald*, 22 April 2006, 6.
45. Hannah Wood, 'Peace at Last', *Evening Herald*, 22 April 2006, 1.
46. Hannah Wood, , 'City Must Honour its Dead', *Evening Herald*, 24 April 2006, 7.
47. Wood, 'My Family Wouldn't Exist'.
48. Hannah Wood, , 'I Lost So Many Classmates that Terrible Night', *Evening Herald*, 3 May 2006, 3.

49. Wood, 'Son's Donation'.
50. Hannah Wood, 'We All Have a Duty to Remember Those Lost', *Evening Herald*, 8 May 2006, 16.
51. Stuart Abel, 'Stone on Site for Memorial', *Evening Herald*, 16 April 2007, 19.
52. Abel, 'A Tribute to the Shelter Victims'.
53. Ibid.
54. Radford.

Afterword

1. J. Cornelius, 'Wise'.
2. Michael McLaughlin, 'A Historian in the Round Tower: Using the Royal Archives to Tell a Local Story,' *The Historian*. May (2026). pp. 63–65.

References

Archives

Ancestry.com

1939 England and Wales Register, Lehi, UT, USA: Ancestry.com Operations, Inc., 2018.

BBC Archive

Chamberlain, Neville, *Radio Address by Neville Chamberlain, Prime Minister*, 3 September 1939. Transcript from the BBC Archive.

British Library Collection

'Map of Plymouth-Devonshire CXXIII.8.18', 1894.

British Library of Information

Churchill, Winston, 'Report on the War', 27 April 1941, <https://www.ibiblio.org/pha/timeline/410427awp.html>. Reproduced with permission of Curtis Brown, London, on behalf of Portland Churchill Ltd © Winston S. Churchill / Portland Churchill Ltd.

The Box, Plymouth

Campbell, Colin, 'ARP Controller's Report for the Air Raids of the 21st, 22nd, 23rd April and 28th and 29th April, 1941.' 16 May 1941. 1495/54.

City of Plymouth, 'Emergency Bulletin No. 2', 25 March 1941; 'Emergency Bulletin No. 3', 26 March 1941; 'Emergency Bulletin No. 4', 27 March 1941; 'Emergency Bulletin No. 5', 28 March 1941; 'Emergency Bulletin No. 6', 29 March 1941; 'Emergency Bulletin No. 7', 30 March 1941; 'Emergency Bulletin No. 8', 3 April 1941; 'Emergency Bulletin No. 9', 8 April 1941. 1561/194.

City of Plymouth, 'Deaths due to War Operations. Air Raids 21st, 22nd & 23rd April, 1941. Bodies Received and Identified at Halwell Street & Weston Mill. & Efford.' 1941. 1714/4/2.

City of Plymouth, *Emergency Committee Minutes*, 22 April 1941. 1561/183.

City of Plymouth, *Emergency Committee Minutes*, 23 April 1941, 4.30 p.m. 1561/183.

City of Plymouth, *Plymouth City Diary*. 22 April 1941. 773/16.

Cole, Percy, Lecture, December 1942. 1714/6/4.

Johns, W.P., *Days of Destiny*, unpublished manuscript, 2001. 4263/293.

Martin, Leslie, 'The Duties of a Mortuary Superintendent', 1942. 1714/6/6.

Ministry of Health, *Circular 1846*, August 1939. 1564/10/1.

Ministry of Health, *Circular 1914*, November 1939. 1564/10/1.

Ministry of Health, *Circular 1949*, January 1940. 1564/10/2.

Ministry of Health, *Circular 2112*, August 1940. 1564/2/16.

Ministry of Health, *Circular 2398*, 1941. 1564/2/16.

Ministry of Health, *Circular 2470*, 1941. 1564/2/16.

Ministry of Health, *Memorandum 222: Civilian Deaths Due to War Operations – Identification, Records and Registration*, revised July 1941. 1714/6/1.

Ministry of Health, 'Draft Conference Syllabus', October 1942. 1714/6/3.

Ministry of Health, 'Six Health Hints'. Poster, *c.*July 1941. 1561/127.

Ministry of Health, 'Public Shelter Rules', 20 March 1941. 1561/127.

Ministry of Health, *War Deaths: Emergency Mortuary and Burial Arrangements*, 1942. 1714/4/5.

Ministry of Home Security. *Air Raids: What You Must Know, What You Must Do*, 1940. 1151/46.

Ministry of Health, *Home Security Circular No 290/1940: Air Raid Shelters*, 11 December 1940. 1561/127.

'Missing Persons List', April 1941. 1714/5/5.

'Mortuary Records: Portland Square Air Raid Shelter', April 1941. 773/16.

Plymouth Blitz 'Bomb Book', 1941. 1555/40.

War Deaths Department, 'Air Raids on Plymouth, 20th and 21st March', Notes, 1941. 1564/2/16.

War Deaths Department, 'Air Raids on Plymouth, 21st, 22nd and 23rd April, and 28th and 29th April 1941', Notes, 1941. 1564/2/16.

Churchill Archives Centre, Churchill College, Cambridge

Churchill, Winston, 'The Prime Minister's Personal Minutes. May, 1941'. Char 20/35/5.

Friends of Ford Park Cemetery, Plymouth.

Brock, Sylvia, 'Sylvia Brock to Charlie Morton,' Tony Rees files.

Mills, Barbara, 'Untitled memories,' Tony Rees files.

Payne, Ena, 'Vain search for family after shelter was bombed,' Tony Rees files.

Phillips, Frank, 'Messenger's memories,' Tony Rees files.

Imperial War Museum Archive, London

'Air Situation Report, 21 April 1941'. Documents.8378.

'Air Situation Report, 22/23 April 1941'. Documents.8378.

'Plymouth City Blitz', <https://www.iwm.org.uk/memorials/item/memorial/25734>.

'Portland Square Air Raid Shelter Victims', <https://www.iwm.org.uk/memorials/item/memorial/46036>.

'This is London Wall.' Object. EPH 9785.

'Visit of their Majesties the King and Queen to Western Approaches Command, Plymouth, 20 March 1941'. Photograph. A3483.

Mass Observation Archive, University of Sussex

Second Report on Plymouth, April 1941. File Report No. 626. Reproduced with permission of Curtis Brown, London, on behalf of the Trustees of the Mass Observation Archive © The Trustees of the Mass Observation Archive.

Third Report on Plymouth, October 1941. File Report No. 903. Reproduced with permission of Curtis Brown, London, on behalf of the Trustees of the Mass Observation Archive © The Trustees of the Mass Observation Archive.

Nancy Astor Archive, Special Collections, University of Reading

Astor, Nancy, 'Nancy Astor to Arthur Penn', 23 February 1941. MS 1416/1/6/119.

Astor, Nancy, 'Nancy Astor to Arthur Penn', 8 March 1941. MS 1416/1/6/119.

Astor, Nancy, 'Nancy Astor to Plymouth Town Clerk', 13 August 1940. MS 1416/1/6/119.

Astor, Waldorf, 'Waldorf Astor to Arthur Penn', 1 March 1941. MS 1416/1/6/119.

Baring Gould, 'Notes of Miss Baring Gould', 3 March 1941. MS 1416/1/6/119.

'Household Notes', 18 March 1941. 1416/1/6/119.

'Letter from Colin Campbell', 18 March 1941. MS 1416/1/6/119.

'Letter from Lord Mayor's Secretary', 18 March 1941. MS 1416/1/6/119.

'Notes for Lady Astor: Virginia House', 18 March 1941. MS 1416/1/6/119.

'Notes for Lady Astor: Y.M.C.A.', 18 March 1941. MS 1416/1/6/119.

Office of the Commander-in-Chief, Mount Wise, Devonport, *Memorandum No. P.357/4: Visit of Their Majesties the King and Queen*, 18 March 1941. MS 1416/1/6/119.

Penn, Arthur, 'Arthur Penn to Waldorf Astor', 29 September 1940. MS 1416/1/6/119.

Penn, Arthur, 'Arthur Penn to Waldorf Astor', 20 February 1941. MS 1416/1/6/119.

Penn, Arthur, 'Arthur Penn to Waldorf Astor', 28 February 1941. MS 1416/1/6/119.

'Queen Elizabeth to Nancy Astor', 23 March 1941. MS 1416/1/4/8.

'Visit of Their Majesties the King and Queen, Groups of Women War Workers Invited to Send Representatives', March 1941. MS 1416/1/6/119.

National Archives, Kew

George VI, 'The King's Speech', audio, 3 September 1939.

Ministry of Health, *Circular 1779*, February 1939. MH 10/143.

Ministry of Health, *Memorandum 222: Civilian Deaths due to War Operations: Identification, Records and Registration*, February 1939. MH 10/143.

'Raids on Plymouth 21st to 23rd April, 1941. Note on Visit to Plymouth'. HO 186/625.

Navy Registers of Seamen's Services, 1848–1939.

Plymouth & West Devon Record Office, Plymouth

City of Plymouth, *Minutes of the Plymouth City Council Public Services Committee*, 21 April 1981. PWDRO, PCC/1/1.

City of Plymouth, *Minutes of the Plymouth City Council Public Services Committee*, 9 June 1981. PWDRO, PCC/1/1.

Royal Archives, Windsor

'Address of the Lord Mayor', 29 October 1947. RA PS/PSO/GVI/PS/VISUK/08717/065.

Astor, Waldorf. 'Waldorf Astor to Alexander Hardinge', 15 March 1941. RA PS/PSO/GVI/WARBOMB/04932/217.

Elizabeth. 'Queen Elizabeth to Queen Mary', 21 March 1941. RA QM/PRIV/CC12/158.

George VI, 'George VI to the Astors', 21 March 1941. RA PS 04932/224.

George VI, 'Private Diary of King George VI', 20 March 1941. RA GVI/PRIV/DIARY/WAR/1941: 20 March.

Great Western Railway, *Notice No. 10*, March 1941. RA PS/PSO/GVI/WARBOMB/04932/234.

Hardinge, Alexander, 'Alexander Hardinge to Waldorf Astor', 10 March 1941. RA PS/PSO/GVI/WARBOMB/04932/214.

Security Control Officer – Plymouth Control, 'Copy of Extract from Fortnightly Intelligence Report', 30 March 1941. RA PS/PSO/GVI/WARBOMB/04932/228.

Books and Articles

Eyre's Post Office Plymouth & Devonport Directory, 1895 (J. G. Hammond & Co. Ltd, 1895). Available at University of Leicester, <https://leicester.contentdm.oclc.org/digital/collection/p16445coll4/id/64277/>.

Front Line: 1940–41: The Official Story of the Civil Defence of Britain (London: His Majesty's Stationery Office, 1942).

Gardiner, Juliet, *The Blitz: The British Under Attack* (London: Harper Press, 2010).

Gill, Crispin, *Resurrexi: I Have Risen Again* (Plymouth: Hitchings & Mason Ltd, 1997).

Hartnell, Norman, *Silver and Gold: The Autobiography of Norman Hartnell* (London: V&A Publishing, 2019).

Johnson, Stephen, 'Plymouth's World War Two Underground Air Raid Shelters', in K. Ray (ed.), *Archaeological Investigations and Research in Plymouth, Volume 1: 1992–93*. Plymouth Archaeology Occasional Publication No. 2 (Plymouth: Plymouth Archaeology, 1995), 41–46.

McLaughlin, Michael, 'A Historian in the Round Tower: Using the Royal Archives to Tell a Local Story,' *The Historian*, May (2026), pp. 63–65.

McLaughlin, Michael, 'Burying the Blitz: The Grief and Politics of Commemoration in Wartime Plymouth', *The Journal of the Institute of Cemetery and Crematorium Management*, Summer 2025, 10–11.

McLaughlin, Michael, 'Churchill Visits Plymouth: 2 May 1941', *Their Finest Hour*, 204 (Winter), 2024, 32–37.
McLaughlin, Michael, 'Civilian Casualty Management in World War II: A Case Study of Plymouth's Halwell Street Mortuary', *Omega – Journal of Death and Dying*, 2024, 1–16. https://doi.org/10.1177/00302228241293827
McLaughlin, Michael, 'Private and Public Civilian Burial in Second World War Britain: A Case Study of the Plymouth Blitz,' *Journal of Mortality*, 2025 (Dec), epub.
Ministry of Information, *Plymouth Blitz*, 1942.
Morton, Andrew, *The Queen: Her Life* (New York: Grand Central Publishing, 2022).
Noakes, Lucy, *Dying for the Nation: Death, Grief, and Bereavement in Second World War Britain* (Manchester: Manchester University Press, 2020).
Noakes, Lucy, 'Valuing the Dead: Death, Burial, and the Body in Second World War Britain', *Critical Military Studies*, 6(2), 2019, 224–242. https://doi.org/10.1080/23337486.2019.1663683
Norman, Vicky, *Scattered Homes, Broken Hearts* (Vicky Norman, 2002).
Owens, Edward, *The Family Firm: Monarchy, Mass Media and the British Public, 1932–53* (London: University of London Press, 2019).
Quigley, Laura, *Bloody British History: Plymouth* (Stroud: The History Press, 2012).
Ramsden, John, 'Churchill: A Man who Believed', *Finest Hour*, 129 (Winter), 2005, 30.
Ramsey, Winston G. (ed.), *The Blitz: Then and Now: Volume 2* (London: Battle of Britain Prints International, 1988).
Ray, John, *The Night Blitz, 1940–1941* (London: Arms and Armour Press, 1996).
Rugg, Julie, 'Managing "Civilian Deaths Due to War Operations"', *History Today*, 55(2), 2005.
Rugg, Julie. 'Managing "Civilian Deaths due to War Operations": Yorkshire Experiences During World War II', *Twentieth Century British History*, 15(2), 2004, 152–173. https://doi.org/10.1093/tcbh/15.2.152
Twyford, Henry Patrick, *It Came to Our Door* (Plymouth: Underhill, 1946).
Twyford, Henry Patrick, *It Came to Our Door*, ed. Chris Robinson (Plymouth: Pen & Ink, 2005).
Van der Kiste, John, *Plymouth: A City at War 1914–1945* (Stroud: The History Press, 2014).
Wade, Stephen, *Air Raid Shelters of World War II: Family Stories of Survival in the Blitz* (Barnsley: Pen & Sword Military, 2011).
Waller, Jane, and Michael Vaughn-Reese, *Blitz: the Civilian War, 1941–45* (London: Macdonald & Co, 1990).
Wasley, Gerald, *Blitz: An Account of Hitler's Aerial War Over Plymouth in March 1941, and the Events that Followed* (Exeter: Halsgrove, 1991).
Wasley, Gerald, *Devon at War: 1939 – 1945* (Devon: Devon Books, 1994).
Wasley, Gerald, *Plymouth: A Shattered City* (Exeter: Halsgrove, 2004).
Watson, J.P., and Patrick Abercrombie, *A Plan for Plymouth: The Report Prepared for the City Council* (Plymouth: Underhill, 1943).
Williamson, A. B., 'The Problem of the Disposal of the Dead after Air Raids', *Report of Proceedings Eighth Joint Conference of Cemetery and Crematorium Authorities* (Portsmouth, 26 June 1939).
Wintle, Frank, *The Plymouth Blitz* (Cornwall: Bossiney Books, 1981).
Worth, Richard Nicholls, *History of Plymouth: From the Earliest Period to the Present Time* (Plymouth: William Brendon & Son, 1890).

Personal Memoirs and Letters

Barretto, Douglas, 'Doug Barretto to John Cornelius', 3 December 1995.
Barretto, Douglas, 'Doug Barretto to John Cornelius', 22 September 1996.

Barretto, Douglas, 'Doug Barretto to John Cornelius', 9 October 1996.
Brickwood, L., 'Report Made by L. Brickwood', (n.d.), courtesy Anne Corry, 11 October 2024.
British Army Form B199A for William John Lang Cornelius.
Chapman, Lilian, 'Telegram, 22 April 1941', courtesy Peter Chapman.
Chapman, Florence, 'Telegram, 23 April 1941', courtesy Peter Chapman.
Cornelius, John, 'John Cornelius to Doug Barretto', 31 March 1997.
Cornelius, John, 'John Cornelius to R. J. Bull', 6 February 1997.
Cornelius, John, 'John Cornelius to Catherine Hunt', 10 September 1993.
Cornelius, John, 'John Cornelius to Catherine Hunt', 1 December 1996.
Cornelius, John, 'John Cornelius to Roland Levinsky', 17 July 2005.
Cornelius, John, 'John Cornelius to Barbara Mills', 5 January 1996.
Cornelius, John, 'John Cornelius to Pamela Selley', 2 July 1996.
Cornelius, John, 'John Cornelius to Noreen Wise', 13 March 1996.
Cornelius, John, *My Journey to the New World*, unpublished memoir (n.d.).
Cornelius, John, *Two Journeys*, unpublished genealogy (n.d.).
Cornelius, Lang, 'Lang Cornelius to Anthony Cornelius', 19 November 1939.
Cornelius, Lang, 'Lang Cornelius to Anthony Cornelius', 18 February 1940.
Cornelius, Lang, 'Lang Cornelius to Basil Cornelius', 18 February 1940.
Cornelius, Lang, 'Lang Cornelius to Marjorie Cornelius', 30 May 1940.
Cornelius, Lang, 'Lang Cornelius to Marjorie Cornelius', 1 June 1940.
Eyres, Nelson, 'N. Eyres to Colin Campbell', 19 September 1941.
Eyres, Nelson, 'Report made by Nelson Edgar Eyres', (n.d.) courtesy Anne Corry, 11 October 2024.
Ford Park Cemetery. 'Portland Square Mortuary and Burial List', courtesy Vivian Warne.
Hollett, Stanley Charles, *Looking Back*, unpublished memoir (n.d.), courtesy Simon Edwin.
Lowe, George, 'Report Made by G.S. Lowe, Chief Constable', (n.d.), courtesy Anne Corry, 11 October 2024.
Lowe, George, *Situation Report for the Fortnight Ending 10 May 1941*, 12 May 1941.
McLaughlin, Michael, 'Interview with Peter Chapman', 10 April 2024.
Mills, Barbara, 'Barbara Mills to John Cornelius', 1 January 1996.
Mills, Barbara, 'Barbara Mills to John Cornelius', 19 November 1996.
Mould, Henrietta, 'Henrietta Mould to Audrey Mould', 9 July 1940, courtesy Anne Corry, 9 November 2024.
Northwood, Lilian, 'The Air Raids on Plymouth', 2 November 2003. WW2 People's War. A1951959.
Palmer, Charles, 'Report Made by Charles Palmer', (n.d.) courtesy Anne Corry, 11 October 2024.
Plymouth: The People's Blitz, 'Faces of the Blitz: Hempkins.' Facebook, <https://m.facebook.com/PlymouthThePeoplesBlitz/photos/faces-of-the-plymouth-blitz-this-lovely-wedding-photo-of-edward-hempkins-and-his/702859976490784/>, 22 April 2015.
Plymouth College and Mannamead School. Sports Standard Certificates, 1938.
Plymouth College and Mannamead School. Sports Standard Certificates, 1939.
Rees, Tony, 'Tony Rees to John Cornelius', 10 July 2005.
Rees, Tony, 'Tony Rees to John Cornelius', 15 July 2005.
Rees, Tony, 'Tony Rees to John Cornelius', 16 July 2005.
Rees, Tony, 'Tony Rees to John Cornelius', 9 December 2005.
Saundercock, Victor, 'Devonport Blitz', 2004. WW2 People's War. A2938421.
Stanleick, Dorothy, Untitled Memories (1989), courtesy of Lesley Allsopp, 2024.
Stevens, Larry, Primary Source Testimony, www.cyber-heritage.co.uk/history/blitz.htm.
Temlett, Gladys, 'Gladys Temlett to Nell', 24 April 1941, courtesy Peter Chapman.
Wise, Noreen, 'Noreen Wise to John Cornelius', 1996.

Newspapers

Cornish Evening Herald

'Plymouth Gets New-Type Double Blitz', 22 April 1941.
'Another Double Blitz on Plymouth Starts Fires, Wrecks Houses', 23 April 1941.

Dundee Evening Telegraph

'Body Recovered from Dock', 8 September 1939.

*Evening Herald (*Plymouth*)*

'A Night of Horrors Changed Lives Forever', 21 April 2001.
Abel, Stuart, 'A Tribute to the Shelter Victims', 6 October 2007.
Abel, Stuart, 'Stone on Site for Memorial', 16 April 2007.
Gill, Crispin, 'Heaps of Rubble Spewed into Road', Blitz Supplement, 6 March 1991.
Freeman, Martin, 'We Must Not Forget the 76 Victims of Portland Square', 26 November 2005.
Morton, Charlie, 'I Didn't Want to Die by Being Buried Alive', 12 March 2001.
Morton, Charlie, 'Shelter Blast Killed Dozens', 15 March 2001.
Morton, Charlie, 'Survivor', 21 April 2001.
Radford, Eleanor, 'A Tribute to 76 Air Raid Victims', 24 April 2009.
Wood, Hannah, 'City Must Honour its Dead', 24 April 2006.
Wood, Hannah, 'For Those Who Died', 22 April 2006.
Wood, Hannah, 'I Lost So Many Classmates that Terrible Night', 3 May 2006.
Wood, Hannah, 'My Family Wouldn't Exist if it Wasn't for Blackie the Spaniel', 29 April 2006.
Wood, Hannah, 'Peace at Last', 22 April 2006.
Wood, Hannah, 'Son's Donation to Blitz Tribute', 6 May 2006.
Wood, Hannah, 'We All Have a Duty to Remember Those Lost', 8 May 2006.
'Fortitude and Strength of Astors Came Shining through Dark', Blitz Supplement, 6 March 1991.
'A Night of Horror that Changed Lives Forever', 21 April 2001.
'I Remember Portland Square', 20 February 2001.
'Memorial Plea for Blitz Dead', 9 December 2005.
"Memorial Soon' for Disaster', 26 November 2005.
'Saddest Duty in Raids', Blitz Supplement, 6 March 1991.
'Seen and Heard', 25 September 1995.
'Shock at University Plan to Close Campus', 9 July 2005.
'They Shall Be Remembered', 22 April 2006.
'Whole Families Killed in the Worst Single Disaster of the Blitz', Blitz Supplement, 6 March 1991.

*The Herald (*Plymouth*)*

'A Tribute to the Shelter Victims', 6 October 2007.

Plymouth Herald

Dodd, Rachael, 'Devastating Air Raid Claimed Dozens of Civilians', 21 April 2018.
McLaughlin, Michael, 'A Plymouth Boy's Blitz Survival Story', 22 April 2025.

McLaughlin, Michael, 'Book gives voice to the effects of Blitz's toll,' 26 May 2026.
McLaughlin, Michael, 'The Forgotten Beginning to Plymouth's Blitz', 5 July 2025.
McLaughlin, Michael, 'How Leader's Visit Helped to Galvanise City's Spirits', 7 May 2024.
McLaughlin, Michael, 'Night the Bombs of the Luftwaffe Blitzed Plymouth', 28 November, 2025.
McLaughlin, Michael, 'The Night the Sirens Were Silent', 28 February 2026.
McLaughlin, Michael, 'On this Day: When the Crown Came to Town – 20 March 1941', 20 March 2025.

The Times (London)

'Court Circular', 21 March 1941.
'Future of Anglo-German Relations', 1 October 1938.
'Heavy Attack on Plymouth', 23 April 1941.
'Heavy Damage at Plymouth', 24 April 1941.
'The King and Queen at Plymouth A Crowded Seven Hours', 21 March 1941.
'Many Homeless in Plymouth', 24 March 1941.
'Prime Minister at Plymouth', 3 May 1941.
'Severe Raid on Plymouth', 22 March 1941.

Western Evening Herald (Plymouth)

Jones, Tom. 'Honour Shelter Victims', editorial, 9 May 1981.
'100-'Planes Raid Starts Plymouth Fires', 21 March 1941.
'Ancient Church is Damaged', 21 March 1941.
'Another Round in Plaque Fight', 30 May 1981.
'Arthur Seeks Air Raid Survivors', 12 March 1981.
'Astor Home Hit', 23 April 1941.
'Blitz Disaster Memorial to Go Ahead', 11 December 1981.
'Blitz Memorial Plan Delayed', 21 November 1981.
'Bomber Shot Down By A.A. Guns in Plymouth Blitz', 22 April 1941.
'City's Blitz Victims Are Laid at Rest', 28 April 1941.
'Decision on Blitz Plaque Put Off', 22 April 1981.
'Fate and Hitler's Firebomb', 11 September 1998.
'Herald Man Meets Queen', 21 March 1941.
'Lady Astor Indicts "Ministry of Inflammation"', 29 April 1941.
'Last Post for Blitz Victims', 23 April 1981.
'Loss to Boot Trade', 28 April 1941.
'Many Killed When Heavy Bomb Hits Communal Shelter', 23 April 1941.
'Memorial Battle Victory', 10 June 1981.
'Memorial to 72 Dead Unveiled', 22 December 1981.
'Mr. Churchill Tours Ten Miles of Blitzed Plymouth', 3 May 1941.
'Nazis Dive-bomb Blazing City in Second Plymouth Blitz', 22 March 1941.
'Plymouth Gets New-Type Double Blitz', 22 April 1941.
'Premier Heartens Homeless in City Centre', 28 April 1941.
'Proud Moment in Royal Visit to Devonport', 21 March 1941.
'Real Object of Nazi Raids', 23 April 1941.
'Royal Visit to City', 21 March 1941.
'Shelter Bomb Killed 72', 21 April 1981.

'Soldier Hero of Raid Tragedy', 26 April 1941.
'Talk of the City', 3 May 1941.
'They Went and Remembered', 23 April 1981.

Western Morning News (Plymouth)

Charleston, Michael, 'The Prophetic Notices for Rebirth of a City', 21 March 1991.
Charleston, Michael, 'When Pain and Death Poured from the Skies', 23 March 1991.
'30,000 for Plymouth', 6 March 1939.
'A Plymouth to Rival Copenhagen', 2 April 1941.
'A.R.P. Parade on the Hoe', 12 August 1939.
'Accelerated A.R.P.', 1 September 1939.
Advertisement: FJ Moore, 28 March 1939.
Advertisement: FJ Moore, 22 April 1939.
Advertisement: Sale this Day, 6 June 1940.
'Air-Raid Shelter for Every House', 2 February 1939.
'Air-Raid Shelters Some to be Built in Middle of Road at Plymouth', 4 May 1940.
'Air Raid Shelter Wardens', 24 May 1940.
'Air-Raid Shelters Wrongly Erected', 20 April 1940.
'Army Cable-Laying', 13 August 1938.
'Bert's Endurance', 3 December 1941.
'Big Raid Shelters Will Have Sick Bays', 18 October 1940.
'Bigger ARP Bill', 20 April 1939.
'Black-Out Offenders at Plymouth', 9 August 1940.
'Bombs Hit Club and Shop', 9 July 1941.
'Brave Plymothians', 16 August 1941.
'Bunks for 1,000', 31 January 1941.
'Cakes Attract Queen', 21 March 1941.
'Can Presume Raid Deaths', 25 March 1941.
'City Council is Still in Control', 27 March 1941.
'City Council to Hear of New Plans', 15 June 1939.
'City Labourer is Awarded B.E.M.', 19 July 1941.
'City Mothers Sing', 21 March 1941.
'City Plans New "Drive" for Recruits', 20 April 1939.
'City Schools After the Blitz', 10 April 1941.
Classified listing: 42 Portland Square, 5 November 1940.
Classified listing: General, 10 June 1904.
Classified listing: General, 26 May 1905.
Classified listing: Girl, 19 April 1909.
Classified listing: Mother's Helper, 13 October 1911.
Classified listing: Nurse, 29 October 1904.
Classified listing: Nurse, 13 September 1906.
Classified listing: Nurse-General, 19 August 1903.
Classified listing: Nursery Governess, 27 August 1910.
Classified listing: Nursery Governess, 27 January 1911.
Classified listing: Stable, 11 May 1915.
'Cold Anger in County', 26 April 1941.
'Country Divided Into Three Groups', 10 January 1939.
'Damage to Air Raid Shelters', 23 October 1939.

'Damaged Shelters', 15 September 1939.
'Damage to Raid Shelters', 9 May 1940.
'Daphne for the Queen', 7 April 1941.
'Death-Roll in Raids', 8 July 1940.
'Direction Signs', 29 July 1940.
'Disinfection of Shelter', 8 October 1940.
'Dogs and Smoking', 6 July 1940.
'Eight Rules for Public', 29 August 1940.
'Employers Thanked', 12 August 1939.
'Enemy Planes Over Three S.W. Towns', 29 November 1940.
'Epic of the 'Blitz'', 5 April 1941.
'Evacuation Area?', 28 April 1941
'Facing Up to Hitler', 15 January 1941.
'Falkland Islands', 9 May 1936.
'Farewell to Parish', 11 January 1939.
'Fire Bombs by the Thousand', 21 March 1941.
'Food Convoys Rushed to Plymouth', 24 April 1941.
'Free Shelters Critics', 14 February 1939.
'Four Killed in Raid in West Town', 8 July 1940.
'Girl Safe in Debris of Home', 22 July 1940.
'Government A.R.P. Policy', 7 July 1939.
'Handshake for Post Office Hero', Photograph, 7 April 1941.
'Impaired Safety Shelters', 1 April 1940.
'In Camp at Cornwood', 13 June 1938.
'In Private Shelters', 17 August 1940.
'Is the West Prepared?', 6 April 1939.
'Less than the Truth', 1 May 1941.
'Locked Air-Raid Shelters', 3 November 1939.
'Lord Mayor's Ball', 7 October 1936.
'Man a Mere Chattel to the Nazis', 28 April 1941.
'Many Fires in Town's Most Severe Raid', 30 December 1940.
'Need for More Operators', 5 December 1932.
'No Jingoism in West Determination', 4 September 1939.
'No Licences', 28 October 1927.
'No Wireless Licence', 28 April 1928.
'Notes in the West', 28 August 1939.
'One Grave for Raid Victims', 28 March 1941.
'Opposed at Plymouth', 14 August 1940.
'Philatelic Lecture', 10 April 1937.
'Plymouth Air-Raid Shelters', 30 September 1939.
'Plymouth Defiant and Carrying On', 15 January 1941.
'Plymouth Goes to Task of Cleaning Up', 24 March 1941.
'Plymouth Has Taken Hard Knock Well', 25 March 1941.
'Plymouth Is On the Danger List', 7 March 1941.
'Plymouth Recruiting', 24 April 1939.
'Plymouth Shows Its Courage', 24 March 1941.
'Plymouth Wireless Sets Without Licences', 9 May 1931.
'Police Help Needed', 3 September 1940.
'Practice to Cease', 24 August 1940.
'Praised by General', 31 January 1938.

'Premier in Plymouth', 3 May 1941.
'Pride in the Forces', 22 January 1934.
'Protecting City in Air Raids', 8 February 1939.
'The Queen Praises Women of Plymouth', 21 March 1941.
'Raid Shelter Key-Keepers', 5 June 1940.
'Receives D.S.O. from the King', 21 March 1941.
'Recruiting Drive', Photograph, 24 April 1939.
'Recruiting for Territorials', 30 April 1937.
'Royal Visitors at Bombed Plymouth', 21 March 1941.
'Sample Shelter', 12 April 1939.
'Services Did Fine Work in City Raids', 29 March 1941.
'Severe Raid on S.W. Coastal Town', 23 April 1941.
'She is a Lovely Lady', 21 March 1941.
'Shelter Amenities', 21 August 1940.
'Shelter Amenities', 20 September 1940.
'Shelters Are On the Urgent List', 15 November 1940.
'Shelter Guards', 25 June 1940.
'Shelters at New Schools', 14 January 1939.
'Shelters in All New Buildings', 12 May 1939.
'Signal Company's Training Camp', 12 July 1939.
'South-West Town Main Nazi Target', 28 November 1940.
'Territorial Army Officers', 1 February 1930.
'Territorial Ball at Plymouth', 14 February 1931.
'Territorial Specialists', 28 January 1935.
'Territorial Units', 31 March 1937.
'That "Short, Sharp Raid" Bulletin', 30 April 1941.
'They "Jumped To It"', 31 March 1941.
'Transport Bearers', 6 May 1941.
'Troops Who Lined the Route', 14 May 1937.
'Throne and People', 21 March 1941.
'Their Grave is Sacred', 29 April 1941.
'Their Hearts are High', Photograph, 5 May 1941.
'To A.R.P. Shelters', 25 July 1940.
'Traders' Tribute', 8 April 1940.
'Trees and Trenches', 19 September 1939.
'Trees Have Survived', 20 March 1940.
'Trenches and Shelters', 11 February 1939.
'Trenches Dug in Crisis', 21 January 1939.
'Trenches for Civilians', 24 February 1939.
'Two Ceremonies Coincide', 25 February 1939.
'Underground Air Raid Shelter', 18 April 1939.
'Unlicensed Wireless Sets', 18 September 1928.
'Vicar Resigns at Plymouth', 7 April 1936.
'Vicious Raid on South-West Coastal Town', 22 April 1941.
'Warden Assaulted During Raid', 12 September 1940.
'Wardens have No Powers', 30 August 1940.
"Warfare' in the Rain', 17 July 1939.
'Wedding: Cornelius-Hill at Plymouth', 24 November 1923.
'Wessex Signals', 11 August 1939.

'Western Police Courts', 15 August 1930.
'Wet Shelters Numerous', 11 November 1940.
'Whitehall is to Blame', 16 May 1939.

Television and Online Resources

'Ben Bennett, a Survivor of the Portland Square Air Raid Shelter Disaster Speaks in 1993, Audio Only', Facebook video, 16.21, 2 December 2017, <https://www.facebook.com/stephen.johnson.54379236/videos/1738580232821522>.
'Churchill Visits Plymouth', YouTube video, 1.04, posted by 'British Pathé', 13 April 2014, <https://www.youtube.com/watch?v=I5Tr-iPL01U>.
'Mr Churchill Visits Plymouth – NO SOUND', YouTube video, 6.33, posted by 'British Movietone', 21 July 2015, <https://www.youtube.com/watch?v=4i49oc0yJ2M>.
'Plymouth: The Blitz Remembered – Portland Square', regional television news programme, March 2001.
'Sir John Anderson Speaks on the Need for Air Raid Precautions (ARP) (1939)', YouTube video, 0.40, posted by 'British Pathé', 10 November 2020, <https://www.youtube.com/watch?v=Ll5f7X15Mdg>.
'Target Swilly 1940, 6th July', YouTube Video, 25.12, posted by Cyberheritage Steve Johnson, 11 November 2022, <https://www.youtube.com/watch?v=4wcjTgyHON0>.

Index

www.ingramcontent.com/pod-product-compliance
Ingram Content Group UK Ltd.
Pitfield, Milton Keynes, MK11 3LW, UK
UKHW010853230826
174704UK00002B/44

9 781784 276744